Messianism, Mysticism, and Magic

Stephen Sharot

Messianism, Mysticism, and Magic

A Sociological Analysis of

Jewish Religious Movements

The University of North Carolina Press Chapel Hill

© 1982 The University of North Carolina Press
All rights reserved
Manufactured in the United States of America

First printing, May 1982
Second printing, January 1987

Library of Congress Cataloging in Publication Data

Sharot, Stephen
    Messianism, mysticism, and magic

    (Studies in religion)
    Bibliography: p.
    Includes index.
    1. Messianic era (Judaism)—Social aspects.
2. Sabbathaians. 3. Hasidism—Social aspects.
4. Zionism and Judaism—Social aspects. I. Title.
II. Series: Studies in religion (Chapel Hill, N.C.)
BM625.S5 1982   306'.6   81-11688
ISBN 0-8078-1491-1   AACR2
ISBN 0-8078-4170-6 (pbk.)

FOR TAMI

Contents

viii   *Contents*

Acknowledgments

I wish to thank Bryan Wilson and Robert Liberles, who read the entire manuscript and gave me the benefit of their critical judgments and attention to details. Paul Flohr read chapter 5 in article form, and I am grateful for his comments. I was lucky to have a number of very good students who attended my graduate courses in the sociology of religion in the Hebrew University. I would like to mention two, in particular, who wrote excellent papers on Hasidism: Ilana Friedrich-Silber and Eva Gobey-Bogan. Another former student of mine, Rachel Kimor, was a superb research assistant. For financial support I would like to thank the Faculty of Social Sciences, the Hebrew University, for two small research grants.

I gathered some useful criticisms when I presented parts of the work in a number of forums: the Department of Behavioural Sciences, Ben-Gurion University of the Negev; the Department of Sociology and Anthropology, Tel-Aviv University; the Department of Anthropology, the University of North Carolina at Chapel Hill; and the BSA Sociology of Religion Study Group.

I wrote a large part of the manuscript during a sabbatical year in the Department of Sociology at the University of North Carolina at Chapel Hill, which provided a most congenial environment. Bruce Geyer, a graduate student in English literature, did an excellent job of typing the manuscript. In its final stage the manuscript benefited from the skillful editing by David Perry at the University of North Carolina Press.

Most of chapter 5 appeared in *Comparative Studies in Society and History* 22 (July 1980). Part of chapter 10 appeared in *Journal for the Scientific Study of Religion* 19 (December 1980).

Messianism, Mysticism, and Magic

1. Sociology and Jewish Historiography

THIS BOOK is a sociological study of popular religious traditions and movements in Jewish communities. It deals primarily with the religion of the Jewish folk or masses; thus it is concerned with the religious doctrines and speculations of the intelligentsia only insofar as they were influential in, or in some way relevant to, popular expressions of religion. Religious phenomena may, of course, have many causes. The explanations suggested here, however, are primarily sociological; thus interpreted, religious beliefs, practices, and movements originate and develop under certain social conditions, and a plausible link can be made between social conditions and religious phenomena.

A focus on popular Judaism and its social determinants has been rare among historians of Jewry. Most historians of Judaism have concerned themselves exclusively with the ideas and works of scholars, rabbis, philosophers, and other intellectuals, and the few historians who have directed their attention to popular religious expressions have rarely taken a sociological viewpoint. It is possible to account sociologically for this neglect. A sociology of knowledge of Jewish historiography would require a work in itself, but with the proviso that a summary account necessarily ignores important differences between individual historians, a brief explanation can be presented.

Modern Jewish historiography developed in the nineteenth century in Germany.[1] The German Jewish historians experienced the conflicting pressures and tensions of the middle- and upper-middle-class German Jews who sought acceptance into the dominant society: they desired to retain a distinctive Jewish identity, but at the same time they tried to show that in their German nationalism and culture they were no different from other Germans. In seeking an entrance into German intellectual circles, the Jewish historians emphasized the rational aspects of Judaism. They ignored popular Jewish religion, the "irrational" mystical trends in Judaism, and social history in their attempt to portray Judaism as an intellectual religion.

In the last decades of the nineteenth century a number of German Jews from highly acculturated and partially assimilated families realized that however much the German Jews stressed their German nationality and culture, they would never gain full acceptance within German society. The rise of political anti-Semitism in Germany strengthened this view and contributed to the rise of Zionism and other Jewish nationalist expressions. A new generation of Jewish historians rebelled against both the assimilated culture of their parents and the rationalist view of the history of Judaism. However, although at least some of the revisionist historians focused their attention on popular religious movements, especially Hasidism, they were no more inclined than their predecessors to emphasize the social determinants of the movements.

Some nationalist historians suggested that Judaism had an essence which gave its history continuity. Some saw this essence as a suprahistorical form, the transcendental God, which meant that history was not a fully autonomous realm. Others saw the essence as a secular force, such as a common nationalist identification or the Land of Israel, which they saw as uniting the Jewish people throughout its history in exile.

Another perspective viewed the history of Judaism as a struggle of forces within the religion. Like the historians who emphasized a single essence, proponents of this perspective advanced both religious and secular versions. The best-known religious, or, more specifically, mythical, version was that of Martin Buber. Buber posited a struggle between an intellectual, rational, rabbinic religion and a national, mythical, folk religion. The latter, a countertradition, was for a long period a subterranean current in heretical groups, but it emerged openly in the Hasidic movement. Although Buber acknowledged a struggle of opposing forces, he wished to capture the essence of one of those forces, the hidden myth of Jewish history, which represented, for him, the true spirit of Judaism. In order to locate this mythical essence in Hasidism, he isolated the movement from its sociohistorical context and presented an ahistorical, mythopoetic account.

The most prominent historian presenting a secular version of conflicting forces in Judaism is Gershom Scholem. Scholem expunges any attempt to discover an essence and presents the history of Judaism as a dialectical struggle of opposing forces: between transcendentalism and mythical ideas that are often close to pantheism or polytheism, between rationalism and irrationalism, and between constructive and destructive forces. The focus of Scholem's research has been the history of the cabbalah, the mystical subterranean tradition in Judaism, which was long ignored or denied importance by Jewish historians. He views the cabbalah not as the essence of the religion but as a powerful countertradition which interacted in dynamic fashion with the prevailing rabbinic tradition. Unlike Buber, Scholem presents a secularized history of Judaism, but it is a history that focuses on the interaction of immanent ideal forces with almost no attention to social contexts and causes.

More so than the mainstream rabbinic scholars, the cabbalists articulated religious motifs found among the unscholarly masses. Yet Scholem's history of the cabbalah is very much a history of the ideas of a small intelligentsia. His most ambitious work, *Sabbatai Sevi*, is a work on a popular movement, but he argues that the movement was the consequence of the diffusion of certain cabbalistic ideas. In short, he presents an idealist history in which religious change is the consequence of immanent developments within Judaism. Developments within the cabbalah resulted in the Sabbatian movement, which in turn prepared the ground for the highly divergent movements of Hasidism and the *Haskalah* (Enlightenment). Whether they are from other religious traditions or from the socioeconomic environment, the influences of forces from outside Judaism are rarely discussed in Scholem's work, and when they are discussed, they are accorded little significance.

Those historians who have concentrated on Jewish social history have rarely shown the interrelationships between the social and the religious histories. The few exceptions have either lacked a theoretical framework or they have been rigid Marxists who have provided a foil for a historian, such as Scholem, to cut down. Marxist historian Raphael Mahler has made important contributions to the social and religious history of the Jews, but even he has restricted his interpretations by imposing a somewhat inflexible framework of substructure (economic forces) and superstructure (religious beliefs).

Interestingly, Scholem has argued that an objective Jewish historiography is possible only in the context of Zionism or the national "normalization" in the state of Israel, where Jewish historians are no longer subject to the political and cultural distortions of the anomalous life in exile. Scholem recognizes that nationalist historians have also presented biased and distorted accounts of Jewish history, but he asserts that the Zionist context at least provides the promise of objectivity. For Scholem, objectivity does not mean attempting to collect all the facts, which was the futile hope of some nineteenth-century historians; instead, it is a selective method which aims at discovering the major historical forces in Judaism.

The nationalism of the revisionist historians made them resistant to an analysis of the social forces in religious developments. In their rejection of *galut* (exile), the nationalist historians ignored or rejected the possible influence that the culture and social structure of the non-Jewish dominant societies, particularly the structure of relationships between Jews and gentiles, had on Jewish religious developments.

This work is an attempt to link the religious and social histories of the

Jews within a sociological framework. As a sociologist, I concentrate on the social determinants and processes of religious change, but I do not intend to substitute a one-sided sociological interpretation for a one-sided interpretation that relies on immanent religious forces. While objectivity is certainly a scientific value, total objectivity is not possible; insofar as this work deliberately concentrates on social causes, it presents a partial analysis. Heuristically, it is often useful to pay special attention to one set of determinants, and this is particularly true when those determinants have largely been ignored. The crucial task of this study is to demonstrate that social forces were among the major determinants of religious phenomena.

However, the attention given to sociological explanations here does not mean that other explanations are ignored. On occasion, psychological processes are considered as intervening factors between social conditions and religious developments. Other explanations considered in this study in some detail account for religious developments by other religious factors, which may be either exogenous or endogenous. Explanations emphasizing exogenous factors view religious change as a response to the intrusion or influence of elements from an external religious tradition: a diffusionist perspective. Explanations emphasizing endogenous factors view religious change as the consequence of a logical progression or dialectic within a single religious tradition: an immanentist perspective.

In acknowledging that religious phenomena cannot be reduced to social phenomena and that religious ideas can develop in an autonomous fashion, this work follows the perspectives of two of the founding fathers of sociology who wrote works that became classics in the sociology of religion: Emile Durkheim and Max Weber. The charge of reductionism has often been leveled at Durkheim, but in his later works, which include his major work on religion, he came increasingly to emphasize the importance of religious beliefs as partially autonomous from, and having important effects upon, the social substructure. In his article "Individual and Collective Representations," Durkheim wrote that once the basic collective representations (common perceptions and beliefs) came into existence, they became "partially autonomous realities," which could combine in various ways and develop further representations. He believed that the evolution of religion provided "the most striking examples of this phenomenon. It is perhaps impossible to understand how the Greek and Roman Pantheon came into existence unless we go into the constitution of the city, the way in which the primitive clans slowly merged, the organization of the patriarchal family, etc. Nevertheless the luxuriant growth of myths and legends, theogonic and cosmological systems, etc., which grow out of religious thought is not directly related to the particular features of the social morphology."[2] In his major work on religion, *The Elementary Forms of the*

Religious Life, Durkheim argued that central religious symbols both express *and* create the recognition of society as a moral force and unity.[3]

Weber was strongly critical of reductionist approaches to religion. He criticized Nietzsche for reducing doctrines of salvation and ethics to a feeling of resentment among the disadvantaged and the Marxists for interpreting religion as a function of economic conditions. Weber agreed that economic and other social factors were important in the interpretation of religion, but he also emphasized the relative autonomy of religion. Religious ideas did not simply reflect the interests, economic or otherwise, of groups or social strata; nor did they only constitute the ideologies of groups and strata. He stressed, however, that religious ideas became important in history only if they had a social "carrier," a group, class, or stratum that supported the ideas. The social carrier selected and interpreted those aspects of the religious doctrines which had an affinity with its interests and life-style. This concept of "elective affinity," the process whereby groups select and interpret from available belief systems those ideas that are congruent with their life conditions, is an important one. It directs attention to the social forces in religious change, but it acknowledges that social forces and religious ideas can develop relatively independently of each other, that the religious doctrines of a particular group or stratum can vary considerably depending on the type of religion that has evolved in the society, and that the affinities that emerge between social units and religious phenomena are likely to involve considerable plasticity.[4]

The focus of this study is religious movements. They are defined in a very broad way as groups or collectivities that seek to bring about, or look forward to, religious change with important social implications. Religious movements may be distinguished by their orientations to the religious traditions and institutions from which they emerged. Some religious movements completely reject the religious traditions into which their members were socialized and adopt foreign traditions or introduce completely new systems of belief and practice. Most movements, however, relate in some way to the traditions into which their members were socialized, and they seek either to promote or prevent change in those traditions. The movements discussed in this work demonstrated two different orientations to their religious traditions. Some brought into prominence or expressed in a dramatic fashion one or more aspects of long-existing religious traditions. Most instances in which Jewish communities expected the imminent coming of the messiah were of this type; such instances were relatively few and mostly short-lived, but they expressed and dramatized an orthodox Jewish belief in the coming of the messiah and a messianic kingdom. Other movements introduced a substantial modification or replacement of elements in their religious traditions. Some millenarian movements were of this type; a number of Sabbatian sects developed in an antinomian direction, rejecting a large part of the religious law and, in some cases, combining novel elements with conversion to non-Jewish religions. Hasidism, the mystical movement that began around the middle of the eighteenth century, respected religious tradition, but it introduced changes in the hierarchy of Jewish religious values.

Respect for religious tradition does not necessarily imply respect for the dominant religious institutions that claim to represent that tradition. Many Christian movements claimed that they represented the true tradition, and they rejected the established churches, which they argued had distorted Christianity. Some sought to reform the churches and seceded only after their failure to do so. Most of the Jewish movements discussed here did not desire separation from the rest of the Jewish community, but in some instances they were forced into separation.

An analysis of the religious movements is preceded in chapter 2 by a discussion of sociological approaches to the three major religious orientations discussed in this work (magic, millenarianism, and mysticism) and, in chapter 3 by an account of the religious context, the Jewish folk religion of medieval and early-modern Europe, in which the movements emerged.

2. Concepts and Perspectives

Religion and Magic

Definitions of religion by social scientists may be categorized as either substantive or functional. The substantive definition, which is the one preferred here, defines religion as those beliefs and actions that refer and relate to supernatural beings, such as gods, spirits, demons, and ghosts and supermundane principles, such as nirvana and cosmic order. The functionalist definition defines religion through its consequences or the needs that it is presumed to meet. One common functionalist definition defines religion as a system of beliefs and practices that are concerned with the "ultimate problems of human life." According to this definition all men experience such issues as evil, pain, injustice, and death as ultimate problems, and they will attempt to find meaning or make sense of these problems. Nontheistic belief systems, such as communism, humanism, and nationalism, that deal with these problems are also included under the rubric religion.[1]

Discussions of the relative advantages and limitations of the substantive and functionalist definitions have stirred much controversy.[2] For the purposes of this study, the mention of a single criticism of the functionalist definition that emphasizes ultimate problems is sufficient: it directs attention away from the relationships that people perceive between the supernatural and their worldly, mundane, everyday affairs, goals, and worries. The functionalist definition reflects, perhaps, the metaphysical and moral concerns of intellectuals, but it ignores important focuses of popular religion—the explanation of events in the empirical world and the achievement of such worldly goals as fertility and health.[3]

The distinction between supernatural beliefs and practices directed toward worldly concerns and those directed toward ultimate problems has been expressed, on occasion, as the difference between magic and religion. Bronislaw Malinowski, for example, wrote that magic had an end or definite practical purpose in view, such as the prevention of death in childbirth. Religion had no such conscious ends or goals but had expressive social functions which safeguarded and reinforced the cultural tradition.[4] In his criticism of Malinowski's formulation, A. R. Radcliffe-Brown wrote that all ritual acts have some expressive or social function. He noted ambiguity in the phrase "definite practical purpose" and asked, rhetorically, if the desire to please God and escape purgatory was not a practical purpose.[5]

Other attempts at distinguishing magic and religion have been made using the distinctions of belief, practice, and organization. One such argument holds that magic and religion present different conceptions of the supernatural: in magic, the supernatural is conceived as an impersonal power, subject to manipulation and control, while in religion the supernatural is conceived as a personalized power, outside man's control. James Frazer argued that magic is the erroneous application of the notion of causality: it is essentially mechanistic, representing an attempt to manipulate the world by techniques and formulas that operate automatically.[6] Frazer's argument that primitive man is unable to distinguish between magic and empirical techniques has been shown to be false, and his evolutionary scheme of magic, religion, and science as three stages of human history is of doubtful usefulness. Nevertheless, many have emphasized the distinction between the mechanical aspect of magical thought and the greater degree of contingency in religious thought. This argument further notes that a decline in magic was associated with the development of monotheism; the belief in one transcendental, omnipotent God may leave little room for magical thought. Weber perceived a move away from magic as religious development proceeded through naturalism, animism, polytheism, and, finally, monotheism. Magic declined as the supernatural conceptions became more abstract and remote.[7]

In this definition of magical belief, magical practices are rituals of manipulation and control, such as spells, incantations, and exorcism. The words, gestures, and objects used in magic must be precisely correct. In contrast, religious rituals are those of communication, propitiation, and supplication, such as prayer, offerings, good conduct, confession, and expiation.

Focusing on the organization of magic and religion, Durkheim made a further distinction. He stressed the individual relationship between magician and client, as opposed to the collective nature of religious action. Religion depended on the common beliefs of a moral community (a "church"), which was absent in magic.[8] Jack Goody criticized Durkheim for confusing two separate features: the assembly of a group and a moral community. Goody argues that magic is also dependent on consensus, and is, therefore, no less social than religion.[9] Weber made a distinction between priests who are involved in the continuous operation of a cult and the magicians who have ad hoc arrangements. The charisma of the priest is dependent on the office he occupies, while that of the magician is personal, tied to the individual. Weber emphasized, however, that many exceptions and cases do not fall neatly into categories; for example, sorcerers may be organized in a guild.[10]

Most modern scholars acknowledge that supernatural beliefs and practices cannot be rigidly categorized into magic and religion, but some wish to retain the distinction as a conceptually useful one: supernatural beliefs and practices may be plotted according to the extent to which they approach the religious or magical ends of a continuum; rituals may include religious and magical elements together; and a single practice or ritual may have a religious meaning for some participants and a magical meaning for others. Others have argued that the distinction is not conceptually useful: it is not possible to separate out the magical and religious elements; one will often presuppose the other; and they are aspects of a single phenomenon. Most leading anthropologists appear to have decided that the distinction adds nothing to their analyses, and they have dropped the debate. The distinction was derived from the great religious traditions, especially Judaism and Christianity, and attempts to impose it on the religions of tribal societies may lead to distortions.

The position taken here is that magic should not be distinguished as something apart, empirically or conceptually, from religion, but that it is useful to distinguish the one particular religious orientation to the world that may be called magical or thaumaturgical. In this we follow Bryan Wilson, who writes that the thaumaturgical response to the world is a demand for supernatural assistance which provides immediate personal relief from sickness, deprivation, and evil powers. The thaumaturgist seeks special dispensation and release from personal, familial, or other specific ills. Thaumaturgy is concerned not with evil as an "ultimate problem" but with highly specific evils, such as particular demons and witches who wish to do harm to the individual and his family. Insofar as the term *salvation* can be used in this context, it is an immediate salvation from a specific problem and has little or no relevance beyond the given case and others like it.[11]

Millenarianism

While the thaumaturgist largely accepts the world and only wishes to obtain special dispensations for individual cases, the millenarian seeks the destruction of the natural and social orders as a prelude to a perfect society and state of being. The millenarian looks forward to major transformations in the world to be brought about by or to take place under the auspices of supernatural beings or processes. Viewed as full of suffering, death, and other evils, the present world will be replaced by a perfectly good and happy one. The change will be ultimate and irrevocable: the millennium is not necessarily limited to the literal sense of a thousand years, but is often perceived as an eternal age. The coming transformation is seen as this-worldly, involving the union of the terrestrial and the transcendental on this earth, and collective, merging the redemption of the individual with the group of faithful or all humanity. In addition to these beliefs millenarian movements have been characterized by a belief in the imminent occurrence of the millennium; it is expected soon or at least during the lifetime of a majority of the members.

Yonina Talmon gave an excellent account of the dimensions that distinguish the differences among millennial traditions and movements.[12] They are:

History or myth. Millenarians differ in their relative emphases on concrete political and social hopes or on a cosmic drama where the image of the millennium is largely divorced from the empirical world.

Temporal or spatial. There are different emphases on perfect time or perfect space. The extent to which redemption is located in a specified area or society is highly variable.

Catastrophe or redemption. In some cases redemption is expected to occur suddenly and miraculously, without any preparatory struggle or cataclysm, but more often redemption is to be preceded by an apocalypse of upheavals, calamities, and wars.

Redemption or redeemer. Millenarianism and messianism do not necessarily coincide. The expectation of a final redemption is not always accompanied by the expectation of a human-divine savior. The millennium may be brought about directly by the spirits of ancestors or by an unseen divine power. Messianism need not be millenarian: a living messiah may offer salvation from existing bodily ills rather than promise salvation in a future state of bliss.

Particular or universal. Millenarians may believe that only a particular group, divinely appointed or otherwise ascriptively defined, will live to enjoy the millennium. Another possibility is that the group will have an elite status within the millennium. Alternatively, millenarians may believe that all members of the human species will live in a state of equality in the millennium.

Restorative or innovative. Some millenarians perceive the millennium as a return to a golden past or mythical age of paradise. An emphasis on innovation and the birth of an entirely new order, with an element of antitraditionalism, is more common. However, movements show substantial differences in the extent to which they

envisage the overthrow of prevailing values and norms.
Hypernomian or antinomian. Some movements emphasize the importance of self-discipline, strict conformity to rules, and ascetic
behavior. Antinomian movements attempt to break with all accepted norms and values, which often include the taboos on sexual
relationships. Millennial movements tend to display highly emotional patterns of behavior, and this is especially the case in
movements that reject traditional values and norms.
Active or passive. Movements vary greatly in the extent to which the
members believe that they have a part in bringing about the
millennium. The passive type believes that supernatural forces
alone will bring the millennium. The more active believe that
members can contribute to the advent, although the kinds of
activities involved will vary greatly, from actions of a purely
symbolic nature to active rebellion.
Amorphous or cohesive. The organizations of movements vary from the
amorphous type, with a cohesive core of leaders and an ill-defined
body of followers, to the cohesive, exclusive, sectlike type.

Mysticism

Sociologists have given far less attention to mysticism than
they have to millenarianism; no work has been done on the common
features and variable dimensions of mystical traditions and movements
which is comparable to Talmon's delineation and typology of millennial
traditions and movements. The common features of mysticism as presented
in the following paragraph are in contrast tó those of millenarianism.[13]
The mystic seeks union, adhesion, or some form of direct contact with
the divine or a superworldly state which goes beyond sense perception
and intellectual apprehension. Unlike the millenarian, who envisages visible, material change in the world, the mystic seeks an ultimate reality and a
transformation of his individual condition not directly perceptible to others. While the millenarian takes an activistic or symbolic revolutionist
stance toward the world, the mystic attempts to escape or withdraw from
the world and is likely to show indifference to its material conditions. The
millenarian may see the millennium as an end to history, but he gives a
place to history in the events leading up to the millennium. The mystic, on
the other hand, takes a timeless stance, seeking the eternal now of the
divine. The focus of the mystic on his personal salvation or individual soul
contrasts with that of the millenarian, who holds that his individual salvation is bound up with that of the group or collectivity.

The following list of dimensions represents an attempt to categorize the major differences among mystical traditions and movements:

Relational or nonrelational. The relational type presupposes a divinity or a transcendental Being, with whom the mystic seeks union or adhesion. The nonrelational type does not postulate a divinity, but the mystic seeks to enter a new ontological state. An example of the latter is found in Buddhist mysticism, where the goal is nirvana: the Buddhist mystic believes that he annihilates suffering by canceling the illusionary phenomenal self of mundane existence.

Absorptive (unitive) or nonabsorptive. In nonrelational mysticism the mystic is likely to perceive himself as absorbed within the super-worldly state of being or ultimate reality, such as the Impersonal Absolute Brahman in Hinduism or the absence of all being in the Buddhist nirvana. Where a divinity is postulated, it is possible to find both absorption, the attainment of full identity of the self with God, or nonabsorption, where the distinction between the self and God is retained. Jewish mystics have tended to conclude from the transcendental, unique, and unfathomable nature of the divine that the mystic may achieve adhesion to the divine but that he cannot achieve deification. In Christianity, where both types are found, a transcendence of the distinction between self and God has been encouraged by incarnational theology, which proposes that Jesus had both human and divine elements.

Stimulation or annihilation. This dimension relates to the means used to achieve mystical communion or unity. The mystic may stimulate his senses by song and dance or by artificial means such as drugs and alcohol. In contrast, the mystic may attempt to become desensitized and empty his mind by contemplation and meditation. He attempts to annihilate the self and become an empty vessel for the infusion of the divine.

Experience or knowledge. A mystic may see his mystical experience as having no features or consequences that can be expressed or have relevance outside the temporal limits of the experience itself. In comparison, the mystic may claim that his experience has given him special insights into the divine nature or ultimate reality and that these can be communicated to others. Unlike the prophet who claims knowledge of divine revelations, the mystic claims knowledge of the character and structure of the divine being.

Radical or conservative. The conservative mystic describes and interprets his experiences through traditional symbols and beliefs. He rediscovers the sources of the tradition, recognizes the eternal validity of the sacred writings, and thereby reinforces religious authority. At the other extreme, the most radical type of mystic rejects all tradition and authority in favor of the new revelations of his mystical experience. Between these extremes is another radical type who accepts the validity of the sacred texts but contends that his experience has revealed new meanings in the texts.

Hypernomian or antinomian. The mystic may perceive his experience as a corollary or part consequence of his strict adherence to religious norms and values. His behavior may take ascetic forms such as fasting and mortification. In contrast, the mystic who feels that he is united with the divine may conclude that he is absolutely free from sin and that the normative standards of good and evil no longer apply to him.

Amorphous or cohesive. It has been argued that the mystic's religious individualism means that he has little desire to form or enter into organized fellowships. Lacking any internal pressure toward the development of an enduring social organization, he is likely to form only a loose association with like-minded individuals. The lack of organization may be reinforced by traditional religious authorities who appreciate the potential for radicalism in mysticism and attempt to keep individual mystics from banding together. On the other hand, the recognition of the dangers of heterodoxy in mysticism has led to the belief that a mystic requires a spiritual guide who represents traditional authority and will guide the mystic's experience into acceptable channels. Therefore, a cohesive organization made up of a guide or guides and disciples and students is possible. In addition, special roles and organizations may be available for the assimilation of mystics into church structures.

Thaumaturgy, millenarianism, and mysticism represent three different religious responses to the world: the thaumaturgist seeks special dispensations within the world, the millenarian seeks revolutionary change of the world, and the mystic seeks escape from the world. Although one response may be clearly prominent in a particular movement, they are often found in various combinations and in tension with one another. They may also be found together with other orientations, and it would be useful at this point to note briefly two other orientations relevant to this study: the conversionist and the introversionist.[14] Conversionists focus on change of the self rather than change of the world, and it is unlikely that they will become engaged in rebellious activities, actual or symbolic. They believe that society will change not by the overthrowing of its institutions and structure but by the saving of souls through evangelization. Introversionists attempt to withdraw from the world, but in contrast to mystics, they emphasize community in separation. They often employ distinctive items of culture, such as clothing and language, and affirm the sacredness of the community; the holiness of the individual is seen as dependent on the holiness of the community.

Interpretations: Magic

Most anthropological and sociological studies of magic may be distinguished by the particular emphasis each puts on the instrumental or symbolic components of magic. The writers who emphasize the instrumental component argue that magical rites are designed to achieve certain ends in nature or in the behavior of people. Malinowski argued that man's material resources and empirical techniques rarely satisfy his needs and that he may turn to magic in an attempt to achieve greater satisfaction. He wrote that the people he studied, the Trobriand Islanders, realized that their mode of subsistence depended on their knowledge and techniques but that they used magic to control the forces over which they had little or no control. Magic was used more extensively in situations that were particularly dangerous or uncertain, such as open-sea fishing, than in safer or more predictable situations, such as lagoon fishing.[15] Instrumental goals in magic fall into three types: the productive, in which the goal is to ensure the successful outcome of a particular activity and create confidence where conditions are uncertain; the protective, in which the goal is to prevent or remove the dangers to an individual or a group; and the destructive, in which the goal is to harm others.

Radcliffe-Brown criticized Malinowski's interpretation of magic on both empirical and theoretical grounds. His empirical critique noted that magical rituals are performed in some societies in situations that carry no apparent dangers. Criticizing Malinowski's theory, he noted that Malinowski assumed that magical rites are performed to alleviate anxiety; however, the concern to perform the ritual correctly actually induces anxiety. If there were no ritual, it is possible that there would be no anxiety. For example, a native feels anxiety when the rituals surrounding childbirth are not properly carried out. A prospective father observes the taboos associated with childhood not because of his anxiety but because he is expected by others to show some symbolic expression of concern. For Radcliffe-Brown, the major functions of the magical precautions at childbirth and death were to express symbolically the importance of birth and death and to inform others of changes in the kinship network.[16]

Symbolic interpretations of magical and other religious beliefs and practices have often gone beyond the interpretations of the participants and have postulated latent meanings of which the participants are not aware. Symbols have been commonly interpreted as expressions of social relationships or features of the social structure. This approach has been criticized by the neo-Tylorians, who argue that many postulated links between symbols and the phenomena they are presumed to symbolize are unconvincing. The neo-Tylorians acknowledge their intellectual debt to E. B. Tylor, who viewed magic as an intellectualistic attempt to postulate direct relationships of cause and effect.[17] Robin Horton states the neo-Tylorian position: the native accounts of events such as illness, death, and the weather as actions of supernatural beings are considered serious attempts at explanation. In modern societies science explains such events; modern Western religion differs from most other religions in that it gives little attention to events in this world.[18]

The instrumentalist approach has been faulted for failing to explain why people involved in magic do not come to appreciate the inefficacy of their rituals. The functionalists have responded to this by postulating latent functions that, although unintended and unrecognized, are said to explain the persistence of magical rituals. Robert Merton argued that the latent function of the Hopi rain dance, its promotion of group solidarity, helps to explain the persistence of the ritual.[19] The problem here is that since the Hopi do not know that the ritual promotes solidarity, it is not clear what motivates them to practice it. From the intellectualist perspective, the Hopi perform the rain dance simply because they believe that it will bring rain or that it is one of the essential factors in bringing rain. In fact, Tylor gave a number of good reasons to explain why the participants in magic do not conclude that their rituals lack efficacy: magical actions are sometimes followed by their intended effects; failure is attributed to breaking taboos or hostile magical forces; notions of success and failure are not hard and fast; and the authority of the magician is supported by custom and tradition.

Since it is possible to assert that magic is both instrumental and symbolic, much of the debate between the neo-Tylorians and symbolists may be reduced to a matter of emphasis.[20] One might add that the relative importance of the instrumental and symbolic components may vary across different social, cultural, and religious contexts.

Interpretations: Millenarianism

The most common interpretation of millennial movements views the movements as providing compensation or seeking a remedy for oppressive conditions, suffering, strain, and tension. A number of scholars, some of whom have taken an explicitly Marxist approach, have interpreted millenarian movements as protests of the economically and politically oppressed who look forward to the overthrow of the existing order.[21] The movements appeal to colonized peoples, to peoples who have never gained or have been dispossessed of political power, and to members of the lower stratum in modern societies who have no access to political power.

Other scholars have interpreted millenarian movements as responses to the disruption of social and cultural patterns, although some cases, such as colonized societies, include both oppression and disruption. One acute instance of disruption is a disaster such as an epidemic, famine, war, or massacre. Following a disaster, persons feel vulnerable, confused, and full of anxiety, and they turn to millennial beliefs in order to account for the otherwise meaningless events. They interpret the disaster as a prelude to the millennium; thus their deepest despair gives way to the greatest hope.[22]

Millenarian and other religious movements are frequently said to arise in conditions of anomie, social disorganization, and relative deprivation. It is presumed that people require norms to orientate their lives, that they require communities for purposes of identity, dependency, communication, and involvement, and that they require a frame of reference within which they feel themselves of worth. When these needs are not met or when the structures that formerly met them are undermined, movements will emerge to provide a normative system, a cohesive community, or new comparative standards of status and worthiness.[23] A less common explanation of this type is that movements arise as a reaction against too much structure: in opposition to a rigidified structure the movements provide an "antistructure" or "communitas" which involves little role or status differentiation and comprises relationships that take more direct, immediate, and spontaneous forms.[24]

Sociologists using the remedy-compensation perspective have argued that strain or tension is a necessary but not a sufficient cause of a religious movement and that other conditions must be taken into consideration. In their analysis of how individuals become members of a religious millennial cult, John Lofland and Rodney Stark presented tension as one of three predisposing conditions prior to contact with the cult; the other two were a propensity to impose religious meanings on events and seekership, a searching for a more satisfactory system of religious meaning. In addition, they described a number of situational contingencies that led to successful recruitment: interaction with the cult occurring at a turning point in the life of the potential convert, his affective bonds with members, the absence of important or influential affective bonds with nonmembers, and, finally, his intensive interaction with members.[25]

Additional conditions have also been delineated by investigators who have paid less attention to the question of why certain individuals join a movement and more to the question of why a particular type of movement originated and spread in a particular area at a particular time. The mode of expression adopted by oppressed or deprived groups varies according to the established norms for resolving dissatisfaction and the presence or absence of viable options. A movement is likely to take religious rather than secular forms if the parent society lacks a tradition of political organization and popular agitation above the local level and the situation offers little hope of remedy by human agencies. The spread of a movement is likely to be influenced by such factors as the existence of channels of communication, the techniques and devices used by leaders to mobilize support, the response of social-control agencies, and the extent to which dominant groups can accommodate or isolate the movement.[26]

The success and spread of a religious movement may depend in large part on its orientations, policies, and organizational characteristics. These may be more important than the social context in which the movement originated. In his study of Jehovah's Witnesses in Britain, James Beckford found no evidence of objective indicators of deprivation, no frustrated mobility, and no economic or social relative deprivation. In addition, he found no evidence that Witnesses had sought a community of primary, affectual relationships or that they had been in a state of anomie. There was evidence that, prior to their affiliation, Witnesses had felt "ethical deprivation," a feeling that a discrepancy existed between what was happening in the world and what they believed should occur. But their moral indignation and concern had lacked sufficient clarity to motivate them to protest against the situation or to seek a movement with an answer. Beckford found that many Jehovah's Witnesses were recruited through members of their families, but that an even more important form of recruitment was the door-to-door evangelism of the movement. The major religious activity and status determinant of Jehovah's Witnesses is to go from door to door to sell the literature of the movement, to explain its ideas, and to convert. Beckford put great emphasis on the systematic evangelism of the movement to explain its success, and systematic evangelism was in turn related to the centralized organization of the movement: the top leaders make all the important decisions and direct the activities of members to the specific evangelical goals of the movement.[27]

Interpretations: Mysticism

There are many anthropological and sociological studies of millennial movements, but very little attention has been given to the social contexts of mysticism. Weber discussed the religion of the privileged intellectuals who seek salvation through mystical and contemplative channels. Unlike the salvation doctrines of the disprivileged strata, which reflect the need to compensate for present conditions, those of the intellectuals stem from an inner compulsion to understand the world, the "metaphysical needs of the human mind." Taken by itself, this is hardly a sociological explanation, but Weber argued that such intellectual needs were likely to operate in a particular social context of demilitarization when a ruling class loses its political power to another class. Since the privileged intellectuals no longer need concern themselves with practical political matters, they are able to turn their attention to other-worldly concerns. They find no significant meanings in the empirical world, and their religion often takes the form of a flight from the world.[28]

Mysticism is often associated with small, elite groups of intellectuals, but the mystic's emphasis on union or fusion with the divine is also found in Pentecostalism, a movement which has spread over many parts of the world. Pentecostalists believe that the Spirit of the Holy Ghost descends and enters their bodies or souls. The typical outward expression of the "baptism" of the Holy Spirit is glossolalia, speaking in "unknown tongues," which is a central part of their highly emotional services.

As it is with millennial movements, the most common explanation of Pentecostalism relies on the remedy-compensation approach: anomie, social disorganization, or relative deprivation. Early in this century Pentecostalism spread in the rapidly growing American cities where the large number of immigrants felt the loss of their traditional communities and found that the norms of the Old World were of little relevance in their new environment. The Pentecostal sects provided the immigrants with a community life and religious practices in which they could express their frustrations and assert their worth.[29] The growth of Pentecostal sects among a more recent immigrant group in the United States, the Puerto Ricans, has also been analyzed as a response to anomie and a quest for community. Thomas F. O'Dea and Renato Publeto argued that Pentecostalism provided both meaningful orientations and a cohesive community to Puerto Ricans who had lost their former normative consensus and whose traditional social networks had been disrupted by migration and dispersion.[30] A study of Pentecostal sects among West Indian immigrants in England interpreted their growth as a response to relative deprivation of status. Clifford Hill argued that the increasing expression of racial prejudice toward West Indians in Britain since about 1964 led to a rise of status deprivation among them, which in turn made them responsive to the compensations of emotional worship and religious status in Pentecostalism.[31]

In their studies of Pentecostalism in the United States and elsewhere, Luther P. Gerlach and Virginia H. Hine expressed their dissatisfaction with disorganization and deprivation theories. They noted that Pentecostalism spread in populations with close and well-adjusted family and community relationships; many Pentecostalists stated that they had been satisfied with the dominant norms and behavior patterns prior to their recruitment to the movement; and while Pentecostalism at the beginning of the twentieth century was particularly successful among migrants and the lower class, from the late 1950s it attracted support from a wide range of socioeconomic and educational backgrounds. After stressing the inadequacy of explanations that view Pentecostalism as a response to pre-existing social conditions, Gerlach and Hine presented an analysis that accounted for the success of the movement largely by features of the movement itself. For example, they argued that the decentralized structure of Pentecostalism and its segmentation into a great variety of localized cells, each essentially independent of the others and each with its own style, goals, and means, contributed to the growth of Pentecostalism in the United States and elsewhere. These organizational characteristics made the movement more difficult to suppress, permitted recruitment across a wide variety of class and cultural boundaries, maximized the possibilities of variation, innovation, and experimentation, and minimized the consequences for other groups of failure in one group.[32]

Summary of Perspectives

The interpretations discussed above, and their relevance in a study of religious movements, may be summarized as follows:

The intellectualist (neo-Tylorian) approach. Religious beliefs represent descriptions and interpretations of aspects of the empirical world, and religious ritual is believed to have instrumental efficacy. This approach has been used particularly with reference to tribal societies, but it is also highly relevant to a study of magic in more advanced societies. The typical social context of thaumaturgy is the tribe, village, or local community, but social change can undermine the traditional context and lead to the emergence of thaumaturgical movements, such as witch-finding movements. Wilson writes that a major problem faced by thaumaturgical movements is the maintenance of a stable commitment of members: the demand for individual service on the part of the magician's clients is not conducive to a strong or stable commitment to a formal belief system and regular ritual practice. However, the persistence of the demand for thaumaturgy has meant that religious movements of many types, including millenarian and mystical, have acquired thaumaturgical functions.[33]

The symbolist approach. In a reductionist interpretation religious phenomena simply reflect economic and social structure, but more sophisticated versions generally postulate some degree of consistency or congruency between different parts of the sociosymbolic system. Religious symbols and beliefs will, therefore, express or be congruent with experience in other parts of social and cultural life. Writers who use this approach differ in the social spheres or institutions that they emphasize as the bases of experience for religious symbolism. The emphasis may be on the general features of the total society, such as the number and characteristics of its constituent groups and institutions, the strength of its social boundaries, and the extent of its role differentiation.[34] Alternatively, the emphasis may be on particular groups or institutions: religion has been viewed as expressing family relationships, the style of life of status groups, or the political structure.[35] This approach has been used more frequently by anthropologists than sociologists. Anthropologists more commonly study relatively self-enclosed, small-scale societies with comparatively low degrees of differentiation between institutions or cultural patterns. Such societies are likely to demonstrate greater interdependence and congruency between religious symbols and social structure.

The remedy-compensation approach. This has been the most common approach in the study of religious movements in the West. Movements are viewed as responses to oppression, disaster, anomie, social disorganization, or relative deprivation, which are often found in various combinations. However, additional dimensions are often taken into consideration in order to account more fully for the type of movement.

The processual approach. In contrast to the interpretations in which movements are viewed either as compensatory responses to social situations or as symbolic expressions of a social situation, this approach emphasizes the characteristics of the religious movements themselves. It may be seen as complementary to, rather than opposed to, the other approaches; it is addressed more to the successful spread of a movement than to its origins at a particular time in a particular place. Its strength is that it demonstrates that movements should be analyzed not as the prestructured results of social, cultural, and psychological conditions but as emergent and processual entities the features of which play a large part in their development and spread.

Charisma and Its Routinization

One further theoretical problem requires discussion: the question of leadership. Religious movements have often been viewed as responses to the appeal of a leader or prophet. Some writers argue that appropriate social conditions, such as widespread deprivation, will not necessarily give rise to a religious movement; a strong leader whose message will be relevant to the situation and whose actions will transform and direct amorphous discontent into a movement is also needed. Other writers have argued that a leader will inevitably emerge when the situation demands it. The discussion of the role of leaders often revolves around the concept of charisma.

Weber applied the term *charisma* "to a certain quality of an individual personality by virtue of which he is set apart from ordinary men and treated as endowed with supernatural, superhuman, or at least specifically exceptional powers or qualities." By reason of his "gift of grace," the divine, heroic, or other extraordinary attributes that are believed to reside in his person, the charismatic leader inspires great devotion, enormous reverence, and absolute faith in his message or revelation. In contrast, a society employing legal-rational authority demands obedience to the legally established impersonal order; one that relies on traditional authority calls for obedience to a person bound by tradition and occupying a traditionally sanctioned position of authority. Since its focus is personal, the charismatic form of authority is naturally unstable: the holder may lose his charisma, be "forsaken by his god." Although he may retain his charisma by giving proof of his powers in miracles or other deeds that benefit his followers, it is important to emphasize that the basis of charisma is not in the signs or proofs of his powers but in the followers' complete faith that the individual has those powers, even if he chooses not to exercise them.

Conceived as a unique gift based on strictly personal social relationships and distant from everyday routine structures, the "pure" type of charismatic authority is necessarily a transitory and intermittent phenomenon. A charismatic movement or following is united by its belief in the extraordinary qualities and teachings of a leader, but if it is to continue as a permanent and stable structure, a transformation of the charismatic type of authority is required. Although the desires of the leader may be relevant, in most cases the ideal and material interests of his staff, disciples, and followers are the decisive factors in the demand for continuation. Those interests are particularly evident when the charismatic leader dies or disappears and the problem of succession arises. Among the various solutions to the problem of succession, Weber distinguished six principal types: a search for a new charismatic leader who conforms to certain qualities; revelation through oracles or other techniques; designation by the original charismatic leader; designation by the administrative staff; hereditary charisma; and transmission by ritual means. In addition to the problem of succession, Weber noted other processes involved in the routinization of charisma: the regulation of recruitment of members; the selection, deployment, and benefices of the administrative staff; and the development of a fiscal organization to provide for the needs of the group.[36]

The concept of charisma has often been given meanings not intended by Weber which have devalued the analytical value of the term. In the popular and vulgarized use of the term, charisma is made a quality of an individual personality: the charismatic leader is a person with extraordinary character and unusual ability. On occasion, Weber has been accused of presenting a "Great Man" theory of history[37] or a psychologistic approach to authority.[38] More moderate critics have accused him of allowing ambiguity in his presentation so that it is not clear where the emphasis lies.[39] However, a close reading of Weber's writings on charisma in the framework of his overall analysis of domination leaves little doubt: for Weber, charismatic authority denoted not outstanding personality but a relationship in which the emphasis is on the followers' recognition or attribution of charismatic powers to their leader.[40] It is possible for men with mediocre personalities or little ability to have charismatic powers attributed to them, and even when the charismatic leader does have unusual personality features and abilities, these are rarely equal to the claims made by his followers.[41]

Some sociologists have defined charisma sociologically, but they have moved a long way from Weber's formulation. Talcott Parsons's definition of charisma made it synonymous with Durkheim's sacred: a quality of things and persons that sets them apart from the ordinary and the everyday.[42] This definition is built upon Weber's comment that charismatic authority is oriented to the satisfaction of extraordinary needs which transcend economic routines, but it divorces the concept from Weber's major concern with types of domination. According to Edward Shils, the charismatic propensity is a function of the need for order, the need to provide coherence, continuity, and justice, and anything that contributes to this order will awaken a sense of awe and reverence. All effective rulers possess charismatic qualities, since they have power over order. Similarly, charisma is located in corporate bodies by virtue of the tremendous power concentrated in them and in various occupations, such as judges, scientists, and artists, by virtue of their central concern with the administration and expression of order.[43]

The advantages of making charisma virtually synonymous with such terms as sacredness and legitimacy are not clear; moreover, in such an interpretation the utility of Weber's discussion on the types and subtypes of domination is lost. Shils is able to write about different degrees of charisma, the reduced intensity of charisma in the rational-legal system in contrast to its concentration in a single person, but it is difficult to see how he could deal with the problem of routinization, distinguish types of charisma, and analyze their combinations with other forms of authority.

If we retain Weber's formulation of charisma, there remains a question of whether the concept has any explanatory value. Peter Worsley, who found considerable ambiguity in Weber's formulation, argued that charisma cannot be used as an explanation of collective social action. He emphasized that followers create and select those leaders who express and promise fulfillment of their interests and desires. In some movements the leaders simply transmit a message that they took no part in formulating; in others the leaders define the message or transform vague aspirations into more specific terms and concrete goals.[44] Worsley's emphasis on the leader as symbol and message-bearer is not in conflict with Weber's formulation. But as Wilson points out, although the message may need to be congenial, it is not everything; there may also be a demand for a man whose supernatural powers are the only guarantee that the followers' desires will be fulfilled. The belief that the message is embodied in or revealed by the charismatic leader gives this form of authority the capacity to overthrow custom, law, and tradition.[45] In addition, the forms of organization that emerge in the process of the routinization of charisma may contribute to an explanation of the success and spread of a movement. Consideration of the routinization of charisma can be related to the processual type of explanation discussed above.

Weber's use of the phrase "routinization of charisma" has been criticized as illogical and contradictory. Something that has been defined as anti-routine and personal, critics argue, cannot be routinized and depersonalized; it is better, they say, to refer to the transformation of charismatic authority into other forms of authority.[46] Weber made clear that charismatic authority becomes traditionalized, rationalized, or a combination of both, and he gave many examples to illustrate this transformation. At the same time, Weber wished to emphasize that the element of charisma, in the sense of "the gift of grace," or supernatural or extraordinary elements, does not necessarily disappear. The distinctive elements of "pure" charisma, the concentration of a unique gift of grace in a single individual and the absence of routine procedures, will necessarily disappear, but the gift of grace may be transformed into a quality that is personally acquirable or attached to an office or to an institutional structure. Weber wrote: "We are justified in still speaking of charisma in this impersonal sense because there always remains an extraordinary quality which is not accessible to everyone and which typically overshadows the charismatic subjects."[47]

3. Religion and Magic in the Traditional Jewish Community

BEFORE ANALYZING popular Jewish religious movements in the medieval and early-modern periods, it is necessary to describe the religious context in which they arose. The past tense will be used throughout, although many of the beliefs and practices are widespread among Jews today. What are far less prevalent today are the beliefs and practices of what may be termed the folk religion, those religious beliefs and practices that fell outside the compass of the rabbinically recognized texts and rituals.

A distinction between folk and official Judaism cannot, however, be made too sharply, for Judaism had no coordinating and sanctifying central authority that bound all Jews to a clearly demarcated system of beliefs and practices. The synagogue was a place of prayer, study, and assembly, but unlike the church, it was not an agent of religious control. Each local *kehillah*, the semiautonomous Jewish community organization, was able to impose sanctions for religious deviance, but in religious matters most communities and rabbis were independent of any higher Jewish organization. The rabbinical hierarchy was a largely informal one based on number of followers and recognition of outstanding religious scholarship. The rabbinical networks and hierarchy were employed to control deviations, to settle controversies, and to establish synods, but these organizations were generally set up for specific purposes and rarely continued for a long time.

Moses Maimonides (1135–1204) argued that entry to the world to come was contingent upon subscribing to thirteen fundamental beliefs, which he delineated, but other medieval Jewish scholars challenged his formulation with alternative creeds or argued that it was impossible to isolate the essential dogmas of the Jewish faith. The precise formulation of doctrine and practice was in the hands of the local religious leadership, and there were, in fact, many local variations in *minhag* (practice).

The majority of Jews accepted the sacred texts of official or rabbinic Judaism. The most important of these are the Bible, the Talmud, and the Siddur, the book of common prayer. The "written law," or Bible, is composed of the Pentateuch (the five books of Moses), the prophets, and a collection of other writings. Expositions and interpretations of the Bible, containing ethical and moral teaching as well as legends and folklore, are known as the Midrash. The "oral law," or Talmud, consists of the Mishnah, a codification of rabbinic collections up to the end of the second century C.E., and the Gemara (literally, completion), which contains clarifications and expansions of the Mishnah with further codifications, completed about 500 C.E. The subject matter of the Talmud is divided into the Halachah, which deals with legal matters and rules of conduct covering every aspect of life, and the Aggadah, which treats homiletical, moral, and allegorical matters, including discussions on history and legend. There is a vast rabbinic literature of further interpretations, additions, and compilations made since the completion of the Talmud. The most famous compilation of Jewish law in the late medieval and early modern period was the *Shulchan Aruch*, written by Joseph Karo (1488–1575), which, together with the additional notes by Moses Isserles (1520–72), became the established code for Ashkenazi Jews.

The majority accepted their religious leaders' interpretations of the sacred texts, and in its prescriptions of the rituals of the day, the Sabbath, festivals, and other holy days, rabbinic Judaism was of central importance in the religion of the Jewish masses.[1] The emphasis placed on the value of religious study for all Jewish men meant that there was no division between a literate minority and an illiterate majority. In comparison with that of the Christian population, the general level of religious knowledge among Jews was very high. Nevertheless, the distance between the religion of the leadership and the religion of the Jewish masses was often considerable. Most Jews had little knowledge of or interest in the purely intellectual studies and debates of scholars, and they held many beliefs and practices that were not part of rabbinic Judaism.

The religious intelligentsia often removed themselves, intellectually and socially, from the masses. This was the case among both the medieval Jewish philosophers and the mystic cabbalists, who were radically different from each other in their intellectual orientations. The famous philosopher Maimonides emphasized the differences between the intellectual and the masses, regarding the common people as foolish and ignorant.[2] In contrast to the philosophers, the cabbalists included the religious behavior of the masses in their religious schemes, but at least up to the sixteenth century, they remained an exclusive and elite group whose doctrines were only comprehensible to initiates. The focus of the rabbinate, who provided the official religious leadership, was the study of the Talmud, especially the Halachah, and the extent to which this activity affected unscholarly Jews was highly variable. A favorite activity of the rabbinate in eastern Europe in the eighteenth century, and one which had little relation to the day-to-day religious life of the Jewish masses, was the technique of *pilpul* (dialectic or hairsplitting). This was a means to find the correct meaning of the text, but it often became an end in itself. In pilpul a rabbi took various passages from the sacred writings which at first glance appeared to be unrelated or to be in contradiction, revealed the inconsistencies in the commentaries on the passages, and then revealed affinities in the texts or reconciled the contradictions.

An important difference between official religion and folk religion was that the latter dealt more extensively with thaumaturgical concerns and used magical practices. This does not mean that all religious scholars disbelieved in magic. The Bible condemned sorcery, but the rabbinic authorities of the Talmud had divided sorcery into several divisions. They condemned idolatrous magical acts—that is, those which did not invoke the aid of a supernatural being—under punishment of death. They also condemned magic with the assistance of demons, but the punishment was less severe. Finally, they permitted magical action that invoked an appeal to the powers of good, since this recognized the supremacy of God.[3]

A parallel can be drawn between the talmudic distinctions between forbidden and permitted magic and the distinctions made by some anthropologists in their discussions on magic and religion. As noted in the previous chapter, magic and religion can be distinguished by their different conceptions of the supernatural: in magic the supernatural is an impersonal power subject to manipulation, whereas in religion the supernatural is a personalized power.

Frazer recognized that this distinction is difficult to use when persons hold beliefs in supernatural intermediaries that can be forced into action by a spell or some other magical action. He suggested a further distinction between types of magic, which was identical to the one made by the talmudic sages: between magic that invokes a supernatural intermediary and magic that invokes no supernatural being. This produced a further problem, however. If magic includes the possibility of a supernatural intermediary, the earlier distinction between magic and religion becomes unusable. It has been suggested that one way to solve this dilemma is to state that in magic the supernatural agent has to obey the orders of the magician whether it wants to or not. There is little personalization in magic; the user of magic believes that the agent has the ability to understand and the power to fulfil the order, but that its own preferences and dispositions are irrelevant. The religious worshiper appeals to a supernatural agency, but that agency is not obliged to act and can accede to or refuse the request depending on its will and relationship to the worshiper.

Distinctions and classifications of magical and religious actions along these lines are often difficult to make. It is difficult to determine the degree of freedom of action that the supernatural agents are perceived to have or to what extent they will simply follow commands. A ritual directed to a single agent may include both requests and commands, both entreaties and admonitions.[4] Most Jewish magical practice in the Middle Ages had recourse to supernatural beings, and the success of magicians was seen to be dependent on their religious piety.

Medieval scholars repeated the biblical condemnation of magic, but admitted the "permitted" categories under a number of terms. In practice, scholars excluded from forbidden magic those forms that were in current use among Jews. While a few scholars in southern Europe condemned magic in toto, this was not the case elsewhere. Some scholars condemned a particular form of magic or the popular misapplication of various teachings, but most admitted the permitted categories when practiced by men of learning and piety.[5]

At the popular level persons had little knowledge of or paid little attention to the distinctions between forbidden and permitted magic, and although the talmudic scholars were often believed to be the greatest miracle workers, it was not uncommon for unscholarly Jews to practice magic. Women were involved in magical activity, such as providing charms and love potions, but where the magician was a distinctive role, it was generally performed by men, since only they had sufficient religious education to know the correct holy names. Magicians came to be known as Ba'alei Shem (Masters of the Name); these became rather numerous especially in Germany and Poland from the sixteenth century. Some Ba'alei Shem were important rabbis and talmudic scholars, but the number of unscholarly Ba'alei Shem increased in the seventeenth and eighteenth centuries.[6]

The following two sections of this chapter provide a brief summary of the major features of the common beliefs and practices of medieval and early-modern Jews in Europe. This includes both those parts of rabbinic Judaism which were also part of the religion of the majority and the nonofficial folk religion.[7]

Beliefs

Pantheon. A pantheon is a society's system of supernatural beings and agencies; it is generally presented as a hierarchy, listing the various agents in order of importance. Monotheistic religions invariably include an elaborate pantheon, but they are distinctive from other religions insofar as one god is given ultimate rule and direction over the various forms which the supernatural is believed to take. Weber wrote: "Only Judaism and Islam are strictly monotheistic in their essence."[8] Other religious traditions that have emphasized a single high god have introduced such principles as the trinity in Christianity and dualism in Zoroastrianism, which may be interpreted to have compromised the monotheistic principle. In the official mainstream of Jewish monotheism, God is defined as an absolute unity; his nature admits no plurality. He is absolutely unique; no other being can in any way be compared to him. He created and sustains the universe; only his existence is necessary, uncaused, and eternal. His will and purposes are supreme; he is not subject to the manipulative powers of magic, and he demands that humans act according to his law. Although he allows the possibility of a direct and personal relationship with man, he is transcendent, ineffable, distant, and mysterious, transcending human apprehension and standing outside the cosmos.

The importance to the history of the West of the differentiation that emerged in ancient Judaism between a transcendental God and a disenchanted world can be little doubted. The religious systems of other ancient societies regarded human behavior and social arrangements as direct reflections or manifestations of the activities and characteristics of divine beings or principles: the ruler was a divine incarnation or an agent of the gods, and the gods participated in social institutions, such as kinship, at a higher level. This mythological scheme and monistic universe was undermined in Judaism, which presented a vast abyss between God, an infinite and transcendental being, and man, a finite creature.[9]

The rabbis of the talmudic period carried this process further: their doctrine of *creatio ex nihilo* represented a definite break with myth; they interpreted the vestiges of myth and anthropomorphism in the Bible in a metaphorical sense; and they developed an antimagical system of legal commandments which divorced the law from cosmic events. Each commandment was a rite of resemblance: in observing a commandment, the Jew was not imitating or affecting divine actions or processes, but was evoking the historical event that established the law. The antimythological tendency was accentuated by the rationalistic stream in medieval rabbinic Judaism. This was particularly true among the philosophers who sought to preserve and reinforce the pure unity of the concept of God and to divest it of all mythical and anthropomorphic elements. The increasingly urban character of the Jewish people aided this development. The Jewish rites developed in the Talmud still reflected an intimate relationship between God and man in nature, but in the diaspora the nature rituals became historical rituals: rituals came to represent historical reminiscence rather than the cycle of the natural year.

Even at the level of the Jewish intelligentsia, however, the picture of an increasingly abstract monotheism in the ancient and medieval periods requires some qualification. Mythological tendencies were not absent in the talmudic period, but for our purposes, it is sufficient to note developments within the cabbalah, the mystical doctrines of the medieval period. The term *cabbalah* is often used to apply to the whole history of Jewish mysticism, but in the more restricted sense of the term the cabbalah began at the end of the twelfth century in southern France and became centered in the thirteenth century in Spain. The most important single cabbalistic work, the Zohar, was written around 1286 in Spain by Moses de Leon (circa 1240–1305), who attributed his work to the famous second-century talmudic teacher Rabbi Shimon Ben Yohai.

In part, the cabbalah represented a reaction to the antimythological and antimonistic world of mainstream rabbinism. The cabbalists retained the notion of a transcendental, infinite God and did not return to a mythical stage of religion. Instead, they presented a dialectical synthesis of mythical and transcendental religion containing many diverse and contradictory elements. The cabbalists expressed the absolute and unknowable aspects of the divine by the term *Ein-Sof* (Infinite), and they built a phenomenally complex and intricate theosophy around the notion of the progressive manifestations or emanations of the Divinity. The successive manifestations of the Divinity were divided into ten fundamental categories, realms, or phases known as *Sephirot*: Crown, Wisdom, Intelligence, Mercy, Power, Compassion, Eternity, Majesty, Foundation, and Kingdom. The Sephirot were correlated to a great number of other symbols, such as the body of *Adam Kadmon* (primordial man), the names of God, the elements, the metals, and the mythical cosmic tree. The mythological theme was pronounced in the symbolic correlations between four Sephirot and a divine family: Wisdom was the Supernal Father, Intelligence was the Supernal Mother, Compassion was their Son, and the last Sephira, Kingdom, was their Daughter. The cabbalists made clear that the members of the divine family were but four aspects of the godhead, but many passages of the Zohar appear to move from the metaphorical to the mythological realm. The members of the divine family had independent feelings, and they conversed and interrelated with each other as separate persons. The Zohar also gave numerous accounts of episodes in their lives and described the relationships between the divine couple and between son and daughter in highly erotic terms.

The cabbalah reintroduced the close interrelationships of mythological religion between events in the divine realm and events in the world. The happy and intense love relationship between the divine son and daughter was disrupted by the sins of Israel, and the divine bedchamber was destroyed with the destruction of the Temple and the exile of the Jewish people. The daughter was also known as the Queen, Lady, *Matronit*, and *Shechinah*. In the talmudic sense the Shechinah represented the manifestation of God's presence on earth, especially in Israel, but the cabbalah identified the Shechinah with both the feminine aspects of the divine and the community of Israel. Thus, the exile of the Jewish people represented a separation of the masculine and feminine principles of the Divinity, and the Redemption of the Jewish people would constitute the reunion of those principles.

The cabbalists stressed not only the interrelationship of the divine and human worlds but also their mutual effects. The observance of a commandment was a concrete symbol of a divine essence, but it also transmitted an effect to that essence. The Zohar stressed that all "upper happenings" required stimulation by "lower happenings." Every religious act performed with the proper *kavanah* (intention) was "for the sake of the reunion of God and His Shechinah." Not only important historical events but also the regular activities of ordinary people were built into the cosmogony. The weekly divine union of the King and the Matronit was the prototype of the traditional weekly union between husbands and wives. According to the cabbalists, when pious scholars coupled with their wives on Friday night, they recognized that they were imitating the union that took place at the same time between the divine beings. If the wife conceived at that time, the child would have one of the pure souls procreated in the divine copulation. The human imitation of the divine act not only sanctified the sexual act but also helped the godhead to achieve mystical unity: the human act caused the King to fertilize the Matronit, who gave birth to human souls and angels.

The cabbalists rejected any charge that they were polytheistic heretics. They claimed that while a passage might appear to be heretical, its true meaning was in conformity with tradition, which would be understood if a person immersed himself in the hidden truths. They argued that their conceptions did not affect the fundamental Oneness of God but that the Shechinah and other elements were symbols that would help men comprehend the divine emanations. The cabbalists were traditional mystics insofar as they accepted the sacred texts and the existing ritual of rabbinic Judaism. They did not reject the literal meanings of the Torah, but they tended to devalue them in favor of symbolic meanings that were hidden in the text. Every word of the Torah was said to have six thousand "faces," or meanings, which were found at different levels of the mystical search and could be ordered in a hierarchy. Likewise, they attributed new meanings to the traditional rituals. For example, they related rituals of the Sabbath and festivals to the sacred marriage, the union of the male and female aspects of the Divinity. The cabbalists did not regard their new interpretations as a break with traditional authority, and they confirmed that authority by claiming that their revelations had come from the Prophet Elijah, whom they conceived as the vigilant custodian of Jewish tradition. Their claim that they had communicated with the Prophet Elijah rather than directly with God was also an acknowledgment that their revelations were lower and less authoritative than the revelations of the past.[10]

Jewish mysticism was relational and nonabsorptive: the complexities of its theosophy were set within the framework of a unique and unknowable God. It was hypernomian rather than antinomian: the cabbalists tended to be highly pious, ascetic men who kept the *mitsvot* (commandments) in a strict fashion. The emphasis was on knowledge rather than experience: the cabbalists were less interested in describing their experiences than in presenting mystical commentaries on the texts. In contrast to the rabbinic tradition, where the object of study was God's revealed will, the object of study of the mystics was the Divinity itself; but the mystics remained traditionalists in following the method of scholarly commentary on the texts, and they generally accepted the rule that mystical practice and speculation should be restricted to fully trained talmudic scholars.[11]

The cabbalists were, therefore, an esoteric elite within an elite, and up to the end of the sixteenth century, they showed no interest in spreading their ideas among the masses. Until the end of the fifteenth century the influence of the Zohar was confined mainly to small circles in Spain and Italy. Its influence gradually spread after the expulsion of the Jews from Spain in 1492, but it took some time before its influence was felt among the Ashkenazi Jews in northwestern, central, and eastern Europe.[12]

The complicated theosophy of the cabbalah remained the esoteric concern of a small elite, but certain elements, doctrines, and practices were absorbed at the popular level. One branch of the cabbalah which appealed to the unscholarly came to be known as "practical cabbalah." This focused on the magical use of the sacred and esoteric names of God and the angels, but the term *practical cabbalah* came to be used to encompass all magical practices in Jewish communities. A number of cabbalistic beliefs, such as the transmigration of souls, became part of folk Judaism, and certain cabbalistic rituals, such as the midnight vigils for the exile of the Shechinah, became widespread.[13] The conception of the Shechinah as the female element within the Deity had an important influence on the masses from the sixteenth century. In its popular expressions the Shechinah was no mere symbol or emanation but a discrete goddess who took on pronounced physical attributes and with whom the people could feel a deep, emotional attachment. Unlike the divine King who had become remote from the people following the destruction of the Temple, the Shechinah shared the exile of the Jewish people and could be approached directly at any time or place.[14]

Quite apart from the influence of certain cabbalistic conceptions, the Jewish pantheon was populated by numerous angels and demons. Weber wrote that in no religion was the existence of spirits and demons permanently eliminated; the need remained for accessible and tangible religious objects that could be brought into relationship with concrete life situations and were accessible to magical influence.[15] Perhaps more than in other religions, the numerous supernatural forms in folk Judaism were subordinated to the will of God. The angels, which were numerous, each having a distinct name and personality, were seen as the means by which God ruled over all aspects of life. Angels had a great influence on events and human behavior, and they could be instrumental in punishing a transgression of the Law. On the other hand, the angels were seen as mediators between man and God, appearing before God either as man's defenders or persecutors and performing many acts on their own accord without special orders from God.

In addition to the angels, the souls of the dead were believed to be able to intercede in heaven on behalf of the living. Spirits of the dead inhabited the earth and came into frequent contact with the living, whom they could help or harm. They retained their bodily forms, and during the night they conversed, pursued their studies, and congregated in prayer.

Apart from a few scholars in southern Europe, almost nobody doubted the existence of demons. Only a few demons were seen to have distinguishing characteristics; some remained from talmudic times, but demons from the non-Jewish environment were adopted en masse in the Middle Ages. Satan, who was known by a number of names, especially Samael, was not as prominent as he was in Christianity. Lilith, the chief female demon, had an important position in Jewish demonology. She was known as a child killer and as a seducer of men, from whose nocturnal emissions she bore many demonic sons.

Demons were somewhat vague entities who combined the characteristics of angels and men: they had wings, but they ate, drank, propagated, and died. No place, time, or individual was exempt from the dangers of an attack by demons, but the risk was greater outside the boundaries of a settled community, in the forests and fields, and in unclean places. The danger was particularly great during the critical stages of life: birth, marriage, illness, and death. For infant boys, the period prior to circumcision was especially dangerous, for demons would attempt to prevent their taking their place in the world to come. Demons would attempt to upset the happiness of a bridal pair, and they would surround a dying man in order to gain possession of his corpse.

The *dibbuk*, a demon, evil spirit, or doomed soul who entered the body of a living person, was an especially common belief among eastern European Jews. A bodiless spirit, the dibbuk wished to acquire a body; once inside the body, he talked through the person's mouth and caused symptoms of mental illness. Ideas about witches, their compact with the devil, and their ability to change form were adopted from Christians. The general belief was that Jews were not witches, but occasionally someone within the community was suspected of being a witch. A further agency of evil was the evil eye, a belief which was very prevalent among east European Jews. The evil eye had two meanings: one was that a person was born with the evil eye, that it could be recognized by the peculiar cast of the eye, and that every glance produced rays of destruction; the other was that a glance that expressed envy or hatred would attract the evil spirits, who would act accordingly.

Like Christians, Jews generally accepted the notion that every person had a star in heaven whose history was coterminous with his own, that the heavenly constellations at any given moment controlled human actions and events, and that the study of the stars would disclose the future. Maimonides was an exception in disputing the truth of astrology, and his writings on the subject were not influential. For the majority, the issue was not whether the stars had an influence but the extent of that influence. Some argued that the influence of the stars was subject to the will of God or that God could modify or change the fate that was "written in the stars."[16]

Myths. In tribal and archaic societies myths chronicle the activities of divine beings, the origins of man, nature, and society, and the relationships between the gods and past members of the society, especially cultural heroes. The cultures of more advanced societies have codified and official mythohistorical narratives, such as the Bible and auxiliary texts. The most central myth in Judaism was the giving of the Torah to Israel through Moses on Mount Sinai. Jews believed that God had revealed at Sinai not only the Ten Commandments but the whole of the Torah, a complete way of life according to God's will. The five books of Moses, or Pentateuch, were transmitted by Moses in writing, but the vast majority of statutes were transmitted orally by Moses to Joshua, and then through the prophets, the men of the Great Synagogue, and finally the rabbis, who committed them to writing after the destruction of the Second Temple.

The Talmud explained that the people of Israel had been chosen by God because of their willingness to bear the yoke of the Torah after other nations had rejected it. Israel was the nation closest to God, the chosen people, the only nation to submit to the 613 mitsvot of the Torah. In return for living in accordance with the commandments, God promised to give Israel the land of Canaan and make Israel a nation above all others. Exile from the Promised Land was a consequence of the people's betrayal of the covenant, but the Shechinah dwelt with Israel even in exile and after the day of redemption the people would return to the Holy Land.

The myth of the covenant on Sinai justified the whole way of life of the Jews, explained why they were the chosen people, accounted for the exile, and promised future redemption.

Apart from the central official myths, popular religion contained many myths that accounted for the origins and characteristics of supernatural beings. For example, the myths gave a number of explanations for the existence of demons. According to a talmudic tradition, God had created a number of spirits in the last stages of creation, but the coming of the Sabbath prevented him from creating their bodies. Another tradition held that demons were the result of the copulation of Adam with Lilith. Demons were also believed to be the spirits of wicked people or the offspring of the nocturnal emissions of men.

Values. The highest value in the traditional Jewish community was study of the Torah. The study of the Torah made full observance of the mitsvot possible, but it was also a religious value in itself. It was possible to criticize a man for spending too much time on his prayers at the expense of his studies.

The value of Torah study applied to men; women's role was to assist men to live according to it. The ideal was that not only the scholarly elite but all Jewish men would study the Torah, perhaps on a certain day of the week or for a fixed time each day. For those who lacked the intellect or education necessary for this study, the rabbis introduced selections from the major religious texts into the synagogue services, so that all could obey the commandment to study, if only symbolically.

The importance of study was clear in the important institutions of the society. Status and prestige depended on level of scholarship. Wealth was not sufficient in itself to achieve the highest status, but wealth and scholarship often went hand in hand. Scholars served as communal leaders, and wealthy young men served as rabbis; moreover, it was the ambition of many to establish a new *yeshivah* (advanced educational institution). A number of educational institutions provided at least an elementary religious education for all males, but their major aim was to produce scholars who would study at the yeshivot. Marriages were often arranged according to the religious scholarship of the prospective bridegroom, and it was not unusual for a wealthy man to support financially his son-in-law while the latter devoted his time to study. The wife of a scholar often managed the family business, thereby giving her husband the time to study.[17]

Theodicy. Two meanings of theodicy may be distinguished. The first, more inclusive definition is that theodicies are attempts to explain and find meaning in "ultimate problems": unjust suffering, unjust rewards, and problems of evil and death. The second, more exclusive definition is that theodicies are attempts to solve the contradiction in monotheistic religions between, on the one hand, evil and unjust suffering and, on the other, a universal, transcendental, omnipotent, omniscient, and benevolent God. It may be argued that if God were both omnipotent and benevolent, he would eliminate evil and suffering.

A problem with the more general formulation of theodicy is that we often need to assume that a need to explain unjust suffering once existed, but that this need no longer exists because a religious solution has been found. There may be no historical evidence that such a need did exist prior to the emergence of the religious beliefs that are assumed to provide the solution. The histories of monotheistic religions may point to the problem of theodicy in its more limited meaning, but it may not be easy to distinguish the two problems. It is necessary to emphasize that the problem of theodicy, either in its first or second sense, is one which is defined by religion itself. Not all religions distinguish a category of unjust, as opposed to just, suffering or define it as a religious problem. Judaism, however, did pose the problems of suffering and justice within the monotheistic context.

Weber distinguished five types of theodicy: a future, perfect world on this earth; compensation in heaven after death; a God who is beyond human comprehension; dualism; and the transmigration of souls.[18] All these types were found in varying degrees of importance in the Jewish religion of the Middle Ages and early-modern period. The first type, the belief in the millennium or messianic age, will be discussed in detail in the next chapter. The classic text for the third type (God is beyond human comprehension, and one cannot apply the criteria of human justice to him) was the Book of Job, but for many Jews this provided no real answer to, or comfort for, their suffering.

The rabbis of the talmudic period continued to be troubled by the problem that God ruled man with absolute justice, and their answer was that God's justice was not bounded by the limits and understandings of man's short earthly existence. Justice could not be fully administered in this world because God wished to give the sinner all the opportunities to repent; justice was to be distributed after death. At the "end of days" the dead were to be resurrected and brought before God for judgment; the righteous would live in eternal bliss, while the wicked perished. An interpretation that conflicted with this one, and which probably reflected a Greek influence, was that the soul was immortal. The contradiction between the two notions was solved when it was proposed that after death an individual's soul would live in another realm (heaven or hell) and that when the dead were resurrected, the soul would rejoin the body for judgment.[19] Both scholarly and popular works gave detailed descriptions of the nature of divisions of hell, its torturers, and the terrible punishments and afflictions that awaited the wicked and unrepentant.[20]

The theodicies discussed above relate to justice and the punishment of wicked deeds, but not to the problem of evil itself. Unlike Zoroastrianism, Judaism did not present a dualistic system of a good God and an evil God; evil was presented as an integral part of the cosmos. Evil was to some extent personified in Satan, but Judaism gave greater emphasis to "the powers of evil," "the other side," or *kelippot* (literally, shells or husks), which were personified in a great number of demons and evil spirits. According to the Zohar, Adam's sin had generated the kelippot, and the people's sins continued to activate them. Most Jews were less concerned with evil as an ultimate problem than with the evil powers that caused misfortune and illness. These were explained by the influence of a demon, the entrance of a dibbuk, a glance from an evil eye, or the work of a sorcerer or witch.

The development and spread of the doctrine of the transmigration of souls (*gilgul*) in the medieval period indicates that not all Jews were satisfied with the available answers to suffering and justice in their tradition. Gilgul first appeared in the late-twelfth-century cabbalistic work *Bahir*, and was further developed by cabbalistic writers. The cabbalists differed among themselves over such questions as whether gilgul governed all humans, the number of possible transmigrations, and whether people were punished by transmigrations into animals, plants, and inorganic matter. The doctrine was adopted into the folk religion, especially in eastern Europe, and was used to explain a wide range of phenomena. If the righteous suffered or if a newborn baby died, they were being punished for their sins in their previous lives; barrenness was a male soul in a female body; and proselytes to Judaism were Jewish souls who had passed into the bodies of gentiles but were restored to their former state.[21]

Religious Practice

Religious behavior in Judaism may be divided into conformity to the commandments in one's everyday interactions with other people, animals, and objects and institutionalized forms of communication directed to the divine. The former included ethical, moral, and legalistic directives. An emphasis on ritual purity was expressed in the dietary laws, the taboos on menstruating women and women who have just given birth, purification by immersion in the *mikveh* (ritual bath), and avoidance of contact or any association with "idolatry," especially anything that was symbolic of Christ.

In rabbinical Judaism ritual that aimed at communicating with the divine could be performed by an individual or a group. Prayer was considered most efficacious when offered with a congregation, and a number of essential prayers could be recited only at a group service. In official Judaism communication between the individual or the group and God was seen as direct, with no human or supernatural intermediary. The important official religious functionaries were in no way intermediaries; the major role of the rabbi was to study and interpret the law, and the *chazan* (reader) led the congregation in prayer. However, in folk Judaism supernatural and human intermediaries were more common. Requests were made to the spirits of the dead to intercede in heaven, and the attainment of a goal through supernatural means sometimes required the employment of a magician who knew the correct formulas or had special power over the agency.

The major means of conveying the messages in ritual was the oral language, the recital or prayer, but symbolic use was also made of the body, numerous objects and actions, and food and drink. No musical instruments were allowed during religious services, but important use was made of vocal music, the traditional cantillation and chants. Some prayers were read silently, others audibly but in a low tone, and others loudly. Parts of the service were read in unison; other parts were read individually. The services were divided into sections where worshipers stood and those where they sat, and worshipers expressed themselves with their bodies by bowing, stepping forward and backward, and swaying to and fro. Dance as a form of worship was restricted to a very few occasions.

The Jewish tradition forbade any visual representation of the deity, and most ritual objects symbolized religious values or historical events. The shape of the synagogue lacked symbolic meaning, and the interior of the synagogue did not contain any bold religious symbols. The central role of the Torah in synagogue worship was shown by the prominence of the *bimah*, the raised platform on which the Torah was read, and the holy ark, in which the scrolls were kept. A light hung in front of the ark symbolized the spiritual light forever emanating from the Torah.

An example of a symbolic form of contact with sacred objects was the kiss. A worshiper kissed the fringes of his *tallit* (prayer shawl) during the recitation of the last paragraph of the *Shema* prayer. When the Torah scrolls were carried from and to the ark, everyone within reach touched the mantle of the scrolls and then kissed the place that had come into contact with the scrolls. Men kissed the *tefillin* (phylacteries) when they took them out and before they returned them to their receptacles. Before entering a house, Jews kissed the *mezuzah* on the doorpost. All these actions of kissing symbolized the love and devotion to the Torah and its commandments. If a Jew accidentally dropped a prayer book, he kissed it to apologize for his carelessness.

Food and drink were important symbols. The meal on the eve of the Sabbath was preceded by the *kiddush*, a benediction recited over a cup of wine, a symbol of blessing and joy, to proclaim the sanctity of the day. Two loaves of bread symbolized the double portion of manna that fell for the Israelites on a Friday during their travels in the wilderness so that they did not need to collect it on the Sabbath. The cloth covering the bread symbolized the protective cover of dew over the manna. During *Pesach* (Passover) leavened bread was prohibited, and *matzot* (unleavened bread) were eaten. This commemorated the hasty flight from Egypt when the Israelites had time to prepare only unleavened bread. The Passover meal, the *Seder*, the most elaborate sacred meal of the year when the *Haggadah* was read, included a dish with a number of symbolic foods: for example, horseradish to symbolize the bitterness of slavery, and *haroset*, a mixture of nuts and apples, to symbolize the mortar out of which the Israelites made bricks for the Pharaoh.

The Jewish ritual year included a number of fasts. Twenty-four-hour fasts were held on *Yom Kippur* (The Day of Atonement) and the Ninth of *Av*. The Fast of Esther and Fast of the Firstborn were held from sunrise to sunset. The very pious fasted far more often. The increasing trend to mortification of the flesh during the medieval period is shown by the increase in the number of fasts, some of which were local, and such practices as flagellation on *Yom Kippur*.

As the above examples of Jewish religious symbols indicate, the important objects and goals of official Jewish ritual were praise and thanksgiving, recitation and affirmation of the religious code, repentance, and the commemoration of past events. Most daily Jewish prayers were *berachot* (benedictions), and the Jewish liturgy provided expressions of praise and thanksgiving for an enormous range of experiences: when rising from sleep, dressing, eating, and drinking; for less routine experiences such as escaping from danger and recovery from illness; and upon perceiving something in nature such as mountains, rivers, and deserts. Prayers referred to far more than the immediate occasion: the prayer after meals gave thanks not only for the food but also for the Land of Israel, the Torah, the covenant, the temple service, and the messianic promise.

The recitation and affirmation of the faith was especially evident in the important *Shema* prayer, read twice daily, and in the annual cycle of the reading of the Pentateuch and lessons from the prophets, which was an integral part of the synagogue liturgy. Confession and repentance were the focus of the most important yearly ritual occasions. *Rosh Hashanah* (New Year) inaugurated a period of ten days of penitence, which reached its climax on *Yom Kippur* when worshipers were expected to recognize and confess their sins, express regret, ask pardon, and abandon sinful behavior. The major focus of other yearly ritual occasions was to commemorate events in the history of the Jewish people. The most important were *Pesach*, commemorating the exodus from Egypt, *Shavuot*, commemorating God's revelation to Israel on Mount Sinai, and *Sukkot*, commemorating the journey in the desert en route to the Promised Land. Among other important religious ceremonies were the rites of passage: circumcision, bar-mitsvah, marriage, and death.

Prayers of petition were not frequent or prominent in official Jewish ritual, and they referred to the people of Israel rather than to the individual alone. The prayers were in the plural, corporate in their formulation, calling for the health, sustenance, and deliverance from persecution, sickness, and famine of the Jewish people as a whole. Important among the prayers of petition were the supplications for the salvation of the people and the rebuilding of Zion and Jerusalem.[22] Thus, official Judaism gave little attention to providing the individual with supernatural assistance to obtain his worldly goals or to protect him from supernatural dangers. However, these were important focuses of folk religion: to protect the individual against illness and misfortune, such as miscarriages, fire, and theft; to cure illnesses and infertility; and to fight against the evil forces, such as demons and the evil eye.

The invocation of the names of God, of the angels, and occasionally of demons was prominent in Jewish folk religion. Some names were taken from the Bible and Talmud, many were derived from the mystical literature, and others were created anagrammatically according to various systems. The Talmud permitted the use of sacred names, since it involved an appeal to the supernatural and a recognition of the supremacy of God, but the masses tended to use the names to manipulate the supernatural in order to control events on earth. On the basis of the belief that a name contained the essence of a being, people assumed that they could control the province over which a supernatural being had authority. Various works listed the holy names and the purposes to which they could be put. One work listed seventy names of the archangel Metatron, each with its particular use. Possessing the names of God was seen to give men great power to manipulate God's world. Some scholars expressed concern over the use of God's names, but most tended to evade the problem; they asserted both the power of God and the power of his names.

Numerous objects, formulas, and actions were believed to provide protection against evil. The typical written amulet began with the invocation "in the name of . . . ," followed by the names of God and the appropriate angels, stated the purpose using a relevant biblical verse, and concluded with the name of the person the amulet was to protect. Objects were also used as amulets, such as the hair of a black donkey, the ashes of the buttocks of a rooster or chicken, or the head of a snake.

The mezuzah was originally a device to prevent demons from entering the house, and although the early rabbis made it a symbol of official religious values, its magical elements were enhanced during the medieval period. In general, biblical verses, and especially the psalms, were believed to be potent protective devices because of the names hidden in each sentence of the Bible. Verses were often recited with additional mystical names, and various techniques were used such as reversing the usual order of reading, transposing words, and dissolving and consuming the writing. Certain numbers, especially three, seven, and nine, were believed to have special potency. And in addition to study and prayer, human saliva, the circle, and the magical properties of numerous objects such as iron, herbs, and water provided protection against demons. During the marriage ceremony the bridegroom stamped on a glass to drive off demons, and during funerals all mirrors were covered and participants threw grass behind their backs. In one ritual of cabbalistic origin ten men danced around the grave to protect the deceased from the children made by demons from his wasted seed (nocturnal pollution and onanism).

Childbirth and illness were important focuses of folk religion. When an infant was ill or a woman in labor pains, a scroll of the Torah was laid upon the sufferer to alleviate the pain. Some amulets were used to promote health and fertility, and biblical verses were used to heal wounds and diseases. Psalm 20 reduced the pains of childbirth: its nine verses corresponded to nine months of pregnancy, and its seventy words were symbols of the seventy pangs experienced during childbirth. Various philters and potions aided in sexual and marital problems; powers were ascribed to animal heads, stomachs, eyes, tongues, teeth, and other parts. One example will suffice: "If you take the tongue of a frog and place it under the breast of a sleeping woman, she will have to answer all that you ask."[23]

Comparisons

The prayer services and religious practices of official Judaism did not cater to the people's this-worldly, individual problems, goals, and fears. The thaumaturgical response was the focus of the folk religion, which used the sacred writings and symbols of official Judaism as well as a wide variety of magical beliefs and practices that had developed in Jewish folk traditions or had been adopted from the non-Jewish environment. While the major beliefs, values, and rituals of official Judaism differed radically from those of the Christian church, Jewish magic was highly syncretistic and overlapped at many points with the magic of Christians. Some beliefs and practices adopted from other peoples had vanished from the native folklore and had been preserved in Jewish practices.

Cultures differ in the extent to which their religious beliefs, practices, and organization are divided between an orientation toward an ultimate salvation and an orientation toward worldly concerns. Scholars of religion in Southeast Asia have disagreed over the question whether Buddhism and the spirit cults represent two discrete religions with incompatible premises, beliefs, and ethics. They appear to agree, however, that Buddhism and the spirit cults differ sharply in the religious goals of their participants: Buddhists are oriented toward attaining a happy rebirth and an ultimate other-worldly salvation, whereas members of the spirit cults are devoted to combating misfortune and augmenting fortune in this world.[24] Official and folk Judaism were not distinct religious systems, for they overlapped considerably in their assumptions and symbols. They were divided in function, however, since official Judaism did not cater to man's ubiquitous desire for supernatural means of control over his earthly environment.[25]

The concentration of magic outside the official ritual system and religious institutions of Judaism was in contrast to the absorption of such practices by the Catholic church. Catholic authorities defined magic as heresy, but in practice, they condemned only those magical practices that were performed outside the church's religious canopy. The church had many means, such as holy water, signs of the cross, amulets, efficacious objects and formulas, to deal with disease, illness, and sterility and to drive away evil spirits. Some churchmen stressed that such means were not constraining on the divine and that, apart from the sacraments, their effectiveness was dependent on the faith and piety of the supplicant. At the popular level, however, these agencies were credited with a compelling power.

When the Protestant churches denied the efficacy of Catholic agencies and removed supernatural assistance in everyday life, the people sought such assistance outside the churches, especially from magicians. But even after the Reformation magic and religion were not two discrete systems in Protestant countries. Religion still retained some of its magical aspects, as shown by the use of Protestant prayers to cure disease, and magic involved religious aspects, such as the importance of piety and prayer in the use of magical power.[26] The interpenetration of religion and magic was even more pronounced in Jewish communities where, in contrast to Protestantism, the problem of removing magic from religion was hardly an issue.

4. Normative Jewish Millenarianism and the First Jewish Millenarian Movements in the Diaspora

A MILLENARIAN MOVEMENT may represent either a break from the normative religion or an attempt to realize normative beliefs. Among primitive peoples influenced by Christianity a millennial movement has often represented a radical departure from their traditional religion, which has contained nothing of millenarianism. Even if a religion contains ideas of a future, this-worldly, perfect age, these ideas may be defined as heretical. Early Christians believed that the second advent of Christ was imminent, but from the fifth century the new orthodoxy of the Christian church taught that the millennium had begun with the birth of Christ and was fully realized in the church, the mystical City of God. The church taught that salvation was not a collective phenomenon to be achieved in a future age but an individual experience achieved by the righteous after death in heaven. In 431, the Council of Ephesus denounced the belief in the coming of a millennium as a superstitious error. Thus, in the medieval period Christian millennial movements were heretical and heterodox, often in rebellion against the religious teachings and authority of the church. In this they contrasted with the Jewish believers in an imminent millennium, who presented their beliefs as a fulfillment of the hopes and expectations of the prevailing tradition in Judaism.

For the majority of Jews in the medieval and early-modern periods, it was an article of faith to hope constantly for the advent of the messiah. The twelfth principle of the best-known formulation of Jewish religious doctrines, Maimonides' "Thirteen Principles of the Jewish Faith," reads: "I believe with complete faith in the coming of the Messiah, and even though he should tarry, nevertheless, I shall wait for his coming every day." The affirmation of this belief was a persistent theme in Jewish prayers: in a number of daily benedictions, in the prayers after meals, during the wedding ceremony, and on festivals and fast days. The Jews frequently reminded themselves that they were in *galut* (exile), and they expressed the imperfection of the unredeemed world by such customs as the incompletion of a synagogue building and the tearing of a new garment. Family and business letters, holiday wishes, and expressions of congratulations often concluded with the wish that the côrrespondents would witness the advent of the messiah and the ingathering of the exiles. Beliefs in the coming of the messiah and the collective salvation of the Jews in a future, this-worldly, perfect age may, therefore, be described as normative in traditional Judaism. Before discussing Jewish millennial outbursts and movements from the medieval period, it is important to describe the features of normative Jewish millenarianism of the traditional Jewish community.

Normative Millenarianism

The characterization of millennial movements as movements that look forward to "total" change has been questioned by some writers. If, for example, one wishes to include the cargo cults of Melanesia as millennial movements, it would be preferable to refer to "radical" or "revolutionary" change.[1] A number of medieval Christian millennial prophecies looked forward to a radical reform of certain institutions (the papacy, for example), rather than to their destruction, and many millenarians would have been discomforted by the idea of a totally new future.[2] However, it is generally assumed that a defining characteristic of millennial beliefs is that changes are expected in nature or the cosmos, often preceded by an apocalypse of punishment and destruction and accompanied by the appearance of supernatural beings. In this sense one interpretation of the Jewish tradition is messianic but not millenarian. This "rationalist" position was classically stated by Maimonides, who wrote that the "only difference between this world and the Days of the Messiah is the subjection of Israel to the nations." The messiah was to restore the kingdom of David, rebuild the Temple, reinstate the ancient laws and sacrifices, and gather the Jews from their dispersion, but there were to be no miracles, no changes in nature, no innovations in creation, and no end to history. The rationalist viewpoint was opposed by Jewish scholars who were millenarians as well as messianists: the revival of the kingdom of David was to be accompanied by changes in nature, in the cosmos, and in man's moral character.[3]

The medieval rationalist view of the messianic age was similar to the future hopes of the Jewish people of an earlier age.[4] During the biblical period the Israelites had concrete social and political hopes, rooted in history, rather than expectations of a cosmic drama. Almost all the biblical prophets, and especially the preexilic prophets, emphasized the political power that Israel would have after the Redemption. This did not necessarily mean the political domination of other nations by Israel, but it did include the ingathering of the exiles, national independence, and security; Israel would no longer be subservient to another people or fear a foreign king. In addition, the borders of the land of Judah and its cities would be extended, especially those of Jerusalem, and peace would rule among the nations, between individuals, and in nature. The prophets differed in their emphases on material prosperity, but all looked forward to greater spirituality as the knowledge of God spread to all peoples. Human perfection would be achieved in Israel, and other nations would praise Israel for its spiritual superiority and ethical qualities. Other common prophecies included a great increase in population, the resettlement of ruined cities, the healing of the sick, and the lengthening of human life.

While many of the prophecies of the preexilic prophets were based on supernatural premises, they did not present a view of the future as an essentially different order from that of the present. The dualistic conception of two worlds, in which the future hope would be realized in transcendental as well as terrestrial realms, was essentially a postexilic development. Its beginnings may be traced to Deutero-Isaiah, who is believed to have prophesied in the last years preceding the conquest of Babylon by the Persians in 539 B.C.E. Deutero-Isaiah's belief that the climactic events in history would presage not a new historical era but a transformation of the world on a cosmic scale was followed by most later prophets. During the classical period of Jewish apocalyptic works, from the second century B.C.E. to the second century C.E., the writers moved toward a view of the future world that was removed from historical reality. Whereas the ancient prophets knew only a single world in which the events of "the Day of the Lord" would occur, the apocalyptic works made a radical contrast between this world and the next, the reign of darkness and the reign of light, and between sin and holiness, impurity and purity. The concrete hopes for political redemption remained a central feature of the millenarian hopes, but from the early third century C.E., with the transfer of Jewish leadership from Palestine to Babylon, the concrete hopes of political redemption became increasingly subordinate to mythical and cosmic fantasies. The dominant millenarian tradition, which was inherited, accepted, and extended by medieval Jewry, was one in which the supernatural elements of the millennium were the most prominent. Not only the Jewish masses but most Jewish scholars conceived the millennium as an entirely new world.

Cosmic change did not necessarily mean final change. A common distinction made in postbiblical literature was that between the "messianic age" and "the world to come." The expression *the world to come* denoted two distinct phenomena: life after death with its rewards and punishments in Paradise and *Gehenna* (hell) and the renewal of the world after the messianic era. Sigmund Mowinckel has argued that the idea of the millennium in its more specific sense of a kingdom lasting one thousand years represented a solution to the tensions between the political, national, this-worldly future hopes and the transcendental, universal hopes of a world beyond. The Jewish millennial kingdom, which incorporated the this-worldly hopes, was to end with a general judgment and destruction of the world in which even the messiah would die. This was to be followed by a new creation, the resurrection of the righteous, and a new state of bliss. The fifth kingdom of the Book of Daniel (written circa 165 B.C.E.) was to be an everlasting one, but much subsequent literature saw the reign of the messiah as preceding God's universal reign on the Day of the Lord.

Talmudic literature did not, however, provide a clear or consistent picture. The terms *the days of the messiah* and *the world to come* were not used in a consistent fashion and were occasionally included within a single reference, *the future to come*. Descriptions of life after death, the messianic age, and the new world after the messianic age overlapped considerably. Some scholars opposed any attempt to describe the other-worldly paradise of the world to come on the grounds that whereas the prophets had described the messianic era, only God had knowledge of the world to come. A more popular layer of thought, represented in unincorporated Midrashim, presented a this-worldly picture of the world to come and canceled any distinction with the days of the messiah: it was a world of feasting and drinking, full of gems, precious metals, and magnificent buildings, inhabited by angels and beautiful people. Concentration on the study of the Torah, made possible by freedom from material necessity, was a common feature of both the days of the messiah and the world to come, and in a number of popular Midrashic paradises God appeared as the director of studies, explaining those commandments whose meanings had formerly remained obscure.

In the millenarian hopes of most medieval Jews the distinction between the messianic era and the world to come had little real significance. For rationalist scholars, such as Maimonides, the messianic age was primarily a period of opportunity in which Jews would be able to study the Torah without disturbance and thereby make themselves worthy to enter the world to come, but for the majority, the coming of the messiah signified the beginning of eternal salvation.

The majority of medieval Jews did not perceive the messianic age as a period of transition, but they did expect a transitional period of catastrophic events prior to the reign of the messiah. Predictions of a period of catastrophe existed in Judaism before millenarianism. The preexilic prophets threatened the destruction of the kingdom of Judah and the terrible punishments of the Day of the Lord, but they differed over whether the punishments would be imposed on Israel alone, on other peoples alone, or on both Israel and other nations. The later preexilic prophets added cosmic disturbances such as earthquakes, fire, great noise, and whirlwinds. These elements became more pronounced in later Jewish eschatological writings, especially those written under Roman domination, which referred to the events preceding the millennium (monsters, demons, plagues, famines, floods, falling stars, earthquakes, wars, revolutions, and so forth) as the "birth pangs of the messiah." The belief arose that the messiah would come at the time of the deepest catastrophe of the Jewish people.

Further Jewish apocalyptic literature was written against the background of the political upheavals and wars at the end of the sixth and beginning of the seventh centuries, especially those between Byzantines and Persians. The most important apocalyptic work written at that time was the Book of Zerubbabel, which was rich in descriptions of the messianic wars against Armilus, the son of Satan. This literature had a great impact on medieval Jewry, and though some medieval Jewish philosophers expected the political deliverance of the Jews without an apocalypse, the apocalyptic view was the dominant one among medieval Jews, who elaborated and built up detailed accounts of the Armageddon between the armies of Gog and Magog and the forces of the messiah. In many accounts the forces of the messiah are almost defeated, and only the direct intervention of God secures their victory.

Normative Jewish millenarianism foresaw a perfect space as well as a perfect time. The millennium had a center, the Land of Israel and, more specifically, Jerusalem, where the most perfect state of being would be achieved. The ingathering of exiles into this perfect space was spoken about in the books of the biblical prophets, but its importance in millenarian thought grew with the destruction of national independence and the ever-greater dispersion of the Jews. According to one common belief, the new Jerusalem would descend from the heavens; its area and height would be tremendous and its gates huge; it would include thousands of towers, fortresses, pools, and cisterns, and its streets would be full of precious stones.

Jewish millenarianism contained universalist as well as particularist elements: national freedom and the ingathering of the exiles were often linked to the emancipation of humanity. Some prophets saw redemption as encompassing peoples and lands in addition to those of Israel, and redemption did not necessarily include the whole of the Jewish people. Most prophets predicted that only a "remnant of Israel" would remain after the punishments of the "Day of Wrath." The rabbinic literature stated that the future bliss would be shared with the righteous among the gentiles and that all sinners, Jews and gentiles, would perish. However, the popular millenarian notions among medieval Jews stressed the particularist rather than the universalist elements: their thinking restricted redemption to the Jews and foretold the humiliation and destruction of their enemies and oppressors.

Their desire for the restoration of an independent kingdom under a messiah who would be a descendant of King David was a restorative element; the ancient Israelites had come to view the age of David as one of unparalleled prosperity and justice. But in contrast to other ancient peoples who emphasized a golden age of the past, the Israelites, with their history of afflictions, looked forward to a future in which they would be free from attack by enemies and would live in peace with all living creatures. The Sinaitic covenant was to be renewed in such a way that a new spirituality was to come into being with a guarantee that the new covenant would not be dissolved.

Some Jewish millenarians believed that men could contribute to the coming of the messiah. Others argued that everything was in the hands of God and warned against human action that dared to attempt to bring about the Redemption. Jewish revolutionary millenarianism, which took the form of military uprisings, developed under Roman oppression. The Zealots, whose revolt against the Romans reached its peak in 66 C.E., believed that the millennium would occur only if they demonstrated their loyalty to God and participated in the divine plan by their rebellion. Jerusalem fell in 70 C.E., but in 132 C.E. another revolt flared up, led by Bar-Kochba, acclaimed as the messiah by the renowned Rabbi Akiba. The failure of these revolts and the subsequent persecution led to disillusionment and the discrediting of militaristic millenarianism.

Nonmilitaristic forms of millenarianism also existed during the periods of rebellion, and these were activistic only in the sense that men believed that their religious actions would bring the millennium closer. The Essenes, who lived at Qumran from around 150 B.C.E. to 68 or 70 C.E., trusted little in the force of arms and believed that the decisive war was to be fought on the transcendental plane, but they also believed that an ascetic life and exact observance of the commandments would hasten the Day of the Lord. After the crushing of the Jewish revolt in 135 C.E. and the Roman paganization of Jerusalem, Jewish millenarianism began to take more passive forms: the rabbis argued that redemption was entirely in the hands of God and that men should not even attempt to calculate its timing. In the diaspora militaristic millenarianism became very rare. Those Jews who believed that men could hasten the coming of the messiah or at least prevent their contributing to his further delay emphasized repentance and the strict adherence to the mitsvot.

Even if men could have no part in bringing about the millennium, they might at least be able to calculate the date of its coming. A number of methods were used: numerical interpretations of certain passages in biblical texts, especially the Book of Daniel; the numerical logic in the periods of previous exiles; *gematria*, the numerical value of letters; and astrology, which came to be used extensively in the fourteenth and fifteenth centuries. The dates given were not always imminent ones, but those who maintained that the date could not be known to man and denounced the raising of false hopes consistently and vehemently opposed messianic calculation throughout the ages.

The pious means that might bring forward the date of the Redemption were matched by the pious picture of the millennium itself: normative Jewish millenarianism was hypernomian rather than antinomian. The millennium would represent the completion and the perfection of the Jewish law, the Halachah; those parts of the Law not realizable under the conditions of exile would be fulfilled in the messianic kingdom. This was clearly the emphasis of the rationalists, who saw the messianic kingdom as a continuation of this world. However, the utopian conception of the millennium, in which man would be totally good and have total freedom, raised questions about the status of the Torah. The laws could hardly be the same in conditions in which the need to separate good from evil would be superfluous. This potential antinomianism remained latent in normative Jewish millenarianism. Even utopians perceived the millennium in conformity with the law of God as they knew it.

By the medieval period normative Jewish millenarianism had come to give a large role to the redeemer, the messiah. This was a gradual development. For a long period the concept of a messiah was either absent or of little importance beside that of eschatological salvation. Many prophetic books spoke of no messiah: God alone was the redeemer. Other prophetic works included a collective messiah, the House of David. The messiah was seen not as a redeemer who would establish the future kingdom but as the future ideal king of that kingdom. The term *messiah* originally meant "anointed with oil," and the idea of a savior or redeemer was at first connected with the king or the high priest. Moses was an important symbol of the redeemer, but the prototype messiah was the second Israelite king, David, who, in addition to his unification of the tribes, was believed to have had outstanding religious and ethical qualities.

The theme of the future ideal king is found in Isaiah and Micah Isaiah, 740–701 B.C.E., and these writings laid the foundation for the royal messianism that became important in the postexilic period. During the Second Temple period Jewish writings referred to eschatological salvation without a messiah, but a variety of messianic figures were drawn during that period. The this-worldly, warrior, Davidic king who would die when his kingdom ended was the most prominent messianic figure, but other figures were also spoken about, figures that contrasted sharply with the Davidic image. The "suffering servant of God," who first appeared in Deutero-Isaiah, was to be despised and rejected; according to Zechariah he would ride upon an ass, which no self-respecting king would do. The "son of man," a preexistent being of divine character, was to remain hidden with God until the time came for him to descend from heaven to save his people. The themes of the suffering servant and the son of man were greatly elaborated in Christianity, but they never became dominant in Judaism. The Essenes expected a specially anointed high priest (the Messiah of Aaron) as well as a specially anointed lay leader (the Messiah of Israel).

After the failure of the last revolt against the Romans, apocalyptic writers began to make a distinction between the warrior messiah of the House of Joseph, who would die in the final battle against Gog and Magog, and the more spiritual messiah of the House of David, who would rule the future kingdom. In addition, they expected certain personages to precede the messiah. The major one was the prophet Elijah, who by his miracles and preaching would bring about the people's repentance and thereby prepare the people for the messiah.

The rabbinic literature presented the messiah as the redeemer, the instrument by which the kingdom of God was to be established, as well as the future ruler of that kingdom. The talmudic literature included, however, many contrasting views, and the middle ages did not inherit a coherent, unified conception of the messiah. Unlike the Christian messiah, the Jewish messiah is not a deity but an ideal man who exemplifies physical and spiritual perfection. Since there were no histories or legends of a real person, the Jewish messiah remained a vague, anonymous figure, enabling a wide range of personality types to claim the role.

Early Millenarian Outbursts in the Diaspora

After the defeat of the Jewish millennial revolt in 135 C.E., Judea was almost depopulated of Jews and was renamed Syria Palaestina. Exile became the lot of the Jews, and subsequent Jewish millenarianism merged the idea of the return to the Land of Israel with the idea of redemption. The notion of the Land of Israel as the center of the millennium, the perfect space, took on far greater meaning in the diaspora. But conservative rabbinic opinion warned against any attempt on the part of the Jews to hasten the return, prophesy its date, or even pray excessively for it: exile was part of the divine intention, an expression of the wrath of God, and the Jews could only wait patiently for the divine action that would restore them to their ancestral home. It is possible that millenarian outbursts occurred which left no historical record, but it appears that a long period passed before imminent millenarianism stirred a Jewish community. Whether this absence of millenarian activity was a result of an acceptance of the conservative view, or simply a matter of loss of hope and accommodation to exile is not known.

Prior to the period of the crusades Jewish millenarianism was confined to an incident in Crete, sometime in the second half of the fifth century, and a series of movements in Persia in the eighth century. At the time of the incident in Crete the island had a substantial Jewish settlement. A certain Moses proclaimed himself the messiah and gained support from many Jews, who neglected their businesses and finally followed him to the sea, where, expecting a repetition of the Red Sea miracle, they threw themselves in. Many drowned, but others were saved by local fishermen and sailors. The messianic pretender disappeared.

No information is available to indicate why this incident occurred in Crete, but many Jews had predicted that the messiah would come in the fifth century. This was based on the calculation that the messiah would come four hundred years after the destruction of the Temple, which corresponded to the number of years of the first exile in Egypt. The barbarian invasions and the decline of Rome sparked millenarian beliefs in the Christian world. It was believed that the Antichrist would appear at the fall of Rome, and Christian oracles predicted that the messiah would come between the years 440 and 470.[5]

Information on a series of Jewish millenarian movements during the period of Islamic conquests is also scanty.[6] Around the year 720 a convert to Judaism, Severus, who promised to restore Palestine to the Jews, gained followers in the region of Mardin in Syria.[7] It is not clear whether Severus maintained that he was the messiah or only a messenger or forerunner of the messiah. Declaring that the days of the messiah had begun and the Redemption was at hand, Severus made a number of alterations in talmudic laws: he abolished the second-day celebration of religious festivals, prescribed new forms of prayer, and made changes in the dietary laws. Many of Severus's followers entrusted him with their belongings, but he was arrested by the authorities and executed.[8]

The most important movements of this period occurred in Persia. In the middle of the eighth century, Abu-Isa, an illiterate tailor who claimed to be the last of five messengers to precede the messiah, attracted a large following, some of whom regarded him as the messiah. Abu-Isa led an armed rebellion against the caliph, Merwan II, and was defeated and killed by the caliph's forces around 755. Some of his followers refused to believe that he had been killed; they claimed that he had concealed himself in the mountains and would reappear to complete his religious task.[9] These followers, the Isawites, formed a sect and migrated to Damascus, where remnants of the group still remained two centuries later. Others accepted the death of Abu-Isa and proclaimed Yudghan of Hamaden, a disciple of Abu-Isa, as the messiah. Yudghan died a natural death, but his followers also expected him to return, and they formed a sect, the Yudghanites, who remained in the area. Mushka, a disciple of Yudghan, continued the millennial revolt; he was later killed in battle.

The majority of Jewish millenarians in Persia were uneducated Jews who were removed from the centers of talmudic learning and subject to the influences of the Muslim environment. They did not deviate radically from talmudic Judaism, but they did make a number of modifications in the religious law. Abu-Isa introduced frequent fasting and seven daily prayer services instead of three, and he prohibited divorce, eating meat, and drinking alcohol.[10] The pious, ascetic way of life was seen as a way of atonement which would help bring redemption, but the most distinctive feature of the movements was their nationalist-militarist nature. Redemption was to be achieved by armed revolt.

It is possible that a century of mutually destructive conflict between the Byzantine and Persian empires had encouraged Jewish hopes for the reestablishment of a Jewish kingdom and that these hopes had received a blow from the Islamic conquests. As real political prospects grew remote, the millenarian hopes became more attractive: this was reflected both in these movements and in the apocalypses written at the time. The political instability and the absence of social order and control in the early period of the Arabic conquests made active rebellion seem a realistic option. The movement led by Severus arose at the time of the Islamic offensive against Byzantium. Constantinople was under siege, and many Jews believed that the messiah would appear in Constantinople to witness the mutual destruction of "Esau and Ishmael." At the same time, Caliph Omar II (717–20) put pressure on Christians and Jews to embrace Islam.

Persia, the center of Jewish millenarianism and sectarianism, was also the center of the militant Persian Shiite sects, which stressed the importance of the messianic Mahdi figure and rebelled against the Arabic conquerors. The Abu-Isa movement emerged at the time of a series of Shiite uprisings against the weakened Omayyad government. The unstable conditions lasted for some time, but Persian political control gradually increased, and resentment of the Arabs declined. With the relative stabilization of power in Persia, the Jewish minority became reconciled to its powerlessness. In the ninth century Jewish sectarian movements, such as the Karaites, stressed legal and ritualistic issues rather than messianism, and by the tenth century the prominence of Jewish sectarianism in Persia had come to an end.[11]

Period of the Crusades

Historical sources chronicle seven millenarian instances among Jews from about 1060 to 1172.[12] Most of the incidents occurred during the period of the first two crusades of 1096 and 1146. The earliest, around 1060–70, in the city of "Linon" was the first recorded incident of millenarianism among European Jews since the incident in Crete in the fifth century. A messianic pretender, who was believed to have the ability to fly, was put to death, together with many of his followers, by the Christian authorities. For some time afterward many believed that he had not been killed, but had gone into hiding. Maimonides, who is the only source we have on the incident, did not make clear whether Linon was Lyons in France or León in Spain.[13] The locations of other recorded incidents of millenarianism among medieval Jews are not in doubt, and it is interesting that none occurred among the Ashkenazim in central and western Europe.

The second incident, in 1096, was centered in Salonika, but appears to have involved Jews over a large area of Byzantium. This incident featured no messianic pretender, but Jews abandoned economic activities and prepared themselves for their imminent redemption by repenting, fasting, giving alms, and beginning the journey to the Holy Land. Visions of Elijah, the forerunner of the messiah, were reported in Salonika, and small groups in Constantinople and across the Bosporus left their homes and assembled in Abydos, near Constantinople, to await the millennium.[14]

Maimonides recorded an incident in Cordova, around 1100–1110, which had been related to him by his father. A number of Jews in the city had calculated by astrology that the messiah was imminent, and they chose one Ibn Aryeh to fill the role. Since Ibn Aryeh did not oppose the attribution, the Jewish leaders of the community fined him, flogged him in public, and put him under a ban.[15]

A document found in the Cairo Genizah relates that in 1120 in Baghdad the "pious daughter of Joseph the physician" declared publicly that she had seen the prophet Elijah in a dream and that he had told her that the redemption of Israel was at hand. The prophecy caused excitement among the Jews of the community: they failed to deliver taxes and contributions to the authorities, and they took off the badges that they were obliged to wear on their clothing. The Jews finally had to pay a heavy fine, but their continued faith was expressed in a story that the caliph had rescinded an order to imprison them following an apparition of the prophet Elijah.[16]

The fifth incident in Fez, Morocco, in 1120–25, was recorded by Maimonides. Moses Al-Dar'i, a pious and learned man, preached that the messiah would appear on the eve of Passover of that year. Many were ruined when they followed his advice to sell their property and contract debts to Muslims with the promise to pay back ten dinars for each one borrowed.[17]

The messianic movement of David Alroy, which was centered in the North Caucasus in the years 1120–47, was the most significant and the least ephemeral of the instances during this period. In contrast to the other instances in this period, but like the eighth-century movements in Persia, it was a military rebellion against the Islamic rulers. The movement began in the mountains of Khazaria under Alroy's father, who called for repentance to prepare the way for redemption. The second stage of the movement, under David, centered around the Kurdistan town of Amadiyah, where, in the second half of the century, Benjamin of Tudela reported two thousand Jewish families. Believed by many to be the messiah, Alroy gathered a large following and a substantial armed force, which he intended to lead to Jerusalem. He planned to conquer the fortress of Amadiyah, which would provide a good basis to attack the crusaders who, according to Benjamin of Tudela, were Alroy's objective. Alroy dispatched messengers to many Jewish communities to prepare the ground for military action. In Baghdad his envoys were reported to have convinced a number of Jews to wait on their rooftops on an appointed day in order to be ready to fly to Israel. At first, the local Muslim commanders viewed the movement calmly, but the mountainous terrain made it difficult to suppress, and it lasted for some time. When the Muslim authorities threatened the Jewish religious leaders that Persian Jews would suffer if they did not use their influence on Alroy, the Jewish authorities in Baghdad threatened him with excommunication, but Alroy and his followers did not accept their demands. Finally, Alroy was murdered and his movement suppressed, but a number of followers in Azerbaijan, known as Menahemites, continued to believe in his messiahship.[18]

The final incident of Jewish millenarianism in this period occurred in the Yemen in 1171–72. After a messianic pretender obtained the support of both uneducated and scholarly Jews in the towns of Yemen, he was arrested by the Muslim authorities. Believing that he would survive decapitation, he requested that his head be cut off. As in many cases some followers continued to believe in his messiahship for some time after his death.[19]

Explanations

This cluster of millenarian incidents, most of which occurred over the fifty-year period from the first crusade to the second, would seem to suggest an explanation connected in some way with the crusades. One possible connection, the influence of the millenarianism of Christian crusaders, can be ruled out, for the areas where Christian millenarianism was important, central and northwestern Europe, showed little, if any, Jewish millenarian activity. Two other possible connections are that Jewish millenarianism was a response to the crusaders' persecution and massacre of Jews or that the Jews interpreted the wars of the crusades as the events that had been predicted to precede the coming of the messiah. As the following discussion will show, however, the connection between the millenarian outbreaks and the crusades was tenuous at best, and no explanation encompasses all the instances.

The crusades were a period of disaster for the Jews in western and central Europe. Large numbers of Jews were massacred; these massacres were the work not in the main of the crusading armies of barons and their retainers but of groups of lower-class Christian millenarians led by popular prophets. The Christian millenarians perceived the Jews as demons, the followers of Satan or the Antichrist, and believed that God would forgive a man his sins if he killed a Jew who refused baptism.[20] The largest massacres occurred during the first crusade in 1096, especially in the towns along the Rhine. These were the first large-scale massacres of Jews in Europe. Some outbreaks against Jews had occurred shortly after the year 1000, but the troubles had quickly subsided, and the comparatively high status of the Jews during the early Middle Ages had been quickly restored. After 1096, the economic position and social status of the Jews in western and central Europe began to decline. Further massacres on a smaller scale took place in Germany and France during the second crusade in 1146 and in England in 1183, shortly before the third crusade.[21]

With the possible exception of the millennial incident in "Linon," which occurred prior to the massacres of the first crusade, none of the Jewish millenarian outbursts occurred in the areas of the massacres. The survivors of the disaster areas interpreted their sufferings within a Jewish religious framework, but they did not turn to millenarianism. A few Jews had predicted that 1096 would be the year of redemption, and it is possible that the massacres put an end to millennial hopes in France and Germany.[22] On the other hand, the massacres could have been interpreted as part of the birth pangs of the messiah. In fact, some Jews did view the persecution in a messianic context,[23] but among the Ashkenazim, this did not become the dominant trend, and they made no preparations for such an event.

The Jewish chronicles of the period show that the Jews understood the persecutions of the crusades as a continuation of the endless sufferings that God had chosen them to endure.[24] They saw precedents to the massacres in biblical narratives, and this archetypal mode of thought possibly militated against any tendency to view the events as signifying an end to history. They believed that their suffering was a just retribution for the sins of the Jewish people and their failure to uphold the law of God. While some declared that their own sins were being justly punished, self-accusation was more a conventional formula than a deeply held belief. Medieval Ashkenazim found little in their own behavior to warrant such punishment, and some concluded that they were being punished for the sins of their ancestors.[25] For them, suffering was a test of faith; it was imposed on a religiously qualified generation which was able to withstand the cruel tests and thereby fulfill the hopes of God. Compensation was to come in the form of an immediate personal afterlife in which proof of religious merit was to be rewarded by happiness in heaven.[26] Ashkenazi rabbis also stressed that the righteous would be resurrected and enjoy the splendors of the ultimate redemption, but they did not introduce any apocalyptic interpretations of contemporary events into their millennial conceptions.[27]

If Jewish millenarianism was not the consequence of direct experience of persecution, the possibility remains that Jewish millenarians interpreted the crusades as a prelude to the coming of the messiah. Jacob Mann, who assumed that Linon was Lyons and dated the incident, for unexplained reasons, in 1087–88, tried to link the incident to events preceding the first crusade in 1096. He noted that the idea of conquering the Holy Land had already spread throughout France; hence it was already known to the masses at the time of the incident.[28] Aaron Aescoly, who dated the incident circa 1060, noted that a Christian pilgrimage left France for the Holy Land in 1064 and debate on the crusades began in 1074.[29] If Linon is León, a possible link is the Christian military descent on the Muslim south, which began about 1060. There are a number of recorded attacks by Christian warriors on Spanish Jewish communities; the attacks in 1063 evoked papal intervention on behalf of the Jews. The link is extremely speculative, since we are not certain of the place or the exact year of the millennial incident.

A direct link to the crusades is most clear in the millennial excitement in Byzantium in 1096. No massacres of Jews took place in Byzantium, but the authorities were sympathetic to millenarians, and the appearance of disorganized bands of crusaders on the borders of Byzantium stirred millenarian enthusiasm among both Christians and Jews. The news of the massacres had not yet arrived, and when one of the advance parties of the crusaders, made up of Franks, arrived in Salonika in the summer of 1096, the Jews were encouraged in their belief that the Christian and Moslem combatants would meet in Jerusalem, destroy each other, and thereby prepare the way for the coming of the messiah.[30]

The millennial instances in Cordova, Baghdad, Fez, and Kurdistan occurred in the period between the two crusades, when a number of Islamic rulers waged war against small Christian kingdoms in the Middle East. The center of this conflict was in Syria and Mesopotamia, and there is no evidence that it influenced Jewish millenarianism. It is possible that events connected with the Christian-Muslim conflict in Spain stimulated the incident in Cordova, 1100–1110. The counterattack by the Muslim Almoravides in the 1080s was accompanied by the pillage and destruction of many southern Jewish communities and followed by the migration of many Jews north to the Christian territories.[31]

The millenarian incident in Fez, 1120–25, occurred at approximately the time when Mohammed Tumart, the first leader of the Almohades, announced himself as the Mahdi who had come to establish divine righteousness in the world. Tumart visited Fez before 1120, and on that occasion he debated with the Islamic scholars and led his disciples to the marketplace, where they smashed musical instruments.[32] Mann argued that the Jews interpreted the commotion caused by Tumart's movement in the Maghreb as a sign of their imminent redemption, but the connection remains a speculative one.[33]

Mann's argument of a direct connection between the second crusade and the David Alroy movement is tenuous. He argues that the Jews in the area saw the Christian and Islamic forces as those of Gog and Magog,[34] but although the Alroy movement lasted into the period of the second crusade, it started some time before it, and it would appear that local factors were more important than the crusade. The movement began at the time when a nomadic people, the Kipchaks, from north of the Black Sea, invaded Khazaria in 1117. The Kipchaks were in turn attacked by the forces of the Russian prince of Kiev and were forced to move to the North Caucasus, which had a large Jewish community. This area became the center of the Alroy movement. The Kipchaks caused great hardship to the Jews, and the problems of the Jews increased when the king of the Georgians used the Kipchaks to strike at his Muslim enemies. The wars interfered with Jewish trade, but they also demonstrated the weakness of the Muslim regimes that were a barrier to the Land of Israel.[35]

A link between the crusades and the messianic outburst in the Yemen is difficult to support. Mann wrote that the Yemenite Jews were in contact with the Jews of Egypt and must have heard of the conflict over Israel.[36] In 1171, Saladin proclaimed the authority of the Abbasid caliphate in Egypt, and the harmony with other Muslim rulers made possible a jihad.

Saladin's forces captured Jerusalem in 1187, and this was followed by the third crusade, 1189–92, but both of these events occurred after the Yemenite movement in 1172. More important for the Yemenite Jews was the attempt by the Shiite rulers, from about 1165, to convert them forcibly to Islam.

Mann finds it surprising that there was no recorded Jewish millennial occurrence during the years 1187–92 when Saladin was waging a holy war against the Christians,[37] but it is clear that throughout the period most of the Jewish millenarian outbursts were not closely related to the crusades. Moreover, as S. W. Baron noted, what is surprising is not the frequency of the movements but their relative paucity and historical insignificance.[38]

Conclusion

Millenarian movements are often interpreted as movements of rebellion against economic and political oppression. This appears obvious when the movements actually take military and other violent action against an economically and politically dominant group. The question remains, however, why some movements of rebellion give an eschatological meaning to their battles against their oppressors and expect a millennium after the destruction of their enemies.

Jewish millenarianism developed from a future hope which did not, at first, have an eschatological and millenarian character. The ancient Hebrews looked forward to the restoration of their national and political independence, an expectation that was rooted in the notions of their election by God and his covenant with them. After repeated disappointments for the restoration of an independent kingdom, the Jews became more desperate in their hopes and began to believe that their situation would be transformed only after a period of cosmic catastrophe. Under Roman oppression millenarianism was strengthened and expressed in many pseudepigraphic and apocalyptic writings. It was believed that even in the most hopeless situation God would provide for a miraculous deliverance. Different views of the efficacy of human action and the effectiveness of military action remained, however. In the first century c.e., many militaristic messiahs sought to mobilize resistance against the Romans, but the failure of the revolts and the destruction of the Second Temple discredited the militaristic forms of messianism.

Christian millenarians completely rejected militaristic messianism. Some scholars argue that Jesus and his inner circle of disciples were in the military messianic tradition and that most of the Jews who awaited Jesus' return after his crucifixion expected him to overthrow Rome and make

Jerusalem the capital of a Holy Jewish Empire. But the writers of the Gospels accommodated the movement to the power of Rome and emphasized a peaceful messiah: they attempted to convince the authorities that their messiah had not had military or political pretensions but had died to bring eternal life to all mankind, and that the Christian kingdom of God was not of this world.[39] Jews retained the image of a militaristic messiah, the this-worldly millennium, and the importance of national independence, but they also accommodated themselves to their powerlessness by emphasizing their dependence on supernatural action and the fruitlessness of military revolt.

In the diaspora the majority of Jewish communities were in no position even to contemplate a military uprising. The exceptions were the series of movements in Persia in the eighth century and the David Alroy movement in the first half of the twelfth century. These movements arose during periods of political instability and conflict which provided favorable conditions for military uprisings.

The desire for national independence remained an important element in Jewish millenarianism, but political subordination was a permanent feature of Jewish life in the diaspora and cannot, therefore, account for the irregular outbursts of millenarianism. Explanations stressing the disruption of social life, especially as a result of religious persecution, appear to fit some instances (Yemen and possibly Spain), but not all. Moreover, the areas in Europe where the greatest destruction of Jewish communities took place were the least millenarian. The reasons for different responses to persecution will be discussed in the next chapter.

Even in the absence of oppression or disruption millennial movements may sometimes be sparked off by an adventitious event or series of events that is interpreted through already-existing, but dormant, millenarian beliefs as a sign of an imminent transformation.[40] The movement in Byzantium appears to demonstrate this case.

To conclude, then, no single explanation can account for all the millennial instances in the diaspora. It must be admitted, however, that as far as these early movements are concerned, the analysis is hampered by the absence of historical information both on the movements themselves and on the circumstances in which they arose.

5. Sephardim, Ashkenazim, and Italian Jews

WITH THE possible exception of the incident in "Linon," which was discussed in the previous chapter, existing records show no instances of collective millenarianism among the Ashkenazi Jews of northwestern and central Europe in the medieval period. Most instances of millenarianism occurred among the Sephardi Jews in Spain or, after the expulsion from Spain in 1492, in Italy. The discussion in this chapter attempts to explain why this was so. The first part of the chapter provides a historical overview of millenarianism among European Jews from the thirteenth to the sixteenth century. This is followed by an attempt to account for the historical location of these instances by testing the general causal theories of millennial movements.

Instances of Millenarianism

Abraham Abulafia, an ecstatic cabbalist and prophet from Spain who announced that he received his first prophetic call in Barcelona in 1271, presented himself to the Jews of Sicily as the messiah and predicted that redemption would occur in 1290. His messianic pretensions and his attacks on the ruling elite of wealthy men and scholars brought him into conflict with the rabbinic authorities. He does not appear to have attracted a great number of followers, but some of his adherents prepared for the messianic journey to the Holy Land, and the community of Palermo turned for advice to the Spanish scholar Solomon Adret, who managed to discredit Abulafia as an imposter.[1]

In 1295 considerable excitement centered on two messianic prophets in the town of Avila and the village of Ayllon. In Avila a reputed illiterate claimed that angels had dictated to him a treatise revealing the imminent future kingdom, while in Ayllon a prophet announced that on a specified day of that year a blast of the messiah's horn would summon Jews out of their exile. Many prepared themselves by fasting, prayer, and giving to charity, and on the day they rose early, dressed in white, and went to the synagogue to await the signal.[2] Nearly a century later, in 1391, a number of prophets predicting the imminent coming of the messiah appeared in

Burgos and Palentia. The fragmentary records of these events do not allow us to establish the extent of the millennial enthusiasm or the identity of the prophets. Some scholars believe that one of the prophets, known as Moses, who was extravagantly praised by the famous scholar R. Hasdai Crescas, was in fact Moses ben Isaac Botarel. In addition to writing a great number of books filled with false quotations from historical and imaginary figures, Botarel appears to have had messianic pretensions.[3]

Some revival of messianic hopes occurred among Spanish Jews after the capture of Constantinople by the Turks in 1453, but millenarianism became more widespread with the expulsion of the Jews from Spain in 1492. Jewish exiles expressed a strong belief in the imminent coming of the messiah, and they saw the Christian-Islamic wars as a sign of their coming redemption. They expected that their expulsion would be fully revenged, but they also believed that the expulsion was a means of redemption, since it resulted in the concentration of Jews in the Turkish empire, closer to Israel.[4]

About nine thousand Spanish exiles settled in Italy which, in the sixteenth century, became the center of messianic speculation and activity.[5] The most important propagator of an imminent millennium among the Iberian exiles in Italy was Don Isaac Abravanel (1437–1508), a widely respected Jewish leader. In a trilogy on the messianic theme, published in Italy in 1496–98, he collected the messianic beliefs common at the time, and on the basis of his interpretations of biblical and talmudic literature, historical events, and astrological calculations, he predicted that the process of redemption would begin in 1503 and be completed by 1531. He noted some disillusionment among Jews that the messiah had not come despite the massacres and expulsions, but he argued that the low state of the Jews indicated that salvation was imminent. The messiah, who had been born before the expulsion, would appear in Rome following a series of wars between Muslims, Christians, and the ten lost tribes of Israel. In the face of his supernatural powers all nations would either yield and pay homage to him or be destroyed. The ingathering of exiles and the resurrection of the dead would follow, and nature would come to approximate to its state at the beginning of creation. The change in nature would be especially felt in Israel, where the Jews, the spiritual elite, would spend their time in worship and the study of the Law while their material needs were met by other nations.[6]

That belief in the imminent coming of the messiah was not confined to Iberian exiles in Italy was demonstrated by the widespread acceptance among Italian Jews of the messianic prophecies of Ascher Lamlein in 1502.[7] Lamlein, an Ashkenazi, announced in Istria, near Venice, that the messiah would come within six months if the Jews repented and prepared for their redemption. Disciples carried his prophecy to many parts of Italy, and widespread repentance was recorded so that long after 1502 the year was known as the year of repentance. According to one source, the disappointment over the failure of Lamlein's prophecy caused such disillusionment that many converted to Christianity.[8]

This disappointment did not stop others from announcing an imminent coming, and millennial expectations continued for at least thirty years after the expulsion from Spain. Rumors circulated that the ten lost tribes were moving toward Israel, and it was calculated that the configuration of the stars was correct for the coming of the messiah. Abraham Ha-Levi, a scholar and interpreter of apocalyptic prophecies, believed that the process of redemption would begin in 1520, and intense messianic hopes were also expressed in the Hebrew poems of the time.[9]

The activities of David Reubeni and Solomon Molcho also stirred millenarian hopes. Arriving in Venice in 1524, Reubeni claimed that he was a prince from one of the ten lost tribes in the "Wilderness of Harbor" and that he had been sent to seek assistance from the pope and the European powers to conquer Palestine. Through the influence of a wealthy Jewish banker, Reubeni received an audience with the pope, who in turn gave Reubeni a letter of recommendation to the Portuguese king. The king received Reubeni, but the enthusiastic reception given to him by the conversos (New Christians)[10] compelled him to leave Portugal. Three years after his return to Italy, Reubeni went with Molcho to the Imperial Diet in Ratisbon to ask the emperor to arm Jews in order to regain Palestine from the Turks. The emperor had them put in prison, and Reubeni was taken back to the Iberian peninsula, where he died, probably in an auto-da-fé.[11]

Reubeni's intentions, at least at first, had no messianic attributions: he claimed to be not the messiah or a prophet but a statesman with political and military proposals. Nevertheless, some Jews interpreted his mission in a messianic context, and he does appear to have given some encouragement to this. While to the gentiles he spoke of joint Christian-Jewish military action against the Turks, to the Jews he spoke of returning to Jerusalem as part of the process of salvation. He maintained that God had ordained him to wage war to redeem the Jews, but he upheld the traditional view that the final act of redemption would be achieved by a miracle.[12]

The romantic nature of Reubeni's career and his contacts with high Christian dignitaries have led many to exaggerate his influence on Jews and his importance in Jewish millenarianism. His appearance in Portugal caused great excitement among the conversos, but his influence among Italian Jews was not so great. He appeared at a time when rumors about the ten lost tribes were common in Italy, but many Italian Jews regarded him as an imposter or a madman. In both Venice and Rome the Jewish communities were divided as to how he should be treated. In Rome the leaders refused to give him support, but he did convince some wealthy Jewish families, who gave him their patronage and financial support. The peak of Reubeni's influence occurred after his audience with the pope, but after his failure in Portugal support and belief among Italian Jews waned.[13]

While Reubeni's influence was declining, Solomon Molcho was gaining a considerable reputation as a messianic prophet. Born into a converso family in Lisbon, Diego Pires took the Hebrew name of Molcho, circumcised himself, and fled from Portugal to Salonika, where he studied the cabbalah. His prophecies, which included the destruction of Rome and the prediction that redemption would begin in 1540, became known in Italy, and following the sack of Rome in 1527, which appeared to give credence to his prophecies, Molcho went to Italy. He appears to have come to believe that he was the messiah, and in conformity with a talmudic legend on the sufferings of the messiah, he sat as a beggar for thirty days by the gates of Rome. Molcho met opposition from leaders of the Jewish community, but he gained an audience with the pope; his reputation was further strengthened when certain prophecies that he was said to have made—a flood in Rome and an earthquake in Portugal—did, in fact, occur. He went to Venice, where he had the support of a large section of the community, but his opponents denounced him to the Inquisition in Rome, and only the protection of the pope saved him at that time from the fire. He was burnt in 1532 in Mantua after the failure of the mission with Reubeni to the emperor.[14] Many refused to accept that Molcho had died, but millenarianism appears to have declined after Molcho's death.

Millennial expectations were renewed in Italy in the 1560s. A number of imminent dates for the coming of the messiah were announced, but the year that was most widely and strongly believed to be the year of redemption was 1575. When that year passed, a leading believer in imminent redemption recalculated the year to be 1608, but he expressed himself with less certainty.[15]

Explanations

Gerson D. Cohen contended that no discernible connection existed between the persecution of the Jews and Jewish millennial movements and that all such movements appeared in areas and periods of relative stability.[16] It is true that among the Ashkenazim persecution was not followed by millenarianism. Among the Sephardi and Italian communities, however, some instances of millenarianism did follow persecution, although among these communities disaster was not a necessary condition of a messianic outburst.

Disaster did not immediately precede the incidents in Castille in 1295; in fact, there is no clear historical or social factor that can account for these events. Some Castilian Jews had fears concerning their future. The last years of the reign of Alfonso X (1252–84) had been marked by the execution and jailing of a number of Jewish courtiers who had become involved in court intrigues, and in 1281 the king had many Jews arrested in their synagogues. Sancho IV (1284–95) reinstated the Jewish notables and gave them important positions as tax farmers and financiers, but the crown was under continual pressure to eliminate the Jews from positions in the state and from various economic activities. With the death of the king in 1295 many Jews feared that they would now be exposed to the persecution of their enemies.[17] Demands were made on the new rulers to exclude Jews from their official positions, but it is not known whether the death of the king aroused great fears among the poorer stratum of Jews, who supported the prophets in Avila and Ayllon.

Avila had a Jewish population of about fifty families, mainly small shop-keepers and artisans who also had some land under cultivation and owned small herds of sheep and cattle.[18] In a village such as Ayllon the economic character of the Jews could not have been very different. Millenarianism did not appear in the larger urban Jewish communities, which were dominated by wealthy Jewish families.

The millenarianism in 1391 had a clear background of disaster: violent attacks on Jews began in Seville and then spread to the rest of Spain. In large part the disturbances represented a social protest on the part of the Christian poor; they singled Jews out for attack since they provided a large proportion of the tax farmers and receivers acting on behalf of the crown and the aristocracy. The majority of Jews were neither tax farmers nor wealthy, but the mobs attacked the Jews as a group and made no distinction between rich and poor Jews.[19]

The greatest disaster to befall Spanish Jewry was the expulsion in 1492. The Jews were given four months to leave Spain, and those that remained were either forcibly expelled or baptized. They were forced to sell their property for very little and forbidden to take gold, silver, precious stones, or certain specified goods. Pillage on land and sea accompanied the expulsion: thieves and pirates murdered many; others died of hunger and disease; and some were turned away from the lands where they had hoped to find refuge. The majority of exiles migrated to Portugal, but the Portuguese king, John II, admitted them on the condition that they leave the country within eight months. When the time ran out, he began to sell them as slaves. John's successor, Manoel I, freed the Jews, but in 1497, as a result of an agreement with Spain, he ordered the Portuguese Jews converted by force.[20]

The Spanish exiles provided an important focus for the millennial excitement among Italian Jews around the turn of the century,[21] but since Italian Jews had not directly experienced any great disaster or persecution, their millenarian excitement requires further explanation. When the Jews have been persecuted and segregated, non-Jewish millennial movements have not stimulated Jewish millenarianism, but during the Renaissance, which was a time of marked social acceptance of Jews in Italy, the Italian Jews shared in the widespread millenarianism among the Italian population. Millennial tension and expectations built up in Italy in the 1480s and 1490s when a number of prophets appeared in various parts of the country, including Venice, proclaiming imminent destruction and the end of the world. This excitement was related to the expectations of invasion, and the actual invasion in 1494, of Italy by the French king, Charles VIII. In France, Charles VIII was seen in the millennial role of a second Charlemagne, and Charles saw himself as an apocalyptic reformer of the church, a new crusader who would conquer the Islamic world. The prophecy that Charles VIII would conquer the Mohammedans and convert them to Christianity circulated in Italy as well as in France, and at first, his Italian conquests did appear to fit the prophecies.[22]

The invasion had a particular impact on the Jews. The second entrance of the French into Rome in 1495 was accompanied by an anti-Jewish outbreak, but once Charles assumed control in the city, he put the Jews under his protection. This, together with the fact that the pope and his cardinals had fled Rome, gave rise to the belief among some Jews that a new era was about to begin. The arrival of the French in Naples in 1495 brought with it the pillage of its numerous and influential Jews, but one Jewish prophet saw Charles's entry into Naples as a sign of the imminent advent of the messiah. In a somewhat confused fashion he calculated that 1490 had been the beginning of the period of sufferings, that in 1495 this period had ended, and that in 1503 deliverance would finally materialize.[23]

The most important focus of millennial excitement in Italy was Florence, where Savonarola, the prior of the Dominican convent of San Marco, preached the coming advent to enthusiastic crowds. Before the French invasion, Savonarola had preached great suffering for Florence and Italy, and following the invasion, when he spoke more of the coming millennium, he spoke with the authority of a prophet whose former predictions had come true. For Savonarola, the tribulations of Florence were a sign of its election as the chosen city, the new Jerusalem, the center of the millennium, and of the Florentines as latter-day Israelites, who would reach new spiritual heights and enjoy great riches, power, and a large empire.[24] We do not know how much impact Savonarola's campaign had on Italian Jews, but B. Netanyahu argues that Abravanel, who was a member of the court of Naples and had to flee from the French, must have been aware of Savonarola.[25]

The millenarianism of Italian Jews in the first decades of the sixteenth century was not the result of direct experience with disaster or persecution; it was rather the consequence of the contemporaneous influence of the Spanish exiles and the Christian Italians and the messianic interpretation given to events in Spain and Italy. The revival of millenarianism among Italian Jews in the last decades of the sixteenth century coincided with the anti-Jewish measures taken by the Italian Counter-Reformation. From the 1560s an increasing number of harsh restrictions were imposed on Italian Jews: they were expelled from many areas, their occupations and economic pursuits were severely limited, they were forced to wear a Jewish badge and live in ghettos, and the Talmud was publicly burnt and prohibited. Reduced to poverty and a precarious existence, many Jews emigrated from Italy.[26] Of those who remained, many appear to have found compensation in millenarianism and mysticism.

While not all incidents of millenarianism in Spain and Italy were preceded by disaster, some of the most widespread incidents followed the greatest tragic events in the history of Spanish and Italian Jewry: the massacres of 1391, the expulsion of 1492, and the persecution by the Italian Counter-Reformation. However, millenarianism was almost unknown among the Ashkenazim, who were subject to a greater number of disasters and periods of persecution. The Ashkenazim were massacred in large numbers during the crusades, at the time of the Black Death, and on a number of other occasions. They were subject to a number of expulsions, particularly in the fourteenth, fifteenth, and sixteenth centuries, and their livelihoods were increasingly restricted by anti-Jewish decrees.[27] While the faith of the Ashkenazim in the eventual coming of the messiah was often strengthened during these periods of persecution, there were no influential predictions of, or preparations made for, his imminent coming.

Most of the popular prophets in Spain were unscholarly men who found support from their own socioeconomic stratum, but the differences between Sephardim and Ashkenazim extended also to the elite rabbinical level. The Sephardi rabbis tended to condemn messianic pretenders and prophets, but they often seemed preoccupied with calculating the date of the coming of the messiah. The Ashkenazi rabbis were influenced by injunctions that prohibited such calculations, and this orientation penetrated to the masses: speculation on the matter remained esoteric and limited to narrow circles. In Spain scholars felt no inhibition in discussing in public the date of the coming of the messiah, and they discussed the problem in a long series of tracts.[28] The millenarianism that followed the expulsion of 1492 infected all strata of Iberian Jewry, the wealthy and scholarly as well as the poor and unscholarly.

Millenarianism was not the only response of the Sephardim to the persecution; other responses included hopeless despair, self-blame for the failure to keep religious law, or the acceptance of Christianity. Nevertheless, millenarianism was one significant response to disaster: through it, the sufferings became the birth pangs of the messiah, and the victims of persecution believed that they would soon find happiness in the millennial kingdom.

The contrast in the responses of Ashkenazim and Sephardim to persecution reflects more general differences in their cultural and religious orientations. The Ashkenazim emphasized sin, guilt, humility, and asceticism; their quiescence and passivity were not conducive to millenarianism. The Sephardim emphasized pride, nobility, self-assertiveness, and, in some cases, Epicureanism. They put great emphasis on the noble status of their families. As it was among the Ashkenazim, descent from scholars was important, but the Sephardi notions of nobility were closer to those of the Christians: nobility was seen to be inherent in the families themselves, and claims were made of descent from the nobility of ancient Jerusalem including, toward the end of the Middle Ages, the House of David.[29]

In general, the Ashkenazim were stricter in their religious practice. Religious laxness and indifference were not uncommon among the rich Sephardim, especially the Jewish courtiers who found that Jewish religious requirements were not always compatible with court life.[30] Averroism, which stressed the superiority of reason over faith, spread among the wealthy Sephardim, although at the same time other wealthy Sephardim were developing cabbalism, an other-worldly ascetic mysticism; these latter attacked their peers for their rationalism and their accommodation to the non-Jewish world.[31]

The secular tendencies among Sephardi Jews explain, in part, why they often acted differently from the Ashkenazim when faced with the alternative of conversion to Christianity or death. Many Ashkenazim, including some entire communities, converted under this pressure, but the majority demonstrated their religious merit and believed that they insured their path to heaven by the choice of death. Martyrdom became an ideology and an institutionalized ritual: for the "sanctity of the name" those Jews faced with the threat of forced conversion first recited benedictions and then killed their children and themselves. This phenomenon did not appear among the Sephardim until the end of the fourteenth century, and then only a small minority took the path of martyrdom; the great majority preferred to submit to conversion.[32] Perhaps the Sephardim often had more choice, for in Germany the mob was intent on pillage and killing, whereas in Spain conversion was the long-range goal of the rulers.[33] Nevertheless, even when they were faced with similar situations, Ashkenazim and Sephardim chose different responses.

Cohen attempted to trace the differences between the passivity of the Ashkenazim and the self-assertion of the Sephardim back to their different beginnings. He argued that Palestine provided the cultural roots of the Ashkenazim and that after the failure of the Bar Kochba revolt the Jews in Palestine remained relatively quiescent: its leaders taught submission and passive waiting for the intervention of God. On the other hand, the cultural roots of Iberian Jews were in Babylonia; there they held two political stances: the cooperation of Jewish leaders with the gentile rulers and the rebellion of dissatisfied groups.[34]

However, this is not a convincing argument. It is true that in the early Middle Ages Franco-German Jewry came under the influence of Palestine through Italy and Spanish Jewry had links with Babylonia through North Africa. It is also true that differences between Ashkenazi and Sephardi rituals stemmed, in part, from their separate beginnings in Palestinian and Babylonian rituals, respectively.[35] But there is no evidence of a transmission of different political and cultural orientations to the wider society, and it is clear that these orientations developed over time, becoming clearly distinctive only in the later Middle Ages.

Mention has already been made of the development of the cabbalah among Sephardi Jews. The possibility that these religious innovations stimulated millenarianism deserves consideration. Certain Spanish cabbalists, such as Abraham Abulafia, were also messianists, but while their mystical experiences and prophetic announcements were closely related, their messianism was not a logical outgrowth of their cabbalistic doctrines.[36] The major part of the most important cabbalistic work of the period, the Zohar, was probably completed between 1280 and 1286,[37] and it is interesting to note that Moses de Leon, the author of the Zohar, lived in Avila at the time of the messianic prophet.[38] The Zohar contains a number of eschatological passages that alluded to the later crusades and to the collapse of the palaces of Rome and apocalyptic calculations that predicted that the exile would end at the beginning of the fourteenth century.[39] However, these passages are only a small part of a vast work or collection of several books concerned with mystical interpretations and secret meanings of the whole world of Judaism. Furthermore, the influence of the Zohar and the cabbalah in general is not evident until the last decades of the fifteenth century, and for some time it remained the esoteric preoccupation of small circles of mystics who had no apparent influence on the millenarianism of the masses.[40]

Ascher Lamlein was influenced by certain cabbalistic doctrines,[41] but only in the second half of the sixteenth century in Italy are there indications of a close interrelationship between millenarianism and cabbalism.[42] Mordecai Dato, a major cabbalistic writer, wrote on millennial themes around the year 1575,[43] and a group of cabbalists tried to hasten the coming of the messiah by introducing new significance into the midnight prayer for Israel's restoration.[44] Many cabbalists in Italy in the last decades of the sixteenth century were also millenarians, but in contrast to the Lurianic cabbalah, which became the dominant form in the seventeenth century, nothing in the doctrines of the prominent cabbalistic system of the period would inspire millenarianism. Moreover, it can be argued that the spread of mysticism was itself a response to the deteriorating situation of Italian Jews.

The different cultural orientations of Sephardim and Ashkenazim have to be seen in relation to the differences in the societies in which they lived and, in particular, to the different natures of their relationships with the dominant gentiles. Until the second half of the tenth century the number of Jews in Germany and northern France was very small, and Franco-German Jewry became firmly established only around the year 1000. Prior to the first crusade, apart from some minor incidents, the Ashkenazim lived in peace, and they achieved high status, mainly as merchants. However, this period of peaceful coexistence with non-Jews and of high status was of comparatively short duration. From the first crusade, in 1098, the economic and social position of the Ashkenazim in western and central Europe declined: pogroms became more frequent; Jews were limited to a narrow range of occupations, especially moneylending; and they were increasingly segregated from the non-Jewish population. This is not to say that over some periods in certain areas the Ashkenazim did not live peacefully and prosper or that friendly relations with Christians never existed, but the pogroms, discrimination, and segregation deeply affected the Ashkenazim, strengthening their cultural distinctiveness and their feelings of separateness from the dominant society.[45]

In contrast, large-scale persecution of the Sephardim began after a very long period of relative peace, prosperity, and status. Apart from a temporary setback as a result of the invasion of the Almoravides in the 1080s, the Spanish Jews under Muslim rule in Andalusia enjoyed prosperity and high status. This lasted until the invasion of the Almohades in 1147, when many Jews migrated north to Christian Spain, where from the beginning of the Christian reconquest in the second half of the eleventh century the already favorable position of the Jews improved further. The Christian princes of the reconquest found the Jews reliable allies, and once territories were conquered, Jewish familiarity with the country was a useful asset.

Kings and nobles appointed Jews to important positions as diplomats, financiers, tax farmers, administrators, scholars, and physicians. In Castile, which was often in a state of political disturbance, kings felt that they could trust their Jewish counselors, who were not subject to the conflicting loyalties of their Christian vassals. Jews occupied a wide variety of professions and occupations, and unhampered by economic discrimination, they were of great importance in the economy of the country: they constituted a large section of the urban population and bourgeoisie, controlling a significant part of Spanish commerce, industry, mining, and viniculture. The ruling elements saw land ownership by Jews as being in the royal interest, and they put no restrictions on the Jewish acquisition of estates. Some wealthy Jews owned castles and villages and even exercised feudal rights in the thirteenth and fourteenth centuries. Secular leaders often ignored or opposed decrees of the church that were intended to segregate and discriminate against the Jews. Some popes complained about the important positions given to Jews in Spain, but in Spain itself churchmen employed Jews to lease, administer, and collect taxes from the ecclesiastical properties.

The majority of Spanish Jews lived in Jewish quarters, but up to the latter part of the fourteenth century this was entirely voluntary, and it was not unusual to find Jews living outside and Christians living inside the Jewish quarters. The Christian kings referred to themselves as the "kings of the three religions," and a pluralistic structure evolved in which a comparatively high level of tolerance characterized relations between the three religious collectivities. There were no clear visible differences between Jews and Christians: they spoke the same language, took similar names, and wore the same style of clothes. The life-style of the wealthy Jews, who carried arms, mixed freely in the royal courts and nobles' mansions, and conspicuously displayed great riches and luxury, had no counterpart among the Ashkenazim. The Jewish community itself displayed a strong social division between a minority, made up of the rich and powerful, and the majority, who were small merchants and artisans, but cordial relations between Jews and non-Jews were not limited to the upper stratum: Jewish and Christian burghers had friendly professional and personal relationships; Jewish advocates represented gentile clients in the secular courts; Jewish artisans had Christian customers or worked for Christian employers; Jewish textile merchants employed Christian workingmen; Jews and non-Jews joined in common processions, shared the public baths, exchanged gifts on holidays and family occasions, and ate occasional meals together. Jews performed the roles of godfather and godmother at Christian baptisms, while Christians performed similar roles at Jewish circumcisions.[46] This is in sharp contrast to the precarious position of the Ashkenazim, their low status as despised moneylenders, and their segregated existence.

Feelings of superiority among the Sephardim did not stem only from their Judaism and Jewishness, as was the case among the Ashkenazim, but also from their status and power within the larger society. Since the Sephardim felt secure in and strongly identified with the dominant culture, any reversal in their situation was bound to create disorientation. Among the Ashkenazim, who rarely identified with the host society and culture, pogroms and expulsions created suffering but less fundamental disorientation: they had a tradition of martyrdom which reminded them that persecution was an integral part of their history and that it was sensible to keep their assets in liquid form, ready to move.

Indications that the position of the Spanish Jews was not inviolable were already present at the end of the thirteenth century. With the reconquest nearly completed and most of the Iberian peninsula united into a few large kingdoms, churchmen and secular rulers began to treat the Jews more as they were being treated in the rest of Christian Europe. In Aragon the change in the policy of the church began in the middle of the thirteenth century, but in Castile, where Jewish influence in the state, and especially in its financial administration, was greater, the status of the Jews remained high and relations between Jews and Christians remained good.[47]

The spread of anti-Jewish sentiment in the fourteenth century was related to a number of factors: the success of the reconquest; the decline in the pluralistic orientation of the Spanish rulers; the increasing influence in Spain of common European cultural and religious patterns; and some development of the Spanish-Christian bourgeoisie. In Aragon the Jews lost much of their political influence and socioeconomic status, while in Castile, despite increasing demands by clergy, burghers, and nobles for the removal of Jews from positions of state, the Jews were not seriously affected until the second half of the fourteenth century. A civil war in Castile in 1366–69 ruined a number of Jewish communities and marked the beginning of the decline of Jewish power in the state. In the last decades of the century discriminatory and segregative measures began to be put into effect.[48]

The pogroms of 1391 were followed, in 1412–15, by discriminatory measures that excluded Jews from certain trades, barred them from service in the royal and urban governments, and reduced their social interaction with Christians. The Spanish kings soon abolished many of the anti-Jewish edicts and tried to restore the Jews to the former status. This improved the situation of the Jews, but it did not return them to their pre-1391 situation: many communities were not reestablished, the Jews' political rank and influence declined, fewer wealthy Jews remained, some discriminatory measures were reinstituted, and the center of Jewish life moved from the large cities to the small towns, where Jews continued as small merchants, shopkeepers, and artisans. Nevertheless, up to the expulsion of 1492, the situation of the Spanish Jews remained considerably better than that of the Ashkenazim in western, central, and northern Europe. Despite the official ban on Jews' holding offices in the royal and urban administrations, they remained important as financiers, tax farmers, physicians, and surgeons, and these rich Jews continued to mix in court and government circles. Although occasional outbreaks continued against Jews, the discontent of the general population was directed more against conversos than against Jews.[49]

Thus, even in the fifteenth century the strong contrast between the Ashkenazim and Sephardim remained: the Sephardim were not confined mainly to moneylending but were found in a wide range of occupations, including the most prestigious; they were not segregated in ghettos but were allowed to mix freely with non-Jews; and they did not feel an enormous cultural gulf between themselves and the non-Jewish population but identified themselves with many aspects of Spanish culture. During the second half of the fifteenth century, the sermons and writings of Jewish scholars, rationalist and antirationalist, continued to express a high respect for the Spanish Christian culture.

A number of discriminatory measures and unauthorized local expulsions in Castile preceded the expulsion edict of 1492, but it came as an unexpected and enormous blow to the Jews.[50] Its effects on the lives and self-image of the Spanish Jews were devastating, far greater than those of any other expulsion of Jews in the Middle Ages. One reason for this, perhaps, was that it was done on a far greater scale than other expulsions of European Jews: expulsions from Germany or France had been either partial or carried out in stages, and the total expulsion of Jews from England in 1290 had affected a much smaller Jewish population.[51] More important, however, the Sephardim felt that they were torn, violently and cruelly, from their homeland. For the Ashkenazim expulsion was a tragedy in the loss of their property and in the problems of migration and resettlement, but it little affected their attachment to a particular society and culture or to focal elements of their identity. For the Sephardim, who regarded themselves as among the cultural elite and who took great pride in their history and achievements in Spain, exile was a great blow to their identity and pride and gave rise to enormous resentment and a desire for revenge. The exiles expressed their concern that the Spanish Jews had accepted expulsion without attempting armed resistance, and some found consolation in the belief that the punishments of the "end of time" were near.[52]

It would appear, therefore, that millenarianism was a response to disaster among a people whose leaders had enjoyed wealth, status, and power, and who had been rejected by a society into which they had formerly been highly integrated, culturally and socially. To illustrate this with an individual case, Don Isaac Abravanel, who served as diplomat and financier to six kings, associated freely with kings and nobles and participated comfortably in both Jewish culture and the culture of the Christian upper stratum. On three occasions, in Portugal, Spain, and Naples, Abravanel was separated from his property, stripped of his honor, and forced into exile. He had shared the false optimism of Spanish Jewry, and although his immediate reaction was to despair of redemption, he came to interpret the expulsion as a part of the birth pangs of the messiah. In his messianic works he emphasized revenge: the redemption of the Jews would emerge from the punishment of the gentiles, especially of the Christians.[53]

The change in the situation of Italian Jewry in the sixteenth century replicated, in many respects, the change that had occurred earlier in Spain. During the Renaissance, in the fifteenth century and the first half of the sixteenth, Italian Jews mixed freely with Christians and adopted many aspects of the dominant culture. Christians, including clergymen, visited synagogues to hear Jewish preachers, and Jewish-Christian friendships, which were especially prevalent among the humanists, were sometimes found between clergymen and rabbis. As had been the case in Spain, gentile friends served as godfathers at circumcision ceremonies. Since it was possible to mix with Christians without abandoning Jewish religious practice, few Jews converted, but there was a decline in religious observance as well as a tendency toward skepticism and freethinking, mainly among the intellectuals. The Jews of the Renaissance emphasized courage and self-esteem; attracted to pomp and solemnity, they concerned themselves with titles, family coats of arms, and the right to bear arms.[54] The measures of the Counter-Reformation in the second half of the century represented a sharp reversal for the Italian Jews: like the Spanish Jews before them, they experienced a sudden fall from wealth and honor and the rejection of a society that had formerly accepted them and whose culture they had, in many respects, accepted. Once again, the sufferings were interpreted as the birth pangs of the messiah.[55]

The Italian Jews, Ashkenazim, and Sephardim were all victims of persecution, but the Spanish and Italian Jews underwent a deeper disruption of their social expectations and cultural order. They experienced a greater deprivation, relative to their past state, in their economic position, social status, and political influence.

6. The New Christians

IN 1391 the majority of those Spanish Jews who were given the choice of conversion or death chose conversion. For the New Christians, or conversos, return to Judaism constituted heresy, and the apostate was subject to the death penalty. The number of conversos increased in the years 1412–14 as a result of the campaign of the preacher Vincent Ferrer and anti-Jewish legislation. In 1412, in Castile, various decrees excluded Jews from holding office, possessing titles, entering various trades, bearing arms, hiring Christians, and socially interacting with Christians.[1]

After 1414 the number of conversions was small until the expulsion decree of 1492. An exact figure of how many Jews chose conversion rather than leave Spain would be hard to calculate, but one estimate is that about 160,000 went into exile, while about 240,000 conversos remained in Spain.[2] Of the exiles, the majority, 100,000 to 120,000, migrated to Portugal, but they were permitted to remain there for only a limited period. In 1497 the Jews who remained in Portugal were forced to convert. Very few were able to flee, and mass baptisms took place. Some of the converts managed to leave Portugal, but a number of enactments were passed to prevent the emigration of New Christians, and in 1542 about 60,000 conversos remained in Portugal.[3]

Millenarianism and Mysticism among the Conversos

Some conversos defended their conversion by pointing to the "senselessness" of Jewish messianic hopes, but messianism found many enthusiasts among the marranos, or secret Jews, who continued to practice at least some Jewish rituals. The millenarian spirit appealed to a number of the conversos of 1391; many tried to leave Spain for Israel. They believed that migration to the Holy Land was one means of bringing about the coming of the messiah.[4]

Messianic hopes increased among the marranos from the middle of the fifteenth century. The capture of Constantinople by the Turks in 1453 encouraged these hopes, and visionaries and calculators of the end of days closely followed the Turkish conquests and victories over the Christians. Stories circulated that the messiah was already born. One New

Christian in Valencia told of a miraculous young boy. who lived on a mountain near Constantinople; apparently, only circumcised Jews could look upon him without being blinded.[5]

After the exile of 1492 a number of millenarian outbreaks occurred among the marranos. The first recorded incident occurred in 1500 in the small town of Herrara in northern Castile, which in the fifteenth century had contained a Jewish community of substantial size and wealth. Ines, the "Maiden of Herrara" and the daughter of a shoemaker, proclaimed that she had been led by her mother, a boy who had just died, and an angel to heaven to a place where she had heard the voices of souls who had been burnt "in sanctity of the name." The majority of conversos in Herrara believed in her, and many conversos came from elsewhere to see her. They ceased work, fasted, and prepared themselves in holiday clothing for the imminent arrival of the messiah. Some said that a town created in heaven would be brought down to earth and that the conversos would dwell there in luxury, eating off golden plates.

There were similar occurrences elsewhere. Maria Gomez, a prophetess in Chillón, a small provincial town in Ciudad Real, claimed that she had ascended to heaven where she had been told that all the conversos who fasted, observed the Sabbath, and kept other commandments would be taken to the Holy Land. In the same province another prophet claimed that he had ascended to heaven where he had met God, Elijah, the Messiah, and the prophetesses of Herrara and Chillón. He said that Elijah would come to Spain to collect all the conversos who gave arms to the poor conversos, believed in the law of Moses, and kept the Sabbath and other precepts. His followers dressed in holiday garb in readiness for the messiah.

Popular prophecy among the conversos occurred in other parts of Spain, such as Córdoba and Valencia. Signs in the sky, political events, and wars were taken as signs that 1500 was the year of the Redemption. Most prophetesses and prophets who appeared at the time predicted that Elijah and the Messiah would soon appear and take the conversos who believed in redemption to Israel on clouds or angels' wings. Several communities of conversos in Castile lived for weeks in a state of exaltation and excitement, leading ascetic lives, fasting regularly, and adhering as rigidly as possible to Jewish observances. Some hastily married off their sons and daughters. The Inquisition learned of the movements and imprisoned and burnt many of those involved.[6]

Not all converso millenarians were marranos. Some were devout Christians. The rise of millenarianism and mysticism in the fifteenth and sixteenth centuries in Spain was related, in part, to the influence of the conversos. The Franciscan Fray Melchoir, born in a converso family in

Burgos, prophesied, in 1512, imminent revolutionary changes: the Holy Roman Empire and the papacy would be overturned; all the clergy would be killed, apart from an elect who would be preserved to accomplish the work of renovation; the church would be transformed and situated in Jerusalem; and all of humanity would live in virtue and happiness. He started conventicles of followers and found disciples among the conversos.[7]

Some Spanish millenarians emphasized the role of the Spanish royalty. From the end of the fifteenth century many Spaniards believed that it was the prophetic destiny of the Catholic sovereign finally to vanquish the Turk.[8] In 1520, Juan de Bilbao, of Jewish descent, claimed that he was Prince John, the son of the Catholic sovereigns and the redeemer of mankind.[9]

The conversos were particularly important in the Christian mystical movement of illuminists, or *alumbiados*. The illuminists criticized excessive formalism in religion and advocated the attainment of direct communication with the divine through prayer, ascetic practices, mortification of the flesh, and passive surrender of the will to God.[10] The beginnings of the movement can be traced to Franciscan friars of converso origin who attracted public notice in 1512. The movement, which grew undisturbed until the early 1520s, included many conversos. Some of the greatest figures of Spanish mysticism were descendants of conversos. A grandfather of Santa Teresa of Jesus was a rich converso who had been persecuted by the Inquisition, and many of Santa Teresa's friends and patrons were also of Jewish descent. The conversos also gave enthusiastic support to the reform movement of barefooted Carmelites.[11]

Many illuminists appeared to deny the efficacy of the sacraments, and in 1525 the Inquisition turned its attention to the quasi-Lutheran beliefs that it detected in their teachings. Some illuminists turned to Erasmism, which stood for a pure, interior, nonritualistic religion, and many of the most eminent Erasmists were of converso origin. The Inquisition began to prosecute the Erasmists in 1529 and extinguished the cause of Erasmus in Spain in the 1530s. A small number of Protestant groups emerged in Spain in the 1550s, and once again, conversos were prominent. Protestantism was eradicated in Spain through a series of autos-da-fé from 1559 to 1562.[12]

In Portugal, millenarianism attracted many marranos. Luis Dias, "the Messiah of Setubal," a poor, uneducated tailor, was a converso living in the seaport of Setubal, south of Lisbon. He came to consider himself first as a prophet and then as a messiah, and he attracted a considerable following of conversos in both Setubal and Lisbon. His followers, including a number of Old Christians, believed that he worked miracles, and they would kiss his hand devoutly. He was arrested after the authorities learned that he was circumcising the children of his followers. He was released after a confession, but when he reverted to his earlier practices, he was arrested again. Together with eighty-three of his followers, he was burned at the stake in Lisbon in 1542. A high government official, an Old Christian who was converted to Judaism under Dias's influence, died at the stake in 1551.[13]

When David Reubeni arrived in Portugal in 1528, he created a stir among the marranos, who believed that there was a connection between their precarious situation and his appearance.[14] Reubeni wrote in his diary that he had tried to convince the conversos that he was a warrior and not a mysterious figure or miracle worker. When the Portuguese king accused him of coming to return the conversos to Judaism, Reubeni replied that he had not come for the sake of the marranos.[15]

In Ancona, Italy, Solomon Molcho attracted many former marranos who had returned to Judaism, and in the same town in 1556, twenty-four marranos who believed in the imminent coming of the messiah were burned.[16] In Ferrara in 1553, Samuel Usque, a former marrano from Portugal, published in Portuguese a book on the coming consolation for those who bore the tribulations of Israel. Usque wrote of the many trage-dies of the Jews, including the expulsion from Spain, the forced conver-sions in Portugal, and the sufferings of the conversos who had escaped from Portugal. He narrated the history of these misfortunes because he believed that the Redemption was near and that the sufferings of the conversos would be the last in Jewish history. The book gained immediate acclaim and spread widely among the Portuguese-speaking marranos and former marranos.[17]

In Portugal, millenarianism continued to hold an attraction for some marranos in the seventeenth century. Among them circulated myths of the appearance of the ten lost tribes, occasional rumors of the birth of the messiah, and beliefs that the messiah would not enter the Iberian penin-sula in the form of a man, since the Inquisition would catch and burn him. One legend had it that the messiah would appear in the form of a fish.[18] Conversos on trial in 1616–17 said that they believed that the messiah would divide the sea for them and that they would go on dry land to Israel. A trial of conversos in 1676 found that they believed that Enoch and Elijah had left Paradise and were in France performing miracles and resur-recting the dead.[19]

In addition to the marranos who believed in a messiah who would come to redeem the conversos, other conversos became involved in, and con-tributed to, Portuguese millenarianism. In the 1530s, in the province of Beira, a cobbler, Goncalo Eannes Bandarra of Trancoso, prophesied the reappearance of a hidden king, the redeemer of mankind. Bandarra was in close contact with many conversos who believed in his prophecies. His prophetic verses were later interpreted as predicting the death of the young king San Sebastian in 1578 and his future return.

Portuguese millenarianism developed after the death of San Sebastian at the battle of Alcazarquivir in Morocco. The decline of the Portuguese empire had been apparent for some time, and the defeat enabled Spain to assume control of Portugal two years after the battle. The king's body was never recovered, and many Portuguese would not accept that he had died. They believed that he was a prisoner of the Moors, who had taken him to a desert island from which he would return to liberate his people. Conversos contributed their biblical knowledge and messianism to Sebastianism and associated the movement with the coming of the "Fifth Empire." Sebastian became the national messiah, and a number of pretenders claimed the role: two appeared in 1584–85, one in 1595, and the last in 1598 in Venice, where a number of exiled Portuguese had settled. By the 1620s and 1630s many Portuguese had started to merge the myth of the hidden Sebastian with the more visible body of a lawful heir. Portugal regained its independence in 1640, but a large part of the empire had been lost, and the myth did not completely disappear. The people desired a return to the past glories of Portugal, and the myth was strengthened each time the independence of Portugal appeared to be threatened or social conditions deteriorated. The belief that Sebastian would return and liberate his people continued well into the nineteenth century.[20]

The Background to Converso Millenarianism

In Spain, until the late 1440s, the position of the conversos was comparatively good: they were not fully accepted into Christian society, but they were able to enter occupations closed to the Jews. Many experienced rapid social mobility: they entered the professions and obtained important offices in the municipal councils, the church, and the state. They provided the chief financial officials at court, and many assimilated with the nobility. In 1449 mobs attacked conversos in Toledo, and from then until 1474 conversos had to endure a series of riots and popular uprisings against them. The background to these attacks was a scarcity of foodstuffs and a sharp rise in prices, beginning in the 1440s. In 1473 a particularly bad wave of anti-converso uprisings and massacres followed a sharp rise in the price of wheat. The agitation was not exclusively against the conversos; it was also directed against tax collectors and taxation. But many conversos were involved in taxation as guarantors to tax farmers, many of whom were Jews. In addition, there was much jealousy of the economic success of many conversos, and they were made the scapegoat of the economic troubles.[21]

The troubles of the conversos increased with the passing of the "purity of blood" statutes, which excluded them from public administration, academic life, religious orders, and cathedral chapters. The greatest blow came with the establishment of the Spanish Inquisition, which began its operations in 1480. The Inquisition directed its activities against the conversos; any converso was automatically suspected of being a secret Jew.[22]

In Portugal, as in Spain, a period of relative tolerance and social mobility preceded one of persecution and a rapid fall in fortune. From the mass conversion of the Jews in Portugal in 1497 to the late 1530s, however, the situation was far better than that in Spain. Some Portuguese blamed the conversos for a famine in 1503, and in 1506, following a plague and famine, mobs killed some conversos. But tensions subsided after the king punished the instigators and pronounced that the sincerity of the conversos' Christian faith would not be questioned. As it did in Spain in the first half of the fifteenth century, conversion to Catholicism in Portugal eliminated the legal disqualifications that applied to Jews and lifted many barriers to social mobility. The Portuguese conversos became physicians, financiers, and commercial entrepreneurs and entered the army, the universities, and the church. In the first decades of the sixteenth century they almost monopolized finance and high commerce in Portugal. Some acquired enormous wealth and intermarried with the nobility.

A few marranos were killed in mob attacks on them in the late 1520s, but the major blow for the conversos came with the establishment of the Portuguese Inquisition in 1536. The conversos tried to limit the powers of the Inquisition, but they did not succeed; in 1540 the first auto-da-fé took place in Portugal in Lisbon, and in 1547 a bull bestowed great authority upon the Inquisition. Thus, in both Spain and Portugal a period of relative security and economic and social success was followed by discrimination and persecution.

The "fall of fortune" became a common experience of the conversos: many who had successfully pursued wealth and honor lost their property, became targets of the Inquisition, or lived in fear of that persecution.[23] Millenarianism appealed more to the poorer conversos who had not experienced wealth and status, but they were no less affected than were their richer brethren by the mob attacks and the persecution of the Inquisition.

The millenarianism of the conversos corresponded with the periods of their persecution. In Spain messianic hopes increased from the middle of the fifteenth century, as the situation of the conversos began to deteriorate, and rose after the violence against them in 1473. The movements in 1500 followed the expulsion of the Jews from Spain, the sudden increase in the number of conversos, and the intensification of the activities of the Inquisition.

In addition to the problems that affected practicing Jew and converso alike, the conversos suffered for an additional reason, one which did not, in the main, affect Jews. The conversos had loyalties to and identified with two religions, but they were accepted by neither. As shown above, they came to be hated and persecuted by Christians, but they found little sympathy among Jews. Most Jews saw the conversos as Christians and as strangers to the Jewish people. The Spanish Jews disputed the arguments of some non-Spanish Jews who defended the marranos as people who had been forcibly converted but who remained faithful to Judaism. The harsher Jewish critics denied the conversos a share in the Redemption.[24]

Historians have disagreed over the extent to which the conversos continued to identify themselves as Jews and to practice the Jewish religion. Some historians have argued that the majority of conversos, including their children and grandchildren, were marranos or secret Jews: they had Jewish prayer books and secretly attended Jewish services; they did not work on the Jewish Sabbath, they continued to observe the dietary laws, the laws of mourning, the fast on Yom Kippur; and they celebrated the Jewish festivals.[25] According to this view, the Inquisition correctly evaluated the character of the conversos when it prosecuted thousands for continuing to practice Judaism. An opposite view is taken by Netanyahu, who argues that by the time the Spanish Inquisition began its operations in 1480, the majority of conversos had become detached from Judaism. He argues that the forced converts of 1391 began to turn from Judaism, and that their children ceased entirely to observe the Jewish law and adopted the beliefs and practices of Christianity. Groups of secret Jews did exist on the fringes of the converso population, but in the main the Inquisition persecuted men and women who were at least semi-Christianized. The persecution of people for their beliefs often intensifies their adherence to those beliefs, and the short-term effect of the Inquisition was to increase the number of marranos.[26]

Judgments on the identity and religion of the conversos require statements of the standards used in determining detachment from Judaism. By rabbinic standards the overwhelming majority of conversos, including the most loyal crypto-Jews, had deviated substantially from Judaism: they violated the Sabbath, ate forbidden foods, and participated regularly in gentile religious ceremonies. The problem, however, is not whether conversos deviated from rabbinic Judaism but whether they behaved in a way that indicated Jewish self-identity.[27]

Up to the middle of the sixteenth century, some marranos in Spain and Portugal preserved their Judaism in an orthodox fashion, but Judaism, a strongly ritualistic religion, was not easy to keep secret, and it became increasingly difficult to retain Judaism in its traditional forms. Some possessed Hebrew prayer books as well as Jewish religious books in Spanish, but the marranos became increasingly dependent on oral transmission. The problem of transferring Judaism to the next generation was particularly acute, and most parents waited until their children were adolescents before they felt safe in introducing them to marranism. This meant that for many years they had to hide their true religion from their own children.

The levels of observance varied greatly, but the Judaism of most marranos weakened and took forms that had elements of Catholicism. Knowledge of Hebrew declined until it was lost completely, and the marranos came to rely on the Latin version of the Old Testament. The absence of prayer books reduced the stock of prayers to a very few, such as the *Shema* and the *Amida*, which were learned by heart and constantly repeated. Some other prayers remained only in the vernacular and in attenuated forms. The services of the marranos consisted of memorized Hebrew prayers, adaptations of Catholic prayers, and original prayers, composed by the marranos.

The observance of the mitsvot among the marranos declined. Circumcision had to be abandoned as too dangerous, but the barmitzvah became an initiation ceremony into the secret religion, and although the marranos had to be buried with Catholic rites, the mourners observed the *shiva* (traditional week of mourning). Some vestiges of the dietary laws remained; the observance of the Sabbath was limited to one or two rites, particularly the kindling of lights on Sabbath eve. Most of the religious holidays were forgotten or neglected. Passover and Yom Kippur retained some importance, but the dates of these holidays were calculated according to the solar calendar, since the Jewish calendar was too complicated to preserve orally. A festival which came to rival Yom Kippur in importance was Purim, which the marranos called the Feast of Esther. The marranos could easily identify with Esther, who had kept her Jewish identity secret and had continued to practice Judaism in a hostile environment.

The influence of Catholicism and the syncretic nature of the marrano religion is obvious at many points: worshipers no longer covered their heads; kneeling during services was prevalent; Catholic prayers were used with only slight modifications and omissions; and prayers were recited rather than chanted in the traditional manner. In some instances the marranos adopted Catholic forms in order to strengthen their Jewish identity. In reciting that salvation was possible only through the Law of Moses and not through the Law of Christ, the marranos used the language of Catholicism to confess their Jewish faith. The victims of the Inquisition were revered as saints according to Christian models: they were incorporated into the liturgy; candles were burnt in their honor; and their intercession with heaven was sought. The growing reliance of the marranos on fasts, increasing the number of fast days and changing some festive occasions into fasts, may also have reflected a Catholic influence, but a more important factor may have been the belief that by fasting they could atone for their sinfulness as apostates.[28]

The attenuation of Judaism led many marranos to center their religion on a few doctrines, especially the denial of the Christian claim that Jesus was the messiah. The belief in a Jewish messiah who was yet to come became a major, sometimes the only, Jewish principle of many conversos. The desperate desire to retain their Jewishness, despite the dangers and fear of the Inquisition, led them to believe in the miraculous appearance of the messiah as their only hope. Their suffering made no sense if the messiah had already come; if Jesus was the messiah, they asked, why had they not been able to assimilate and find peace and honor? They were saved from despair only by their belief in redemption. The marrano sang: "Has the redeemer already come? No—*this one* is not the redeemer; the redeemer is yet to come."[29]

The conversos were not a closely unified group. They ranged from the fanatical convert who took part in the persecution of Jews to the crypto-Jew who attempted to practice as much of his traditional faith as possible. In some districts converts assimilated quickly with the Old Christians; in others they maintained close connections with Judaism, either because they lived in large communities of their own or because, prior to the expulsion, they lived near Jewish communities. One factor differentiating the conversos was the extent to which a conversion had been a forced one. The converts of 1391 had death as the only alternative; the converts of 1412–15 had converted to escape discrimination; and the converts of 1492 had converted to escape expulsion. Some converted freely to achieve social mobility. Another factor differentiating conversos was the state of faith prior to conversion. A section of the Jewish upper-class, the Averroists and other intellectuals who emphasized a religion of reason, was already highly assimilated into Christian society and was not essentially changed by conversion. Some conversos saw Christianity as even more inconsistent with a religion of reason than Judaism, and they were an important element in the rationalist groups in sixteenth-century Spain. Those who were traditional Jews before their conversions were more likely to be crypto-Jews after it.[30]

But the conversos had great difficulty in being conventional Christians. Even if they became devout Christians, they were open to suspicion from Old Christians and persecution from the Inquisition. They could not take Christianity for granted, for the knowledge of a different religion which presented a different definition of reality remained with them. Some conversos may have become mystics, Erasmists, or Protestants because of their experiences with or knowledge of the persecution by the Catholic establishment. Perhaps more important, they were intellectually open to the acceptance of a divergent belief system. The experience of having broken with one religious tradition caused some to be prepared to accept a radical reevaluation of another.

An important distinction should be made between the conversos of Spain and Portugal. For a whole century in Spain, from 1391 to 1492, a substantial converso population lived in a society with a substantial Jewish population. The expulsion of the Jews and the persecutions, spoliations, and emigration of conversos left only small, isolated crypto-Jewish groups in Spain. The great majority of the fourteenth- and fifteenth-century Spanish conversos who remained in Spain were assimilated into Spanish society.[31]

In Portugal, the whole Jewish population was converted in one sweep, and all Jewish energies were immediately directed to the organization of a converso community. Whereas in Spain many conversions had an important voluntary element, in Portugal it was entirely forced, and the converts included the most tenacious Jews, who had chosen exile from Spain. The fact that conversion was the norm in Portugal increased the cohesion and solidarity of the Portuguese converts. In addition, the Portuguese conversos lived through a period of tolerance in which they were able to strengthen their Judaism. The ravages of the Inquisition were greater in Portugal than in Spain, but from 1497 to 1538 conversos laid the foundations for a marrano religion. For these reasons, crypto-Judaism was stronger and lasted longer in Portugal than in Spain. After Portugal was annexed by Spain in 1580, some conversos migrated to Spain to escape the Portuguese Inquisition and the country's declining economy. The activities of the Spanish Inquisition were renewed, and Portuguese conversos became its principal target in the seventeenth century.[32] Portuguese conversos emigrated from Portugal and Spain, and in a number of societies they were able to return to Judaism. These were to have an important influence on the further development of Jewish messianism.

7. The Sabbatian Movement

THE LARGEST and most significant messianic outburst in Jewish history was the Sabbatian movement in the seventeenth century. In 1666 a great many Jews were convinced that the messiah had arrived in the person of Sabbatai Zvi. Beginning in Gaza, Palestine, the movement spread to many communities throughout almost the whole diaspora. This chapter considers the movement in 1665 and 1666, before the totally unexpected conversion of Zvi to Islam. The following chapter will discuss the sectarian developments after Zvi's conversion.

In analyzing the Sabbatian movement, we have the benefit of Gershom Scholem's vast work on Sabbatai Zvi, probably the greatest history of a messiah and a messianic movement. Scholem is a superb historian, his scholarship is awe-inspiring, and his book has received much acclaim.[1] The critical reviews have been few, although he has been taken to task from a religious point of view. He has been accused of subverting traditional Judaism by claiming that Sabbatianism was a central episode in Jewish history and that the Sabbatian theology was as important as normative rabbinic thought.[2] But Scholem's claim that the majority in most Jewish communities believed in Zvi in 1666 and his explanation of the movement have received little questioning. Most commentators have accepted Scholem's idealist argument that the events of 1666 were an outcome of developments in the cabbalah and that nonreligious factors were of little consequence. Scholem's massive scholarship has blinded many scholars to the absence of a strong foundation for many of his general statements and his causal analysis.[3] His biography of Zvi, his description of the train of events, and his excavation of the historical sources on which they are based are exhaustive, but the wealth of information that he provides also contains much evidence that can be used to question his fundamental thesis and to support alternative explanations. The discussion here does not present new historical material on the movement itself, but it does relate the evidence to factors to which Scholem either gives little attention or entirely ignores.

On the eve of Pentecost 1665, in Gaza, Palestine, a young scholar, Nathan Ashkenazi, fell into a trance during the religious service and made a number of utterances, including a reference to an acquaintance, Sabbatai Zvi. After coming out of the trance, Nathan explained that he had been chosen by God as a prophet and that the meaning of his utterance was that

Zvi was the messiah. At the end of May 1665, Zvi accepted Nathan's prophecy and announced that he was the messiah; to signify the break in history, he announced that the Fast of the Seventeenth of Tammuz would be a day of rejoicing. Zvi traveled from Gaza to Jerusalem, where he was expelled by the rabbinic authorities after he ate forbidden animal fat. He then went to Aleppo; in his absence, enthusiasm grew among the communities in Palestine, and miracle stories were communicated to other communities. In a number of towns, such as Aleppo, Smyrna, Safed, and Damascus, the presence of Zvi produced great enthusiasm, but the acceptance of Zvi as the messiah spread far beyond the area of activities of Zvi and Nathan.

Many Jews in Gaza came to accept Zvi as the messiah, but in the first months following Zvi's acceptance of Nathan's prophecy, Nathan, Zvi, and their followers appear to have made little effort to spread the tidings. The movement spread not by organized missionary activity but almost entirely by letters and rumors. Nathan and his group began making definite efforts to spread their message from the middle of September 1665, but only two emissaries were sent from Palestine, one to Egypt and another to Italy, and it is doubtful that even they had a formal mission. Enthusiastic letters from Aleppo, where Zvi stayed for a while, began to arrive in Constantinople in September 1665, and in the following months the messianic tidings spread rapidly to many other communities under Islam. The first reports to reach Christian Europe arrived in Italy at the end of October and beginning of November. From Italy the news traveled to Germany, Holland, England, and the rest of the continent. The news entered Poland from Turkey, via the Balkans.

The commercial and family ties between Jewish communities, especially those in Turkey, Italy, and Holland, greatly facilitated the spread of the message. Amsterdam, which received reports as early as December 1665, became an important center for the transmission of the news. Parts of letters received in Amsterdam were put together and then sent on to London, Germany, and Poland. During 1666 in many Jewish communities each mail brought many letters and created great excitement. As the news passed from one community to another, new interpretations and additions often transformed its content. There were often wide gaps between the teachings of Nathan, the events around Zvi in the Middle East, and the content of the news.

Nathan did not expect the Redemption to take place through military action: he did not expect Zvi to take the role of warrior, and vengeance on gentiles was to be limited to those responsible for the massacres in Poland in 1648 and the following years. Nor did Nathan expect a sudden occurrence of miracles: he argued that believers should have faith without a sign or miracle, and those who denied the messiah, however orthodox they might be, would be condemned. He predicted that the reign of the messiah would begin in 1667, but this did not include the ingathering of the exiles. The only miracle at that time would be the rulers' acknowledgment of Zvi as the messiah, which would allow the Jews to live in peace and honor in their societies. The period of messianic woes would begin in 1672, and the miraculous events of the apocalyptic legends would then follow.

The letters and rumors told of miracles and mythological and apocalyptic events occurring in the present, presaging an imminent return to the Holy Land and the Redemption. The earliest reports received in Italy told not of specific events in Palestine but of the ten lost tribes marching on Gaza. Letters from Egypt on the appearance of the lost tribes in Arabia and the conquest and destruction of Mecca were received in Amsterdam. At the end of 1665 the believers in Palestine also began to include legendary material in their letters. They told of a fiery cloud encompassing the prophet, of a voice of an angel emanating from a cloud, and of Christian churches sinking into the earth. The earliest reports received in Amsterdam stated that Zvi had confirmed his messiahship by miracles: he had predicted accurately the sudden death of certain people, a day of darkness, and a storm of great hailstones, fire, and brimstone, and he had entered a fire without harm. News of miraculous events continued after Zvi's imprisonment by the Turkish authorities. Letters told that Zvi had resurrected the dead and had passed through the locked and barred doors of his prison. Christian news reports in the form of small pamphlets were dependent on Jewish sources, but they added distortions, exaggerations, and embellishments of their own. Jews took note of the impression that the movement made on Christians, and they quoted from their reports.[4]

Reports of the appearance of a messiah and signs of an imminent redemption spread throughout a large part of the diaspora. However, Jewish communities differed in the proportion of believers in Zvi, the strength of the community's commitment, and the forms of messianic activity. In some, the great majority were believers, commitment was high, and individuals participated in mass ecstatic behavior, a common feature of millenarian movements. In a second group, a majority or a substantial minority were believers, commitment varied, and repentance was the main expression of the beliefs. In a third category, only a small minority were believers, and, as in the second type, repentance was the main activity. For a number of communities sufficient evidence to place them firmly in one category or another is lacking.

The first category takes in a number of communities in the cities and towns of the Ottoman Empire: Aleppo, Smyrna, and Constantinople are clear cases. In two of these, Aleppo and Smyrna, mass enthusiasm was stimulated in part by Zvi's presence. Zvi's arrival in Aleppo caused a wave of penitence and prayer: many ceased business to devote themselves to prayer, and some went into trance and prophesied. From Aleppo, Zvi went to Smyrna where, at first, he kept to himself. During a period of illumination he revealed himself as the messiah, and this, together with the arrival of a delegation from Aleppo to pay him homage, led to even greater enthusiasm than that which he had encountered in Aleppo: business life stopped; feasts, dancing, and processions alternated with penitential exercises; reports of miracles and visions were common; many went into trance; and incidents of mass prophecy occurred, mainly consisting of ecstatic outbursts of biblical phrases and references to Zvi. A significant proportion of the wealthier stratum in Smyrna, rabbis and important laymen, opposed the movement or kept aloof, but after one of the two major rabbis became a supporter, the other rabbi was dismissed and Zvi's authority was unchallenged. The messianic fervor in Smyrna lasted for about three weeks.

Without Zvi's presence the response in Constantinople to the messianic reports was instantaneous, and the excitement lasted longer than it had in Smyrna. There were many prophets, some acting as if they were possessed, and visions and reports of miracles added to the feeling that the end of time was near. A minority opposed the movement, and clashes occurred between believers and nonbelievers. Other communities in the Ottoman Empire, especially those in Palestine, such as Gaza, Hebron, and Safed, might be included in this first category, since they demonstrated such features as majority support, the combination of severe penitence and exuberant rejoicing, and the appearance of prophets. They did not, however, reach the level of the frenzied enthusiasm in Aleppo, Smyrna, and Constantinople.[5]

The evidence on Salonika and other Balkan communities is sparse. One report refers to an economic crisis and the impoverishment of the wealthier classes in Salonika as a consequence of the movement, but overall the evidence suggests that Salonika and some other Balkan communities belong to the second category: the available evidence indicates widespread belief and penitential activity, but no outbreaks of mass ecstatic behavior, and the movement appears to have passed without serious economic dislocation. The same may be said for other Jewish communities under Islam, although often the evidence is not sufficient to make a clear judgment on the effects of the movement. There appears to have been widespread belief and penitential activity in the Yemen, certain Moroccan towns, and possibly also parts of Persia and Kurdistan. Cairo was a center for the distribution of messianic reports, but most of the rabbis in Cairo were opposed, and daily life continued without disruption.[6]

The picture is clearer for Christian Europe. No community there demonstrated the mass ecstatic behavior that occurred in some cities and towns of the Ottoman Empire. The European communities that clearly fall into the second category are Amsterdam, Hamburg, and a number of Italian communities, especially Leghorn, Ancona, and Venice. With somewhat less certainty, one might include Frankfurt, Vienna, and Prague. The opposition was significant in these communities, but at least a significant minority, if not a majority, were believers.[7] The believers engaged in demonstrations of rejoicing, but they focused their religious activities on acts of penance and mortification. The reported acts of repentance included fasting for a whole week or number of days, regular immersion in ritual baths, lying naked in the snow and rolling in it for a quarter or half hour, self-inflicted scourging with thorns and nettles until the body was covered with blisters, and dripping boiling liquid down naked bodies. Some of the more painful acts of penance were reported in travelers' tales, which were prone to exaggeration, and they were probably not common. Moreover, acts of repentance did not always indicate belief in Zvi as the messiah: many traditionalists supported penitential demonstrations whatever the motivation and believed that the cleansing of sins would hasten the coming of the true messiah.[8]

The believers made little preparation for a return to the Holy Land. The Amsterdam community made some preparation for the removal of the dead from their graves in order to transport them to the Holy Land, and in Hamburg the liquidation of community property was at least contemplated. Some neglected their businesses, as they spent more time on prayer, meditation, and repentance, and some sold or contemplated the sale of goods and belongings. But the evidence does not indicate that sale of property went on on a significant scale or that economic dislocation was widespread. Moreover, the minute books of Hamburg, an important center of the movement, cast some doubt on the strength of commitment of many believers. At the height of the movement in Hamburg, the community still demonstrated a concern with everyday mundane matters, such as business between members and medical services, and with long-range plans, such as the enlargement of the synagogue and cemetery.[9]

The third category includes the communities in Poland, Bohemia-Moravia, Hungary, France, and most of the Germanies. For these communities, the evidence that Scholem presents does not support his general statements of majority support.[10] Certainly, some in these areas were fervent believers, but for the great majority the happenings in the Middle

East were simply a matter of news, and many were concerned that the news of a Jewish messiah might encourage attacks on Jews.[11]

Scholem writes that in Poland little was known about Zvi or the events connected with him. "Legend reigned supreme and nourished the messianic hunger of the masses."[12] Leaflets appeared with new directions and prayers for repentance, the people talked of miracles, and Jewish communities sent a few messengers to see Zvi, but the case for widespread belief and enthusiasm in Poland is not supported by the evidence that Scholem presents, which is thin and sometimes in contradiction with his argument.[13] Bernard Weinryb, a historian of Polish Jewry, writes that the records of the Polish communities in 1666 reflect a concern with their long-term interests in Poland and do not give the impression that anything out of the ordinary was occurring. He concludes that out of 100,000 or more Jews in Poland, only one or two dozen were highly committed Sabbatians in 1666.[14] Although Weinryb certainly overstates his case here, the thinness of the evidence in relation to the size of the population suggests that only a small minority in Poland were committed Sabbatians.

The Messiah and the Prophet

The spread of the belief in Zvi as the messiah had little to do with Zvi's personal qualities. Scholem notes that Zvi had received a fairly good traditional religious education, but that he was by no means an outstanding scholar and he had no literary talent. He had some personal charm, and he attracted a number of friends and disciples even before he claimed to be the messiah, but his charisma as messiah was in no way dependent on his personality characteristics or talents.

Zvi was a manic-depressive: his moods alternated between joy and dejection, enthusiasm and melancholy. Yet his mental sickness did not destroy his personality or affect his intelligence, and it is not uncommon for such psychological types to take on religious roles. During his states of exaltation, Zvi had strong suggestive powers over others, but this power did not continue after the condition had ended. In the Jewish tradition such psychological characteristics would be likely to cause doubts concerning the suitability of the person for an important religious role, but the majority of believers in 1666 were ignorant about Zvi's personality, and those close to Zvi were able to interpret his sickness in a way that reinforced his fitness for the messianic role. They interpreted the manic phases, when Zvi appeared in a state of ecstasy, as communion or union with God, while they saw the depressive phases as part of his fight with evil. They defined Zvi's transgressions of the religious law during his manic phases as "strange or paradoxical actions" which were important to his messianic role and whose meaning would be understood at a future date. During the height of the movement, Zvi's "strange actions" were not widely known, and they became an important element in the movement only after his conversion to Islam.[15]

Scholem argues that the major cause of the outburst in 1666 was the diffusion of the cabbalah of Isaac Luria and his followers. Zvi studied the cabbalah, but he was not influenced by the Lurianic cabbalah, and he remained non-Lurianic in his mentality. Scholem writes that this shows that "the course of the movement was determined by the public climate more than by the personality or the inner life of the young kabbalist."[16] However, as a secondary cause, Scholem emphasizes the role of the prophet Nathan of Gaza (1644–80) in the success of the movement. The division of roles between a messiah and a prophet is a common one in messianic movements, and in the Sabbatian movement it was the prophet who gave the initial spark to the movement.

One thing is clear: the acceptance of Zvi, rather than some other individual, as the messiah by the first group of believers in Gaza was largely Nathan's doing. Zvi had previously proclaimed himself messiah in 1648, although he had probably only made the claim to a few friends and then only intermittently. The year 1648 was mentioned as a possible date for redemption in the Zohar, and this, together with the massacres in Poland in that year, accounts for the timing of Zvi's announcement. At that time he was not taken seriously and was considered ill or possessed by an evil spirit. Zvi moved a lot between the cities of the Balkans, Egypt, and the Middle East; as a consequence of his transgressions of the religious law, he was forced to leave Smyrna, Salonika, and Constantinople, where in 1658 he was flogged. He first approached Nathan in Gaza to seek help to overcome his transgressions, and Nathan had to convince Zvi that he was the messiah and that he should proclaim himself. Even Zvi's friends and disciples were only persuaded that he was the messiah by Nathan's prophecies. Some rabbis who came to see him accepted the validity of Nathan as a prophet, and their letters made a great impression on other rabbis elsewhere. There was a greater willingness to accept a prophecy that came from the Holy Land. The Jewish community in Palestine was small, with a large proportion of rabbis and poor people: it consisted of only a few thousand, of which the majority were supported by donations from the diaspora. Scholem argues that the spiritual prestige of the Holy Land was enhanced by the new Lurianic cabbalah, which originated in Safed in the sixteenth century.[17]

Explanations Rejected

Before examining Scholem's argument that the diffusion of the Lurianic cabbalah was the major cause of the movement, it is necessary to look at two explanations that Scholem rejects. The first views the movement as a response to a specific incident of persecution: the 1648 massacres in Poland. The second views the movement as a response by the lower stratum in the Jewish communities to its economic oppression.

In the past, many historians emphasized the importance of the 1648 massacres as an important cause of the messianic outburst in 1666. Ukrainian peasants and Cossacks led by Bogdan Chmielnicki swept through large areas of Poland, killing Polish nobles, Catholic clergymen, and Jews. The uprising was an expression of religious, ethnic, and economic class divisions and conflicts: the Orthodox Ukrainian peasants were rebelling against the Polish Catholic landowners and their Jewish administrators and middlemen. The wealthier members of the Polish nobility were absent from their huge estates, living in grand style in cities such as Warsaw and Paris, and although most Poles in the regions overrun by the Cossacks were killed, the Jews often bore the major brunt of the attacks. It is probably impossible to obtain an accurate estimate of the loss of Jewish life and wealth in 1648. Some estimates put the number of victims in the hundreds of thousands, but the contemporary sources exaggerated, and Weinryb believes that a reasonable estimate is forty to fifty thousand, or 20 to 25 percent of the total Polish Jewish population. A further five to ten thousand fled Poland. In some regions, such as Podolia, the proportion killed was much higher. The invaders rarely gave the Jews any alternative to death, and the killings often took horrible forms, such as skinning the victim alive. The troubles of Poland continued with the Swedish invasion of 1655–60, the Russian invasion of 1654–67, and outbreaks of pestilence and famine in the 1650s and 1660s. The Polish economy, and the position of the Jews within it, deteriorated sharply in this period.[18]

It is grimly ironic that some cabbalists had calculated from a passage in the Zohar that the messiah would come in 1648. Some Jews viewed the massacres as part of the birth pangs of the messiah, but as Scholem notes, the widespread nature of messianism in 1666 cannot be explained by local factors. The movement was successful among communities, such as the Moroccan, that were far from the area of the massacres and had heard very little of the events.

Scholem states that local conditions shaped and colored the movement in many places and maintains that one should not underestimate the effects of the massacres on the state of mind of Polish Jews.[19] As noted above, the evidence does not support Scholem's claim that the majority of Polish Jews accepted Zvi as the messiah. The Polish Jews demonstrated the traditional nonmessianic responses of the Ashkenazim to persecution: they condemned the perpetrators of the killings and identified the victims as martyrs, but they also stated that the moral and religious deficiencies of the Jewish people had unleashed the wrath of heaven. There were strong warnings concerning the observance of the mitsvot, further restrictions were placed on dress, penitential prayers were composed, and additional fasts were instituted. Not all the gentiles were condemned: the Ukrainians and Cossacks were blamed and despised, but there was little or no criticism of the Polish state and nobility who were depicted as being concerned with the well-being of the Jews.[20]

Scholem also rejects a Marxist interpretation which views the movement as a religious expression by the lower economic stratum to their oppression. Many scholars and wealthy Jews were prominent and active in the movement, and their participation was a consequence not of pressure from the poorer Jews but of a genuine enthusiasm. The conflict between believers and unbelievers did not follow clear-cut class lines, but Scholem acknowledges that in some communities a greater proportion of the upper stratum was opposed. Some wealthy Jews were satisfied with their comforts and positions and viewed the messianic outburst with distrust, or they were caught in a dilemma between their economic self-interest and their religious inclinations. For example, in Smyrna, the birthplace of Zvi and an early center of the movement, the majority of the poorer Jews joined, and those that accompanied Zvi were from the lowest class. Many of the rabbis and more prominent laymen in Smyrna kept aloof, but from the beginning, his supporters included wealthy merchants, elders, brokers, and rabbinic scholars.[21]

A booklet published in Amsterdam in July 1666 included a Yiddish poem by a poor school teacher who recorded the feelings of the "common people" among the Ashkenazim. The poet wrote that the Jews had suffered in exile for more than fifteen hundred years and that they would soon return to Israel where they would study the Law and serve the land. The poem also included an element of social protest: those rich people who took the poor with them to the Holy Land would be honored, but the rich who did not heed the poor and thought nothing of redemption would "perish here on a dung heap."[22] Social protest against the upper Jewish stratum was not a prominent feature of the movement, and while in some communities the opposition came from a section of the upper stratum, in others scholars and lay leaders took a leading part. In Leghorn, an important commercial town where the poor were probably a minority in the Jewish community, the majority, including most rabbis, accepted Zvi as the messiah. Among the most prosperous Jewish communities, Amsterdam was particularly responsive to the messianic message.[23]

If the movement was not an expression of an oppressed class within the Jewish community, it might still be interpreted as a response to the political oppression of the entire Jewish community or as a prepolitical protest of a politically powerless people. Scholem seems to suggest something of this when he writes of the insecurity experienced by Jewish communities: "In the peculiar conditions of Jewish existence, messianism was the expression not so much of internal Jewish struggles—class or otherwise—as of the abnormal situation of a pariah nation. The sense of insecurity and permanent danger to life and property, affected the upper classes no less than the lower; in fact, the former often had more to fear."[24] The movement certainly included elements of a political character, especially among the poor, who emphasized the imminent catastrophic period in which the gentile persecutors of the Jews would be suitably punished; however, this does not account for the timing and distribution of the movement. The communities that enjoyed most freedom, such as Salonika, Leghorn, and Amsterdam, included high proportions of very enthusiastic adherents. Jews did not have their own autonomous nation, but some Jews did have political power and influence: the lay leaders exercised political power over their communities, and some, such as the court Jews, used their wealth and connections to influence the decision making of the gentile rulers.

The Religious Factor

Scholem's major argument is that the ready acceptance of Sabbatai Zvi as the messiah was the consequence of the diffusion of the Lurianic cabbalah throughout the diaspora. In the early stages of the development of the cabbalah, there was little interest in messianism; the cabbalists were less concerned with redemption than with creation, on finding their way back to the original unity of the cosmos, prior to Satan's first deception. The path back to the primordial beginnings involved a contemplative life in communion with the divine, and redemption was a concern of the individual, who would remain aloof in his private meditations.

A change in the cabbalah occurred after the expulsion from Spain. Isaac Luria Ashkenazi (1534–72) and his disciples formulated a new messianic cabbalah in the town of Safed in Palestine. Luria and his original disciples did comparatively little to spread their ideas, but other disciples and followers broke away from the elitist and esoteric traditions of the cabbalists and sought to influence the masses. Cabbalism as a whole became increasingly popular in the second half of the sixteenth century; before 1550 popular works showed little or no trace of the influence of cabbalistic beliefs, but after that date many writers propagated cabbalistic doctrines. The propagation of the Lurianic cabbalah began in the last decade of the sixteenth century, and Scholem claims that by the middle of the seventeenth century it had become the dominant school in Jewish thought.

The decisive innovation that gave the Lurianic cabbalah its great appeal was the transposition of the central concepts of exile and redemption from the historical to the cosmic and divine plane. The historical exile and coming redemption of the Jewish people were concrete expressions of a spiritual reality: an inner, mystical process within the Godhead ultimately produced the outer material creation and terrestrial events. Everything on the terrestrial plane was a symbol of a reality within the divine: the exile of the people of Israel was a reflection of the exile of God's sparks of holiness.

The Lurianic system began with the assumption that God is everywhere. God did not make the world out of nothing, because nothing, a place without God, did not exist. God made room for the world by abandoning a region within himself. The existence of the universe was made possible by the shrinkage, contraction, or withdrawal of the divine into himself. This provided the first symbol of Jewish exile: God had banished himself from his totality.

This contraction was followed by the emanation of the divine lights, by which God projected his creative powers outside himself. The first and highest being which emanated from the divine was Adam Kadmon, primordial man, and from him the lights of the Sephirot, the spheres of divine emanation, burst forth. Emitted in an "atomized" or isolated form, certain of the lights had to be caught and preserved in special "vessels" or "bowls," which were created for that purpose. The light of the lower six Sephirot broke forth all at once, and the impact was too great for the vessels, which broke and shattered. Some of God's lights remained stuck to the fragments of the shattered vessels. They were in exile. The powers of evil developed out of the shattered fragments of the vessels, which sank into the lower depths of primordial space.

The process of *tikkun* (cosmic mending) that then began was completed with the creation of the earthly Adam, the Adam of the Bible. But Adam sinned and destroyed the restored harmony, and the Shechinah (divine presence) was again in exile. The Adam of the Bible corresponded on the anthropological plane to the cosmic being Adam Kadmon, and his original sin repeated on the lower, earthly level the cosmic event of the breaking of the vessels. When Adam sinned, the world fell from its spiritual state and the divine lights became mixed with the realm of evil, the kelippot, or "shells." The material world came into being, and man became part material, part spiritual.

Since the breaking of the vessels, exile had been a fundamental aspect of all existence; it had taken place within the Deity. The all-important goal was to purge the divine light of its impurities and to restore the ideal, spiritual order. The lights of the divine emanation could not bring about the process of tikkun by themselves. Man had a major part in this process; by performing the mitsvot of the Torah, men could contribute to the progressive separation of good and evil. Prayer was a vehicle of the soul's mystical ascent to the divine and a part of the process of tikkun. The true worshiper could exercise tremendous power over the divine worlds. In Scholem's words, "Luria's doctrine of mystical prayer stands directly on the borderline between mysticism and magic, where the one only too easily passes into the other." By their prayer and observance of the mitsvot, Jews had an important role in the enthronement of God, in the perfection of their maker.

As popular preachers mediated the Lurianic ideas to the masses in the seventeenth century, they emphasized and elaborated the more dramatic and spectacular aspects of the belief system. Symbols that Luria and his disciples had regarded as metaphors were given literal interpretations by the popular preachers, who especially emphasized tikkun and its messianic implications. The preachers proclaimed that the whole process of restoration or cosmic repair was almost complete and that adherence to the Lurianic teaching was a means of bringing the messiah. Once they had successfully implanted the doctrine of tikkun into the popular consciousness, "the eschatological mood was bound to grow."

The Lurianic ideas provided an answer to the fundamental question of the exile of the Jewish people: exile was rooted in the process of creation, and the struggle to become free from exile involved purging the cosmos of evil. Exile was a mission: the Jews had to raise the scattered, holy sparks and liberate the divine light from the realm of evil, which was represented at the material level by the oppression of the Jewish people. Thus, the cosmic redemption of raising the sparks merged with the national redemption of Israel; both were encompassed by the phrase "the ingathering of the exiles."

The advent of the messiah was the sign that the Jewish people had fulfilled their sacred mission of tikkun. Luria and his disciples believed that the final stages of tikkun had been reached, and both Luria and his leading disciple, Hayyim Vital, claimed messianic status. Salvation was at hand, and men were now faced with the difficult task of extracting the last sparks from the realm of evil. In its descriptions of the period before the Redemption, the Lurianic school preserved many of the catastrophic traits of the apocalyptic writings. These aspects were important among the masses, and they were also emphasized within the movement in 1666.[25]

The message of Nathan the prophet appealed both to the masses and to the small elite groups of scholars and cabbalists, for he combined the traditional, popular, and apocalyptic with his interpretations of Lurianic cabbalism. In September 1665, Nathan proclaimed that the kingdom of the messiah would become manifest in a year and some months. As a result of the people's religious acts and the struggle of the messiah against the demonic powers, the cosmic tikkun had been achieved. No sparks of the Shechinah were left in the shells, and the forces of evil could not subsist for long after the light of holiness had been withdrawn.

Nathan also gave a cabbalistic interpretation to Zvi's illness. He wrote that following the breaking of the vessels the soul of the messiah had also fallen into the abyss, where he was tormented by the "serpents." The messiah struggled with the serpents, but on those occasions when illumination departed from him, the serpents took possession and he fell into depression. Zvi's manic phases occurred when his illumination had overcome the serpents or "dragons." For Nathan, Zvi's psychological state was the proof of his messiahship, but these interpretations were not widely known in 1666. In that year, Nathan's speculations appeared as legitimate elaborations of the Lurianic teachings, and Scholem argues that the appeal of the message to the cabbalists was of decisive importance, since they were the most active religious group. Nathan and his friends spoke the language of the cabbalists, who were satisfied by the similarity between the terminology and symbols of Lurianism and Sabbatianism.[26]

Scholem's argument, then, is that where the Lurianic cabbalah was accepted, messianic expectations rose, accompanied by a readiness to accept a messianic claimant. A question remains: Was the influence of the Lurianic cabbalah as widespread as Scholem claims? Scholem writes that for a whole generation after Luria's death in 1572 his disciples remained in esoteric groups and did little to spread their beliefs. The propagandizing of the Lurianic cabbalah began only at the end of the sixteenth century with the journey of Israel Sarug, who had not been one of Luria's pupils, to Italy and Poland. Up to about 1620 the European cabbalists were largely under the influence of other cabbalistic schools from Safed, especially that of Cordovero. The Lurianic works began to appear in print from 1630; by the middle of the seventeenth century, they "had spread to all parts of the Diaspora."[27]

If we accept, for the moment, the claim that the Lurianic cabbalah became widely diffused and popular, the question remains why this occurred. What were the circumstances that made Jews ready to substitute the Lurianic beliefs for other cabbalistic and noncabbalistic religious beliefs? Scholem does not address this question adequately, but he does note the relationship between the expulsion from Spain and developments within the cabbalah. He emphasizes that the consequences of the catastrophe of 1492 were not confined to the Jews then living; in fact, the expulsion initiated a historical process that took almost an entire century to work itself out. This event did not give rise immediately to a mass messianic movement, but it did encourage the belief among many that the Redemption was near. These viewed the expulsion as the beginning of the birth pangs of the messiah, and cabbalistic works written around 1500 found many apocalyptic meanings in important religious texts. With the passing of time the expulsion ceased to be regarded in a redemptive light, but the event and its consequences were recast in cabbalistic thought. The messiah had not come, and the expulsion had not been the immediate prelude to redemption, but in the Lurianic cabbalah the event was assimilated into the notion of exile, which was now seen as a cosmic as well as human event. The traditional explanation of persecution as the consequence of the sins of the Jewish people held little appeal among the Sephardim, and the implication of the Lurianic cabbalah was that men should not feel guilty concerning the exile in general or the expulsion in particular. Man's predicament was a reflection of a cosmic process: God's sparks were themselves in exile.[28]

The expulsion from Spain goes some way toward explaining the development of the Lurianic cabbalah and its diffusion, at least among the Sephardim. Luria was from a German family, but the majority of the population in Safed were exiles from Spain and Portugal. Their influence was such that Spanish became the language of the town's schools, and even the native Jews began to call themselves Sephardim.[29] The influence of the Safed cabbalists was marked in Aleppo and Hebron, which were to become centers of Sabbatianism. Exiles from Spain started to arrive in Aleppo at the beginning of the sixteenth century, and the leadership of the community gradually passed to the Sephardim.[30] Hebron was also a center of Spanish exiles, and toward the end of the sixteenth century and the beginning of the seventeenth some of the most important cabbalists of Safed moved to Hebron.[31] In Salonika, a center of Sephardim from the early sixteenth century, the cabbalah was studied avidly, and even before the influence of Luria, it was often associated with messianism. There, many regarded the Zohar as being as sacred as the Bible, and some believed that it was superior to the Talmud. It was common for families to read a passage from it each evening. According to common belief, knowledge gained from the Zohar could be used to cure diseases, manipulate the occult forces, exorcize demons, and provide protective formulas for amulets. On the basis of certain passages, some Jews in Salonika expected the messiah in 1540 and 1568. They used the Lurianic cabbalah for both thaumaturgical purposes and messianic speculations and attributed great supernatural powers to Luria and his disciple Vital. It was believed that they were able to make gold, that they talked with animals and flowers, that they had battled successfully against legions of demons, that they could fly, and that they had visited Paradise.[32] In a number of other communities, including many in North Africa, the Sephardim assimilated with the indigenous populations, and this may have been a factor in the spread of the Lurianic cabbalah.

Scholem also claims that the Ashkenazim adopted the Lurianic cabbalah, but apart from noting that many Ashkenazim also had memories of expulsion, he gives little indication of anything in their recent historical experience that would have made Lurianism attractive to them. The impression he gives is that the power of the Lurianic ideas, their dramatic expression of the fundamental Jewish experience of exile, was sufficient to gain them support.

Weinryb has questioned Scholem's claim that the Lurianic cabbalah was influential in Poland, the major center of the Ashkenazim in the seventeenth century. Scholem writes that a genuine demand for cabbalistic literature in Poland is demonstrated by the number of cabbalistic works printed on the presses of Cracow and Lublin from the end of the sixteenth century.[33] Weinryb finds, however, that no more than 10 percent of the nearly three hundred titles published in the two towns from 1547 to 1660 belongs to the category of cabbalistic or mystical literature. Scholem's quotations from writers of the period who emphasized the importance of the cabbalah in Poland are countered by quotations collected by Weinryb which present the cabbalah as having minimal importance.[34]

More damaging to Scholem's argument is a point that he himself emphasizes concerning the special character of the cabbalah in Poland. The Polish cabbalists were highly syncretistic, combining different cabbalistic systems, gematria, and a preoccupation with the demonic. They used Luria's name as a source of legitimation, but their own writings had little to do with the Lurianic ideas, and they displayed a lack of interest in the theoretical aspects of Lurianism, such as the notion of tikkun. The emphasis in Poland was on each person's personal struggle with individual demons and evil spirits. Pious behavior and magical safeguards were the weapons used against evil beings. Scholem admits that it was only within the Sabbatian movement that the first attempts were made in Poland to deal with Lurianic ideas in a systematic way.[35]

Thus, if the Sabbatian movement was important in Poland, as Scholem claims it was, it cannot be explained by the influence of certain Lurianic ideas. If neither the relevant Lurianic ideas nor the Sabbatian movement was important in Poland in 1666, it is still possible to reject Scholem's claim that Sabbatianism was a mass movement in all major Jewish concentrations in Europe but retain his argument that Lurianism was the major cause of the movement. To confront this possibility, we need to examine the influence of the Lurianic cabbalah in the communities in our first two categories, where the majority or a substantial minority were enthusiastic supporters of Zvi.

The influence of the Lurianic cabbalah does correspond somewhat to the response to the messianic call in 1666. The Lurianic cabbalah was more important in the Sabbatian centers of Palestine, other parts of the Ottoman Empire, and Italy than it was in Poland and most of Germany, where only a minority were caught up in the excitement in 1666. Scholem's evidence does not, however, support his contention that "the growing dominance of the kabbalah on the popular consciousness of the time, and particularly among the fervently religious, must be seen as the general background which made the movement possible."[36] Only some of the Lurianic books published in Europe stressed the messianic implications of the doctrine, and no evidence indicates that the notion of tikkun spread beyond small groups of Jewish mystics. When Scholem discusses the support for Zvi among unscholarly Jews, such as the wealthy merchants in Hamburg or a poor teacher in Amsterdam, he admits that they were far removed from cabbalistic speculations.[37] To explain the movement as a result of contact with the Lurianic cabbalah, one must show that the small cabbalistic circles had a considerable influence on the Jewish masses in 1666. But the evidence shows no such decisive influence, and as Scholem shows, the cabbalists were themselves divided over Zvi's claim.[38]

The Former Marranos

The influence of the Lurianic cabbalah was a contributing factor to the messianic outburst, but it cannot be regarded as a sufficient or even major cause. The centers of Sabbatian enthusiasm in 1666 show a closer correspondence with another factor: the geographical distribution of the Iberian exiles and, in particular, the distribution of the former marranos. As already discussed, millenarianism was more important among the Sephardim and the marranos than it was among the Ashkenazim, and the Sabbatian movement was not an exception to this comparison. The argument here is that the former marranos, in particular, provided an important nucleus for the success of Sabbatianism.

Scholem does not ignore the former marranos. He notes that they and their descendants were concentrated in such towns as Salonika, Leghorn, Venice, Hamburg, and Amsterdam, that they "everywhere appear among the leading supporters of the movement," and that many desired to atone for their marrano past in the messianic enthusiasm.[39] Since Scholem argues that the movement was widespread throughout almost the whole diaspora, he does not discuss the former marranos as a major factor in the support of the movement. The argument here is that Scholem's own evidence demonstrates that communities may be distinguished by their levels of support; the classification below of the communities in categories one and two, in which the majority or a substantial minority were believers, shows a strong correspondence with communities that had concentrations of former marranos.

> *Category one.* Firm placing: Constantinople, Aleppo, Smyrna. Less firm placing (possibly closer to category two): Gaza, Hebron, Safed, Damascus.
> *Category two.* Firm placing: Salonika, Leghorn, Ancona, Venice, Amsterdam, Hamburg, Tripoli, Alexandria. Less firm placing: Frankfurt, Vienna, Prague, Yemen, Cairo, and some parts of Morocco, Persia, and Kurdistan.

The emigration of marranos from Spain began after the forced conversions of 1391, but that was a short-lived movement. The emigration increased in the second half of the fifteenth century, especially after the establishment of the Inquisition in 1481. From Portugal there was a larger emigration of marranos; it began after the forced conversions of 1497, increased after the introduction of the Inquisition in 1536, and accelerated with the intensification of persecution after 1630.[40]

A large proportion of the marranos settled in Muslim countries. Morocco was a refuge from the end of the fourteenth century, but from the end of the fifteenth century, the majority settled in the Ottoman Empire. The victories of the Turks during the reigns of Selim I (1512–20) and Suleiman the Magnificent (1520–66) resulted in a vast empire, rich in resources, with a large population and many urban centers, but the empire lacked an innovative entrepreneurial class. The Sephardim who migrated to the Ottoman Empire after the expulsion from Spain were involved in the traditional forms of trade and commerce that they had known in Spain. The marranos had become in Spain, and especially, Portugal an innovative entrepreneurial class, skilled in industry, distribution, marketing, and finance. The Ottoman rulers welcomed the marranos and had no objection to their returning to Judaism. In fact, in some cases they demanded that the marranos publicly renounce Christianity and return to Judaism. This made the former marranos heretics in Europe and guaranteed their loyalty to the Turks. For some marranos the return to Judaism was an entrepreneurial decision.[41]

The important settlements of the marranos in the Muslim world were Salonika, Constantinople, Smyrna, Safed, Tripoli, Aleppo, Ankara, Alexandria, and Cairo. In many of these communities, particularly in Constantinople and Salonika, the Sephardim had already settled in large numbers, and many were employed by the marranos as merchants and artisans. Salonika, a predominantly Jewish city in which almost all the important commerce and industry was in Jewish hands, had the largest marrano community: the number of former marranos eventually exceeded the population both of other Jews and of non-Jews.[42]

The correlation between the centers of Sabbatianism and concentrations of former marranos is particularly evident in Christian Europe. Among the Christian European countries, the marranos first migrated to Italy. After antimarrano campaigns broke up two early marrano centers, Ancona and Ferrara, the former in 1559, the latter in 1581, Venice became the major center of the marranos. The Venetian government passed decrees of expulsion against the marranos in 1497 and 1550, but in 1589 it permitted the marranos to live in Venice provided they openly declared their Judaism, lived in ghettos, and devoted their energies to international trade. The stream of marranos into Venice increased, and the Jewish population of the city rose from about 1,000 in 1600 to 4,870 in 1655, after which it began to fall. The former marranos maintained their Iberian culture; the bankers and international merchants among them were the wealthiest and dominant section of the community.

Leghorn also gained a large marrano community, second only to Amsterdam in Christian Europe. The city became a free port in 1593, and the city authorities invited the marranos. They established a synagogue in 1602, and the number of Jews in the city rose from 114 in 1601, to 1,175 in 1642, and to 3,000 in 1689. The former marranos absorbed other Jewish migrants in the city, including Jews from other parts of Italy.

Marranos settled in southern France, especially Bordeaux, but in France they were not able openly to return to Judaism. The two other important centers of marranos in Christian Europe were Hamburg and Amsterdam. The marranos began settling in Hamburg at the end of the sixteenth century; the community was officially recognized in 1612, when there were 125 adults, on the condition that it did not congregate for public worship. A synagogue was established in a private house in 1627, but it was not until 1650 that Jewish public worship was officially permitted in Hamburg.

The first marranos arrived in Amsterdam about 1590, but they did not openly reveal themselves as Jews. Jews had been forced to leave the

Netherlands in the second half of the fourteenth century and again in the fifteenth, and the marranos had first migrated to Belgium. Some wealthy marrano families had settled in Antwerp, but they had been expelled in 1550. In 1598 the first synagogue was built in Amsterdam, and a second synagogue was opened in 1608; after some vacillation the Dutch government officially recognized the Jewish community in 1615. The settlement of former marranos increased after the end of the war between the Netherlands and Spain in 1648, and by the middle of the seventeenth century about four hundred Jewish families lived in the city.[43]

All the urban concentrations of the former marranos had familial and economic links with each other,[44] and the Sabbatian movement in 1666 was important in all of them. Even where the marranos were unable to return to Judaism, indications are that there was some response to Sabbatianism. In the Iberian peninsula a special watch was put on the ports to detain those marranos who intended to join Zvi.[45]

However, the movement was successful in some places where the marranos were not important or were entirely absent. In general, the correlation between concentrations of marranos and Sabbatian enthusiasm was closer for Christian Europe and the Ottoman Balkans than for other Muslim areas. Marranos and former marranos settled in Morocco and Palestine, but they counted for a smaller and less important segment of the Jewish population than they did in the Christian European and Balkan centers of the movement. Neither the marranos nor other Sephardim were present in the Yemen. Exactly how strong the movement was in these Muslim areas is difficult to calculate, a problem which also appears for the three possible exceptions in Europe: Frankfurt, Vienna, and Prague. Thus, there were exceptions, but the correlation requires explanation before the exceptions are discussed.

In the previous chapter, the messianism of the marranos in the Iberian peninsula was related, in part, to their persecution by the Inquisition. For many, only Jewish messianism was able to give meaning to their sufferings. In the countries of refuge some marrano communities lived in conditions of relative freedom and prosperity, but their past sufferings and the continuing sufferings of those marranos who remained in the Iberian peninsula still posed problems of religious meaning. In the 1640s and 1650s the Inquisition accused hundreds of conversos of being secret Jews and burned dozens at the stake. Their relatives in the marrano diaspora learned with great pain of the persecutions and killings.

The former marranos may be termed the first modern Jews: some were familiar with developments in philosophy, and they continued to mix in Christian circles even after their adoption of Judaism.[46] Familiarity with non-Jewish culture and social participation in the Christian world did not, in the seventeenth century, necessarily lead to deviance from Judaism. Nor was scientific knowledge seen to be in contradiction with messianic and millennial beliefs. Some of the most advanced scientists among the Christians believed that both science and religion converged to indicate an imminent end to the world.[47]

A prominent example in the Jewish community of a widely read man who was also a fervent messianist was Menasseh ben Israel (1604–57). Menasseh was baptized in Madeira, a Portugese territory, and his family moved to Holland, where they openly returned to Judaism. His father had lost everything as a result of the Inquisition, and the family lived close to poverty. Menasseh became a rabbi and the head of a yeshivah in Amsterdam; in addition to his knowledge of rabbinic and mystical literature, he was widely read in classical literature and Christian theology. His friends included not only the elite of the Jewish community, among whom were many physicians, but also Christian theologians and other scholars in Holland, Sweden, Germany, and France.

Menasseh became convinced that the Indians in the mountains of Ecuador were descendants of the ten lost tribes, and he corresponded on this with Christian scholars, many of whom were messianists. He perceived a connection between the discovery of the remnant of the ten tribes and messianic deliverance, and he expressed his views in *The Hope of God*, a book published in Amsterdam in 1650. He believed that redemption would take place only when the Jews were dispersed in all parts of the world. The formal admission of the Jews to England appeared to him as a vital prelude to the Redemption, and in 1655 he went to England, where he petitioned Cromwell to admit the Jews. The massacres in Poland and other events, such as the Thirty Years' War, the revolt in England, and the execution of the king, were interpreted by Menasseh as birth pangs of the messiah, a view shared by many of his Christian friends. But the tragedy that Menasseh felt most closely was that of the marranos. Not only his own family but also the majority of his Jewish friends in Amsterdam were former marranos and their descendants, and the reports of autos-da-fé in Spain, Portugal, and their dependencies made a deep impression on him.[48]

It is interesting that the first Jewish communities to become secularized in the eighteenth century, Hamburg and Amsterdam, were among the most messianic in the seventeenth. Secularization was largely the consequence of the movement out of the ghettos and greater social interaction with Christian circles. The former marranos were among the first Jews to have extensive contacts with Christians, and the question arises of the possible influence of the widespread Christian millenarianism in their environment.

Scholem completely rejects the possibility of Christian influence on the

Sabbatian movement, but his arguments are mainly directed against the view that Sabbatai's father, Mordecai, heard rumors from English merchants about the millennial date of 1666 and passed them on to his son. Scholem writes that propaganda for the date 1666 appeared in Dutch and English literature only in the 1650s.[49] In fact, as early as 1597 one English writer had fixed on 1666, calculated from the number of the Beast (666) in Revelations, as the date when the Antichristian Rome would fall; moreover, there was widespread discussion in England on the date both before the 1650s and continuing up until 1666, and elsewhere in Europe, hopes were focused on that year.[50] Sabbatai was a well-traveled man, and he might have heard about the Christian millenarian beliefs from a number of sources;[51] but speculation regarding Christian influence on Zvi is largely beside the point. More important is the possible influence of the widespread millenarianism among the Christian contacts of the former marranos and other Sephardim.

Scholem notes that while most Christian writers disparaged the movement, some Dutch Christian millenarians were enthusiastic and contrasted the penitential revival of the Jews of Amsterdam with the laxness of the Christians. Peter Serrarius, a leading Flemish millenarian who had contacts with Protestant millenarian circles all over Europe, expected the conversion of the Jews, but he also sympathized with the Sabbatians and had visions of Israel's glory in the new kingdom.[52] Serrarius had many Jewish friends in Amsterdam, but Scholem does not infer from such facts that Christian millenarians may at least have provided a stimulus to Jewish millenarianism. To recognize such a factor would be to go against his consistent emphasis on "the imminent development of eschatological traditions in rabbinic and kabbalistic Judaism."[53]

While they cannot be ruled out as a possible factor, Christian sources could have had at most only minor influence on the responses of some Jews in a few communities, particularly Amsterdam, to the messianic call. More important were the religious, social, and psychological problems of the former marranos. Scholars have noted the contradiction that many marranos encountered between their expectations of Judaism prior to their "return" to Judaism and the reality that they found after it. For the majority "return" was the espousal not of a religion in which they had previously been members but of the religion of their ancestors; they had been baptized, and most had had a Catholic upbringing. Many had been introduced to the marrano religion in their adolescence; others had turned to Judaism only when they were persecuted by the Inquisition or were discriminated against. Most knew little of Hebrew, the Talmud, or the rabbinic traditions, and the limited knowledge that they did have was often distorted.

Some historians have argued that the Jewish knowledge of the marranos was confined to the Bible and that they expected Jewish life to conform to the "Law of Moses" of the Old Testament. According to this argument, they were shocked to discover the sharp contrast between the religion of the Bible and Judaism as it was actually practiced. Many had risked their lives for something quite different from the religion to which they were now expected to conform.[54]

But, in fact, Jewish knowledge among many marranos was not confined to biblical Judaism. They had known in their native lands that the development of Judaism had not ended with the Bible, that the Talmud existed, and that Jewish communities respected a rabbinic tradition and lived according to that tradition.[55] But most marranos knew little of its content and particulars, and many found it difficult to accept and practice the complex and intricate ritual system.

It was not an easy or simple matter to step over the religious gulf between Catholicism or the marrano religion and rabbinic Judaism. Males had to undergo circumcision, and they had to acquire a considerable knowledge of ritual practice and religious law. Some accepted without question their new religion. Others resented the elaborate system of rituals, many of which appeared to be irrational and unjustified, as well as the authority of the rabbinate. The more educated marranos, many of whom had been students and teachers in Spanish universities, at that time among the most advanced scientific and philosophical centers of Christendom, particularly resented these strictures. They had rejected the authority of the church and the priesthood, and they were now expected to accept the discipline of the Jewish community and its rabbis, to whom many educated marranos felt intellectually superior.[56]

The historian Yosef Yerushalmi has stated that, given the earlier life of the former marranos in a Catholic environment, what is surprising is not that some failed to adapt to Judaism but that the majority succeeded.[57] It is true that the great majority remained in Judaism, but just as the first-generation marranos, whatever their commitment to Catholicism, were not able to be ordinary Catholics, so their descendants who adopted Judaism could not be ordinary Jews and take either their Judaism or their relationships with other Jews for granted. In a number of communities, such as Constantinople, where the Jewish community was substantial even before the marrano influx, Jews were suspicious and distrustful of the former marranos. They were offended by the ignorance of the former marranos regarding Jewish rites and customs, and they often treated them with sarcasm or pity. Some Jews accused the former marranos of secretly remaining Christians and hiding their crucifixes. Others defended them, arguing that the marranos had never been true Christians and that their faithfulness to Judaism should not be questioned.[58]

Even in the communities, such as Salonika and Amsterdam, where the former marranos formed the dominant section of the Jewish community and other Jews did not question their status, their experiences as former marranos gave rise to perplexity, self-questioning, and deep problems of identity. The former marranos had gone through the experience of what Peter Berger has termed *alternation*: they had passed between logically contradictory meaning systems. Alternation is a phenomenon of the modern world, when people are able to choose between varying and sometimes contradictory intellectual universes.[59] What was peculiar about the former marranos was that they experienced alternation in a largely traditional society, a society of closed and binding world views in which people were assigned definite and permanent identities. The Christian and Jewish worlds in the seventeenth century were separated by legal, cultural, and social barriers; Jews and Christians had little contact beyond formal economic and political relationships, and each group regarded the other as another species of being. In such a society alternation caused acute problems of identity and location in society. Many former marranos retained a nostalgia for the land of their births, and a few returned despite the dangers. Some retained a fondness for Catholicism, a few returning to the religion of their childhood. Others, identifying strongly with Judaism, felt an overwhelming sense of guilt and sought pardon for their Catholic past by such practices as wearing hair shirts.[60]

In the Christian European centers of the former marranos, Amsterdam, Hamburg, and Venice, one response to the marrano experience among the intellectuals was heresy. Among the most prominent heretics were Uriel da Costa and Baruch Spinoza. Uriel da Costa had rejected Christianity in Portugal and had concluded that the only true religion was that based on the Old Testament. Although he knew something of rabbinic Judaism, he was disillusioned in Hamburg when he found that Judaism differed radically from that of the Bible. He moved to Amsterdam, where he openly denied the oral law, doctrines such as the immortality of the soul, and many rituals. He was excommunicated twice, and twice recanted, but he committed suicide after many harassments and humiliations.[61]

Spinoza developed his critique of religion solely within the intellectual context of the Jewish community and prior to his reading of the new scientific and philosophical works in the Christian world. For some time, Spinoza continued to conform externally to normative Jewish practice, but in 1655 he began to make his opinions public, and in 1656 he was excommunicated from the Jewish community.

Excommunication was not an uncommon sanction in the Amsterdam Jewish community. It was used against a variety of deviant individuals and groups, and not only against such prominent cases of heresy as those of da Costa and Spinoza. Its use reflected the tensions and conflicts in the Amsterdam community. Excommunication was the ultimate sanction in most traditional Jewish communities, but it was rarely used, since persons there acted with a high degree of conformity to Jewish religious norms. In Amsterdam, a greater number were unwilling to accept certain religious laws, such as those of *shechitah* (ritual slaughter of animals), and disputed the authority of the rabbinic authorities. Faced with the task of incorporating the refugees from the Inquisition, the community leaders could not afford to tolerate acts that challenged the tradition. The excommunication of Spinoza and other heretics and deviants was part of the continuing struggle to integrate the former marranos into Judaism and unify the community.[62]

The society of the former marranos, with its conflicts, tensions, and problems of identity, produced both heretics and a high level of messianism. Having rejected one religious system, a few former marranos rejected another and chose to remain outside or on the margins of both the Christian and Jewish societies. This could involve social isolation and great strain, and a heretical thinker like Jean de Prado preferred to outwardly accept the norms and remain within the Jewish community. However, the majority committed themselves to Judaism, and in 1666 many found an immediate cure for their problems of doubt, the conflicts they felt between their childhood socialization and their adult resocialization, their feelings of guilt over their Christian past, and the tensions involved in adopting a new religion and a new identity. By their belief in Zvi the former marranos declared their full commitment to Judaism and immediately put behind them the problems of adopting a complex system of religious rituals. The commitment to the Jewish messiah was the decisive test; their past was to be forgiven and forgotten, and they were now assured of redemption.

In the Ottoman Empire and in some Italian communities the major support for Zvi came from native Jews and Sephardim who had not been marranos. In some cases these may have been influenced by the enthusiasm of the former marranos, but the latter were not always present in numbers that could achieve such an impact. The contention here is that the movement would not have been so widespread and important without the former marranos, but at the same time other economic and social factors, entirely ignored by Scholem, help to account for the support in certain areas of all Jews. These factors are discussed below.

The Crisis of the Seventeenth Century

Both Jewish and Christian millenarianism in the seventeenth century must be set against the background of what many historians have termed the "crisis of the seventeenth century."[63] The crisis included economic decline, especially in the Mediterranean area, a fall in banking profits and prices, political instability, and social revolts. E. J. Hobsbawm wrote that the "general crisis" began about 1620 and reached its most acute phase between 1640 and the 1670s. As an aside, Hobsbawm wrote: "It may not be wholly accidental that the greatest messianic movement of Jewish history occurred at that moment, sweeping the communities of the great trading centers—Smyrna, Leghorn, Venice, Amsterdam, Hamburg—off their feet with special success in the middle 1660s as prices reached almost their lowest point."[64] Hobsbawm's chronology of the crisis and of prices has since been described as a somewhat premature estimation that does not give sufficient attention to the variations in different areas. For example, prices began to fall in Germany in the 1620s and in Italy and Holland around the middle of the century, but nearly the whole of Europe experienced similar monetary disasters, and these were related to the economic and political troubles of the middle decades of the century.[65]

Hobsbawm presents an explanation of the crisis within a Marxist theoretical framework. He argues that the crisis was the result of early-modern capitalism operating within a feudal framework. A capitalist class was emerging, but the triumph of capitalism required radical changes in the social structure of feudal or agrarian society: the redistribution of resources from agriculture to industry, the growth of a wage-earning class, and the formation of large and expanding markets for goods. These changes had not yet taken place on a great scale, and capitalists had to depend on traditional feudal markets and to operate within the framework of feudal economic and social relationships. The expansion of commerce and industry within feudal society was sure to create its own crisis. Hobsbawm's interpretation is just one among many that have been presented by historians on the nature and the causes of the crisis. A few historians have criticized the whole notion of a "crisis," but for our purposes, it is sufficient to note that there is a wide consensus among historians that the economic boom of sixteenth-century Europe came to an end during the first half of the seventeenth century and was followed by a period of economic stagnation. About mid-century, even Holland, which was enjoying a position of economic hegemony in Europe, began to experience economic contraction.

The Sephardim, including marranos and former marranos, were especially involved in the commercial developments of the sixteenth century, and their position made them particularly susceptible to the economic and political crises of the seventeenth century. The most dramatic economic declines occurred in the Ottoman Empire and Italy, two areas of major Sephardi settlement. The Ottoman Empire reached the limits of its expansion in the sixteenth century, and the Sephardim were the builders of its commercial and industrial structures. A network of Jewish merchants stretched over the whole empire, Jewish industrialists built up the cloth trade, and Jews were prominent among the tax-farmers, physicians, diplomats, officials, and courtiers of the sultans. The decline of the empire began in the last decades of the sixteenth century; it suffered naval defeats, revolts of the army, a shrinking economy, struggles of power, palace intrigues, a corrupt administration, and the increasing ineffectiveness of central control. The establishment of Dutch and British power in Asia and the transfer of world trade routes to the open seas deprived the empire of the greater part of its foreign commerce. The flow of precious metals from the New World and western Europe at the end of the sixteenth century brought financial disruption and economic distress. The decline of the empire greatly affected most of its Jewish communities, and from the end of the sixteenth century they suffered a decline in prosperity and a loss of influence in the state.[66]

Since Salonika was not only an important center of Sabbatianism in 1666 but also its principal center after that year, it is worthy of special attention. Jos. Nehama wrote that Salonika's golden age lasted from 1536 to 1593. The Jews and marranos created great prosperity, developing the cloth industry, commerce, and a port which came near to rivaling Venice. Thousands of Jews were engaged in all stages of the production, distribution, and selling of cloth, the wealthy stratum maintained an opulent lifestyle, and the town's physicians, jurists, philosophers, poets, musicians, and scholars constituted a brilliant intellectual elite.

The town was relatively prosperous up to the 1660s, but from the beginning of the seventeenth century signs of decline had begun appearing. The community suffered from a series of financial crises, the depreciation of money, and the heavy taxes, extortions, ransoms, and dispossessions of a corrupt administration. Unstable political conditions and increasing competition from England and Holland caused a decline in the cloth trade. From the middle of the century the financial crises worsened, and commercial failures became frequent. A contemporary wrote that all the population was under the burden of debts and taxes and everyone ran to escape his creditors, and he bemoaned that God had decreed that the city would be crushed by misfortune. Other documents of the time, letters and memoirs, also indicate an atmosphere of desperation. Nehama noted the parallel developments of millenarianism and mysticism in the city: each added suffering was interpreted as a sign of the coming of the messiah, and greater numbers devoted themselves to ritual ablutions, flagellations, and the study of the cabbalah.[67]

Italy, the European center of late-medieval and early-modern commerce and manufacture, fell into a deep decline. At the beginning of the seventeenth century, central and northern Italy were still among the most highly developed regions in Europe, but by about 1680 industry had collapsed, leaving a backward region. Competition from nations who were expanding their industrial, banking, and maritime activities led to a drastic decline of Italy's exports and a consequent withdrawal of investment from industry, banking, and shipping.[68] Chapter 5 described the persecution and economic decline of Italian Jews in the second half of the sixteenth century; in the seventeenth century most Italian Jewish communities continued to suffer segregation, discrimination, and impoverishment.

The only two exceptions were Venice and Leghorn, where the former marranos were concentrated. In the second half of the sixteenth century, the Venetian Jews suffered along with other Jewish communities in central and northern Italy, but in the first decades of the seventeenth century the new, mainly marrano, Jewish settlers enjoyed a prosperous existence and friendly relationships with gentiles.[69] Leghorn was virtually the only place in Italy where the Catholic reaction made little impression; the town had no ghetto and required no Jewish badge, and the community enjoyed great wealth. However, neither Venice nor Leghorn was immune from the general decline of the Italian economy, and after reaching their peaks about the middle of the century, they, too, began to decline.[70] Thus, although many of the centers of Sabbatianism in the Ottoman Empire and Italy were comparatively prosperous communities, they had passed the height of their economic prosperity, political freedom, and social accomplishments, and they had experienced often sharp and drastic declines in their situations.

The German economy was also in decline in the seventeenth century, but the Hamburg community showed no sign of a radical economic decline. Industrial development was evident in Holland, and the Amsterdam community reached the pinnacle of its wealth in the middle of the century. Holland did, however, undergo commercial crises and experience a fall in its international trade. Colonial expansion also faced problems: the Dutch Empire underwent a great expansion from 1600 to 1640, but in the next thirty years it shrank considerably. Dutch trade reached its peak in the 1640s and encountered stiff competition in the second half of the century. The economy suffered from the disturbances of war and the protectionist policies of neighboring states, but despite some signs of decline, the Dutch Republic retained much of its economic predominance in Europe well after 1700.[71]

The argument here does not require that all the centers of former marranos suffered from economic decline; in many cases, their cultural anomie and social and psychological strains were sufficient to make them responsive to millenarianism. Moreover, the crisis in the wider society was not confined to economic matters but was evident also in an effusion of competing intellectual systems and in a series of revolts and political conflicts over the issues of local autonomy and centralization. Holland's economic prosperity did not make it immune to tensions over political centralization, and the country's comparative tolerance encouraged the expression of intellectual controversies over fundamental matters of religion and philosophy. The social situation and cultural orientations of the former marranos had unique components, but they may be viewed as acute manifestations of what was, according to Theodore Rabb, a general phenomenon in Europe at the time: a period of transition, involving disruption and disorder, was countered by vigorous efforts, ranging from millenarianism to science, to reassert harmony and order.[72]

Finally, it is necessary to discuss briefly the exceptions: those communities where neither former marranos nor other Sephardim were present in any number or at all. A common element in these communities was their poverty and persecuted state. The Yemenite community was desperately poor; together with the Moroccan communities, it was among the most persecuted in the Muslim world.[73] Frankfurt and Prague, together with many other German communities, suffered from the Thirty Years' War. The Frankfurt community suffered a decline in wealth from 1630: its poverty increased during the course of the war, and its population and resources continued to diminish after the war.[74] Following the war the authorities in Prague were influenced by the Counter-Reformation: they segregated the Jews in ghettos, took measures to reduce their numbers, and forced them to pay high taxes.[75] One source reports a messiah appearing in Prague in 1650 and gaining considerable support.[76] The community in Vienna not only suffered economic distress, which was made worse by the immigration of Polish Jews after 1648, but also faced an expulsion order issued by the emperor in 1665.[77] Of course, other poor and persecuted communities were not conspicuous in their support of Zvi, and other factors, such as geographical location and the communication networks of the Jewish communities, were no doubt relevant. Vienna, for example, was close to the Ottoman border.

In conclusion, this discussion does not claim to have accounted in full for the distribution of messianic support and enthusiasm in 1666, but it does claim to have gone some way in explaining the general pattern. It points not to one cause but to a convergence of factors. My argument has been that although the developments in the cabbalah were relevant, this is not a sufficient or even the major explanation. More general cultural and psychological considerations, especially those that affected the former marranos, as well as social and economic factors, were of great importance.

8. Developments in Sabbatianism

Sabbatai Zvi: Imprisonment, Conversion, and Death

Excitement in many Jewish communities reached a pitch early in 1666 when Sabbatai Zvi sailed from Smyrna to Constantinople. They expected that he would remove the crown from the sultan, assume the rule over the Ottoman Empire, and inaugurate the messianic era. On 6 February 1666, however, Turkish authorities intercepted his ship and brought him ashore in chains. Revolts were frequent in the empire, and rebels or suspected rebels were usually speedily executed. Although the Turks had little reason to fear the Sabbatian movement, they may have wished to avoid making Zvi a martyr. Whatever the reason, they showed unusual restraint in his case by putting him in prison. They took him to the fortress of Gallipoli. There, with the help of bribes, he managed to meet with his followers and to hold court in some style for several months. In September, Zvi came before the divan in Adrianople, who gave him the choice between immediate death and conversion to Islam. Zvi denied having made a messianic claim and chose conversion.

The Turks considered Zvi an important convert, and he was granted the honorary title of "keeper of the palace gates." They expected Zvi to act as a missionary, but together with a group of followers who settled around him in Adrianople and who, under his influence, also became converts to Islam, Zvi led a double life of outward conformity to Islam and the secret practice of Jewish and special Sabbatian rites. In 1672, Zvi went to Constantinople, where, at first, the Muslims treated him with respect. However, his enemies used bribes to have him arrested. Turkish authorities then accused him of denying and reviling Islam and banished him to the fortress of Duleigo, in Albania. Zvi died in 1676.[1]

Responses to Disconfirmation of Prophecy

In their study *When Prophecy Fails*, Leon Festinger, Henry Riecken, and Stanley Schachter examined the conditions that result in an increase of fervor among religious believers after their predictions fail to materialize. They studied a small group who believed that a cataclysm would occur on a certain date and that they would be rescued by flying saucers. The belief was sufficiently specific to make it open to refutation by common rules of evidence, and when this occurred, the members experienced cognitive dissonance, an inconsistency between two cognitions, which produced feelings of confusion and discomfort.

People can attempt to reduce or eliminate cognitive dissonance in a number of ways. One way is simply to discard the belief that has been disconfirmed, but this may be too painful if commitment is very strong. Another way is to deny or ignore the event that has disconfirmed the belief. The disconfirmatory evidence may, however, be undeniable and impossible to blot out. A third response is to find a reasonable explanation that will reconcile the apparent failure of the prediction with the belief system. If this is done, it is possible for the believers to become more convinced than ever of the truth of their beliefs. This is more likely to occur if the believers find social support and confirmation of the explanation among others who have experienced the same dissonance. In order to increase social support believers are likely to increase their proselytizing activities. If more people can be convinced that the system of beliefs is true, then it must be correct.

In the group studied by Festinger and his associates a prophetess claimed that the group's long vigil on the night of the predicted cataclysm had caused God to save the world. The highly committed believers who found social support among other members accepted this explanation, and a number attempted to convince others of their beliefs.[2]

In his study of Jehovah's Witnesses, Joseph Zygmunt found that the level of evangelistic activity tended to decline immediately after a prophetic failure. A series of prophetic failures precipitated both crises of faith in the total belief system and crises of mission, since the movement conceived of its evangelistic operations as temporally limited. Before they resumed their proselytizing activities, the members rationalized the apparent failure and redefined the beliefs and identity of the movement. One response to apparent prophetic failure was to argue that the prophecy had been partially fulfilled: a supernatural event, which was not open to confirmation, was said to have transpired on the date. In the case of the Jehovah's Witnesses the major source of identity of the movement shifted from millenarian prophecies to an emphasis on the evil in the world, the divinely chosen elite status of members, and militant evangelization.[3]

Four events occurred which were apparent refutations of the belief in Zvi as the messiah: his imprisonment, his conversion, his death, and the absence of any change in the material world which could have been taken as a sign of the process of redemption.[4] Although the major messianic tradition made no mention that the messiah would be imprisoned, Zvi's imprisonment in Gallipoli was not recognized as a disconfirmation of prophecy. His followers saw the fact that he had not been executed and was held in a comfortable state as a confirmation of his mission. They explained the imprisonment as a deep mystery, and it did not diminish their enthusiasm. In fact, the heights of excitement occurred after Zvi's imprisonment, in July and August 1666, when the believers awaited great events.[5]

Zvi's totally unexpected conversion in September 1666 represented the most unequivocal disconfirmation of his messianic role. An apostate messiah was sure to cause cognitive dissonance among his followers. Zvi's believers were shocked and confused, and the first response was to refuse to believe it. Reports confirmed the event, but among many circles of believers it was some time before they would accept the truth. After clear confirmation of the apostasy, the great majority admitted that they had been mistaken in believing Zvi to be the messiah. The disillusionment of some European believers was so great that they converted to Christianity, but the majority were able to return to the "normal" state of exile. The policy of religious and communal leaders was to restore calm by pretending that little had actually happened. This was especially the case in Turkey, where Jewish leaders were concerned that the Turkish authorities would act against them for permitting preparations for a messianic revolt.

A minority did not admit that they had been mistaken about Zvi. In most previous Jewish messianic movements believers had accepted the disconfirmation of prophecy and had returned to everyday life. The widespread belief in Zvi in some communities, and the ecstatic behavior that accompanied it, led some to believe that the new era of history had already begun; in their minds, the imminent redemption had become a realized redemption. The mass prophecy, the wave of penitence, and the visions and trances had given an extraordinary inner sense of freedom. Some believers could not admit that their personal experience had been false, and it appeared impossible that so many Jews had had a false experience.

Scholem writes that Zvi's conversion presented believers with a contradiction between their subjective experience and the objective historical facts. The believers were divided: whereas the majority accepted the verdict of history and believed that the events of the exterior world were decisive, a minority were unable to tolerate the split between the exterior world and their interior experience. For these latter, if their vital subjective experience was contradicted by facts, then those facts required explanation. Scholem argues that, despite their differences, all Sabbatian beliefs after Zvi's conversion were directed toward explaining the gap between internal and external reality and toward enabling believers to live in the state of tension that this involved.[6]

Scholem's formulation makes too much of a confrontation and divergence between subjective experience and objective fact. Believers had experienced the events prior to the conversion as objective facts; subjective feelings had been confirmed and reinforced by the expressions of belief and actions of others. To characterize those who remained believers after Zvi's conversion as those who were unable to tolerate the split between subjective experience and the objective world places too much emphasis on random psychological differences. From the point of view of the believer, there was a dissonance at the level of the real, material world: Zvi was the messiah and the Redemption was near, but Zvi had converted to Islam. This cognitive dissonance was, of course, accompanied by a dissonance in emotions: belief in Zvi and an imminent redemption had brought a sense of freedom, but the conversion had brought confusion and anxiety. The believers who remained after the conversion accepted explanations that presented new "facts," reduced or cancelled the confusion, and allowed them to retain the feeling of liberation.

One early explanation of the conversion was that Zvi had disguised himself in order to achieve greater success. Another was that Zvi was in hiding and that someone of Zvi's description had converted. Yet another was that Zvi was in heaven and that it was his shadow that had converted to Islam. The most common explanation, and one which came to be generally accepted by the believers, was that Zvi's messianic role made it necessary for him to enter the evil realm represented by Islam. This explanation appeared independently in several places, but it was Nathan and his disciples who gave it a theological foundation by relating it to cabbalistic concepts and beliefs.

When Nathan received the news of the conversion in November 1666, he immediately announced that it had deep mystical meaning. He argued that the doctrine that all the divine sparks had been rescued from the kelippot was mistaken and that it was the supreme task of the messiah to lift up the remaining sparks, which were dispersed among the gentiles and concentrated in Islam. Only the messiah could redeem some sparks, and to complete the extraction, he had to descend into the realm of the kelippot and assume the form of evil. Outwardly, the messiah had to submit to the demands of the realm of impurity, but actually he was conquering the kelippot from within and rescuing the sparks that were imprisoned there. The final stage of tikkun had to be realized in pain and suffering; only a descent into evil would exhaust the full potential of evil and lead to its collapse. Nathan linked this explanation to his earlier explanation of Zvi's personality and his "strange actions" that deviated from the mitsvot. Such actions as eating forbidden meat were part of the fulfillment of the messiah's mission. Nathan and others searched and found in the Bible and in rabbinic and cabbalistic literature allusions and references to the mystery of the apostasy. Through their own ingenious interpretations, they convinced themselves that all the religious writings pointed to the apostasy of the messiah.[7]

The distribution of Sabbatian groups who remained after Zvi's conversion supports the perspective of cognitive dissonance: most of the believers who accepted the explanation of Zvi's conversion lived in communities that had demonstrated the greatest conviction and commitment prior to the conversion. The largest groups of believers were found in the Turkish communities, especially in Salonika, Smyrna, and Constantinople, but Sabbatianism also survived in many Balkan communities. Morocco remained for some time a center of Sabbatianism, and small groups of believers continued in Amsterdam, Venice, and Leghorn. There were also believers in Poland, especially Lithuania.[8] In the last chapter it was argued that Scholem's evidence does not support his contention of mass support among Polish Jews in 1666, but the Jewish population of Poland was so large that if even a small minority had become Sabbatians, small groups of believers would have remained after Zvi's conversion to Islam. In fact, the major centers of Sabbatianism in Poland were not remnants of the support in 1666, but developed in the eighteenth century in the southern provinces of Poland, a large part of which was under Turkish sovereignty. Sabbatianism also spread in the eighteenth century to German communities, especially in Bohemia and Moravia.

Support for Sabbatianism continued to be concentrated in communities that contained many former marranos and their descendants. Like other Jews, most former marranos abandoned the movement after Zvi's conversion, but since they had been among the most highly committed, many were ready to accept an explanation that justified Zvi's action. However, another factor made the former marranos particularly willing to accept a religious interpretation of Zvi's conversion: his action was a repetition of their own biographies and family histories.

If Scholem underestimated the importance of the marranos in the movement in 1666, he fully acknowledged their prominence in the movement after the conversion. He writes that the key to Sabbatianism at this stage was the paradoxical religious feelings of the former marranos and their children; without their disposition, he writes, it is doubtful that the doctrine of the apostate messiah would have been adopted. They could easily accept that the conversion was not real but was the mask of a marrano: they had also led a double life—the religion that they had professed was not the one that they believed. "The idea of an apostate messiah could be presented to them as a religious glorification of the very act which had continued to torment their own conscience." At first it was argued that the conversion occurred under such pressure that Zvi was left with no choice but to become a marrano. This was, of course, how most former marranos had seen their own conversion to Christianity. At a later stage, the paradox was declared more openly: it was argued that the messiah had become a marrano of his own free will. This interpretation enabled the former marranos to reinterpret their own conversions and to assuage their guilt still further; perhaps, like Zvi, their conversion had not represented an admission of weakness or cowardliness but had been part of a cosmic process working toward redemption.[9]

The marrano ideology was expressed clearly by Abraham Cardozo, a former marrano who had returned to Judaism in Leghorn. In Smyrna, from 1675 until he was expelled by the rabbinic authorities in 1681, Cardozo took a leading place among the Sabbatians, and in other Turkish Sabbatian groups his influence was second only to that of Nathan. He argued that, in consequence of their sins, all Jews were originally destined to become marranos before they could emerge from exile. Only the soul of the messiah was strong enough to bear the role of the marrano without hurt, and in his greatness, Zvi had assumed the punishment of the whole people. In a letter to his brother, Abraham wrote that "the messiah was destined to become a Marrano like me," and he emphasized that the Jewish tradition taught that the messiah would be degraded, maligned, and apparently rejected by God.

The Jewish tradition included a motif of a suffering messiah, but this had never become a dominant messianic theme in Judaism; Cardozo's emphasis on a messiah who suffered for the sins of the people had an obvious Christian influence. Abraham's brother, Isaac, accused him of heresy and attacked Sabbatianism with arguments that Jews used against Christianity. The law was eternal, it would remain intact in the messianic age, and Zvi's strange actions and conversion were clear signs that he was a false messiah. In addition, no fulfillment of the this-worldly messianic prophecies had taken place. Abraham responded by citing biblical passages that Christians had always applied to Christ, and like the Christians, he attacked his opponents' interpretation of the messianic prophecies as materialistic. Yerushalmi writes that Abraham's opponents realized that to concede a suffering messiah was to accept a major motif in Christianity, and it became no more absurd to accept the crucified messiah than the apostate messiah.

The stands of the brothers Cardozo to Sabbatianism demonstrate that the marrano experience could lead to diametrically opposed positions. Yerushalmi points out that the marrano was not only a man who had lived a double religious life but also one who had repudiated Christianity, including the image of a suffering messiah. For Isaac Cardozo, the grounds for rejecting Zvi were similar or identical to the grounds that had justified his rejection of Christianity, and Abraham Cardozo had sufficient knowledge of Christian theology to recognize the similarities between his defense of Zvi and the Christian polemics against Judaism.[10] It is possible that Abraham and other former marranos were attracted to a faith that reminded them, consciously or unconsciously, of the faith of their childhood, but their readiness to accept a messiah whose own actions explained and justified a past that they had previously remembered with guilt and sorrow seems more important.

Nathan had predicted that the period of final revelation would begin in September 1667, and the passing of this date presented believers with another situation of cognitive dissonance. One Sabbatian argued that, following Zvi's conversion, the Jews had discontinued their repentance, and this had delayed the Redemption, which God would now bring without the help of the people.[11] Nathan distinguished between the revelation that he had received that Zvi was the messiah and the inaccurate calculations of the time of the Redemption. After making recalculations, Nathan and other prophets announced several new dates. A common belief was that the messianic process had a temporal sequence and that the sequence had to be calculated using a period of either seven or ten years. Since some counted the period from the date of Sabbatai's manifestation, while others counted it from his apostasy, a number of different dates from 1672 to 1675 were announced. The followers around Zvi in Adrianople believed that the messiah would manifest his power and glory in 1673–74. In Amsterdam some believers saw the termination of the war between Holland and England in February 1674 as a messianic portent. In Morocco a prophet announced that the messianic kingdom would begin on the eve of Passover, 1675.[12]

The possibility of mistakes in the calculations of the date of the Redemption was generally accepted, but the death of Zvi in 1676 presented a disconfirmation which had not been anticipated. Abraham Cardozo believed that the Christians were correct in presenting a suffering messiah, but that they were mistaken in their belief that the messiah must die.[13] The death of Zvi without any outward sign of the arrival of the Redemption caused some believers to leave the movement. Festinger, Riecken, and Schachter wrote: "When people are committed to a belief and a course of action, clear disconfirming evidence may simply result in deepened conviction and increased proselyting. But there does seem a point at which the disconfirming evidence has mounted sufficiently to cause the belief to be rejected."[14] Each successive event of disconfirmation reduced the number of believers in the Sabbatian movement. Yet the most acute test of commitment had been Zvi's conversion; the believers who had continued in their conviction after that event had invested their psychological resources in their beliefs, and they were likely to face up to less devastating challenges of disconfirmation.

Nathan announced that the death of Zvi was not real, but was a further occultation. Another explanation was that Zvi may have been the Messiah ben Joseph and not the final redeemer, the Messiah ben David. Mordecai ben Hayyim of Eisenstadt (1650–1729) claimed in Italy that Zvi had been the Messiah ben Joseph and that he, Mordecai, was the Messiah ben David. More common was the belief that Zvi would return, and a number of claimants to the role of Messiah ben Joseph arose to fill the interregnum between the first and second manifestations of Zvi. Joshua Heshel Zoref (1633–1700), the most important figure among the Sabbatians in Lithuania, considered himself the Messiah ben Joseph and saw his role as the revealer of the secrets of redemption prior to the second coming of Zvi. Judah Leib Prossnitz (circa 1670–1730) also claimed to be the Messiah ben Joseph, and he attracted a number of followers in Moravia, Vienna, and Prague. In Smyrna, Abraham Cardozo called himself Messiah ben Joseph.[15]

After Zvi's death new dates were announced for the beginning of the Redemption: 1679 and, after that, 1682. It was believed that the process of redemption in the latter year would begin in Constantinople, and a group collected in the city to await the great events. Some Sabbatians believed that Zvi would reappear in Jerusalem, and in 1700, Judah Hasid, a Polish preacher, led a group from Europe to Palestine to await Zvi. Judah was the leader of a "holy society" whose asceticism and mortifications had made an impression in Germany and Austria, where Hasid urged communities to repent and financially support the emigrants. His death very soon after his arrival in Jerusalem was a bitter disappointment to his followers. Following Judah's death, a leading member of the group, Hayyim Molach, announced that the messiah was about to come, and the believers carried a statue of the messiah to a synagogue, dancing before it as they went.

The disappointments of this group continued: many died during their first year in Jerusalem, others returned to Europe, and those that remained, including Molach, were expelled from Jerusalem. Some converted to Islam. One group who returned to Europe but remained Sabbatians settled in Mannheim and contributed to the spread of Sabbatian ideas in Germany and Poland. Molach spent some time among Sabbatians in Salonika, where he claimed that, just as Moses sojourned forty days in heaven and then returned to earth, so Zvi would return forty years after his death and complete the Redemption. A popular date for the return of Zvi among the remnants of Judah's group in Palestine was 1706.[16] This was also the view of Judah Leib Prossnitz, who, in preparation for the event, gathered a group of ten followers who studied with him and practiced extreme mortifications. Some years later in Padua a group of young men influenced by Sabbatians and led by Moses Hayyim Luzzatto (1707–46) dedicated themselves to tikkun. They believed that the process of redemption had begun and would reach its culmination in a few years. Luzzatto saw himself as a reincarnated Moses who stood above a number of messianic roles which were distributed among the members of his group. He saw his marriage in 1731 as the marriage of Moses to the Shechinah, uniting the masculine and feminine elements in the divine world, and thereby contributing to the process of redemption.[17]

The Sabbatian movement immediately following Zvi's conversion demonstrates the hypothesis that one response of believers to a crisis of disconfirmation is to increase their proselytizing. At first, the believers openly conducted propaganda for the apostate messiah. Nathan left Gaza and expounded his ideas to the Jewish communities of the Balkans. He visited Rome and Venice and then returned to the Balkans. Other Sabbatians also traveled widely to find followers and support. The group around Zvi in Adrianople believed that they had to spread their faith even among the gentiles.

The period of open proselytizing did not, however, last for long. One reason was that the prophecy of the Sabbatians, that Zvi would return in triumph from the realm of evil, did not materialize. More important was the persecution of Sabbatianism by the Jewish religious and lay leadership. In Turkey the Jewish authorities were furious with the Sabbatians for endangering their position, and they drove them underground, forbidding them to make public pronouncements or to organize. After Nathan's excommunication by the rabbis of Brussa he restricted his contacts to fellow believers. In Poland, the central Jewish organization, the Council of the Four Lands, excommunicated the Sabbatians in 1669 and reaffirmed its action in 1671. At that time the Sabbatians in Poland were devout Jews, continuing the ways of repentance, but the rabbis felt a challenge from preachers who took their authority from a different source, and they may have recognized the potential antinomianism in Sabbatian ideas.

The excommunication in 1671 made the first reference to the "sect of Sabbatai Zvi," and this was an accurate representation of developments within Sabbatianism. The Sabbatians had begun to meet in secret and to build a clandestine communication network. Many Sabbatians admitted their faith only to fellow believers. Their writings contained only hidden allusions and references to Sabbatianism, and they often prefaced a presentation of Sabbatian ideas by an attack on the faith. As the persecution gathered strength the Sabbatians increasingly saw themselves as the true

Israel, the "elect of God," the "pioneers" of the new world. A socioeconomic motif entered the beliefs of the movement. The rank-and-file Sabbatians were uneducated, but they saw themselves as the true spirituals and prophesied that dire punishment awaited the rabbis and scholars who rejected the messiah. Nathan and other Sabbatians attacked the rich, since it was often the wealthy lay leaders who promoted the persecution of the movement.[18]

Thus, the Sabbatians erected barriers between themselves and the wider society. This was, in part, to protect themselves from persecution, but it also represented a defense against the refutations of nonbelievers. Within the enclosures of a sect the Sabbatians found the social support of fellow believers, and this was especially important following the events that refuted the prophecies. The explanations of the events could be worked out, confirmed, and reconfirmed without the conflicting influence and pressures of nonbelievers. Unlike the group studied by Festinger, Riecken, and Schachter, which began as a self-enclosed circle and sought proselytes only after the disconfirmation, Sabbatianism began as a movement and, following persecution and successive disconfirmations, evolved into a sect. Like the Jehovah's Witnesses, the Sabbatians came to conceive of themselves as a divinely chosen elite, but unlike the Witnesses, they largely abandoned proselytizing and concentrated their activities on beliefs and rituals that legitimated and expressed their elite status. Sabbatianism was a loosely organized sect, composed of groups and circles, most of which were very small, but many Sabbatians supported and reinforced their beliefs by exchanging visits and letters with fellow believers.

As Sabbatians drew in upon themselves, they developed increasingly nonorthodox beliefs. The focus of their beliefs shifted from imminent prophecies and the role of the messiah to the character of the Redemption, which some believed had already begun, and the status of the believers within it. The problem of the nature of the Torah in the perfect state of the millennium had long been recognized, but few had challenged the orthodox view that the Torah would be observed perfectly and in its entirety. The problem was reexamined with the appearance of a messiah who had himself committed an act that was radically paradoxical.

In their attempts to account for an apostate messiah, the Sabbatian thinkers produced some radical ideas. Abraham Cardozo wrote that "the Torah as it now exists will not exist in the messianic age." Since the observance of the mitsvot contributes to the perfection of the messianic world, the status of the Torah must necessarily change within that world. Cardozo referred to two trees of Paradise, the Tree of Life and the Tree of Knowledge of Good and Evil, which correspond to two Torahs. The dominion of the Torah of the Tree of Knowledge is the unredeemed world in which distinctions between good and evil, commandment and prohibition, holy and profane, pure and impure are necessary. The Torah of the Tree of Life was hitherto unrealizable because of the sin of Adam, and only redemption would restore it as the Torah of the messianic age. Cardozo continued to observe the mitsvot and argued that as long as the messiah had not returned from his mission, others could not follow him. Apostasy was specific to the messiah, since only he could enter the evil realm without spiritual impairment. Nathan also remained loyal to the tradition and emphasized the particularity of the messiah's action. He argued that, since the beginning, the messiah had been bound to the Tree of Life and had never been subject to the Law of the Tree of Knowledge. Only the messiah stood beyond good and evil, and the messiah's actions appeared scandalous only to mortals subject to the Tree of Knowledge.

These moderate Sabbatians argued that the apostasy of the messiah was not intended to serve as an example to others. As long as Israel remained in exile and the exterior world remained unchanged, no commandment of the Torah was to be violated. All the mitsvot remained intact apart from those few that Zvi had personally canceled. The Law of the Tree of Life would become visible with the end of exile and the final and complete redemption of the cosmos. Among the moderates were people of extreme piety who differed from other pious Jews not in their religious practices but only in their theological speculations.

The radical Sabbatians were antinomians and used two somewhat contradictory ideas to justify their antinomianism. One idea was that all the believers had to descend into the evil realm in order to conquer evil from within and hasten salvation. Another was that it was impossible for those whose souls were already in the messianic world to sin. With the arrival of Zvi the sin of Adam had been corrected, and the new Torah had become law. Both ideas had the same practical consequence: it was holy to sin. Actions that bore the outward appearance of sin were, in reality, pure and holy. Believers saw themselves as an elite whose special relationship with the spiritual realm made it their duty to deny the commandments. The violation of the Torah was to promote or express a truer Torah, which had been in a state of concealment during exile.

Knowledge and rumors of antinomian behavior contributed to the persecution of the movement by Jewish authorities, and this persecution in turn strengthened the sectarian orientations of the believers. All Sabbatians, however orthodox and pious in their behavior, were identified with the radical wing and accused of antinomianism. The Sabbatians emphasized the importance of secrecy and justified it theologically. The true believer was seen to express a religious value in not revealing his true beliefs and practices. It was argued that, just as redemption was intrinsically real but not yet visible, so true belief must be held in secret. As Scholem notes, the religious justification of dissimulation appealed to the former marranos, who had already experienced a double life; the true deed, performed in secret, canceled the falseness of public behavior.[19]

The moderate form of Sabbatianism existed in small groups over a large area: in Morocco, Germany, Bohemia, Moravia, Italy, Poland, Turkey, and the Balkans. The radical form began in Salonika in 1683 when two to three hundred families converted to Islam, and it remained largely restricted to Salonika, southern Poland, and a few small offshoots in central Europe. Zvi had urged members of his circle in Adrianople to convert to Islam. One group emphasized the need to obey the messiah and converted, but another group believed that the messiah was testing his followers to the point of demanding their conversion and that they needed to refuse. After Zvi's death many of the converts moved to Salonika, where a large number of believers remained. The converts in 1683 maintained that apostasy would bring redemption and claimed that revelations and visions of Zvi had pointed the way. There was disappointment in 1682 when the messiah failed to appear, but in 1683 pestilence, earthquakes, and fires in Constantinople, Izmir, Adrianople, and Salonika were interpreted as confirming signs of an imminent redemption. Not all the Sabbatians in Salonika apostasized. One group that did not wish to convert migrated to Italy, but some nonapostate Sabbatians remained in Salonika, and a few apostates later returned to Judaism. The conversions continued for a few years, and most apostate families from other cities in Turkey migrated to Salonika.

The apostates, who came to be known as *Doenmeh* ("converts," in Turkish), led a dual life: they attended the mosques and outwardly observed the tenets of Islam, but they privately observed a mixture of traditional and heretical Judaism. They lived in separate quarters in Salonika and married only among themselves. Their numbers were estimated in 1774 at about 600 families; from 1880 to 1924 between 5,000 and 10,000 individuals remained, constituting approximately half of the "Turks" in Salonika.

The Doenmeh did not intend to break completely with the traditional patterns of rabbinic Judaism, but a series of internal divisions and developments led many in a clearly antinomian direction. They made a distinction between the Torah of Creation, the Halachah, which was a manifestation of revelation in the lower realms, and the Torah of Emanation, which could be comprehended in the upper worlds and also in the state of redemption. The messiah, who was to replace the Torah of Creation with the Torah of Emanation, had already appeared, but he had not completely fulfilled his mission. The two states of the world overlapped and existed side by side, and the anarchic freedom of the spiritual Torah was observed only on certain occasions, during the secret festivals and rituals of the Doenmeh.

Schisms divided the Doenmeh into three subsects: the Izmirlis, who claimed to be the only faithful disciples of Zvi; the Jacobites, who believed that the soul of Zvi had entered his brother-in-law, Jacob Querido; and the Konyosos, the most radical group. The Konyosos began at the beginning of the eighteenth century when a new young leader, Baruchiah Russo, was proclaimed by his disciples to be the reincarnation of Zvi. Baruchiah, who was declared a divine incarnation in 1716, taught that the new messianic Torah entailed the complete reversal of values and that the most severely punishable prohibitions, including those on "unnatural" sexual unions and incest, had become positive commands. All three groups had antinomian elements, but Baruchiah's sect was the most extreme. Their secret rituals included eating forbidden food, and the transgression of sexual prohibitions was used as an initiation rite. Ceremonies of ritual fornication took place mainly during the ritual of the "extinguishing of the lights," celebrating the Festival of the Lamb at the beginning of spring.[20]

Antinomianism is a more common development in those religions that hold to a belief in the possibility of identity or continual communication with the divine. People who define themselves as divine may believe that they are no longer subject to the moral code of mere mortals. This belief was rare in Judaism, and when it did arise, it was usually found among single individuals and not in an organized context.

Scholem accounts for the development of antinomianism in Sabbatianism by two factors: the psychological makeup of Zvi, and, more important, the immanent development within the religious beliefs. Under the influence of manic enthusiasm, Zvi had felt compelled to commit "strange or paradoxical actions" that were in contradiction to the religious law. These actions, which were Zvi's "specific contribution to the Sabbatian movement," were given theological meaning by Nathan. In his state of illumination, Zvi represented the paradox of the holy sinner, and "this and nothing else is the true heritage of Sabbatai Sevi."[21]

The Sabbatians believed that the messiah had come, but they acknowledged that his kingdom had not become manifest in the outer world. It was, therefore, the inner realities that were true, and there was a need to reject the outer realities, including the religious law. Everything was permitted for a spiritual elite that trusted in the mission of Zvi and knew secrets that had not yet been generally revealed. The members of the most antinomian Doenmeh sect believed that their leader was God, and if God said that everything was permitted, then it was so. It should be emphasized, however, that many Sabbatians remained moderates and did not develop or accept antinomianism. Sabbatian beliefs made antinomianism a possible option, but it was not a necessary development. An explanation must include some consideration of the social context in which the individual's identification with a spiritual elite might prove attractive.

The nucleus of antinomian developments in Sabbatianism was Salonika, which was also the largest center of former marranos. It was difficult for former marranos to gain status in the Jewish community, but in Salonika many had at least become prosperous. From about 1669 the textile industry in Salonika entered a sharp slump. The wealth of most of the Jewish communities under the Ottomans was much reduced with the decline of the empire, but the economic distress in Salonika was particularly great. Salonika was unable to compete with the textile industries of the West, and much of its other economic activity was transferred to Smyrna. The economic decline of Salonika became acute after 1679 and reached its depths between 1683 and 1689. Economic distress was evident in all classes: the richest families were ruined; merchants and bankers went bankrupt and turned to manual work; and thousands of artisan-weavers became unemployed and entered more humble, precarious occupations. During the same period the taxes on the Jewish community rose greatly, and by becoming a Muslim a Jew could free himself from the heavy taxes.[22] Thus, the claim to a spiritual status above the world's distinctions of good and evil emerged in a community that was experiencing a precipitous fall into poverty.

The Doenmeh: A Postscript

Economic and social differences between the three sects developed between 1750 and 1850. The Izmirlis included rich merchants and professionals, and from the end of the nineteenth century they had a tendency to assimilate into Turkish society. The Jacobites included civil servants at middle and lower ranks, while the Konyosos, the most antinomian sect, drew its members from artisans and the proletariat. Each sect lived in a separate section of the city, they did not intermarry, and each had its own institutions and services, such as mutual-aid societies and medical treatment. In the early period the males had different haircuts: the Jacobites shaved their scalps and grew beards; the Izmirlis did not shave their heads, but shaved their beards; and the Konyosos grew beards, but did not shave their heads. In the later period the Izmirlis and Jacobites participated in the Turkish intelligentsia, the Young Turks, and one became a prime minister. The Konyosos improved their economic position and became mostly merchants. After the exchange of population that followed the Greco-Turkish war of 1924, the Doenmeh left Salonika and settled in Istanbul and a few other cities, such as Izmir and Ankara. The move from Salonika and their distribution in a number of communities contributed to their assimilation into Turkish society.[23]

9. Millenarianism
and Mysticism in
Eighteenth-Century
Poland

AROUND THE middle of the eighteenth century two Jewish religious movements arose in Podolia, a region of the western Ukraine in southeast Poland: the millennialist, Sabbatian movement of Jacob Frank and the mystical Hasidic movement. Neither Jacob Frank (circa 1726–91) nor Israel ben Eliezer, the Ba'al Shem Tov (circa 1700–1760), the founder of Hasidism, attracted more than a few thousand followers of the forty to fifty thousand Jews in Podolia, but while the Frankist movement rapidly declined after the death of its leader, the Hasidic movement grew to encompass the majority of Jews in a large part of eastern Europe.

In Podolia the peak period of the Frankist movement lasted from 1755, when Frank was accepted as leader by the Sabbatians in Podolia and elsewhere, to 1759–60, when a large proportion of the Frankists in Podolia converted to Catholicism. Small groups of Frankists continued in Podolia in the second half of the eighteenth century, but following Frank's release in 1772 from twelve years of imprisonment, the center of the movement moved with its leader to Moravia and later to Germany. After Frank died, his daughter Eva and her two younger brothers assumed the leadership, but the movement quickly declined, and Frank's children were reduced to poverty. The Frankists who had remained Jews either returned to the traditional fold or, in central Europe, became secularized and reform Jews. The baptized Frankists in Poland appear to have retained some distinctive identity after the death of Eva in 1816: a preference for marriage within the group continued into the third generation, and even later in some cases. However, the majority abandoned their distinctive sectarian beliefs and shed their Jewish identity and culture. Most were finally assimilated into Polish Christian society.[1]

The influence of the first Hasidic leader, the Ba'al Shem Tov (Besht being the common acronym), did not extend beyond Podolia and adjacent districts. His successor, Dov Baer, "the Great Maggid," of Mezhirech, who led the movement from 1766 to his death in 1772, resided in the province of Volhynia, north of Podolia. The move to a more central province of Poland facilitated the spread of the movement, and under Dov Baer,

Hasidism began to spread northward to Belorussia and Lithuania and westward to central Poland and Galicia. The most rapid growth and spread of Hasidism, in the last decades of the eighteenth and first decades of the nineteenth century, occurred after the death of Dov Baer when the movement divided into many segments, each with its own *zaddik* (righteous man) as a leader. By the middle of the nineteenth century Hasidism was dominant in most Jewish communities in the Ukraine, central Poland, and Galicia, it had large followings in Belorussia and northern Hungary, and it had attracted a significant minority in Lithuania. From a movement of perhaps a few thousand at the time of the death of the Besht, it quickly became one of hundreds of thousands after 1772, and, in the nineteenth century, one of millions.[2]

Social Background

The economic decline and political disintegration of Poland began with the uprising of the Ukrainian Cossacks and peasants in 1648. This was followed by the invasions of Russia (1654–67) and Sweden (1655–60), and at the end of the Great Northern War (1701–21), which was accompanied by a civil war in Poland, the power of the Polish state was much reduced. The invasions and internal wars resulted in a decline in population, a devastation of villages, a deterioration of towns, a fall in foreign and internal trade, and mounting conflict between classes, political factions, and religious and ethnic groups. The wealthy nobles gained power at the expense of the crown, but they struggled between themselves, and from 1764, when a new king was appointed, the country fell into a chaotic state of warring factions. The weakness of Poland enabled Russia, Austria, and Prussia to divide most of the state in the three partitions of 1772, 1793, and 1795.[3] After the Congress of Vienna in 1815 the remaining part of Poland, Congress Poland, was made a semiautonomous kingdom under Russian rule.

The consequences of the decline of Poland on the Jews were particularly grave. The Polish Jews, who numbered over half a million in 1750, occupied an interstitial position between the nobility and the peasant masses. The peasants made up almost three-quarters of the total population, and about 85 percent were serfs. The nobility and gentry (*szlachta*) constituted about 8 percent of the population, but it is important to distinguish between the few, wealthy, large landowning families, the middle gentry, who were not rich but were educated, and the "barefoot" szlachta, who owned perhaps a few acres and were often illiterate. The clergy, who represented about .5 percent, were drawn from the ranks of the nobility.[4] The Polish middle class was very small, and merchants tended to be either Jewish or German ethnics.

A census of Polish Jewry in 1763–64 found that nearly a third of the Jews lived in villages, but in a predominantly peasant society with very few large towns the Jews made up a significant section of the urban population.[5] It has been estimated that in 1790 only about 500,000 Christians out of a total population of nearly 9,000,000 lived in the towns, while approximately 535,000 Jews out of a total Jewish population of 800,000 were urban dwellers. In some large towns, Brody, for example, the Jews were in the majority, and in a number of smaller towns the Jews constituted 80–90 percent of the population.

The 1763–64 census shows that the distribution of Jews in villages and towns varied between the provinces of Poland. In general, the eastern areas were the more rural and had a greater proportion of Jews living in the villages. The areas of Frankism and early Hasidism had fairly high proportions of village Jews: more than 23 percent of the Jews in Podolia and close to 28 percent of the Jews in Volhynia lived in villages. The proportion of village Jews in these areas was much higher than in central and western Poland, but in other Ukrainian and Lithuanian areas the proportion of village Jews was more than a third.

A significant proportion of the urban Jews resided in small towns. Of the 431 Jewish communities in the Ukrainian regions, 111 were in small towns with less than 100 Jews, 153 had between 100 and 300 Jews, 66 had between 300 and 500 Jews, and 73 had between 500 and 1000 Jews. In the Ukraine and in western and central Poland 71–86 percent of all Jewish urban settlements were small Jewish communities with less than 500 Jews. According to the census, 44 towns had more than 1000 Jews (the true number was nearer to 60), and 12 towns had more than 2000. Most of the large urban settlements were in the western areas (East Galicia, Greater and Lesser Poland) and included the very large communities of Brody, with over 7000 Jews, and Lemberg, with over 6000. Lithuania and Belorussia had few large urban settlements, but the important center of Vilna had, together with two suburbs, about 4000 Jews. Volhynia had two towns with more than 2000 Jews, while Podolia had none. (Together with the Jews in their vicinity, two Podolian towns had more than 2000 Jews.)[6] Thus, Frankism and Hasidism arose in areas where the majority of Jews lived in villages and small towns, but in other eastern areas of Poland which did not immediately respond to Hasidism the Jewish population had a very similar rural-urban distribution.

Most Jews in Polish villages were either arrendators, who leased the rights from the nobles to produce and sell alcohol, bread, and milk, or their employees. Only from 10–15 percent of village Jews were not involved in leaseholding, innkeeping, or bartending. A small proportion of the arrendators, who leased directly from the nobles, were wealthy, but the economic situation of the vast majority of arrendators, many of whom were subleaseholders, was no better than that of the peasants. The economic state of the urban Jewish population was little better, but the urban Jews differed from the rural Jewish population in their occupational distribution. A large section of the Christian urban population was involved in agricultural pursuits, whereas the two largest Jewish urban occupational categories were the merchants, mainly medium and small merchants, peddlers, and hawkers, and the artisans. The small towns had a lower proportion of merchants than the large towns, about the same proportion of artisans, and a larger proportion of leaseholders and publicans. In the Ukraine the proportion of artisans and merchants was much less than it was in central and western Poland; a very large proportion were leaseholders and publicans, not only in the small towns but also in the medium-sized towns. The only other area in Poland with a similar Jewish occupational distribution was Belorussia: a census in 1794–95 found that about one-half of the Jews with occupations in large towns and three-quarters in small towns were leaseholders and publicans.[7]

Unlike the nobles, many of whom lived away from their estates, the Jews lived in close proximity to the peasants, and since they served as the middlemen and agents of the nobles, the peasants often vented their frustrations on them. This was particularly true in the southern provinces of Podolia and Volhynia, where class tensions overlapped with ethnic and religious differences: the nobles were Roman Catholic Poles, whereas the peasants were Orthodox Ukrainians. These were also the areas of the Cossacks, a semimilitary, semipeasant class with its own autonomous structure. The Polish government had given the Cossacks the task of warding off Tartar attacks, but the Cossacks had become the spearhead of Ukrainian peasant rebellion and political banditry. During the 1648 massacres, when about a quarter of Polish Jewry was destroyed, the toll among the Jews in the Ukraine was particularly heavy. In the eighteenth century the southern provinces, and to a lesser extent Belorussia, were subject to the attacks of the Haidamaks, rebel bands composed of Cossacks and peasants who often came from the Russian side of the Ukraine. The attacks increased in the 1730s and reached a climax in 1768 when many thousands of Jews and Poles were massacred in the town of Uman.

In addition to the pogroms, which destroyed whole communities in Podolia and Volhynia, other developments deepened Jewish suffering and insecurity. The number of ritual murder trials grew and became particularly numerous from the 1730s to the 1750s. Economic restrictions introduced by the clergy, town burghers, and merchant guilds forced many Jews out of the towns. The migration of Jews to the villages increased the competition for leases and provided the nobles with an opportunity to increase rents. The situation was exacerbated by the poorer nobles, who saw leaseholding as a means of retaining some measure of gentility. Lacking any means of livelihood, many Jews joined the increasing numbers of wandering, destitute Jews and bands of Jewish robbers. At the same time that Jewish income was declining, the authorities imposed enormous tax burdens on the Jewish communities. All these external pressures contributed to the weakening of the Jewish kehillot and the growth of tensions within the communities.

After a period of decline the central and regional Jewish communal autonomy came to an end in 1765 with the dissolution of the Council of the Four Lands. The local autonomy of the kehillot remained, but this had also been greatly weakened. To pay the tax burden the kehillot borrowed from the nobles and the monasteries, and in their state of great indebtedness they could do little to defend the interests of their members. In the past each kehillah had regulated the right of residence and had imposed all kinds of restrictions on nonresidents, but the pogroms, general insecurity, and its own weakened state prevented the kehillah from stemming the influx into its community. The kehillot also lost their authority in the regulation of competition between the arrendators. The nobles opposed such regulation, since it was a constraint on the raising of rents through competition, and they were able to counter it effectively by supporting individual arrendators against the kehillah.

The kehillot were especially weak in the regions of southeast Poland, and their failure to protect and regulate the large number of arrendators was particularly evident in those areas. More generally, the failure of the kehillah to fulfill the tasks that gave it legitimacy made it appear a purely exploitive body concerned only with the imposition and collection of taxes. The literature of the period included many complaints against the kehillah, its fiscal measures, its economic settlements, and its administration of justice. The literature also points to considerable tension within the community: a lack of cooperation and conflict between members; the emergence of individuals who lied and cheated, in contradiction to the mitsvot; and an increase in unjust acts by the rich. While the majority were falling into poverty, a new stratum of rich Jews, who owed their position to their contacts with the nobles, rose to prominence. These "court favorites" often imitated the nobles in their ostentatious way of living and contempt for their subjects. The weakened communities were less able than they had been in the past to oppose the imposition of the nobles' favorites upon them, and a decline in the number of electors strengthened the oligarchy in Jewish communal government.

Internal opposition within the kehillah was not a new phenomenon, and many regulations existed to prohibit public criticism of the kehillah's activities and prevent the undermining of its decisions or disrespect toward its leaders. The reformulations of and additions to these regulations, together with the increase in penalties and sanctions, point to the strength of opposition in this period and the failure to suppress it. In the towns the *hevrot* (societies), particularly those of the artisans, tried to increase their autonomy from the kehillah and defend the individual against its pressures. The kehillah, in its turn, tried to prevent the formation of new hevrot and took action, such as forbidding additional members, against those already in existence. In a number of towns, especially in Belorussia and Lithuania, the artisans, who were excluded from the electorate, actively resisted the kehillot and attacked their offices.

Opposition was also expressed against the official rabbis, many of whom were closely associated with the court favorites and whose status had greatly declined. The standard of education in the yeshivot had fallen, and it had become possible to purchase ordination and a rabbinic position. In a number of cases Christian authorities were bribed to appoint particular men as rabbis. There were relatively few respected rabbis in Podolia: the province had never recovered from the toll on its religious leadership in the 1648 massacres, and in the eighteenth century scholars preferred the talmudic centers of the north to the intellectual wastelands of the south. Over the whole country the religious distance between the rabbinic elite and the masses had widened: the religious discussions and pilpul of the rabbis were remote from the daily life of the masses, and many rabbis spurned or berated the people for their failure to observe their strict demands for religious observance.[8]

In summary, Frankism and Hasidism emerged during a period of widespread suffering and social disorganization. While adverse conditions were widespread throughout Poland, the situation in the southeastern provinces was particularly acute. The attacks of the Haidamaks, the weak state of the kehillot, the impoverishment of the large proportion of arrendators, the disruption of traditional norms of status, and the absence of an effective religious leadership made these areas particularly receptive to the religious teachings of charismatic leaders.

Religious Leadership and Teachings: The Frankist Movement

Joseph (Jacob) Frank was born in a small town in Podolia. His father was a contractor and merchant, a respected Jew and observant of the laws. Although his father sent him to a *heder* (religious school), Frank gained little religious knowledge. At the age of twelve, Frank went to Bucharest, and after a period as a servant in the house of a Polish Jew, he became a merchant in cloth and precious stones and traveled to Constantinople and Salonika. Frank's contact with Sabbatianism began in his youth, and during his stay in Salonika he became involved with Baruchiah.

Frank attracted his largest following in Podolia, but his leadership was also acknowledged by many Sabbatians in other parts of the Ukraine, Galicia, Hungary, Bohemia, and Moravia. Encountering the official Jewish community's excommunication and persecution of Sabbatians, the Frankists in Podolia sought the protection of a Catholic bishop, but after the death of the bishop and the renewal of persecution, Frank and many of his followers fled to Turkey. Following a royal decree of protection in 1758, the majority returned to Podolia and gathered in and around the small town of Iwanie, where Frank himself arrived in 1759. In an attempt to seek further protection the Frankists declared to the king and ecclesiastical authorities that they were prepared to accept baptism if they would be allowed to retain many of their Jewish customs, such as Jewish garb and the prohibition on eating pork, and retain their separate existence by inmarriage and settlement in a special area in east Galicia. The Polish authorities refused this request, but in 1759 they organized a public dispute in Lemberg between the "talmudists" and the "contra-talmudic" Frankists.[9] The major outcome of the dispute was the baptism of Frank and more than five hundred of his followers, nearly all from Podolia.

Although Frank waged an open struggle against the rabbis, neither he nor the majority of his followers had intended to become Christians, and conversion was initially a way to avoid persecution. Few Frankists outside Podolia converted, and according to Scholem, even in Podolia most Frankists remained Jews, although they continued to recognize Frank as their leader. Catholic priests were suspicious of the genuineness of the conversions, and on the basis of confessions that revealed that the Frankists saw their leader as an incarnation of God, they had Frank arrested in Warsaw in 1760 and exiled to the fortress of Szestochowa under the jurisdiction of the church. During Frank's imprisonment, which lasted for twelve years, a group of his followers settled near the fortress and continued to practice their special rites and devotion to Frank. After his release by the Russians in 1772, Frank continued his leadership in Bruenn (Brno) in Moravia until 1786, and then in Offenback, near Frankfurt, until his death in 1791.[10]

The major religious components of Frankism were Frank's divine status, millenarianism, and antinomianism. Frank taught that the world had been created not by God but by an evil force, which blocked the road to the hidden "Good God" or the "Great Brother," who had no link with creation. Frank referred to himself, and was recognized by his followers, as the true messiah, the messenger of the "Great Brother," and as a living embodiment of this true God's power. He was a despotic leader who demanded absolute obedience, and he imposed various sanctions, including corporal punishment, for disobedience. His claims to divine status were reinforced by his widespread reputation as a great sorcerer and the tales of his magical deeds. Alongside his own divine incarnation, Frank emphasized a female component of the divine, and Christian influence is evident in his reference to the Shechinah as the "maiden" or the "virgin." The maiden was worshiped in the form of Frank's wife and, after her death in 1770, in the form of his daughter. In Iwanie, Frank appointed twelve "brothers," who were considered his major disciples, and twelve "sisters," who mainly served as his concubines.

Frank taught that the Good God would reveal himself and his Torah only through the destruction of all that exists in the present world. Since the world was created by an evil power and was enslaved by unjust laws, the laws of death, the road to life was through nihilism, the rejection of all religions and morals. Destruction was a force of redemption; it was a necessary descent in order to ascend. Men had not only to abandon all religion and laws but also to perform "strange deeds," which were intended to negate man's self-respect. Sin became sacred, and among the Frankists, as among other antinomian groups, this principle was expressed in deviant sexual behavior and orgiastic rites. Frank emphasized that redemption would be achieved through sin only if it was performed in secret. Christianity could, therefore, be used to conceal their true beliefs: members could outwardly demonstrate their Christian allegiance, but they were forbidden to intermarry or mix with Christians. Baptism, the lowest point of the descent into the abyss, was the prelude to the ascent.

Frank expected a "great war," a general revolution and a renewed world in which he and his followers would rule over an autonomous Jewish territory with great wealth. Frank promised his followers that they would replace the wealthy Polish nobles as the aristocracy: they would have princely titles and wear swords and beautiful clothes, while the Polish nobles would become poor cobblers and tailors. In his millenarianism, Frank also deviated from the traditional Jewish beliefs: it was not Israel but

Poland which was the promised land for the future Jewish state. The French Revolution, in which the destruction of existing laws became a real historical event, was taken as a sign of the truth of the Frankist beliefs, but after Frank's death the sect dropped its radical beliefs. Some believed that the messiah would come through the transmigration of Frank's soul, but the nihilistic theories and the demands to sin were discarded, and Christianity became for the baptized Frankists their true religion rather than a cover for their secret religion. Frank's teaching on revolution and on Poland as the chosen land encouraged the participation of the baptized Frankists in Polish culture and patriotic revolutionary activities and made them receptive to assimilation into Polish society.[11]

Religious Leadership and Teachings: Hasidism

Reliable information on the biography of the founder of Hasidism is scarce and is difficult to disentangle from the legends that quickly grew around him. The Besht communicated his teachings orally, and we know his teachings only through the works of his disciples, particularly Jacob Joseph of Polonnoye, who published the first Hasidic book in 1780, twenty years after the death of the Besht. The legends, no doubt mixed with factual material, were collected in the book *In Praise of the Besht*, published in 1815, fifty-five years after his death.[12] Some historians have used this book as a major source, but although the book indicates the nature of the Besht's appeal, it cannot be relied upon as a factual source. It included events and behaviors that are common in the biographies of many religious founders and reformers. A prominent feature is solitude: the Besht is said to have sat alone in the forest in his youth, and legend relates that it was during a long period of solitude in the high Carpathian mountains that the true mysteries of God were revealed to him.[13]

The sources on the Hasidim written during the lifetime of the Besht are few, and the references to the leader of the movement are somewhat ambiguous. Problems with the sources have led one historian to argue that Israel ben Eliezer was not the original leader,[14] and another to claim that the Besht was a legendary figure who raised no great interest in his lifetime and had no important influence on the development of the movement.[15] There can be no doubt that the Besht's reputation grew and spread after his death, but Scholem's careful analysis of the sources shows that the Besht was a charismatic leader during his lifetime.[16]

Israel ben Eliezer was a Ba'al Shem (Master of the Name), a folk-healer whose knowledge and use of divine names, together with other techniques, such as the use of herbs, was believed to work cures and exorcise demons. He became known as a Ba'al Shem Tov (Master of the Good Name), but the appellation Tov was also used with regard to other Ba'alai Shem. It was unusual for a Ba'al Shem to teach particular religious doctrines or to have any religious influence on the people on whom he worked his cures, but from the beginning of his activity among the people, sometime between 1730 and 1738, the Besht was accepted as both a magical healer and a religious teacher, a man of vision who wished to spread his beliefs on the correct way to come close to God.

A central focus of the teachings of the Besht and his disciples was *devekut*, the cleaving or adhesion of man to God. In pre-Hasidic cabbalistic thought devekut, in the sense of communion rather than union with God, was an extreme ideal, the last step in the ascent to the divine of those rare men who could attain such heights. Hasidism made devekut more immediate and accessible. Some Hasidic teachings held that every Jew was capable of directly cleaving to God. However, the more prevalent notion among the early leaders was that there was a fundamental difference between the devekut of ordinary people and the devekut of the spiritually endowed. The divine was directly accessible to the latter only, but the masses could achieve the heights of devekut if they cleaved to these spiritual men.

For the spiritual elite devekut was attainable not only through specifically religious acts, such as prayer and study of the Torah, but also through everyday activities such as eating, drinking, sexual relations, earning a living, storytelling, and traveling. Any act, including those concerned with physical pleasure and the achievement of material needs, became a religious act if the intention was to cleave to God. "Worship through corporeality," religious achievement through involvement in the concrete, material world, was a radical notion in Judaism, but the Hasidim did not draw antinomian inferences from the doctrine.

The Hasidim believed that devekut was achieved in a spirit of joy. Although joy as a religious value is found in pre-Hasidic cabbalistic literature, the Hasidic emphasis on joy and opposition to asceticism represented an important change of emphasis in Judaism. The Besht taught that joy indicated complete belief and trust in God, whereas fasting, self-affliction, and sorrow expressed an ingratitude to God and were impediments to cleaving to the divine.

Devekut through material and physical activities was possible because of the immanence of God in all creation. Although pantheistic tendencies were present among the early Hasidim, many scholars prefer to designate the Hasidic belief as panentheistic: God and the universe are not identical but God's divine power emanates into the world so that everything is included and embodied within God. The divine is hidden in the garments and barriers of the material world, but everything is created out of God's essence. Even sin and the pleasures derived from it are derived from God. The immanence of God had been expounded by a number of important Jewish mystics and cabbalists, but the direct and enthusiastic forms in which it was expressed by early Hasidism were something new.

In expressing God's immanence the Hasidim took a number of cabbalistic ideas and terms and attached different meanings and emphases to them. A major Lurianic idea was that many divine sparks had fallen into the sphere of evil and that the religious actions of Jews contributed to the returning of the sparks to their divine source. The Hasidim turned away from the Lurianic emphasis on the evil spheres and emphasized instead that every object and activity contained a spark of divinity. In contrast to the traditional dualistic beliefs of a division between the realms of good and evil, between the spiritual and the material, Hasidism presented a monistic system in which absolute evil had no independent existence and in which the spiritual was only a higher level of the material. Sin, punishment, hell, and the devil were minimized. It was the task of man to uncover or penetrate the appearance of evil in order to see and have contact with the real. The Besht taught that man could lift up the divine sparks only through contact with, and transformation of, the material world; a descent into evil was a necessary precondition to an ascent to the good.

The links between the belief in the immanence of God, the insistence on joy, and the practice of devekut in everyday affairs are clear, but religious experience was not seen as uniform; it took deeper and more ecstatic forms on certain occasions, particularly during prayer. The proper form of prayer, involving intention, contemplation, joy, and enthusiasm, was regarded as the ideal means to achieve devekut. The Hasidim retained the traditional prayers, but they differed in their techniques and mystical interpretations of the prayers. The need to be in the right frame of mind for prayer, to clear the mind of unworldly thoughts and the body of impurities, was considered so important that the halachic rules for the special times of prayer were sometimes overlooked. As an aid to concentration and as an expression of their joy, the Hasidim engaged in highly demonstrative movements during prayer. Swaying movements during prayer were widespread among Jews, but some Hasidim went much further by shouting the prayers, throwing themselves around the prayer house, and whirling and turning somersaults. The heights of ecstasy that could be attained in prayer were expressed by some Hasidim in erotic terms such as "copulation" with the Shechinah.

The method of the Besht to achieve devekut in prayer was by "attachment to the letters": one contemplated and meditated on each letter until they lost their contours, and their concreteness dissolved; then the divine attributes became visible, and the soul cleaved to God. Since the letters of the Hebrew alphabet were endowed with creative power, Hasidic prayer could participate in and assist the process of divine unification.

The centrality of prayer in Hasidism represented a restructuring of the hierarchy of Jewish religious values. Mystical fervor was considered more important than scholarship, and scholarship without devekut was worthless. The view of Menahem Mendel of Peremyshlany (born 1728), a disciple of the Besht, that the study of the Torah and religious devotion were incompatible was not typical, but many early Hasidim challenged the notion that religious study was the major religious value, and some argued that too much study might interfere with the attempt to achieve devekut. In the teaching of the Besht, the technique of attachment to the letters applied to study as well as prayer. Since by this technique the text was atomized and the literal meaning lost its importance, study became a contemplative rather than an intellectual pursuit. To approach the Torah with love and enthusiasm was more important than to learn its precise meanings. With regard to the mitsvot the early Hasidim adopted a lenient approach and stressed that it was quality rather than quantity that was important. If a man fulfilled only one commandment but did so with kavanah and cleaving to God, it was as though he had fulfilled all the commandments of the Torah.[17]

It is difficult to say what part of the appeal of the Besht derived from his curing and exorcising and what part from his teachings. One of his first disciples, R. Arye Lieb (died 1770), was attracted by the Besht's miracles rather than by his teachings. There can be little doubt that the Besht's reputation for miracle making was accepted as an important proof of his charisma and his teachings. The first Hasidic book on the life of the Besht puts great emphasis on his magical powers: he exorcises and banishes demons, he makes wondrous cures, he brings an end to a period of drought, his amulets offer great protection, and he is able to see into the future and into a man's secret past.[18]

Later Hasidic literature did not doubt the Besht's magical powers, but it did try to erase the image of the Besht as a professional magician and to emphasize instead that he was a great scholar. It is clear, however, that the Besht never abandoned his magical activities and that he was a comparatively unscholarly religious teacher who taught by means of simple stories and parables. Although the Besht had no qualifications or aspirations to be a brilliant scholar, he was not an ignoramus; he was familiar with the basic religious literature, he was not opposed to learning, and he tried with some success to obtain the support of some scholars. The scholars among his disciples did not expect from him new or original interpretations of the Halachah; they looked upon him as a pneumatic whose direct communication with the divine enabled him to preach fundamental truths without the benefit of scholarship.

The immediate circle of the Besht believed that he had exceptional spiritual qualities, and they reported that light and fire emanated from him, especially when he prayed. The special qualities ascribed to the Besht were not necessarily regarded as unique, and several of the Besht's associates saw themselves as charismatic in their own right; they had their own followings and viewed the Besht as an equal or even as a rival and inferior to themselves. The relationship of the masses to the Besht is difficult to evaluate on the basis of the available sources. The Besht was certainly well-known outside his circle of disciples, and it is reported that his clientele became so large that he had to employ a full-time scribe and, in later years, two scribes. However, the majority of the Jewish population in Podolia joined the Hasidim sometime after the death of the Besht.[19]

Little evidence remains of the religious background of the Besht's close disciples and followers, but it is clear that some were known as hasidim before they came into contact with the Besht. In the first half of the eighteenth century a number of small groups of pious men known as hasidim came together to pray, study, and perform the mitsvot. These groups had no prominent leaders and little influence on the public, and they varied widely in their religious character: ascetic and ecstatic, learned and unscholarly, halachic and cabbalistic, traditional and Sabbatian. The ascetic groups, which were found in most Jewish communities, emphasized fasting, repentance, and study, and they had little in common with the Hasidism of the Besht. The nonascetic groups, some of whom were Sabbatian, held many beliefs and practices that became associated with the Hasidic movement: shaking the body, enthusiastic dancing and singing, and a communal Sabbath meal. For the most part, Hasidism did not introduce new ideas and practices, but rather popularized and spread certain cabbalistic ideas and enthusiastic practices that formerly were found only in small circles.

It was particularly from the nonascetic groups that the Besht drew his first disciples and followers, although he also attracted a number of men who had not formerly been hasidim.[20] The Besht converted a number of ascetics to his religion of joy, but some of the ascetic, scholarly groups repulsed or opposed him. A story in the collection *In Praise of the Besht*, although possibly apocryphal, points out that to attract scholars the Besht had to demonstrate that he was above his profession as magician. The story tells that when the Besht came to the town of Medzibezh the hasidim of the town regarded him as unimportant, since they considered that the name *Besht* was not an appropriate one for a pious man. After the Besht demonstrated his knowledge of heaven and his foreknowledge of who would be sent there, the group accepted him as their leader.[21] The Besht had less success among scholarly circles in other towns.[22]

The successor to the Besht, Dov Baer (1710–72), was the son of a poor teacher in Volhynia, but in contrast to the Besht, he became an erudite scholar of the Talmud and the cabbalah.[23] Following a period of employment as a teacher in a small village, he became a *maggid* (preacher), and after the death of the Besht, he settled in Mezhirech, where he attracted many young scholars, rabbis, and cabbalists. Dov Baer was not a folk-healer or miracle-worker, his teaching was more sophisticated than that of the Besht, and he was stricter in his religious practice. His preaching on Sabbaths attracted large audiences, but his greatest influence was on his circle of close disciples, whom he taught on Sabbaths and weekdays in his house.

Dov Baer continued the immanentism and monism of the Besht, but he gave the Hasidic ideas greater depth and complexity by relating them in novel ways to cabbalistic concepts. Dov Baer taught that the divine both permeates his creation and exists beyond it, and that matter is the lowest of all levels, the "dross" in the divine hierarchy. He interpreted *zimzum* (contraction) not as the divine regression of the Lurianic cabbalah but as a necessary means of emanation in the creation of the world and of man's apprehension of the divine. God contracted himself not in the sense of leaving an empty space for the world but in the sense that he weakened his infinite light through barriers and veils. The world could not have borne directly the monumental impact of the divine light, and man was unable to comprehend or express the essence and infinity of God. As a result of the divine zimzum, man could understand God in the biblical sense of the Lord God (Adonai or Elohim). Just as man can look at the sun only through a filter, so the light of divinity can be received only through a veil in the form of Elohim. The breaking of the vessels was part of the divine plan from the beginning; it was not a cosmic catastrophe but a stage in the emanation of the divine into the world.

Dov Baer expressed a common theme of religious mystics when he argued that union with the divine could be achieved only if man put himself, by extreme spiritual concentration, into a state of "nothingness," completely extinguishing his reflective consciousness. When the worshiper reached a state of passive receptivity, it was possible for the divine to govern his speech and speak through his mouth. This should be distinguished from glossolalia, for the words uttered are the fixed Hebrew prayers. Dov Baer had no wish to change or abandon the traditional prayers, but his view that the object of prayer was to escape from materiality had to be reconciled with the petitionary prayers that entreated God to satisfy man's material needs. Dov Baer dealt with this problem by arguing that the purpose of petitionary prayer is not a request to God to satisfy personal needs but a means to satisfy the needs of the Shechinah, particularly in the role as giver.[24]

Social Base and Appeal

The major social carrier of Frankism and early Hasidism in Podolia and Volhynia was the impoverished, lower-middle class of rural and small-town Jews: the arrendators and their employees, innkeepers, bartenders, small shopkeepers, peddlers, hawkers, and the unemployed. Outside Poland the individuals and small groups of Sabbatians who accepted Frank as their leader tended to be wealthier and better educated than their fellow believers in Podolia. In Moravia and Bohemia, Frank's supporters included a number of upper-class families, important merchants, and state monopoly leaseholders. Frank's followers in Hungary included some important community members. Not all the Sabbatians in the countries under Austrian rule accepted Frank as leader, and of those that did, very few joined him in his conversion to Catholicism. Even in Podolia not all of Frank's supporters were ignorant and poor; they included a few rabbis of small communities as well as relatively comfortable merchants and craftsmen, such as silversmiths and goldsmiths.[25]

Some of the occupations the Besht is said to have had may have been the invention of the early legend makers, but they give an indication of the movement's social base: assistant to a village teacher, slaughterer, servant, watchman for a school, clay digger, and bartender. The Besht's major field of activity was in the villages and small towns of Podolia, and some evidence indicates that he was repulsed when he tried to perform his activities in one of the largest towns in the area.[26]

The rural arrendators were the most frequent characters to appear in the Hasidic legends about the Besht and his associates. Artisans, on the other hand, rarely appeared. The Hasidic legends also distinguished between the wealthy arrendators, who leased directly from the nobles, and the subleaseholders and taverners who were dependent upon them. Although most of the Besht's contacts were with the poorer Jews, he did attract some wealthy and powerful leaseholders.[27] The Besht and his disciples helped to organize relations between the arrendators, weaken the competition among them, and obtain the reduction of rents. Their success in this area depended not on legal procedures but on moral exhortation and the common belief that the magical power of holy men could be used to punish a transgressor.

The early Hasidim were also involved in the ransoming of arrendators. The Jewish middlemen were dependent for their revenue on their peasant clients, and when conditions prevented the peasants from fulfilling their payments, the Jews were unable to pay the nobles. The nobles used a number of violent methods to obtain their rents, but the most common was to imprison the leaseholder and to hold him to ransom. By performing such functions as the ransoming of prisoners, which the kehillot, in their weakened state, could no longer perform, the Hasidim attracted the common people, even if the people did not always fully comprehend the Hasidic religious innovations.[28]

The principal social carrier of both Frankism and early Hasidism was the Jewish stratum with the greatest amount of contact with the peasant masses. The question of possible Christian influence is a controversial one, particularly in relation to Hasidism, and requires some comment. The possible sources of non-Jewish influence may usefully be divided into two overlapping but distinguishable elements: the general folk-peasant culture and the more specifically Christian culture in both its Orthodox and sectarian forms. It cannot be denied that Hasidism incorporated elements of the peasant culture, but the Jewish movement often transformed the meaning of these elements, interpreting them through Jewish concepts and symbols. The most obvious example was the adoption of peasant folk tunes, which the Hasidim interpreted as containing divine sparks that could be lifted from the sphere of impurity of the gentile world. Other themes, such as the Besht's love of nature and horses, the importance of song and dance in religious gatherings, and the fondness for wine and tobacco, which were used by some to induce religious ecstasy, also indicate the influence of the peasant culture.

The influence of more specific Christian religious doctrines and forms, Orthodox and sectarian, is less clear. There has, however, been some speculation on this issue, particularly on the possible influence of the Raskol (Old Believers) and other Russian sects. The persecution of these sects in Russia led to an extensive settlement of sectarians in the Ukraine, generally, and Podolia, in particular, during the 1730s. In certain areas the sectarians represented a considerable part of the population, and the Jews appear to have known about them and to have had some contact with them. Before their conversion to Christianity the Frankists held to certain doctrines that were clearly reminiscent of both general and sectarian Christian beliefs: a divine triad, a female incarnation (the virgin), twelve apostles, and a messianic leader. The doctrine that one could profess any religion as long as one remained secretly faithful to the true religion was also found among the Dukhobors. Perhaps the Christian sect most resemblant of Frankism was the Khlysty, although no evidence directly connects the two movements. The members of this sect believed that by ecstatic singing and dancing they prepared themselves for the entrance of Christ into their souls. For most of its history the Khlysty was an ascetic sect with an emphasis on sexual continence and self-mortification, but the doctrine that the divine came to dwell in them led some groups in an antinomian direction. The Khlysty also venerated some of their leaders as Christs.

Parallels with Hasidic doctrines may be found in both Orthodox and sectarian Christianity. Russian Orthodox mystics taught that the most complete union with God could be achieved in joy and ecstatic rapture. Some sects also maintained the immanence of God and the union with God through prayer and observed the ecstatic forms of worship, such as shouting, clapping, jumping, whirling, leaping, and turning somersaults. However, these doctrinal similarities are beliefs that are found in most mystical movements and are too general to indicate any mutual influence. Moreover, while Christian influence on the ecstatic forms of worship cannot be excluded, it is more likely that the similarities are the consequence of a similar expressive response to a deprived condition rather than of direct cultural imitation.[29]

The belief systems of Frankism and Hasidism differed radically, but they can both be interpreted as having a compensatory function for the groups they appealed to. To the arrendators, publicans, and middlemen, who were subject to the gloom of impoverishment and the cruelties of persecution, Frankism offered the traditional compensations of millenarianism: a new society in which the Jews would be wealthy and politically independent. In addition, absence of religious knowledge and learning became a positive indication of status rather than an impediment to it. Frank, himself, boasted that he was an ignoramus. Not scholarship but a noble spirit was important.

The Frankists formed a spiritual elite who were obliged to destroy the traditional laws. However, only a small minority of Jews in Podolia were willing to follow Frank in his revolutionary abandonment of all laws and regulations. Antinomianism held an appeal to individuals from all social strata, and perhaps it had a special appeal to those scholarly Jews whose lives had been strictly and minutely regulated by the mitsvot, but who yearned for the free expression of their hitherto inhibited desires and impulsès. The total rejection of tradition opened up fantastic vistas of freedom of thought and action, but only a few were psychologically prepared to take this radical step. To follow Frank meant not only a radical resocialization but also a break with the Jewish community. Moreover, the freedom of antinomianism was a confined freedom: the Frankist rituals had to be observed in great secrecy, while outwardly one had to conform rigidly to the demands of traditional Judaism or, in the case of the converts, of Christianity.

The more abstract notions in Hasidism, particularly those adopted from the cabbalah, may have been little understood or even known among the mass of followers, but certain religious emphases in Hasidism help to explain its appeal to rural and small-town Jews. The emphasis on joy and ecstatic practices provided an emotional outlet and some respite from a world of increasing insecurity and poverty, and the sense of communion with God through ecstatic prayer or a spiritual intermediary was very comforting. Without any pretense to a deep knowledge of the sacred texts, the spiritually endowed were able to approach the divine in their everyday activities. Moreover, since it was recognized that not all men had the ability to attain devekut through contemplation, it was permissible to use stimulants such as alcohol. These remarks seem to suggest that Hasidism was a response to the relative deprivation of status among non-scholarly Jews and that they rejected status based on religious scholarship for status based on the ability to cleave to God.

But while this may account, in part, for the appeal of Hasidism among the Jewish masses, it does not help to explain why Hasidism arose in the eighteenth century. In the eighteenth century the rejection of religious scholarship as a religious value was a rather moot point, for the standards of the rabbinate had declined until a rabbinic ordination or position was no longer a guarantee of a man's scholarship. Jacob Joseph of Polonnoye (died circa 1782), himself a rabbi, criticized his contemporary scholars on a number of grounds. In the 1780 work *Toledot Ya'akov Yosef*, Jacob Joseph wrote that many scholars studied the Torah not for its own sake but to display their brilliance and knowledge and to attain fame and self-glory. He noted the rivalry and bitter quarrels between scholars, and he argued that the scholars' concern with their personal welfare led to their corruption and subservience to the rich, whom they flattered in order to achieve a good position and material advantages. Moreover, the scholars concerned themselves only with their own salvation and neglected the people, whom they viewed with contempt because they had little time to study and were ignorant of the details of the ritual code. Jacob Joseph believed that the division between the rabbinate and the people had dire cosmic effects: it led to a rupture within the divine forces.[30]

Benzion Dinur has argued that the early Hasidic movement was closely connected to the opposition to the official community. Most of his evidence points not to active opposition but only to the fact that the early

Hasidic leaders were not from the ruling elite and that their activities were outside the framework of the kehillah. We have no exact picture of the disciples of the Besht, but the majority appear to have been itinerant preachers, *shochetim* (ritual slaughterers), *chazanim* (cantors), and *melamdim* (schoolteachers). The Besht's disciples numbered two or three ordained rabbis among them, but the lower stratum of religious functionaries was clearly predominant. Some historians have particularly emphasized the itinerant, or "wandering," preachers as representatives of opposition within the Jewish community. In their preaching and writings they criticized the general moral decline, the injustices of the rich, and the absence of an effective religious leadership. Even if they had a stipend attached to an official position, most preachers were not able to make a living in a single community; they moved around the country giving sermons and living an insecure existence from the donations of their audiences. In general, although often regarded with honor, they did not have high status, and they lived at the same level as that of the Jewish masses. According to these historians, the itinerant preachers were encouraged to seek change in the social order because they were viewed with suspicion and treated as inferior by the rabbis.[31]

The importance of the wandering preachers in early Hasidism has been questioned by S. Ettinger. He finds no evidence that the majority in the Besht's immediate circle were wandering preachers. Moreover, some of his disciples gave up relatively stable positions to follow him, and some of the most prominent early opponents of the movement were also preachers. Ettinger also doubts that wandering preacher, as opposed to permanent preacher, was any special social category or that there was any sharp dividing line between an upper intelligentsia of rabbis and a secondary intelligentsia. Not all rabbis were connected to the ruling class, and some supplemented their incomes by performing the roles of ritual slaughterer or wandering preacher.[32]

However, these reservations do not fundamentally alter the picture of the Besht's disciples. There was a hierarchy of religious functionaries, even if it was not divided into two or three distinctive strata. The lines within the hierarchy were unclear, and it is often impossible to place an individual clearly and unambiguously at a particular level, but this does not alter the point that *most* of the early Hasidic activists were from the lower levels of the hierarchy. Although rabbis were not entirely absent from the early leadership, it is rare to find any movement that is totally homogeneous in the social composition of its following or its leadership; there will always be exceptions, but from a sociological point of view the predominance of a group or stratum is significant.

Even given this predominance of the lower religious functionaries in the early leadership of the movement, we still cannot conclude that Hasidism represented, or was closely connected to, the opposition within the community. The most rebellious and vocal opponents of the official community, the artisans in the large towns, remained largely outside the movement. Hasidism had no program to reform the kehillah, nor did it propose any radical restructuring of the social structure. Although the Hasidim criticized rich Jews for their lack of charity and irreligious ways, they made no suggestion that the division of wealth should be abolished or that the poor should take the place of the rich. Hasidic leaders involved themselves in the daily life of the people, but Hasidic teachings gave little importance to social matters, and in questions of livelihood they believed that man had to depend on the will of God, although this could be influenced by religious action.

Millenarianism or Mysticism

Frankism and Hasidism were two very different religious movements that arose in the same social milieu and drew their major support from the same social stratum. Whereas Frankism represented an open attack on the Jewish tradition, the Hasidim emphasized their roots in that tradition. With few exceptions, the Hasidim upheld the accepted talmudic and cabbalistic texts and observed the complex system of Jewish rituals.[33] The immanentism of the Hasidim, their emphasis on ecstatic experience as more important than religious study, their rejection of asceticism, their focus on joy, and their violent motions during prayer represented significant changes for East European Judaism, but most of these changes built on themes found in the Jewish tradition. Hasidism may be described as a revitalization movement, but in contrast to Frankism, it was neither a revolutionary nor a millenarian movement.

The place of messianism in early Hasidism has been a topic of dispute among historians. The early Hasidim repeated the traditional statements of the Jewish hope and belief in the coming of the messiah, but the question is whether they believed in and worked for the imminent coming of the messiah. A letter from the Besht to his brother-in-law which touches on this question has been subject to conflicting interpretations. The Besht wrote that in a dream he was taken by the teacher of Elijah to heaven, where he saw such wonderful things that he was afraid to write about them. In the lower part of heaven he saw the souls of the living and the dead, who expressed delight that the Besht had arrived in heaven. The Besht then entered the sanctuary of the messiah, and he asked the messiah when he would come to earth. The messiah replied: "By this you shall know: When your teaching—which I have taught you—has been revealed and spread in the world and the waters from your well have been scattered about." Dinur writes that this letter is the most important evidence to support his contention that Hasidism was, from the beginning, a messianic movement, preparing for the final redemption. Dinur argues that there are hints in the early Hasidic literature of the messianic nature of the movement, and he accounts for the absence of explicit messianic statements by the fear among the Hasidim that they would be accused of Sabbatianism.[34] Scholem, on the other hand, argues that the Besht was saddened by the messiah's reply, for he realized that the spread of his teachings would take a very long time. By relegating the coming of the messiah to the distant future the Besht contributed to the "neutralization" of messianic tension.[35] Dinur's point that the Hasidim believed that it was possible to shorten the period before the coming of the messiah does not contradict the evidence that the early Hasidim did not envisage an imminent millennium.

Part of Scholem's argument is that the presence of heretical millenarians, such as the Frankists, who were condemned and persecuted by the majority of Jews, suggests that Hasidism had to neutralize millenarianism if it was to become a popular movement. Isaiah Tishby questions this argument and shows that the areas in which Hasidism was popular also contained non-Sabbatian cabbalistic writers who calculated imminent dates for the coming of the messiah and propagated actions to hasten the advent. The presence of these cabbalists who opposed the Frankists but felt no need to reject millenarianism seems to belie the notion that Hasidism was compelled to keep a check on its millenarianism.[36] Although it is possible to agree with Tishby that Hasidism was not forced by its environment to neutralize messianism, the fact remains that it was the Hasidim, and not the millenarians, who obtained a popular following. The argument that Hasidism would have been less successful if it had not neutralized the messianic element is a persuasive one.

In contrast to millenarianism, the Hasidic emphasis on devekut, which could be realized everywhere at any time, represented a focus on the personal level of salvation. Although many Hasidim believed that absolute spiritual perfection had to await the coming of the messiah, they stressed the achievement of perfection that was possible in the unredeemed world. The action of "raising the divine sparks," which had messianic implications in the Lurianic cabbalah, was given individualistic connotations in Hasidism. Each man could lift the sparks that belonged to his soul, and by good deeds he encountered those sparks in his immediate environment—in his food, clothing, home, and business. A journey for an economic or other mundane purpose had a spiritual significance if the place to be visited contained a number of the individual's sparks which he could redeem.

Hasidism took the apocalyptic tension out of the lifting of the sparks, for in contrast to the Lurianic focus on the redemption of the sparks of the Shechinah from the spheres of evil, Hasidism emphasized the redemption of sparks attached to the individual soul. The salvation of each individual soul had to precede collective salvation, and this was bound to take a very long time.[37]

The focus on redemption *in* exile rather than *from* exile is particularly evident in the thought of Dov Baer of Mezhirech and many of his disciples. Such concepts as *galut* (exile) and *Zion* (the Holy Land) lost their concrete significance and were spiritualized: galut referred to the exile of the Shechinah in the material world, and Zion was identified with the Shechinah or Torah study. While the Land of Israel remained a central focus, Hasidism strengthened the general mystical tendency to see the Land of Israel less as the future site of the messianic kingdom and more as an eternal sacred place, a spiritual center, where pious Jews should settle to live the religious life and be buried in the sacred soul.[38]

Hasidism was not a millennial movement, but the question of its relationship to Sabbatianism remains to be discussed. The majority of Polish Jews had shared in the condemnation of the Sabbatian movement after the conversion of Zvi to Islam, but in Podolia and its environs Sabbatian groups continued an underground existence, and Frankism was only the last and most extreme of these groups. From 1694, Haim Molach propagated the idea of a new Torah in which all that had previously been forbidden was made a positive commandment. Molach gathered a following in Podolia, and a number of extreme Sabbatian groups were organized under his influence. Not all Sabbatian groups took an antinomian direction. Tensions and movements between traditional piety and antinomianism, between extreme asceticism and licentiousness, were sometimes found in a single group or even a single individual. In other parts of Poland the Sabbatian movement declined from about 1725, but the weak organization of the kehillot in Podolia meant that excommunication and other measures taken against the Sabbatians had little effect in that area.[39] The relative strength of Sabbatianism in Podolia was related to its proximity to Turkey, the major center of Sabbatianism. Podolia was under Ottoman rule from 1672 to 1699, and in the eighteenth century commercial relations continued between the Jews of Podolia and Turkey.

A number of Sabbatians in Podolia passed over to Hasidism,[40] but the argument that Hasidism grew out of Sabbatianism is not supported by the evidence. None of the major early Hasidim had been Sabbatians, and there were no mediators between the movements. Although the Besht praised certain works which, unknown to him, were written by Sabbatians, the Hasidim clearly expressed their opposition to Sabbatianism.[41] One

Hasidic legend relates that Sabbatai Zvi came to the Besht to ask for redemption. The Besht was afraid, for he knew that Zvi was a terribly wicked man. When the Besht was asleep, Zvi came to tempt him, but the Besht hurled Zvi to the bottom of hell, where he landed on the same place as Jesus.[42]

Certain Hasidic ideas bear a formal similarity to radical Sabbatian ideas, but Hasidism was successful in inhibiting their possible antinomian implications. One such Hasidic idea was the transformation of evil into good through the raising of "strange" or "alien" thoughts, such as those of a sexual nature, during prayer. The question of how to deal with alien thoughts had been a grave religious problem long before Hasidism, and teachers had proposed various ways to rid the self of the thoughts. The early Hasidic teachers believed that such thoughts were fallen sparks that could be saved, and the Besht taught that the thoughts should not be repulsed but should be "mended" and raised to their divine root. Visions of a beautiful woman, for example, could be traced to the divine root of beauty, and it was with this absolute beauty that the Hasid would seek to unite. However, this subject caused some confusion: while some thoughts were to be mended, others were to be rejected, and some of the Hasidic instructions differed little from non-Hasidic approaches.[43]

It was possible to conclude from the teaching on the transformation of alien thoughts that it was legitimate deliberately to arouse such thoughts in order to contribute to the process of redemption. Lieb Melamed of Brody argued that it was suitable during prayer for the worshiper to think of a woman standing before him, but most Hasidic teachers warned against intentional strange thoughts, since he might not be able to raise them and would descend further into evil. Hasidic leaders did not, however, distance themselves completely from the "sacredness of sin." Many argued, in the name of the Besht, that the Shechinah was found within sin. Jacob Joseph of Polonnoye wrote that worldly desires and the evil drive were a basis for spiritual desires and the love of God, that the pleasure from sinning was drawn from the fallen sparks, and that evil and sin were a "chair to the good." But Jacob Joseph defined as heresy the idea that one should deliberately commit a sin in order to be able to follow the obligation to repent. This idea had preceded Sabbatianism, but it had appeared in major Sabbatian works and was strongly connected to the messianic theme that stressed the importance of repentance as a necessary condition of salvation. The idea had also appeared in contemporary non-Sabbatian writings, and its clear rejection by the Hasidic leaders demonstrates their opposition to antinomian tendencies.[44]

The Sabbatian doctrine of the necessary descent of the messiah into the evil realm in order to fulfill his redemptive role corresponds somewhat to the Hasidic doctrine of the "descent of the zaddik." The Hasidic leaders taught that the zaddikim, the holy men who cleaved closest to the divine, had a duty to descend from their union with the divine in order to associate with and redeem sinners. The idea of the descent of the zaddik can be traced back to the Zohar, but in that work the descent occurs in the supernatural realm: after his death and before his soul rose to paradise, the zaddik descended into hell in order to save the souls of sinners. This idea continued to be discussed in cabbalistic works in terms similar to that of the Zohar up to the period of Hasidism, but certain works gave indications that a zaddik worked also to save the souls of living sinners. In Hasidism the descent of the zaddik was clearly set in this world, but in contrast to the Sabbatian messiah, the zaddik descended to the sinners and not to the sin. In order to raise the sinners with him, the zaddik had to retain his piety throughout. The descent carried with it great dangers, and the zaddik came only as close to evil as was absolutely necessary. According to Jacob Joseph, for the sake of the people the zaddik might have to commit an unintentional transgression. On other occasions the zaddik might be required to initiate a transgression, but these were carefully limited and circumscribed, and the zaddik derived no pleasure from them. For example, in order to mingle with the people, the zaddik neglected his study of the Torah, but he did this only if he had a possibility of helping the fallen.[45]

In summary, Hasidism was a redemptive movement which, although it criticized aspects of the society, directed its efforts to changing the individual rather than the society. The moderation of Hasidism, the fact that it kept millenarian and antinomian tendencies in check, was a precondition of its subsequent growth. The traditional East European Jewish society had been subject to strain, but its major religious and cultural features remained largely intact. It experienced no cultural disintegration that might have been favorable to a radical, transformative movement such as Frankism. Messianism had failed, and it had become associated with heresy and antinomianism, which were anathema to the majority. Certain Hasidic features, particularly the relative devaluation of religious study, aroused violent opposition in some areas, but most Hasidic ideas, including its attitude toward learning and its criticisms of rabbis, were also found in non-Hasidic writings of the period, including some that were accepted by the *mitnagdim* (opponents of the Hasidim). Opposition to the Hasidim arose because the Hasidim did not stop at preaching their ideas, but also put them into practice in religious cells outside the framework of the official kehillah.[46]

Previous mystical movements in Judaism began in closed elitist circles, and if their ideas spread to the masses, they did so only after a considerable period had elapsed and often in contradiction to the intentions and desires of their originators. From its beginnings, Hasidism was associated with the Jewish masses. In the full sociological sense of the term *movement* Hasidism was the only large mystical movement to appear in Jewish history. This can be explained, in part, by the social, economic, and religious background of the movement in eastern Europe, but this has to be supplemented by an analysis of the generative processes within the movement, particularly as they relate to the routinization of charisma.

10. Hasidism and the Routinization of Charisma

THE PROBLEM of this chapter is to account for the spread of Hasidism throughout eastern Europe in the last decades of the eighteenth century and first half of the nineteenth century. It is important to note, however, that apart from certain eastern areas of the Habsburg Empire Hasidism did not spread beyond the boundaries of the former kingdom of Poland. Following the partitions of Poland a small proportion of Hasidim in Posen and Pomerania came under Prussian jurisdiction, but the vast majority of Hasidim were found under three governments: Russia, the Habsburg Empire, and the semiautonomous Congress Poland.[1]

It is not difficult to understand why Hasidism did not spread into central and western Europe. Hasidism revitalized and strengthened the traditional culture, securing its boundaries and its distinctiveness from the non-Jewish culture. An introversionist orientation held no appeal to Jews in central and western Europe, where an ever-increasing number were moving from separateness to various degrees of cultural accommodation and social integration with gentile society. Progress toward civil emancipation in central and western Europe was uneven, but the clear trend from the end of the eighteenth century was a decline in segregation: freedom of residence enabled Jews to migrate to the cities and move out of the ghettos, and Jews displayed a high level of social mobility and entered a wide range of occupations. Moreover, the decline in the functions and social control of the semiautonomous Jewish communities meant that Jews were subject to fewer restrictions on their activities in the wider society.[2]

In contrast to this changing situation in central and western Europe, the place of the Jews in the social structure of eastern Europe remained basically unaltered: the Jews continued as a distinctive interstitial urban stratum in a feudal society. The Russian urban population rose slowly (from 4.4 percent of the total population in 1812 to 7.8 percent in 1851), and in those areas where the Jewish population was most concentrated, the Jews accounted for 75 to 80 percent of urban residents. The 1851 census found that 89.3 percent of the Russian population were peasants, 1.3 percent were nobles, 0.8 percent were "merchants" (members of guilds), and 6.8 percent were "townsmen." The census found that 3.2 percent of the Jews were in agriculture, 5.5 percent were "merchants," and 91.3 percent were "townsmen." About a quarter of the total Jewish population and more than a third in the towns were artisans, but only a very small proportion were involved in industry.[3] The occupational distribution in Congress Poland and Galicia was similar: very few Jews worked in agriculture, and the largest occupational categories were merchants (mainly middlemen and small shopkeepers) and artisans. About 80 percent of the population of Congress Poland in the middle of the nineteenth century lived in the countryside, but more than 80 percent of the Jews lived in urban areas and accounted for more than 40 percent of the entire urban population. A small minority of East European Jews were wealthy, but the vast majority lived in various degrees of poverty.[4]

Under all three authorities the Jews were subject to policies of segregation and discrimination, together with efforts to destroy their distinctive culture and force them to adopt one of the dominant cultures—Russian, Polish, or German. By law, the Jews were a distinct group, subject to limitation on residence, special taxes, and economic discrimination. The majority of Russian Jews were confined to the "Pale of Settlement," most of which comprised the provinces taken from Poland. In an attempt to weaken Jewish religion and culture, the authorities took measures to discourage Jews from wearing their distinctive dress, to prohibit the use of Yiddish in education, and to strip the Jewish communal organization of its authority and autonomy. The most extreme steps were taken in Russia, where many Jewish youths mutilated themselves to escape harsh recruitment and long service in the Russian army. The official policies of forced acculturation only served to strengthen the Jewish resolve to defend their culture and institutions.

A small minority of wealthy "privileged" Jews, who were exempt from the discriminatory laws and lived in the principal cities, supported the *Haskalah*, the Jewish Enlightenment, that spread from Germany to eastern Europe in the early years of the nineteenth century. The early East European *maskilim* (adherents of the Haskalah) adopted the German language and culture, but they espoused a more moderate rationalism than that of the German Jews; they stressed the need for scientific knowledge, but they were normally orthodox in their religious observance. From about the middle of the century they advocated the adoption of Russian or Polish culture, and the need for East European Jews to abandon their "ghetto culture." Even the moderate maskilim encountered fierce opposition from the traditionalists, and the reconciliation of the Hasidim and mitnagdim in the early nineteenth century was, in part, a defense against the exponents of enlightenment.[5]

The major social carrier of early Hasidism, the impoverished lower middle class, an intermediate class between the nobles and the peasants, remained the most important support of Hasidism in its spread throughout eastern Europe. Raphael Mahler has shown this in detail for Galicia. His analysis of official documents and Hasidic and non-Hasidic Jewish sources demonstrates that the major support for Hasidism came from the "simple masses" or petite bourgeoisie: the publicans, middlemen, shopkeepers, peddlers, and the poor without any occupation, the "beggars in rags." This class was dependent on the feudal economy, and its already precarious position was being further undermined by the policies of the absolutist governments and the slow but continuing encroachment of modern capitalism.

Under the Polish regime the landowners had rented out the right to manufacture and sell spirits to the Jews, but in Russia the production and sale of spirits was a government monopoly that was given to a few large rentiers, who were opposed to any competition from Jews. In the Polish areas Christian merchants and poor noblemen sought to take over the alcoholic drink business, and they encouraged the authorities to remove the Jews. The Russian government made some attempt to encourage Jewish agricultural settlements, but the major policy was to force Jews out of the villages by expulsions and by prohibiting the traditional Jewish rural occupations. In addition to the loss of the alcoholic drink business, they also became less involved in tax-farming and money-lending, as the state took over tax-collecting and commercial banks, to some extent, took over money lending. The development of local industry and the increase in tariffs in the nineteenth century impoverished many Jewish merchants, who had profited from the scarcity of locally produced goods. Hasidic stories frequently tell of those on the edge of hunger, of the burdens imposed by the authorities, of the sorrows of the galut. Few artisans are found in the Hasidic tales, and it is clear that they did not constitute a principal support of the movement. Some artisans, mainly from the small towns, were Hasidim, but the artisans from the larger communities tended to be either mitnagdim or more secular.[6]

Hasidism spread, however, over almost the entire range of Jewish occupations and levels of wealth and learning. The further it spread from its original centers in Podolia and Volhynia, the more heterogeneous the movement became in the economic, social, and educational standing of its members. Since it encompassed wealthy merchants and scholars, explanations that emphasize deprivation of either economic class or status are not sufficient. An analysis of the success of Hasidism must view the movement in relation to the social structure of eastern Europe and the position of the Jews within it, but an emphasis on the social background must be supplemented and interrelated with an analysis of those features of Hasidism which transformed its environment and contributed to its spread. These features are discussed below in the framework of the routinization of charisma.

The Zaddik

Following Weber's typology of religious leaders, the zaddik is best described as a mystagogue. Like the magician and prophet, the mystagogue has personal charisma, as opposed to the charisma of office of the priest. Unlike the prophet, whose charisma is based on his reception of divine revelation, the charisma of the mystagogue is largely dependent on his magical powers. Unlike the magician, the mystagogue has a special congregation around him. Weber wrote that dynasties of mystagogues had frequently developed on the basis of hereditary charisma, and he gave examples, such as the guru in India and the hierarch of Taoists in China.[7]

For the Hasidim the zaddik filled three interrelated roles: he was cosmic redeemer, redeemer of the individual soul, and protector of men from evil spirits and agent of change in the material conditions in this world. It was believed that in his cosmic role the zaddik rescued the divine sparks from their captivity within the material and evil world. The zaddik's devekut and tikkun influenced the higher spheres to work toward the concomitant redemption of the Jewish people and the cosmos. The cosmic role was often emphasized in the Hasidic religious writings, usually by the zaddikim themselves, but most adherents concerned themselves more with what the zaddik could do for their individual spiritual and material states. A central notion was the "descent" of the zaddik from the heights of his devekut to redeem the fallen souls of sinners. The soul of the zaddik and the souls of his followers were believed to be related, but the zaddik had to establish contact with his followers in order to raise and redeem their souls in his subsequent ascent to the divine. This secured the Hasidim a happy afterlife and a place in the "world to come." The personal connection between the soul of the zaddik and those of the sinners who had listened to him in this world continued after death, and the zaddik could, therefore, use his influence to prevent a sinner from being sent to hell. Perhaps even more important for most Hasidic groups was the ability of the zaddik to work miracles in this world; he could protect his followers against the multitude of evil forces and secure for them health, children, and a livelihood.

This belief in the zaddik as one who fulfilled all three roles crystallized in the third and fourth generations of Hasidism and represented an important focus for the stability and routinization of the movement. In the teachings of the Besht and Dov Baer the zaddik was an important idea, but it was not a central focus, and the zaddik as institution developed only after the death of the Great Maggid. A number of Dov Baer's disciples formulated an ideological basis for the preeminence of the zaddik, but many refrained from making the zaddik the center of their teachings. It was only in the following generation that the zaddik became the central focus of the Hasidic belief system and took on importance as the major institution of the movement.[8]

Whereas the portrayal of the zaddik in the Hasidic belief system underwent considerable change from the time of the Besht to the fourth generation, subsequent generations repeated and reinforced the beliefs about the zaddik with little change. The belief system of the Besht and his circle emphasized the distinctive qualities of the zaddikim, but the distance between zaddikim and other men in their teachings was undeveloped and qualified compared with that which developed later. The Besht believed that there were a number of steps in devekut and in raising thought to its divine source. The zaddik was able to ascend to the highest step, and he provided an intermediary for those men who were unable to achieve such heights. The prayer and actions of the zaddikim, including their everyday activities such as idle talk, represented the most important contribution to the tikkun of the cosmos, but neither tikkun nor devekut were restricted to the zaddikim. The common man could raise the divine sparks attached to his individual soul, and in moments of spiritual enthusiasm, he could reach an exalted level.[9]

Among the Besht's closest disciples, Jacob Joseph of Polonnoye wrote in most detail on the role of the zaddik. In his writings on the subject, which he presented as the teachings of the Besht, Jacob Joseph emphasized the role of the zaddik as a spiritual redeemer of Jewish souls. He believed that the zaddikim could fill the vacuum left by the absence of a genuine religious leadership and thereby cure the spiritual malaise of his time. He described the zaddik as a mediating principle, joining the people with heaven, from which they were otherwise set apart and opposed, and as a "channel," transmitting and clearing the way for the spiritual outpourings of heaven to the people. The zaddik appreciated that the concern of ordinary people with earning a living allowed them little time for religious study and prayer, and he descended to the people that they might have a chance to reach heaven by cleaving to him. It was the genius of the zaddik to be able to move between the higher and lower realms, and in his descent he was willing to endure suffering and expose himself to great danger for the sake of the people. In emphasizing the responsibility of the zaddik for the people, Jacob Joseph and other Hasidic leaders adopted the traditional belief in the organic unity of the Jewish people. The people and the zaddik were spoken of as body and soul, as body and head, or as representing the two halves of God's name, each incomplete without the other and each dependent on the other. The sins of the masses lowered the stature of the zaddik, and if the zaddik had sinful thoughts, these stimulated others to commit actual sins.[10]

As a Ba'al Shem the first Hasidic leader involved himself in the everyday concerns of those who believed in his powers, but Jacob Joseph did not envisage such activities as the curing of illnesses and the exorcism of dibbukim as part of the zaddik's role. In his concern to establish the Besht as a zaddik, a purely spiritual leader, Jacob Joseph may have wished to turn attention away from the fact that his teacher had been a Ba'al Shem.

Dov Baer of Mezhirech also conceived of the zaddik in almost purely spiritual terms. One of the Great Maggid's disciples, Israel of Kozienice, reported that Dov Baer said that the zaddik needs to pray for the health and livelihood of his followers, but the focus of Dov Baer's teachings on the zaddik clearly discounted any involvement in worldly affairs, and his disciples took care not to bother him with small everyday matters. Nor did Dov Baer stress the necessary involvement of the zaddik with the ordinary people to redeem their souls. He taught that the zaddik had to descend from his holy state in order to arouse repentance and good actions, but he believed that the zaddik could raise the masses without any direct contact with them.

Dov Baer drew an enormous gulf between the zaddikim and ordinary men, and he spoke almost exclusively of the zaddik in his cosmic role. He described the zaddik as the "foundation of the world"; God had created the world because of his love for, and expected pleasure from, the zaddikim. Everything that descended from the higher spheres to earth was brought by the zaddik, who could annul the decrees of God and call forth changes in the order of nature. The higher worlds depended on the zaddik, and what the zaddik did in this world affected the upper spheres. If, for example, the zaddik awakened love on earth, love was also awakened at all levels of the divine. The zaddik cleaved to God with great devekut, and unlike other men, he raised the divine sparks not only by his prayers, Torah study, and mitsvot but also by his everyday activities, such as eating and drinking. Dov Baer taught that the zaddik saw only the divine energy that sustains all things, and he was able to repeat the creative process in reverse: God created the world out of nothing, and the zaddik converted the creation back into divine nothingness. In his prayers the zaddik was able completely to immerse himself in divine nothingness, and he should not, therefore, have practical needs in mind when he prayed.[11]

While Dov Baer emphasized the cosmic role of the zaddik, his description of the zaddik's enormous supernatural powers provided an important ideological foundation for the institution of the zaddik which was established by the following generation. All the most difficult and important religious tasks, which had formerly been open to many men, became the exclusive preserve of the zaddik. For example, it was argued that only the zaddik should attempt to transform evil into good; the ordinary Hasid did not have the qualities to withstand the dangers of contact with evil and to enter a struggle the outcome of which could not be predicted or assured.[12] Many of Dov Baer's disciples concluded that the supernatural powers of the zaddik could and should be used to achieve worldly goals, and they found that an emphasis on the "practical" activities of the zaddik attracted a larger following. Thus, the magical activities of a Ba'al Shem were incorporated, both in practice and in theory, into the role of the zaddik.

The earliest and most important legitimation of "practical zaddikism" was written by the highly successful zaddik Elimelech of Lyzhansk (1717–87), a disciple of Dov Baer. In his book *Noam Elimelech*, which appeared two years after his death and was widely read among the Hasidim, Elimelech wrote that God had given the zaddikim powers to influence the higher spheres and determine the fate of men, both in this world and the next. Like Dov Baer, Elimelech saw an absolute gulf between the zaddik and ordinary men; the level of the zaddik, who was sanctified in the womb of his mother, was higher than that of the angels, and all the mercies in this world were due to the zaddik. Since men were not capable of withstanding the enormous power that would flow from the direct influence of God, divine power was mediated through the zaddikim.

Elimelech distinguished two types of zaddikim: the ascetic type removed himself from the world and concentrated on the purification and "correction" of his own soul, but the more important type concerned himself with the troubles of the Jews and called down benefits from the higher spheres to the world. Through his prayers the zaddik united with the Creator, but in his descent from the higher worlds the zaddik sacrificed his pure spirituality in order to identify with the ordinary individual, abolish his sins, and transform evil into good. If the zaddik were free of all sin, he would have no influence on a sinful world and would not be able to approach the level of ordinary men. In his mercy, God sent a small sin to the zaddik, enabling him to associate with ordinary men and bring about their personal redemption.

Elimelech taught that by the power of his prayers the zaddik provided his followers with health, children, and livelihood: he healed the sick, made barren women fertile, guaranteed success in business, provided protection from persecution, freed captives, and could even nullify a decree by God that a person should die. The zaddik would always be successful as long as his followers spoke of him with respect, believed fully in his powers, and supplied him with his material needs. To utter harsh words against the zaddik was equivalent to blasphemy, and if the zaddik was not successful in attaining the request of a follower, this was a sign that the follower's belief was not sufficiently strong. The followers' material support of the zaddik bound them to him, protected them from the evil inclination, and gave his prayers on their behalf a greater chance of success.[13]

While some zaddikim emphasized their spiritual roles to a greater degree than others, the majority of zaddikim involved themselves in the worldly goals of their followers. This was an important factor in the spread of Hasidism in eastern Europe. More accurately, this combining in the zaddik of the roles of mystic, redeemer, and magician was what drew the masses to Hasidism.

The zaddik is an unusual type of religious leader: a mystic who is active in the world. Weber noted that in its consistent form mysticism demands an absolute minimization of all activity. The mystic believes that he can become a passive vessel of the divine only if he avoids everyday mundane activities and every type of purposive behavior. This flight from the world would normally exclude any religious leadership or indeed any concern with the salvation of others. Receiving his material needs from the labors of others, the mystic believes that he is one of an elite and demonstrates no concern with the fate of the masses.[14] Ernst Troeltsch similarly noted that the mystic's concentration on his own spiritual perfection meant that he was not concerned with evangelization and organization. The only organized forms that mystics may adopt are loose and provisional, based on such needs as companionship, instruction, and protection from persecution.[15]

The typical other-worldly mystical orientation described by Weber was clearly expressed by Dov Baer, who taught that union with the divine could be achieved only if man put himself, by extreme spiritual concentration, into a state of "nothingness," completely extinguishing his reflective consciousness. The description of the zaddik as a superior man who achieved the highest levels of devekut by removing himself from all corporeality, annihilating the intellect, and becoming a passive vessel of the divine would appear to exclude the zaddik as the leader of an organized community. Dov Baer believed that the zaddik had a cosmic role the implications of which went far beyond his own spiritual perfection, but the contribution of the zaddik to the redemption of the cosmos remained an other-worldly activity. Dov Baer restricted his interaction with other men largely to his closest disciples, but he did concern himself with the spread of the Hasidic faith, and he sent some disciples to various areas to preach that faith. His emphasis on withdrawal from the material world was largely confined to the cosmic role of the zaddik during prayer and was not inconsistent with an interest in organization and evangelization. Nevertheless, if the disciples of Dov Baer had not extended the roles of the zaddik to include practical zaddikism, it is highly unlikely that Hasidism would have spread as fast and as widely as it did.

Despite his emphasis on practical zaddikism, Elimelech of Lyzhansk made a strict distinction in his writings between the zaddik and the magician: unlike the magician, the zaddik understood that he had no coercive power over the supernatural, and he marveled at his success, which he interpreted as answers to his prayers and not as the consequence of mechanical operations. However, this distinction had little relevance for the majority of Hasidim, whose devotion to their zaddik was based in large part on their belief in his thaumaturgical powers. A large proportion of Hasidic stories are miracle tales which tell of the satisfactory resolution of a Hasid's petition to his zaddik, who is described in hagiographic and mythological terms. The Hasidic tale, which developed rapidly after the institution of the zaddik had become fully established, was concerned with crucial events such as birth, marriage, illness, calamity, and death. Among the most common tales were those in which the zaddik healed the sick and fertilized barren marriages.[16] Those zaddikim who disclaimed any ability to work miracles or who argued that miracle making was not part of the zaddik's role were not always successful in stemming their followers' requests for health, wealth, and protection from evil spirits.

Bryan Wilson has pointed out that the demand for thaumaturgy, a demand for supernatural assistance which provides immediate personal relief from sickness, deprivation, or evil powers, is a persistent one among mankind. Thaumaturgical elements have declined in western religion in the nineteenth and twentieth centuries, but most new religious movements in premodern societies are likely to acquire thaumaturgical functions.[17] Among the East European Jews, untouched by the growth of empirical and rational explanation in western Europe, subject to an unrelenting persecution and pauperization, and suspicious of messianic pretenders, the appeal of the thaumaturge was great.

As it had in other important religious traditions, thaumaturgy had persisted in Judaism, but it had taken diffuse forms, it had lacked a center or community focus, and it had been practiced by ordinary people or itinerant magicians with little status or authority. The traditional religious leader, the rabbi, was a scholar, an interpreter of the law, and while some rabbis gained reputations as miracle makers, this had never been institutionalized within the rabbinic role.

With the rise of Hasidism thaumaturgical powers were now seen to be concentrated in the zaddik, a man who was the "foundation of the world," an intermediary who ascended to the highest spheres and descended to "repair" the world, a pneumatic whose spirituality and great devekut guaranteed the success of his prayers. Some zaddikim became official rabbis, but in most communities the rabbi continued to hold a separate office with exclusive authority over ritual matters. In his combined roles of mystic, redeemer, and magician the zaddik had a multiple appeal: the different sectors of the Jewish population could emphasize any of the roles according to their religious inclinations. More important, however, was the appeal of a combination of powerful roles that had formerly been separate and largely divorced from leadership.

The Court of the Zaddik

An important part of the process of routinization is the creation of an administrative staff and the stabilization of financial support. Weber wrote that it was not possible to meet the costs of permanent administration by booty, gifts, and hospitality and that the problem of transition from the original charismatic community to an administration concerned with everyday conditions was a more fundamental one than that of succession.[18] In Hasidism the locus of the routinization of finance and administration was the court of the zaddik. Like other Ba'alai Shem and maggidim (preachers), the Ba'al Shem Tov and his disciples had traveled from place to place, receiving gifts in return for their magical work, sermons, and other services. In later life the Besht settled in a community, but he continued to rely on gifts, and his residence did not become a court.

The zaddik was the center of a court which varied in size according to the number and wealth of his following. The majority of a zaddik's followers lived in the region close to his court, but adherence to a particular zaddik was not based solely on residence: it was not uncommon for a Hasid to follow a zaddik who lived some distance from his home rather than the zaddik in his immediate vicinity. The zaddik's court contained the living quarters for the zaddik and his family, including his married sons and daughters and their families, and his servants and guests, a synagogue and study room, a bathhouse with mikveh, kitchens, and stalls for his horses.[19] Some large courts were similar to self-sufficient manors with their own ritual slaughterers, carpenters, shoemakers, and other artisans and merchants. In addition to the members of his family the permanent members or staff of the zaddik included his personal servants, his children's teachers, cantors, officials, and, in a few cases, a court jester. The most important official was the *gabai*, who managed the zaddik's affairs.

A Hasid perceived a pilgrimage to the zaddik as a sacred obligation. The zaddik was often described in various terms reminiscent of the notion of sacred space: Zion, Temple, or the Holy of Holies. The Hasidim did not substitute the zaddik for the geographical Jerusalem or the Holy Land, but he was an additional locus of the divine presence, and his place of residence became an important sacred center. A song of the followers of Menahem Mendel of Kotsk included the chorus:

> To Kotsk one doesn't travel
> To Kotsk one may only walk.
> For Kotsk stands in the place of the Temple,
> Kotsk is in the Temple's place.
> To Kotsk one must walk as does a pilgrim.

The followers of Israel Friedman of Ruzhin described Sadegora, the later site of his court, as "the place of the Temple," and when Nahman of Bratslav arrived in Bratslav, his disciples saw the town as a new Zion.[20]

A Hasid tried to visit the court of his zaddik at least once a year. Most courts did not fix dates for visits, but followers were more likely to come to the court on a Sabbath or, more especially, on the High Holy Days and religious festivals. The court of a popular zaddik drew several thousand followers on the High Holy Days. On occasion women accompanied their husbands or traveled alone to the court, but the common practice on the important religious days of the year was for the male to take his sons, if they were old enough, and to leave his wife and other children at home. Most followers visited the court for a few days at most, but some stayed for longer periods; they supported themselves or lived on small contributions which they received from the wealthier visitors to court.

The most important event for a Hasid in his visit to the court was his private audience with the zaddik, and many would first purify themselves by prayer and study. On his arrival at the court a Hasid called on the gabai who, in return for a payment, wrote a *kvitl*, a short note, stating in a standard form the name of the petitioner and the nature of his problem or request. The gabai arranged a time for the audience and delivered the kvitl and an oral report to the zaddik. During his reception hours the zaddik had the notes before him, and when the petitioner appeared, he read the kvitl "in a high way" as opposed to "the simple way" of ordinary men. A number of beliefs developed around the kvitl; for example, there were dangers if it fell to the ground or contained written mistakes. Numerous kinds of problems and requests were brought before the zaddik. Advice and blessing were sought in such matters as the marriage of a child, family disputes, a separation or divorce, business matters, a change of job or residence, a journey, or a proposed cure. On those occasions when the petitioners were too numerous for the zaddik to see them individually the kvitls were collected for a general blessing. Kvitls were also sent by post to receive the zaddik's blessing and reply. Besides giving his advice and blessing, the zaddik distributed medicines and amulets, such as coins that he had blessed or cabbalistic formulas on parchment. Some Hasidim took the zaddik into partnership for important business ventures; in return for his blessing, the zaddik received a share of the profits.

In most cases a major source of income was the *pidyan* (ransom or redemption), a monetary contribution which accompanied the kvitl and which in some courts was placed on the zaddik's table together with the kvitl. As its name suggests, the pidyan had great symbolic meaning and value; it united the Hasid with his zaddik and was, therefore, necessary if the zaddik's prayer on the Hasid's behalf was to be heard by the divine powers. The amount of the pidyan was not fixed and was expected to vary according to the wealth of the Hasid, but there were regular methods of calculation. The amount was often a variation on the number eighteen, which is the numerical value of the Hebrew word for life. Alternative methods were calculations based on the numerical value of the name of the supplicant or the numerical value of the word for the particular request ("son," for example). It was supposed that the pidyan was given voluntarily, but a petitioner and the gabai would frequently bargain and argue over the amount.

The pidyan was a major source of income for most courts, but it was absent in some courts (for example, Radamsk), and in others (for example, Satmar) it was used primarily for charitable purposes. Sometimes, the gabaim collected regular yearly payments from supporters in their homes. A few zaddikim who had official rabbinic positions supported themselves in part from their salaries and fees.

A Hasid visited the court not only to submit his petition and obtain a private audience with the zaddik but also to meet other Hasidim, arrange business deals and marriages, and participate in the communal activities of the court. During the Sabbath the zaddik and his court observed four ritual communal meals: on Friday evening, on Saturday after the morning prayers, at dusk following the afternoon prayers, and late Saturday night.[21] These meals were restricted to males, and the women ate with the zaddik's wife. The zaddik, usually dressed in white, sat at the head of the table with his family nearest to him and the other Hasidim seated according to religious and economic status. The meals were generally gay occasions with drinking, singing, and dancing. An important ritual was the distribution of the zaddik's *shirayim* (remains). The zaddik was served extra large portions, but he ate only a little, and the remainder was divided among those present. The procedure differed in different courts. In some courts the zaddik cut his food into pieces and distributed some to "chosen ones," while the others present struggled to grab what remained. In other courts the zaddik handed out the shirayim to all those present, giving a piece to the nearest person, who passed it on to the next, and so on, until it reached the end. It was believed that the zaddik took the spiritual content on which he survived from his food and left intact the material content, which represented the promise of material benefits to his Hasidim. To take the zaddik's leftovers was a mitsva and a remedy for any trouble.

The most important part of a meal was when the zaddik "gave Torah," and this was usually a regular feature of the third Sabbath meal. The zaddik expounded his Torah with metaphors and parables, and he interpreted a quotation from the weekly portion of the Pentateuch in mystical and ethical terms. At the fourth communal meal, the *melaveh malkeh*, the Hasidim told and listened to the tales of Hasidic saints and zaddikim. Storytelling was also an important feature of the meal on the anniversary death of a zaddik, when the Hasidim celebrated the elevation of the deceased's soul with song, dance, drinks, and tales of his deeds.[22]

The routinized form of the Hasidic community provided many satisfactions for the individual Hasid. At a time when the traditional community organizations, the kehillot, were weakening, Hasidism provided an important focus for integration at local and regional levels. In their local *shteebels* (prayer rooms) the Hasidim gathered for prayer, study, and socializing, and in the courts the Hasidim were able to forget the restraints of everyday life, express their piety in song and dance, and enjoy the atmosphere of a constant Sabbath.

On the journey to the court and in the court itself the Hasidim created a form of society which Victor Turner has called *communitas*. Turner argues that the pilgrimage is an example of communitas, since it provides an interval from involvement in a life structured by roles and statuses; social differences are ignored and relationships become direct, immediate, and spontaneous. The pilgrimage brings together people from different statuses and areas, and structured social relationships are attenuated, if not eliminated.[23] The mixing of social strata was a feature of the annual pilgrimages to the zaddikim on the important religious holidays: wealthier Hasidim invited the poor to join them in their carriages, share their meals, and stay in their lodgings. In the courts and towns of the zaddikim, an atmosphere of informality prevailed.[24] The extent and mode of participation of the individual Hasid were largely unstructured: in most courts the Hasid was allowed to choose the times and frequency of his visits, and in communal prayers he could choose his pace, the pitch of his voice, and the degrees and form of bodily movement.

In certain conventions, such as the seating pattern during the ritual meals, the differences in rank were indicated, but the general tendency was to forget the social differences that prevailed outside the court and to indicate solely the distance between the zaddik and his followers. This distance was taken to an extreme by Israel Friedman of Ruzhin (1797–1850), who, for example, did not eat in public, but most zaddikim attempted to strike a greater balance between contact with and distance from their followers. In his description of the court of the Belz zaddik prior to World War I, Jiri Langer noted that during prayer the Hasidim would come no nearer than about eight feet to the zaddik because they believed that their thoughts of the material world would upset the zaddik's pure spiritual concentration. Langer also describes the Hasidic dance, in which the men formed a large circle by holding hands or by putting their arms around each other. The men danced a rocking step which gradually increased in pace and could last for hours until the dancers were exhausted. The Belz zaddik danced little, and then only on solemn festivals; when he danced, he danced alone, holding a palm branch or a parchment of the scroll of the law.[25] Thus, the pattern of dance expressed the cohesion and lack of differentiation among followers as well as the basic division between Hasidim and their zaddik.

Charismatic Succession

Weber wrote that the types of charismatic succession differ not only in their development in a traditional or legal-rational direction but also in the extent to which they retain the elements of "pure" charisma. For example, the personal element in charisma is more likely to be retained if a successor is designated by the members of an administrative staff, who are concerned to appoint a person endowed with charismatic qualities, than if he is chosen by hereditary succession or by charisma of office. Whatever form succession takes, the routinization of charisma can be a lengthy process. The death of the original charismatic leader may be a critical stage in the process, but it is unlikely that charismatic authority will be transformed immediately into the legal-rational form, and it cannot, by definition, immediately become traditional authority. Weber illustrated the slow process of depersonalization when he noted that in the early Christian church the bishop of Rome was believed to hold a precarious gift of grace and that only the bureaucratized church of modern history transformed the position into a charisma of office, differentiating between the office and the incumbent.[26]

Weber wrote that routinization is rarely free of conflict and that conflict between personal charisma and charisma of office or hereditary status is a typical process in many historical situations. Weber did not, however, consider in any detail the coexistence of and conflict between two principles of succession in a single movement or the gradual replacement of one principle of succession by another. The case of Hasidism illustrates these processes with respect to two forms of succession, designation of a disciple and hereditary charisma, which Weber noted were the most frequent forms of routinized succession.[27] Hasidism also illustrates the rare phenomenon of multiple succession: charisma was transferred from a single leader to a number of leaders, each with his own personal following, but all remaining within the broad frame of a single movement.

In the early generations of Hasidism the designation of a successor by followers took precedence over hereditary succession. The Besht had a son, Tzevi Hirsch, but there is no evidence that he was ever considered as a successor. A story in the first published collection of tales about the Besht relates that when the Besht was dying, his son was not able to understand what the Besht was saying to him.[28] The son was reported to lack the qualities required to assume his father's position. The successor to the Besht, Dov Baer of Mezhirech, was a comparatively late disciple of the Besht. His teachings differed from those of the Besht in a number of significant respects, and unlike other disciples, he never referred to the Besht as his teacher. Following the death of the Besht, it took a few years before the legitimacy of Dov Baer's succession was established, and even then only a few of the Besht's disciples accepted him as leader. Jacob Joseph of Polonnoye, who was among the most senior and closest of the Besht's disciples, at first opposed Dov Baer and came to accept his leadership only after it was firmly established.[29]

Dov Baer's succession appears to have been based not on the decision and approval of the majority of the Besht's other disciples but on the success of Dov Baer in attracting a large number of disciples, mostly young scholars, to his center in Mezhirech. The succession was legitimized by a story that the Besht had blessed Dov Baer and had made Dov Baer bless him in return,[30] but it is likely that this was invented after Dov Baer had already established his authority. Dov Baer's leadership did not, however, represent an important stage in the depersonalization of charisma. Most of his disciples revered him not principally as the successor of the Besht but as a man of extraordinary attributes whose every action had divine significance. A disciple, Aryeh Leib Sarahs (1730–91), expressed this well when he said that he went to visit Dov Baer not to learn the Torah from him but to watch him tie his bootlaces.

Dov Baer attracted a heterogeneous body of disciples who varied greatly in their social backgrounds, beliefs, and scholarship. After his death, these differences caused the disciples to draw apart and disperse to different parts of Poland, many to those areas where they were already known through their propagation of Hasidic teachings. A number of the disciples succeeded in attracting followings and established themselves as zaddikim.

The gathering of a following around a zaddik was clearly dependent on the recognition of a "pure" type of charisma, but a claim to be a descendant or a disciple of the Besht or Dov Baer was an important reference of legitimation, and most of the zaddikim of the third generation Hasidim were disciples of the first two Hasidic leaders, especially of Dov Baer.

Abraham "the Angel" (1741–76), the son of Dov Baer, was a solitary ascetic who had no desire to organize a movement or attract a large following. Abraham clearly had himself in mind when he wrote of the type of zaddik who is at such a high spiritual level that he is unable to descend to the level of the masses, who cannot tolerate such spiritual perfection. Yet he did not oppose those disciples of his father who became Hasidic leaders, for he recognized the legitimacy of the zaddik who descended to the people in order to provide them with a path to the divine.[31] In contrast, Baruch ben Jehiel (1759–1810), a grandson of the Besht, established himself as a zaddik in Medzibezh, the Besht's former community, and claimed that he was the single legitimate leader of all the Hasidim by right of his descent.[32] This claim was not recognized outside Baruch's own following, but a general belief that succession to the position of the zaddik was a matter of inheritance spread among the zaddikim and their followers.

There was no early agreement among the Hasidim over whether one was born a zaddik or could achieve that status by his religious efforts. Moses Hayyim of Sadylkow (c. 1740–1800), a grandson of the Besht, argued that God had made the zaddik as a special creation and that he was governed by rules and laws that were different from those that governed ordinary people. In contrast, Nahman of Bratslav (1772–1811), a great-grandson of the Besht, attributed his status as zaddik to his religious achievements, especially his fasting and self-mortification. The doctrine that a man was a zaddik by birth rather than by achievement was likely to lend itself to a doctrine of hereditary succession, but there was no necessary connection between the belief that a zaddik was predestined by God and the hereditary principle. No detailed theology was developed to justify the dynastic principle, but it was believed that the holy thoughts of the zaddik at the time of conception would bring down an exceptional soul from heaven and that a child conceived and brought up in holiness would himself be holy.

Although regarded as zaddikim, many of the disciples of the Besht and Dov Baer had no successors; neither their sons nor their disciples retained their following.[33] Of those disciples who had successors, some were succeeded only by disciples, but the majority were succeeded by both sons and disciples.[34] It was usual for one successor, usually a hereditary one, to continue in the place of residence of the zaddik who had died, while the other successors established themselves in other locations, often adding to the following of their predecessor.

In the early stages of routinization of charisma within the movement it was possible for a disciple to break away and attract followers from his master. Jacob Isaac, "the Seer" of Lublin (1745–1815), broke away from Elimelech of Lyzhansk and established his own Hasidic following. In his turn the Seer experienced the defection of his one-time closest disciple, Jacob Isaac, "the Holy Jew" of Przysucha (1766–1814), who left Lublin to establish his own court after some tension with the Seer and harassment by the Seer's disciples, who regarded him as a competitor to their master.

However, the establishment of a court by a disciple during the lifetime of his zaddik was a rare event even in the early stages of the movement. A more frequent source of tension was the question of succession after the death of a zaddik. In some cases this tension took the form of a conflict over whether succession was hereditary or through discipleship. The death of Schneur Zalmon of Liady (1745–1813), a leading disciple of the Great Maggid, who established the Habad branch of Hasidism, was followed by a split between those who supported one of his sons, Dov Baer of Lubavich (1773–1823), and those who supported Aaron Ha-Levi, Zalmon's favorite disciple.[35] Aaron Ha-Levi set up a separate court in Starasselje, and both groups claimed to represent the single authentic interpretation of Zalmon's teachings. In support of Aaron, many argued from precedent that up to that time it was generally the disciple and not the son who succeeded as zaddik, but an influential disciple of Zalmon distributed a letter in which he claimed that he had been present when Zalmon had promised the succession to Dov Baer. Zalmon's brother, Judah Leib, wrote to Aaron, rebuking him for his ambitions and claiming that Zalmon's following had a higher opinion of Dov Baer. Following the death of Dov Baer, his son-in-law (who was also his nephew) Menahem Mendel (1789–1866) was proclaimed successor. When Aaron died ten years later, some of his followers accepted his son Hayyim Raphael as their zaddik, whereas others transferred their allegiance to Menahem Mendel. Hayyim Raphael died without leaving a successor, and while some of his followers preferred to remain without a zaddik, the majority became followers of Menahem Mendel or other zaddikim.[36]

The coexistence of the hereditary and discipleship principles of succession was most clearly evident during the period of rapid growth. Of the disciples of the Great Maggid who established important Hasidic branches, two were succeeded by disciples, three were succeeded by family heirs, and seven were succeeded by both disciples and family heirs. From the fourth generation, however, hereditary succession became the normative mode in most areas. For example, Jehiel Michael, "the Maggid" of Zloc-zow (1731–86), a disciple of both the Besht and Dov Baer of Mezhirech, was succeeded by five sons, one son-in-law, and four disciples. Three of the sons were succeeded by one or more of their sons, and three of the disciples were succeeded by one or more of their sons. In Congress Poland succession by a disciple remained an operative principle over many genera-tions, but it became more and more the exception, and by the end of the nineteenth century hereditary succession had become the exclusive mode in all areas.[37]

The early dominance of the hereditary principle in most areas is perhaps not surprising. Lineage was an important basis of status in Jewish society; the zaddik was likely to favor inheritance by a member of his family; and as a permanent member of the zaddik's household, the son was in a good position to obtain support. In some dynasties it was considered important for not only the zaddik but also his wife to be of pure lineage. First-cousin marriages strengthened the "holy seed" of the next zaddik.

Weber noted that lineage charisma does not always ensure the unam-biguous identification of a successor and that further rules of succession, such as primogeniture, are required.[38] Among the Hasidim, the eldest son was generally favored as successor, but this rule did not apply in all cir-cumstances. Weber wrote: "Once the belief is established that charisma is bound to a blood relationship its meaning is altogether reversed. If origi-nally a man was enobled by virtue of his own actions, now only the deeds of his forefathers could legitimate him."[39] The personal form of charisma in Hasidism did not entirely disappear, but was confined within limits set by the hereditary principle. The principle of primogeniture could, for example, be offset by the personal element: a younger son regarded as more suitable than the eldest son could succeed his father. Conflict over the claims of different sons often resulted in a fission in the community, with two or more sons setting up separate courts. Following the death of the Lubavich zaddik Menahem Mendel in 1866, a quarrel over leadership split the succession among five brothers. The youngest son, Samuel (1834–82), continued the court in Lubavich, while his four brothers established their own branches in other towns. It took some time before all the branches were reunited. The branch of Judah Leib (1811–66), who set up a court in Kopys, continued through one of his sons, followed by another of his sons and a grandson, but the absence of a successor to the grandson, who died in 1926, led most followers to join the Lubavich branch.

The expansion of a dynasty through multiple succession is illustrated by the eight sons of Mordecai of Chernobyl (1770–1839), who became zad-dikim in various communities in the Ukraine. Disputes broke out among the brothers, and the relations between their courts took on a competitive and hostile character. The size of the courts varied considerably, and the element of personalized charisma was no doubt a factor here. The eldest son, Aaron (1787–1872), continued his father's court in Chernobyl with a considerable following, but another son, David of Talna (1808–82), had the largest following. All eight sons had hereditary successors: two were followed by four sons and two by three sons. Another example of multiple succession was that of Israel Friedman of Ruzhin: six sons became zaddikim, five of whom were followed by hereditary successors.

The continuing importance of the personal factor within the hereditary framework was demonstrated when dissatisfaction with a zaddik led followers to leave him and follow another. After the death of the Sighet zaddik in eastern Hungary in 1926, his fourteen-year-old son became heir, but the followers found him unsatisfactory and transferred their allegiance to Yoel Teitelbaum (1888–1979), the younger brother of the late zaddik.[40] In other cases, however, the young age of an heir was not considered an obstacle to hereditary succession. Moses Leib of Sasov (1745–1807) was succeeded by his seven-year-old son, and Asher the Second (died 1873) of the Karlin dynasty was followed by his four-year-old son, Israel, "the Babe" of Stolin. In those cases most followers were willing to wait until the heirs were old enough to fulfill the roles of the zaddik, but this waiting imposed a particular strain on older members. When the zaddik of the Karlin and Stolin Hasidim died in 1955, his grandson, Baruch Schochet, whom the zaddik had proclaimed his successor at the boy's circumcision, was only one year old. While the younger Hasidim remained loyal to the direct heir, many older members transferred their allegiance to the zaddik of the Lelov dynasty, whom they now called the zaddik of Lelov-Karlin. The investiture of a "foreign" zaddik was seen as a threat to the continuation of the Karlin dynasty and strongly opposed by those who supported the child. Families were rent by this dissension, and the conflict between the two groups led to a series of lawsuits in Israel over the ownership of a yeshivah and the collection of funds under the name of Stolin.[41]

The forms of succession in Hasidism may be summarized as follows: (1) *Succession by one disciple.* This was, of course, the earliest type, but exceptional thereafter. (2) *Succession by a number of disciples.* (3) *Succession by a disciple and a son (sometimes a son-in-law or grandson).* (4) *Succession by a number of disciples and one son.* (5) *Succession by a number of sons and one disciple.* (6) *Succession by a number of sons and a number of disciples.* This mode was typical in the early stages of the movement (the successors of the second, third, and, to a lesser extent, fourth generation). (7) *Succession by one son.* This became a common pattern, but only in a few cases did the whole history of a dynasty conform to it.[42] (8) *Succession by a number of sons.* This also became a common pattern. (9) *No successor.* In most cases when a zaddik had no successor, most of his followers transferred their allegiances to another zaddik, possibly a member of the late zaddik's family or another zaddik in the vicinity of their homes. It was rare for a group to continue without a living zaddik. The followers of Raphael of Bershad (1816–26) remained a distinct group without a zaddik after his death, but the most important exception is the Bratslav Hasidim, whose only zaddik, Nahman of Bratslav, died in 1810. The Bratslav Hasidim grew considerably after the death of Nahman, and they have remained an important group up to the present day.

Segmentation and Religious Heterogeneity

The variety and multiple forms of succession in Hasidism led to the decentralization and segmentation of the movement: it had no centralized leadership, and the movement was composed of autonomous, mainly localized groups. In their analysis of Pentecostalism in the United States and elsewhere, Gerlach and Hine account for the decentralized organization of Pentecostalism by the personal and diffused forms of charisma in the movement: charisma often moves from one member to another, various participants exhibit relative degrees of charisma, and there is often simultaneous recognition of a number of charismatic figures.[43] In contrast, charisma in each Hasidic group was concentrated in the zaddik: there were no relative degrees of charisma within each group, and there was no simultaneous devotion to a number of zaddikim. Unlike the charismatic succession in Pentecostalism, succession in Hasidism took routinized forms, and these forms largely account for the fact that Hasidism was even more decentralized and segmented than Pentecostalism.

Hasidism also had less reticulation and fewer cross-cutting ties than Pentecostalism: groups shared familial and local community ties with members of other Hasidic groups, but within the movement itself, there were no common ritual activities or important national or regional associations. Some zaddikim had familial and personal ties with other zaddikim, but they rarely visited each other's groups, and the majority of zaddikim attempted to keep their followings as separate as possible from other groups. After the death of Dov Baer of Mezhirech, Hasidism was one movement, but only in a weak sense; while the various Hasidic groups had certain common religious features which distinguished them from other cultural streams, such as the mitnagdim and the maskilim, each group was nonetheless wholly autonomous in an organizational sense, and the differences between the groups appeared to the Hasidim themselves as more important than their similarities.

Gerlach and Hine account for the segmentation of Pentecostalism by four factors: the Pentecostalist ideology of personal access to power; preexisting personal and social cleavages; personal competition; and ideological differences.[44] With some modifications largely related to the routinization of charisma, these factors also contributed to the segmentation of Hasidism. In Pentecostalism any believer may achieve personal access to knowledge, truth, and power through the baptism of the Holy Spirit, and any person who is spirit filled can preach the word of God. Hasidism distinguished between levels of devekut and taught that only exceptional individuals, the zaddikim, could attain the highest level of devekut. Thus, in contrast to that of Pentecostalism, leadership in Hasidism was restricted to an elite of "exceptional men," and over time the recognition of an exceptional man became highly circumscribed by ascriptive factors. Nevertheless, there was no ideological restriction on the number of zaddikim, and the belief that any man who was able to rise to the highest level of devekut was a zaddik contributed to the segmentation of the movement.

Personal rivalries between zaddikim and their disciples, between several sons, between different disciples, and between the sons and disciples resulted in the formation of new independent groups. The dissemination of the movement to new areas was often accomplished by a son or disciple who had been passed over as the successor of some late zaddik's community. Decentralization was further reinforced by the Jewish tradition of local community autonomy, the partitions of Poland, and the differences in economic conditions, social stratification, and religious education and scholarship of the Jews, both between and within the various regions of eastern Europe. These differences will be discussed later with reference to religious heterogeneity within Hasidism.

Personal competition in Hasidism was primarily a competition between zaddikim for followers, for authority in the larger Jewish community, and for funds to support their courts as well as their charities, such as the support of Jews who settled in the Land of Israel. Each group of Hasidim supported its zaddik in this competition, and intrigues and persecutions between groups were not uncommon. Conflicts were particularly acute between Nahman of Bratslav and other zaddikim. Nahman's move to the town of Zlotopolye represented a clear violation of the territory of the miracle-making zaddik Aryeh Leib, "the *zeide*" (grandfather or old man), who held his court just two miles away in Shpola. Aryeh Leib went to Zlotopolye, where he publicly denounced Nahman as a false leader. Although most of the town people took sides against Nahman, he stayed there for two years and tried to counter the constant accusations of Aryeh Leib. Following an attempt by the zeide to obtain letters of denunciation against Nahman from leading zaddikim, Nahman sought public support to excommunicate him for the crime of having publicly shamed a scholar. In 1802, Nahman settled in Bratslav, which was some distance from Aryeh Leib's territory, but here he came into conflict with his uncle, Baruch of Medzibezh, who at that time was living in Tulchin, two miles from Bratslav. Nahman had no compunction about taking Hasidim from what he termed a "false" zaddik who kept men from discovering the truth. But Baruch saw himself as the legitimate heir of the Besht, and his bitter conflict with Nahman continued until Nahman's death.[45]

The religious differences between the Hasidic groups, which were both a cause and a consequence of the movement's decentralization, went beyond ideological differences; they may be divided into two broad types: the differences in the roles and life-styles of the zaddikim and the differences in the ideology, values, and religious practices of the Hasidic groups.[46] Zaddikim differed in the emphasis they put on their responsibility to their followers as opposed to their own spiritual perfection, the extent to which they stressed the material problems of their followers in addition to their spiritual states, the extent to which they led ascetic or Epicurean lives, and whether they had messianic self-conceptions or not.

Most Hasidic groups conceived of the zaddik as an intermediary who was responsible for his followers. According to common belief the zaddik brought man to God and God to man, he was a channel between the divine and material worlds, there was no belief or worship of God without belief in and attachment to the zaddik, and the zaddik endangered his own soul to raise the souls of sinners. On the High Holy Days the Hasidim asked their zaddikim to forgive their sins and enter them in the Book of Life.

A few zaddikim, however, isolated themselves from the world and from their followers. Two religious goals directed some zaddikim to self-isolation: a concern with self-perfection through mystical contemplation and independent study and an emphasis on the cosmic role of the zaddik. The tension between the need for solitude and the social mission of the zaddik was expressed in the writings of the first theoretician of practical zaddikism, Elimelech of Lyzhansk, and toward the end of his life he closed himself in his room and ignored the demands of his large following.

A more extreme example of self-isolation was the zaddik Menahem Mendel of Kotsk (1787–1859), who, for the last twenty years of his life, locked himself in a room near the study house of his disciples. Food was passed to him through a window, and apart from rare occasions, he was seen by only his family and closest disciples. Menahem Mendel was interested only in a select few who were willing to leave their families and stay in Kotsk for weeks or months, where they would devote themselves to a religious life of study and prayer. He attracted many followers, and the less he made them welcome the more they came. The followers wished to be near a man who in his isolation was believed to be conducting a great struggle with evil which would hasten the coming of the messiah.[47]

Schneur Zalmon, the founder of Habad Hasidism, emphasized the importance of the zaddik in the repair of the cosmos; he did not perceive the zaddik as an intermediary between the upper and lower worlds, and the idea of the zaddik raising his Hasidim to the upper spheres was made indistinct in Habad. Zalmon taught that the zaddik descended not to redeem sinners but to partake of an interval between his rise from one step in the divine spheres to another. Zalmon's rejection of the role of the intermediary led him to restrict the number and forms of contact with his Hasidim, but he did not isolate himself, since he saw the zaddik as a supervisor and teacher of morals.[48]

The cosmic role of the zaddik was of great importance in the Hasidism of Nahman of Bratslav, who saw himself as the great and final premessianic redeemer. Nahman believed that his work of tikkun required great contemplation, free from the distractions of daily contacts with other men. On occasion, Nahman regretted that he was the leader of a group, since this made complete detachment impossible, and he often thought that he should flee from his disciples and live in hiding.

While many zaddikim expressed their longings for the final redemption of the Jewish people, the majority directed their energies to the temporary forms of salvation that they believed were possible to attain in the diaspora. Moses Eliakum of Kozienice (died 1828) claimed that, by the force of his religious action, the zaddik had the ability to repeal the harsh and evil decrees that the authorities were planning against the Jewish people. He argued that the zaddikim were superior to the angels because, unlike the angels, each with his own specialized sphere of influence, the zaddikim concerned themselves with many spheres at the same time. Together with other zaddikim, Moses bemoaned the current humiliations and sufferings of the Jewish people, but they believed that the existing harsh measures would be repealed only with the coming of the messiah. Others claimed, however, that the zaddikim could improve the general economic position of the Jewish people. They argued that the "stream of abundance" in the diaspora had been reversed from its natural direction, for the Jews were in a poorer economic state than the gentiles, but that the zaddikim could re-reverse the stream to some extent.

In the main, practical zaddikism was directed to the problems and sufferings of the individual Hasid: the majority of zaddikim said blessings, provided medicines, and distributed amulets to overcome illnesses, infertility, and evil spirits, and they spent much time comforting and guiding their followers in their everyday material concerns. Jacob Isaac, "the Seer" of Lublin, argued that it was necessary for the zaddik to help others attain their material needs, since material abundance was a precondition of spiritual wealth. Some zaddikim, however, restricted their role to that of spiritual teacher and guide and refused to work miracles or advise on material matters. Menahem Mendel of Vitebsk (1730–88) told the Hasidim not to believe that the blessings of the zaddikim would be fulfilled, and in reply to a disciple who asked him to pray that the disciple would have a child, Mendel wrote that only the Besht had been great enough to have his prayers answered in that way.

Schneur Zalmon taught that the role of the zaddik was to assist the Hasid to find his individual way to God, and he attempted to restrict his personal association with his Hasidim to the spiritual sphere. Zalmon had a hard time convincing his followers that he had no wish to act as an intercessor or listen to their material problems, and to stem the constant stream of followers who came to see him, he put forth a set of regulations to govern visits to his court: a follower could not come more than once a year; each visitor had to come with a testimony written by the gabaim of his town to the effect that a year had passed since his previous visit; and there were strict rules on when to return home. Despite these rules the stream of visitors grew and a revised set of regulations made further restrictions: no one was allowed to enter Zalmon's study to speak to him privately; each Hasid could submit a written outline of his problem so that Zalmon could remember it in his prayers, but the Hasid was not to ask for advice; and if a Hasid believed that he had a matter of extraordinary importance that made it necessary to ask Zalmon's advice, he had first to submit it to three leading Hasidim in his community, who would decide whether the issue was of such importance to require Zalmon's attention. Zalmon believed that although he was capable of making miracles, this was not his proper role; but it was reported that he ordered a mixture of wines to be given as a healing potion for the sick as well as for bereaved mothers and childless women. Zalmon's successors did not consistently follow his attempt to restrict his personal association with his Hasidim to the spiritual sphere, and after Menahem Mendel of Lubavich, the Habad courts incorporated more magical practices, such as the distribution of amulets.

Considerable controversy arose when the zaddikim who emphasized the spiritual role criticized and mocked the "miracle-workers." In Congress Poland a lengthy conflict over the proper role of the zaddik began when Jacob Isaac of Przysucha rejected the practical zaddikism of his former master, Jacob Isaac of Lublin, and attracted many Hasidim who wished to emphasize the spiritual aspects of their religion. The Przysucha Hasidim believed that the zaddik was first and foremost a teacher who educated his followers to a life of Torah and faith and that in material matters the most the zaddik could do was to give advice.

It was among the miracle-workers, such as Baruch of Medzibezh and the dynasties of Ruzhin and Chernobyl, that were usually found the zaddikim who lived in great luxury. These zaddikim imitated the life-style of the wealthy nobles, including splendid courts, many servants, opulent carriages drawn by four horses, and expensive clothes. Some had court jesters and brought to their courts folksingers and musicians of the region. Baruch claimed that the zaddik who worshiped God in his eating, drinking, and other physical acts was superior to one who "only" prayed and studied the Torah. Israel Friedman, who founded the Ruzhin dynasty, maintained that both the soul and the body of the zaddik were united with God and that the zaddik could reach God through the pleasures of the world, as well as through Torah and prayer. The influence of the zaddik was always for the good, and if he lived in a confined way, his influence would be confined. Israel Friedman believed that his indulgent style of life was proof that he was above all other zaddikim in his generation. At the other extreme to Israel Friedman, who taught that fasting and self-mortification endangered the soul, were the ascetic zaddikim, such as Menahem Mendel of Kotsk, who taught that the zaddik could serve God only by utterly despising worldly concerns as worthless.

Israel Friedman believed that he was a descendant of the House of David and hinted at certain times that he was the messiah. After his death his sons encouraged the belief that the messiah would come from their family. The zaddik Isaac Judah Jehiel Safrin (1806–74) believed that his soul was a reincarnation of all previous great fighters against evil, such as Isaac Luria and the Besht, and that redemption of the world would come when he had succeeded in purifying his soul from evil. The theme of the messianic role of the zaddik was, however, central only to the Bratslav Hasidim. Nahman of Bratslav did not claim that he was himself the messiah, but he maintained that he was a great redeemer whose task was to redeem men from sin, especially the evils of sexuality, and thereby prepare the world for the messiah. Nahman admitted that all true zaddikim had divine inspiration but he argued that in each generation a single zaddik stood in the place where Moses had stood in his generation and where the messiah will stand at the end of time. He, Nahman, was the single true zaddik of his generation: he was the general soul and cosmological center of that generation, he embodied the dialectical structure of material and spiritual reality, he contained all the defects and necessary repairs of the cosmos, he was the single channel of all spiritual blessings, and since he was transcendental and mysterious, no man could fully comprehend him.

Nahman was critical of other zaddikim, some of whom he believed to have been appointed by Satan, and he argued that their ability to obtain material benefits by their prayers only confirmed their lower status. Since Nahman saw it as his task to prepare for the messianic kingdom, he proclaimed that he could not waste his energy on the distribution of petty blessings.

After the birth of his son, who at some point he believed to be the messiah, Nahman and his followers concentrated their activities on preparing for an imminent redemption. Nahman began to wear white clothes, and he revealed the particular "corrections" of the soul, such as fasting and celibacy, that were required from each of his disciples. Nahman's teachings had formerly been kept in secrecy within his group, but he now sent out important disciples to the surrounding areas to spread his teachings and collect money for the movement. His great hopes from all this activity were disappointed: his son died in infancy; his disciples failed to gain followers or finance; and he encountered intense opposition and persecution from other Hasidic groups. These setbacks were interpreted by Nahman as expressions of the Evil One. Although he no longer claimed to know the exact date of the coming of the messiah, he continued to believe that he had a messianic role.

The belief in Nahman as a great redeemer was used to explain his "strange actions" in the last year of his life, when he talked and stayed with maskilim in the town of Uman. Nahman's close contact with the maskilim was in apparent conflict with his strong opposition to any form of secular knowledge or behavior, and his secretary, Nathan Herz, who led the Bratslav after Nahman's death, interpreted this contact as the action of a great soul and redeemer. While some of Nahman's disciples opposed his contact with the maskilim, Nathan and others argued that Nahman had descended into the evil spheres in order to struggle with impurity, remove the vital life from the evil forces, and gather, cleanse, and raise the holy sparks from the souls of sinners.[49] Thus, Nahman's paradoxical actions in the last year of his life were signs of his special standing as *the* zaddik, and it is this emphasis on his unique role which explains why he had no successors and why the Bratslav continue to regard him as the center of their faith. The Bratslav believed that Nahman continued in his messianic mission after his death and that he would return to earth to conquer his enemies and the evil powers.

The Bratslav put an enormous emphasis on the sacredness of Nahman's stories, which were written down by Nathan. The stories or wonder tales were believed to have, in addition to their lower simple meaning, a higher sacred meaning of great mysteries and revelations. Interpretation of the stories was holy work for the Bratslav, but they claimed that to read them even without understanding the higher meanings would draw out the spiritual wealth within them. The Bratslav believed that the propagation of Nahman's teachings would hasten the coming of the messiah, but in order to avoid persecution, which continued and even increased after Nahman's death, the Bratslav felt that they also had to hide the truth. Thus, the writings of the Bratslav contained hints of extraordinary truths which would only be revealed to others when the messiah came.[50]

In addition to the differences that centered on the role of the zaddik, Hasidic groups differed also in a number of religious beliefs and practices: an emphasis on immanence or transcendentalism; the approach to evil; the place of scholarship and asceticism; the degree of ecstaticism and formalism in prayer; and the attitude toward messianism.

No Hasidic group presented the divine as totally pantheistic or totally transcendental, but they did have important differences in their relative emphases on immanentalism and transcendentalism. Certain zaddikim, such as Menahem Nahum Twersky of Chernobyl (1730–87) and Levi Isaac of Berdichev (1740–1810), affirmed the presence of God in his creation, while others, such as Nahman of Bratslav and Menahem Mendel of Kotsk, asserted that God stood outside of and confronted his creation. Most Hasidic groups stressed the immanence of the divine, but contradictory approaches to immanence sometimes appeared within a single group or a single teacher. Some followed the Lurianic conceptions: sparks of the divine light had fallen from their root into the material and evil realm, and it was man's task to purify and return the sparks to their origin. Others believed that the presence of the divine in the world represented not a fall but a positive presence in the world, providing a basis for contact with the divine, even in the material realm.

A key point of difference between the transcendentalists and the immanentalists was their conception of evil and their understanding of man's relation to that evil. The former viewed evil as an autonomous realm to be overcome and destroyed, whereas the latter perceived evil as a distorted aspect of the divine which had to be transformed into good. Concerning man's body or materiality, some believed that man's body was an integral part of the evil realm and that the individual had, therefore, to free himself from his materiality, while others saw the body as a reflection of the divine which had undergone a fall but which could be raised to its previous sacred position. A few argued that the body could be raised even above the level of the soul.

The effect of these divergent views can be easily seen in the problem of "alien" or "strange" thoughts, such as sex, self-pride, irreligion, and irrelevant secular matters, which would occasionally enter a man's mind during his prayer. These thoughts were dangerous because they were an obstacle to the worshiper's kavanah, they prevented the achievement of devekut, and they could be captured by the devil to aid the evil powers. Those Hasidic teachers who saw the sacred and evil realms as essentially opposite maintained that the worshiper should reject the alien thoughts by pushing them out of his mind. The contrary approach was to keep the alien thoughts in mind but elevate them to their source in the divine. Thus, thoughts on a woman's beauty could be traced to the divine source of all beauty, against which a women's attractions were only illusory, and thoughts of self-pride could be converted into a concentration on God's majesty. Some zaddikim, such as Nahman of Bratslav, argued that only the zaddik was obliged to elevate alien thoughts and that the ordinary Hasid should totally reject such thoughts. Isaac Judah Jehiel Safrin took an extreme opposite position; he maintained that the rejection of alien thoughts was equivalent to the destruction of the divine sparks that were immanent within the thoughts. He taught that the raising of alien thoughts was a sacred obligation for every Jew, but he acknowledged that a man could reject the thoughts if he felt that he did not have sufficient strength to effect their transformation. In the second half of the nineteenth century, Isaac Judah's view was not typical; the later tendency was to stress rejection of alien thoughts or simply to ignore the problem.

Somewhat contradictory approaches to immanentism, evil, and alien thoughts are found in the writings of the early Habad zaddikim. It has been argued that Habad teaching had two sides: the exoteric, surface ideas presented in a moderate and restrained fashion for the larger community and the esoteric, hidden ideas revealed to a limited circle. In his popular work *Tanya*, Zalmon wrote that the divine penetrates the world; material things have no reality of their own, and their existence is due wholly to the divine sparks. God is both immanent and transcendent, both in the world and beyond it, but in this world our perception of the divine is limited, since man can bear the divine light only when it is veiled. Here, Zalmon followed the Great Maggid's conception of zimzum as the means by which man is able to withstand the divine light through the filter of barriers and veils. Since God's presence is everywhere, man has no need to look for God beyond this world; he is not required to raise divine sparks, but finds a quiet revelation of God in his fulfilment of the mitsvot. In other works, however, Zalmon returned to Lurianic conceptions of zimzum as a shrinkage of the divine to allow creation, and he emphasized the distance between God and the world. Some attempts were made to reconcile these views—for example, a distinction was made between the divine light of affinity, which fills the world, and the divine light of infinity, which is hidden and transcendental, but this was not always made a strict distinction in Habad circles.

The manifest position of Habad regarding alien thoughts was to restrict the work of transformation from evil to good to the zaddikim. Habad distinguished three types of men: the zaddik, the average man, and the evil man. Since the zaddik had already won his struggle with the satanic powers and since the evil man would never repent, the primary concern was the purification of the soul of the average man. But in his constant struggle to purify his soul, the average man should attempt only to repress and not try to elevate his alien thoughts. In other writings the average man is given an important role in the transformation of evil into good. The divine sparks are found at all levels of reality, including such depths as the bestial (as opposed to the divine) souls of Jews, the souls of non-Jews, and deviant sexual acts. In one sense the religious acts of the average man were seen as more important than those of the zaddik because the greater the materiality and evil from which the divine sparks are raised, the more powerful the effects on the upper sphere. The importance of repentance among ordinary Jews, especially sinners, was particularly stressed, since this would bring messianic redemption. Aaron Ha-Levi claimed that the love of God for evil men who repent exceeds even his love for the zaddik. He was careful, however, to close the opening to antinomianism: it was forbidden to commit a sin in order to raise the divine sparks in evil, since this involved a descent from holiness into evil.

An important issue of controversy in Hasidism was the value of religious scholarship. In Congress Poland such zaddikim as Jacob Isaac of Lublin put little or no value on scholarship, whereas the zaddikim of the Przysucha, Kotsk, and Gur dynasties emphasized the study of the Talmud and narrowed the gap between the Hasidim and the mitnagdim. In Belorussia and Lithuania the emphasis on study by Zalmon was opposed by Solomon of Karlin (died 1792) and Aaron of Vitebsk, who were contemptuous of the form of talmudic study among the mitnagdim. At the opposite extreme to Habad Hasidism was the Berezna dynasty, which ignored talmudic scholarship and left no book or written record. An emphasis on scholarship in a group often corresponded to a relatively negative attitude to miracle making, but this was not always the case, as is shown by Israel Hofstein of Kozienice (1736–1813) and the Belz zaddikim in Galicia, who combined learning with magical practices.

With respect to religious behavior the Hasidic groups differed in their levels of asceticism, ecstaticism, and formalism. The early Hasidic value on worshiping God in joy remained important in most Hasidic groups, but self-mortification and frequent fasting were advocated by such zaddikim as Phinhas Shapiro of Korets (1726–91), Joseph Meir Weiss of Spinka (1838–1909), and Nahman of Bratslav. The Przysucha Hasidim were unworldly and ascetic and emphasized the importance of the mind controlling the physical drives. Among the zaddikim who lived in luxury some restricted the religious value of Epicureanism to the zaddik: Mordecai of Chernobyl and Baruch of Medzibezh taught their followers the importance of fasting.

Ecstatic and highly demonstrative prayer was characteristic of the Hasidim,[51] but some dynasties, such as the Gorodok, practiced a sedate style of prayer. Ecstatic prayer was an issue in the conflict between the two successors of Zalmon: his son, Dov Baer of Lubavich, objected to emotional demonstrations, recited his prayers in complete silence, and emphasized the need to overcome the self in divine worship; Zalmon's favorite disciple, Aaron Ha-Levi, encouraged ecstatic prayer even if it meant risking spurious ecstasy and argued that what is sham ecstasy for one is authentic for another of lesser attainment in the mystical order. It is appropriate to mention here the differences between the Hasidic groups in music and dance. The Karlin Hasidim believed music and dance to be on the same level with study and meditation. Music was of great importance for the Hasidim of Kuzmir and Modzitz, but played a minor role among the Hasidim of Przysucha, Kotsk, and Gur. Song was very important for the Hasidim of Lublin and Bobov.

Phinhas Shapiro expressed a formalistic approach to religious practice. He argued that the observance of the mitsvot raised the divine sparks and should be performed for their own sake. The Hasidim of Przysucha and Kotsk opposed formalism in the mitsvot and prayer; they argued that since the main point of prayer was its meaning, its timing was not too important. It was necessary to wait until one was in the right frame of mind for prayer, and it was possible, therefore, to say the morning prayers in the evening and the evening prayers in the morning.

Messianism was not central to the life and teachings of most zaddikim. While they acknowledged that full spiritual attainment was not possible in the premessianic world, most zaddikim concentrated their energies on the degree of perfection that could be attained in their imperfect world. The zaddikim of Apta and Kozienice taught that the messiah represented the combination of all the souls of the Jewish people, and every stain in a Jewish soul directly stained the messiah. The messiah would appear only when all the Jews had repented and their souls had been purified. Meir of Apta (died 1831) maintained that if the zaddik repented, it was as though the whole people had repented. But although most zaddikim believed that the zaddik had a special role in bringing the messiah, this was not the focus of their activities. Some found certain spiritual advantages in the galut. Elimelech of Lyzhansk argued that it was easier to obtain the gift of the spirit in exile: the Shechinah was in exile with the Jewish people and was prepared to enter a man who was free of sin.

Apart from the Habad and Bratslav Hasidim, who expected the messiah in many periods, messianic expectations among the Hasidim were mostly limited to the period of the Napoleonic wars and to the year 1839–40. A number of Jews had seen messianic implications in Napoleon's summoning of the Sanhedrin and his earlier proposal for a Jewish state in Palestine. The zaddikim were divided between those who saw Napoleon as an agent of redemption and those who saw him as a threat to the traditional Jewish religious life. Some Hasidim viewed the military successes and defeats of the Napoleonic forces as outcomes of the battles between the supernatural powers of their respective zaddikim. The year 1839–40 marked the beginning of a new century in the Jewish calendar; it was a date mentioned in the Zohar as a possibility for the coming of the messiah, and it was also the year of the reinterment of Napoleon's remains.[52] The *tarniks*, those who expected the messiah to come in 1839–40, included a number of zaddikim,[53] but other zaddikim warned against the messianic expectations. Menahem Mendel of Kotsk stressed that the process of repentance, which was the only way of bringing salvation, was a long one, and he expressed fears that the disappointment over the year 1839–40 would start a new Sabbatian movement. Apart from the Bratslav, the question of the coming of the messiah appears to have been a concern mostly of the zaddikim and to have made little impression on the majority of Hasidim. There is no evidence of widespread preparations for 1839–40 or of religious repercussions following the failure of the prophecy.

Religious and Social Differences and the Spread of the Movement

The decentralization of Hasidism and the religious differences between its segments were important for the spread of the movement. In the third and fourth generations the multiple forms of succession by both sons and disciples made possible the rapid spread of the movement, and even after the principle of hereditary succession had become firmly established, multiple succession by several sons contributed to further growth. The religious differences between the Hasidic groups aided in the penetration of the movement across class and educational boundaries. Hasidism made little impression on the small number of modern capitalist merchants, many of whom joined the Haskalah movement, or on the artisans in the large towns, but it spread to all levels of wealth and religious education within the Jewish community.

It is possible to distinguish areas of eastern Europe according to the type of zaddik and form of Hasidism which were most successful. In the Ukraine and Galicia the practical, miracle-making zaddik was the dominant type; the religious faith of the Hasidim was unsophisticated with little or no emphasis on religious scholarship. In Lithuania and Belorussia, where the Hasidim were in a minority, Habad Hasidism with its sophisticated theology and emphasis on spiritual matters and scholarship was dominant. No one form was predominant in Congress Poland: the practical zaddikim, such as those of Kozienice and Apta, were found together with the more exclusively spiritual zaddikim, such as those of Przysucha and Gur, who emphasized the importance of scholarship. In general, the miracle-making zaddikim, including those who lived in great luxury, appealed to the poor, unsophisticated, lower middle class of the small towns, whereas the scholarly zaddikim, who spurned magical practices, appealed to the wealthier and more educated strata. The variation in the dominant forms of Hasidism cannot, however, be explained simply by economic class differences between the areas. The regions differed little in the degree of urbanization and occupational distribution of their Jewish populations. The average amount of Jewish capital was somewhat larger in the northwestern districts of the Pale, where the more scholarly Hasidim was found, than in the southwestern districts; but the dominant trend in all areas was the pauperization of the Jewish masses.[54]

The regions did differ according to the presence or absence of unbroken scholarly traditions in urban centers and the relationship of these centers to the small-town communities. Religious scholarship in the Ukraine, which had few large urban concentrations, had never recovered from the massacres of 1648. The centers of religious scholarship in Lithuania had continued an unbroken tradition and had even become stronger in the second half of the eighteenth century and the first half of the nineteenth century. These centers, particularly Vilna, exercised considerable authority and influence over the smaller communities, and in the first half of the nineteenth century a new network of yeshivot became central institutions in many small towns in Lithuania.[55] The importance of religious scholars and their opposition to Hasidism mitigated against the spread of the movement in Lithuania, but the more scholarly form of Hasidism attracted a substantial minority, including some important scholars.

Galicia and Congress Poland contained important urban concentrations, but cultural differences between the Jewish communities in the cities and the small towns were greater. This was particularly the case in Galicia, where in the large commercial capitalist centers—Lemberg, Tarnopol, and especially Brody—the Jewish wholesalers and bankers controlled the trade between Russia and the markets in Berlin, Dresden, Vienna, and Leipzig. The rising Jewish upper middle class in the important commercial towns of Galicia supported the Haskalah, emphasized the importance of cultural adaptation to the dominant society, and strongly opposed Hasidism, which they perceived as the major obstacle to their cultural and social aspirations in the wider society. Thus, in Galicia the socioeconomic division between the commercial capitalists of the cities and the economically traditional petty bourgeoisie of the small towns overlapped considerably with the religious and cultural division between the Haskalah and Hasidism.

There were social and cultural divisions in Congress Poland between the Jewish communities of the cities and the small towns, but these divisions took a somewhat different form from those in Galicia. From the 1820s development of capitalist industry and agriculture in Congress Poland was more substantial than it was in the other regions. Jews were very important in Poland's trade, and a small group of rich Jewish merchants, concentrated mainly in Warsaw, were sharply polarized from the vast majority of impoverished Jews. Most of the members of the new Jewish plutocratic class in Poland were not, however, attracted to the Haskalah; Poland lacked "enlightened government officials," who in Galicia played an important role in introducing the ideas of the Enlightenment to rich Jews, and the cultural reference group of the rich Jews who wished to assimilate into Polish society was the Polish nobility. Unlike other cities of eastern Europe, Warsaw did not become a center of the Haskalah, and when the Haskalah finally arrived, it took a highly assimilationist form.

The relative absence of the Haskalah in Poland had implications for the forms that Hasidism took among certain strata. Elements of rationalism and individualism that elsewhere were expressed in the Haskalah were found in Poland in certain Hasidic groups, particularly Przysucha and Izbica, which appealed to the nonassimilationist members of the wealthier strata. These groups retained the traditional notion of the unity of the Jewish people, but they saw wealth as a sign of faith and poverty as a consequence of sin. Combining elements of predestination with an emphasis on the benevolence of God and submission to his will, Izbica Hasidism demonstrated some parallels to Calvinism.[56]

The contrasts between Hasidism in the Ukraine and Galicia and Hasidism in Lithuania were clear, but all areas offered a variety of forms. In Podolia the miracle-making zaddikim, such as those of Shpola and Talna, were the most numerous and the most successful, but the region included also the Savran Hasidism, who emphasized study, and the Bratslav, who were messianic. In Galicia the miracle makers, such as those of the Sadegora dynasty, were opposed by the Zanz and Halberstam Hasidim, who emphasized traditional learning together with ecstatic prayer. In Lithuania-Belorussia, close to the center of the scholarly Hasidism of the Habad in Lubavich, was the practical zaddikism of Vitebsk. In Polesia the Karlin and Stolin Hasidim practiced ecstatic forms of prayer, and the Gorodok, largely composed of artisans, observed decorum in prayer. The variety of forms of Hasidism in most areas permitted its spread through all the social strata of the Jewish community; most Jews were able to find Hasidic groups that were congruent with their economic positions, social statuses, educational levels, and life-styles.

A further consequence of the decentralized organization of Hasidism was that it minimized the effects of failure from opposition or internal causes. Only in Lithuania was the opposition of the mitnagdim sufficiently strong to act as a brake on the spread and growth of Hasidism, and it is in Lithuania that we find a clear example of failure of a particular dynasty. The Amdur Hasidim in western Lithuania lasted for only two generations, until the end of the eighteenth century. Shemuel of Admur (died circa 1798), who followed his father as zaddik, was not able to counteract the attacks of the mitnagdim, and his following declined during the last years of his life. Neither of his two sons held the position of zaddik, and two of his disciples were unsuccessful when they tried to establish courts in Lithuania. Even without opposition some dynasties or particular lines within a dynasty came to an end as a result of inadequacy in leadership or the absence of a successor, but these failures were of little consequence for Hasidism as a whole. If Hasidim of some group were disappointed with their zaddik or were unable to find a successor, they could simply transfer their allegiance to another zaddik.

In conclusion, the spread and growth of Hasidism in eastern Europe was, in large part, a consequence of the particular forms of routinization of charisma in the movement. The multiple forms of succession resulted in the continual formation of new groups, a decentralized and segmented structure, and a wide variety of religious forms. Structural segmentation and religiocultural diversity allowed Hasidism to fulfill many different psychological and social needs and to attract Jews from a wide range of backgrounds.

11. Hasidism in Modern Society

BEFORE WORLD WAR II the main strongholds of Hasidism were societies where the Jews were separated, legally, economically, and socially, from the wider society. The persecution and discrimination of the East European Jews reinforced a separate way of life, but the Hasidim also felt threatened by secularizing and modernizing groups within the Jewish communities. From about 1815 the Hasidim had formed an alliance with their former enemies, the mitnagdim, against the maskilim. The eastern European Haskalah attracted only a very small minority of the Jewish community, mainly wealthy merchants and professionals. Toward the end of the century, however, a greater threat to the Hasidim was posed by the secular Jewish socialist and Zionist movements, which found support among the Jewish masses. Certain Hasidic dynasties declined in some areas, but Hasidism remained by far the largest Jewish social movement in eastern Europe. The mass emigration of East European Jews to western Europe and the United States began in the 1880s, but Hasidic leaders believed that the comparatively open and secular societies of the West held great danger to their way of life, and they attempted to dissuade their followers from joining the migration.

After World War I the largest concentration of Hasidim was found in the newly independent state of Poland, which had over three and one-half million Jews in 1939. The political representatives of Poland to the Paris Peace Conference had signed minority clauses giving Jews full equality, but these proved worthless, and Polish Jews continued to suffer from legal and economic discrimination, political anti-Semitism, social rejection, and pogroms. There was some development of capitalism and a Christian bourgeoisie in interwar Poland, but the country remained predominantly agrarian, and despite a loss in their share of trade and commerce, the Polish Jews remained a socially distinct urban middleman class. Only a small minority of assimilationists adopted Polish culture with enthusiasm, and these suffered considerable psychological strain from the refusal of the Poles to accept them.

The major division within the Polish Jewish communities was between the religious Jews, largely Hasidic, and the secular Zionist and Jewish socialist movements, which had their own political parties, educational systems, communal organizations, youth movements, and press. The Hasidim responded to the new opportunities for political expression in the Polish state and to the threat of Jewish secular movements by organizing political parties and by participating in the municipal and parliamentary elections. Most of the Hasidic leaders were associated with the Agudat Yisrael (the League of Israel), formed in 1912 and based on the Hasidic dynasties of central Poland. The Agudah announced its loyalty to the state and its support of Poland's parliamentary government, and in 1926 it managed to win some concessions, such as official recognition and support for its schools, by allying itself with a comparatively liberal government. However, the Polish governments defaulted on their agreements, and after 1935 the failure of Jewish political accommodation was made obvious by the passing of anti-Jewish laws and the absence of official protection against the increasingly violent attacks on Jews.[1]

Only a fraction of the Hasidim survived the Holocaust, but the leaders who escaped were determined to continue the Hasidic way of life in new environments, particularly New York and Israel. However, the prospects for the continuation of the Hasidic movement appeared doubtful. Not only were their numbers much reduced, but they were now relocated in comparatively open societies that had no legalized discrimination, were far less anti-Semitic, and offered considerable opportunities for Jews to assimilate into the dominant societies.

Hasidim entering New York after World War II began to settle in three neighborhoods in Brooklyn: Williamsburg, Crown Heights, and Borough Park. Today, the largest Hasidic groups in New York are the Satmar, centered in Williamsburg, which has a total congregation of about thirty thousand, and the Lubavich, centered in Crown Heights, which include about one thousand families.[2] The Lubavich community is less geographically concentrated than the Satmar, and with an estimated two hundred and fifty thousand adherents it is the largest Hasidic sect in the world. New York also has several smaller Hasidic groups, such as the Bratslav, Stolin, Vishnitz, and Bobov, most with less than one hundred families.

Concentrations of Hasidim in Israel are found in the area of Mea Shearim in Jerusalem and B'nai Brak, a suburb of Tel Aviv. The number of Hasidim in Israel is difficult to estimate, but they constitute a large proportion of the approximately fifty-five thousand "ultra-Orthodox" Jews who either support the Agudah party or remain outside the political framework of the society.[3] Perhaps the most important Hasidic sect in Israel is the Gur, whose late zaddik was the dominant figure in ultra-orthodoxy in Israel for eighteen years: he was the head of the "Committee of the Great Men of the Torah," the most important organization of the Agudat Yisrael, which is the most orthodox of the religious parties in Israel. Outside Israel and New York, there are a few smaller centers of Hasidism, including Stamford Hill, in north London, with over one thousand Hasidic families,[4] and Antwerp, which in 1970 was calculated to have a total of thirteen hundred Hasidim.[5]

In the post-World War II period the Hasidim have had to become more consciously introversionist. The majority now live in large cities in open societies which include considerable social and cultural diversity. According to Bryan Wilson's typology an introversionist sect is distinguished by an overriding concern with separation from the world: members have a strong sense of the sacredness of the community, and social relationships are confined within the group.

Most of the Christian introversionist sects, such as the Amish and Hutterites, have maintained their religious and cultural distinctiveness in rural environments, where it is easier to preserve the boundaries of the community and isolate it from the larger society. Apart from some limited trade with local merchants the Amish and Hutterite communities are self-sufficient; the community bears full responsibility for its members, and they do not vote, pay taxes, or accept public services. Members who move away from the rural communities lose their identities, and it is unusual to find a Christian introversionist sect which has maintained its distinctiveness and cohesion in an urban environment.

An exception is the Exclusive Brethren, who have maintained a rigorous separation from the wider society by strict rules that prohibit association with outsiders apart from necessary economic contacts. The Brethren emphasize the spiritual purity of their community, and they seek to maintain that purity by a system of tribunals which admits worthy candidates and expels those accused of false doctrine or conduct.[6]

The Hasidim have no formalized procedures for the acceptance and expulsion of members, but they have achieved great success in maintaining their distinctive way of life. They have almost no defections to the non-Hasidic world, and because they have a high birth rate and, in some cases, recruit from the outside, their number continues to grow. This success may be discussed with reference to three sets of mechanisms: insulation, commitment, and social control.

Insulation

Introversionist groups clearly distinguish between their members and outsiders: the Amish refer to "our sort," as opposed to "other sorts of people," and the Hutterites distinguish between themselves and the "worldly people," that is, all those who live outside their communities. Hasidic groups emphasize their separation from the non-Jewish world: gentiles are never befriended or invited into Hasidic homes. Hasidic groups differ, however, in the extent to which they insulate themselves from non-Hasidic Jews.[7] At one extreme are the Satmar, who stress their social and intellectual isolation and are suspicious toward outsiders who visit their synagogues. The Satmar believe that to even talk to an outsider is to risk the dangers of contact with the impure, and they clearly distinguish themselves from most other Jews in their opposition to Zionism and the state of Israel. They believe that a Jewish state must await the messiah, and in Israel they avoid any contact with the institutions of the state: they do not vote, carry the identification cards which are required for all citizens, or make use of the country's courts or legal system. At the other extreme are the Lubavich, who attempt to draw other Jews into orthodox Judaism. The Lubavich have described themselves as "a mission to Jews by Jews," but they also emphasize their distinct identity as a movement within Jewry.

One important means of insulation is the use of distinctive dress and language to symbolize identity. Like the Amish, the Hasidim wear distinctive clothes, the styles of which undergo little, if any, change from one generation to the next. The Satmar and most other Hasidic men wear the traditional clothing of East European Jews, which was originally derived from the clothing of Polish nobles: long black topcoats and wide-brimmed black hats. From the age of three, boys have their heads shaven periodically except for sideburns, which grow into long dangling curls. Men also grow beards. Most Lubavich men do not wear the traditional clothing, but they tend to dress in the modest and conservative manner typical of many non-Hasidic orthodox Jews: a narrow-brimmed hat, a dark suit, and a beard. Most Lubavich men do not grow sidelocks, and those that do generally tuck them behind their ears. Female dress in all Hasidic groups is not as distinctive as male dress, and as among non-Hasidic orthodox Jews, it is governed less by traditional styles than by rules of modesty: arms are covered at least to the elbows, dresses and skirts cover most of the legs (slacks are never worn), and dark stockings are worn even in summer. Women have their heads shaved at marriage, after which they wear a head scarf or wig, but in urban environments, where a considerable number of women wear wigs, this is hardly distinctive. Orthodox Jewish women are more easily recognized in the summer than in the winter, but Hasidic women are not distinguishable from other orthodox women by their dress.[8]

All Hasidic groups use Hebrew as the language of prayer and Yiddish as the language of everyday discourse. In the West the Lubavich are more likely to be fluent in English than are other Hasidim. In Poland nearly all

Jews spoke Yiddish, but in the West and in Israel Yiddish has reinforced Hasidic separation. In Israel, where Hebrew is the everyday language of the majority, Yiddish serves to symbolize the separation between religious and secular life. It is not unusual for immigrant groups to maintain their language, and many non-Hasidic Jews speak Yiddish, but unlike most immigrant groups, the Hasidim have successfully transferred their language as the first language of their children. Insulation by means of language is found also among Christian introversionist sects: the Amish use Pennsylvanian Dutch for everyday discourse and High German for prayer, and the Hutterites use Tyrolese for everyday discourse and High German for prayer.

In the urban environment the intrusion of the outside world is a constant threat, but the Hasidim attempt to limit its influence as much as possible. They have a sense of righteousness in their exclusivity, that they are observing the correct way of life, and that others are living in disobedience to God. They point to crime, drugs, sex, and materialism as signs of the decadence and degeneracy of the outside world, although they are mainly concerned with the consequences of such phenomena on the Jews.[9] Most Hasidic groups do not allow their members to own televisions and radios, attend theaters and cinemas or read non-Hasidic newspapers, fiction, or scientific writings in religiously sensitive areas, such as evolution. In New York some of the Lubavich have television sets, which they watch with moderation; many, especially the women, attend movies; and some of the women occasionally go to concerts and the theater. The stricter attitude of other groups was demonstrated in Mea Shearim, where a woman who bought a television was stoned and required hospitalization. Social contacts with individuals outside the community are discouraged, and endogamy within each Hasidic group is the rule. Since it is presumed that a woman will follow her husband's beliefs, it is sometimes possible for a male to gain approval to marry an orthodox female from outside his Hasidic group.[10]

The Hasidim have achieved a considerable degree of institutional self-sufficiency, which reduces their dependence on outside agencies and groups. For example, apart from their synagogues, burial society, mikveh, butcher shop, and bakery, the institutional complex of the Satmar in New York includes a school system, an employment agency, a hospital and clinic with female gynecologists, an emergency ambulance and oxygen service, a special nursing service, a large loan society, which gives interest-free loans, a publishing enterprise, which prints a weekly newspaper and books, and a private bus service, which connects the communities in Brooklyn with the Manhattan diamond center on Forty-seventh Street.[11]

The provision of goods for consumption entails a high level of insulation. When purchasing products such as meat, matzah, and bakery and dairy products, the Satmar do not trust anyone except other Satmar and closely related groups. The Hasidim in general put great emphasis on the preparation of kosher foods, and businessmen will sometimes claim that their kosher preparations and provisions are more reliable than those of their competitors. Specialized articles and shops also contribute to economic distinctiveness. For example, leaven-searching sets are produced to prepare for Passover, when the house has to be completely cleaned of leaven. The sets contain a kosher candle, two feathers, a wooden spoon, and a leaflet explaining the laws related to the searching of leaven. In his promotion of the sets, the manufacturer emphasizes that he has exclusive rights within the Hasidic community.[12]

Although the Hasidim produce and prepare their own articles of consumption which have important religious meanings, they are far less self-sufficient and insulationist in their patterns of consumption than the rural Christian introversionist sects. The Amish reject items, such as the automobile, that are part of modern technological society, and their adoption of innovations is slow and likely to involve conflict. The Hutterites select innovations that are consistent with their communal living: they are likely to adopt agricultural innovations, but reject luxury items and labor-saving devices in the house, which are in conflict with their religious standards and work ethic. In contrast to the Amish, the Hasidim do not reject modern technology, and in contrast to the communitarian Hutterites, the Hasidim feel a need to achieve individual economic success. The community makes many demands on the financial resources of the individual, particularly in the area of charity; moreover, the importance of earning a reasonable income has grown with the influence of middle-class patterns of consumption.[13]

Rather than reject modern consumer goods produced outside the community, the Hasidim have transformed some of them from purely secular items to items with religious meaning. Objects that elsewhere have no relationship to religion are adapted for religious purposes and given concrete reference to community values. For example, the Hasidim use an automatic timer on their refrigerators which turns on the motor and prevents the motor from turning on when the refrigerator is opened. This is important on the Sabbath, since starting an electrical current is interpreted as a desecration of the day of rest. Thus, the timer becomes the *shabbos zeiger* (Sabbath clock). The long, black, heavy-gauge stockings ("Hasidic stockings") are another example of the infusion of symbolic meaning into everyday objects; these prevent the exposure of the woman's legs to public view and allow her to be truly modest. An example of the use of technology to reinforce religion is the *shatnes* laboratory, which tests clothes for the forbidden mixture of wool and linen. In its advertisements the laboratory announces that shatnes testing involves skill and that a reliable test can be made only with chemicals and a microscope.[14]

The Hasidim find it harder to maintain their separateness when they enter the urban environment to make a living. The choice of occupations is limited by religiously relevant factors such as the Hasidic clothes, food regulations, and the observance of religious holidays. The limited secular education that most Hasidim receive and the need to reside within the Hasidic community further restrict their occupational choices. A study of the Lubavich in Montreal found that 54 percent of the men were involved in religiously oriented occupations, 20 percent were independent businessmen, and 4 percent were wage earners who mostly worked in companies owned by other Lubavich.[15] Studies of the Satmar in New York found that about one-half worked with outsiders and that a large proportion were engaged in manual labor as operators on piecework rates. As operators, the Hasidim try to make enough money to establish themselves in business within the Hasidic community.[16] An important area of employment in New York and Antwerp is the diamond industry, which provides continuity with the traditional artisan and commercial character of East European Jews.[17]

In addition to their economic involvement in the wider society, and in contrast to the Christian introversionist sects, the Hasidim have taken advantage of social security benefits, external welfare provision, and other governmental programs. The Hasidic community welfare and charity programs are of great importance, and the collection and distribution of money is a regular activity, but even the Satmar in New York have made increasing use of the welfare structure of the dominant society. The Hasidim also participate in the wider political system. At the local level they form a strong voting bloc and have been able to benefit from community-based, city-funded projects. Although in Israel the Satmar reject any involvement with the state, in the United States they make full use of the franchise.[18]

Contact with the wider secular society has required some changes in the organizational structure of the Hasidim in the United States. The Satmar zaddik recognized his limitations in secular matters and appointed an overall community manager to run the affairs of the Satmar court. Since the community manager is a sophisticated man who has contacts and experience with the outside world, he serves as a "culture broker" for the entire community, mediating between the Satmar and the wider society.[19] The Lubavich zaddik, unlike most zaddikim, received a secular education as well as a religious one: he studied mathematics and science at the Sorbonne and was trained as an electrical engineer. With the assistance of a small office staff he directs Lubavich affairs throughout the world from his head office in Brooklyn. The Lubavich are able to point to their zaddik as a man whose familiarity with secular knowledge enables him more fully to appreciate its limitations and dangers.

Solomon Poll has argued that the urban setting has contributed to the growth and development of the Hasidic way of life. Opportunities for the manufacture and sale of the articles and foodstuffs required in their religious style of life are greater in the city because of the accessibility of raw materials and the sizable market. It is doubtful whether the Hasidim could be economically successful in a rural area in modern society, since their economic activities have always been of an urban nature.[20] Problems have arisen, however, in the Hasidic areas in New York City. Williamsburg and Crown Heights, the two major Hasidic areas in Brooklyn, have become areas of major population shifts and centers of the urban crisis in recent years. At the beginning of the 1950s the population of Brooklyn was over 90 percent white, with a large proportion of Jews. During the following two decades the white population declined by 30 percent, and the number of Jewish residents declined considerably. During the 1960s three-quarters of the white residents of Crown Heights moved out and the area became 70 percent black. On one side of the Hasidic neighborhood in Williamsburg is the East River; the other side is the black ghetto of Bedford-Stuyvesant. While most non-Hasidic Jews moved out of these areas, the Hasidim had to consider their need to live in close proximity to each other, their heavy investments in the neighborhood, and the institutions that they had built.

Although some of the smaller Hasidic sects moved out of Brooklyn, the Satmar and the Lubavich decided to remain, and they organized to face the mounting tension in the streets. Friction between blacks and Hasidim began to grow in Crown Heights from the early 1970s. The blacks alleged that the Hasidim received favored treatment in employment and in government loans to small businesses, and their bitterness increased when Crown Heights was divided into two districts after Hasidic leaders expressed a desire for a bigger voice in the affairs of their neighborhood. The blacks organized demonstrations to protest the allegedly cruel treatment of blacks by groups of young Hasidim who patrolled the area; they characterized the Hasidim as "terrorists" and "oppressors," but the violent rhetoric did not develop into mob attacks. In May 1979 an effort was made to halt the hostility by the formation of a coalition of black and Hasidic leaders, but tension rose again in October when a sixty-eight-year-old Hasid was shot dead and robbed by a black youth. A third area of Hasidic settlement, Borough Park, has retained a larger middle-class population of Jews and Italians, but in December 1978 an elderly man was robbed and stabbed after attending Friday night prayers at a service of the Bobov Hasidim. The Hasidim met to demand increased police protection, and they converged on a police station, where a fight broke out with the police.[21]

The attitude of the Hasidim and the blacks toward each other appears to be one of mutual hatred. The Hasidim see the blacks as the "ultimate goyim,"[22] and the proximity of such a negative reference group may reinforce the social cohesion and feelings of superiority of the Hasidim. However, despite the desire of the Hasidim to be near their zaddikim and the concern of the leaders for their followers to remain in the neighborhood, the physical deterioration and dangers have prompted a number to move out.

Attempts have been made to establish communities outside the city. In 1962 the Satmar bought five hundred acres in Mount Olive Township, New Jersey, thirty-five miles west of Manhattan, but proper zoning for housing was refused. In 1974 they made another attempt in a small town near Middleton, New York; eight apartments and twenty-five single-family houses were built. A successful move from Williamsburg was made by the Squarer (Skvira) Hasidim to a suburban country community in Rockland County, forty miles from Manhattan. The first twenty families moved there in 1957, and after some conflict with the local authority over zoning restrictions and other matters, they achieved incorporation as a village in 1961. The zaddik's house, the synagogue, and the boys' school are found at the center of the village, and one corner of the village is occupied by a shopping center and light industry. Many of the residents continue to work in Manhattan, and they have their own bus to take them there.[23] Finally, though, the large Hasidic sects are likely to remain concentrated in the city, and their suburban offshoots will be heavily dependent on the central communities.

Commitment

Although the majority of Amish and Hutterites are born within the communities, full membership is dependent on adult baptism, which not only signifies the commitment of the individual but also requires the approval of the community and its recognition that the individual is living in accordance with its rules and ideals. No such formal rite of entrance is found among the Hasidim, but acceptance within the community is dependent on conformity to a strict religious orthodoxy and a commitment to the particular zaddik. The prerequisites for membership in the Satmar, as stated in its bylaws, include the following: to observe the

Sabbath properly; to behave according to the Torah and not willfully vio-
late its prescriptions; to bring up one's children according to the Torah;
and, for married women and other women over eighteen, to conform to
the prohibition against wearing one's own hair.[24] The strongly introversionist Satmar make few attempts at recruitment, and the line between
members and outsiders is clearly drawn. In comparison, the boundaries of
the Lubavich are less clear-cut, and it is possible to distinguish Lubavich
Hasidism by past family commitment and present commitment. Most of
the core group, those who have the closest personal and organizational ties
to the zaddik, come from Lubavich families; they are likely to be most
resistant to the cultural influences of the outside world. Among those who
come from non-Lubavich backgrounds, it is possible to distinguish the
members who were raised in orthodox homes from the *ba'alai tshuvah*
("repentants" or "converts"), who came to Lubavich to learn Jewish law
and ritual. Interaction between the three categories is considerable, but
members tend to marry within their category. A further category on the
outer perimeter includes persons with a wide range of commitments, from
those who participate frequently in Lubavich ritual and send their children
to a Lubavich school to those whose affiliation is limited to a financial
contribution.[25]

Hasidic children are socialized entirely within the community. The agencies of socialization, the family, peer group, and formal educational institutions, emphasize the same values and reinforce each other. The Hasidim
have basically two age sets: childhood and adulthood; adolescence is not
culturally recognized as a distinct phase of the life cycle, and there is no
autonomous youth culture. The Hasidic schools both insulate the young
from the non-Hasidic world and help to integrate the community by socializing each generation to the distinctive values, norms, and patterns of
behavior.

The Satmar want their schools to serve primarily as agencies to prevent
undesirable acculturation. For the boys the schools are a training ground
for the study of the Torah, and for the girls the schools are places to learn
the knowledge that they will need as adult Hasidic women. Only in a
minor way do the Satmar see their schools as places to impart knowledge
that will be helpful in any practical sense, such as earning a living. The
Satmar are forced by law to provide some secular education, but the boys'
school places a heavy emphasis on religious knowledge and gives little
respect to secular studies. Since the boys know that lack of attention or
interest in secular subjects is unlikely to result in the disapproval of their
parents, they tend to be undisciplined in the secular classes, which are
taught by outsiders. Young men are encouraged to continue their religious
studies, and the yeshivah is a central institution in the community. The

Satmar have no tradition of teaching Torah to girls, but the state law requires that girls attend school until they are sixteen years of age, and despite the opposition of the more extreme conservatives, they have a school for girls. The tradition does not provide guidance for an effective Jewish curriculum for girls, and their religious education is kept to a simple level. The secular classes for the girls operate better than those for the boys.[26]

In Brooklyn there are three Lubavich schools for boys, and each family can decide which school it prefers. The most prestigious school has no English studies program; teaching is entirely in Yiddish, and the curriculum is more completely Jewish in orientation. This school is preferred by the core Lubavich members, and it is also preferred by some of the recent converts, who wish to establish their credentials and status within the community. One of the bilingual schools has the advantage of being located in a section of Brooklyn that has better housing and a lower crime rate than Crown Heights. The third school is for college-age boys who have had little or no previous Jewish learning. The one school for girls teaches Jewish studies and an English program that concentrates on reading and mathematics, with little attention to other subjects.[27]

In his study of the Lubavich in Montreal, William Shaffir notes that the Lubavich schools seek to attract students from the larger Jewish community and that only 25 percent of the students are from Lubavich families. Most of the non-Lubavich students come from homes that observe at least the Sabbath and dietary laws, but in contrast to the Satmar, the Lubavich are not selective in their recruitment of Jewish children, since they wish to familiarize children from less religious homes with orthodox Judaism. The inclusion of non-Lubavich children means that greater consideration is given to a secular curriculum, but although some Lubavich regard the secular studies as an important part of the education, the major emphasis is on Torah education. The school has two streams: in one, instruction is in Hebrew in the morning and English in the afternoon; in the second, instruction is entirely in Hebrew. The community is able to staff the Jewish departments, but it brings in outsiders to teach the secular parts of the curriculum. The risks of Lubavich students continuing their secular studies to the level required for teaching are believed to be greater than any possible deleterious influence from non-Lubavich teachers. The secular staff is expected to remain strictly within the boundaries of their subjects, and directions are given on what they should not teach. The curriculum does not include biology, and any reference to evolution or millions of years is forbidden. A rabbinic college for students between fourteen and twenty-two years of age provides an intensive program of religious studies, and students are strongly discouraged from pursuing a college education outside the community.[28] The Lubavich zaddik grants some children permission to receive a college education if he believes that they are strong enough to resist the secular temptations and that their education will prove useful to the community.[29]

It is important to emphasize what is not included in Hasidic socialization. Children are not taught the skills and knowledge that would enable them to participate successfully in the non-Hasidic world. More important than the lack of a good secular education is the lack of familiarity with the normative patterns of behavior in the larger society, and especially with the more informal and subtle aspects of interpersonal relationships. Young Hasidic adults are ill prepared to handle sociosexual interaction with members of the wider society. The sexes are segregated at an early age, and in some groups there is no period of courting. Most marriages are arranged in part by the parents. Sydelle Levy reports that when the Lubavich parents feel their child is ready for marriage (between eighteen and twenty years for girls, twenty to twenty-four years for boys), they arrange a meeting in the presence of a married couple who know both of them. If the boy wishes to see the girl again, he may call her directly, but while they are dating, they are expected not to touch each other. If they decide to marry, they need only to gain the approval of the zaddik.[30] Israel Rubin notes that the Satmar have little experience in making their own decisions and finds that they are likely to feel threatened if they have to do so. Up to the time of marriage everything is decided by the parents, and upon marriage they transfer this dependence to the zaddik.

The Hasidim are distinguished from other ultra-orthodox Jews by their commitment to, and relationship with, their zaddikim. The bylaws of the Satmar state that the zaddik is "the sole authority in all spiritual matters. His decision is binding for every member."[31] Shaffir writes that when the Lubavich are asked to comment on what characterizes a Lubavich Hasid, they emphasize the recognition of the zaddik as the central figure in their lives and their willingness to conform to his views and directives. As soon as a child is born into a Lubavich family, the father phones the zaddik. Children are taught to revere the zaddik; there is likely to be a portrait of him in the house as well as collections of his writings. The Lubavich refer to their zaddik in everyday conversation with great frequency; they discuss his teachings and directives and his extraordinary powers of perception and wisdom, and they relate miraculous stories about his activities. They place great emphasis on attending the gatherings at the Lubavich center in Brooklyn on holy days, when the zaddik expounds his teachings. When possible, the zaddik's discourses are transmitted to Lubavich communities around the world, and on the Sabbath and holy days, when broadcasting is forbidden, those present attempt to memorize his words and pass them on to their communities. The process of becoming a member of the Lubavich is characterized by an increasing orientation to the zaddik—an interest in his teachings, a letter to ask for his blessing or specific advice, or a request for a personal audience. A new recruit to the Lubavich community is only considered emotionally and intellectually committed to the movement when he places himself completely under the zaddik's direction and authority.

Hasidim also stress a familiarity with the lives, works, and teachings of the earlier zaddikim. The heritage of the movement is seen principally through the works of those zaddikim, and among the important gatherings of the Lubavich are those that commemorate events in the lives of the movement's zaddikim. The present zaddik, Menachem Mendel Schneerson, was born in 1902 and married in 1926, but is childless. The Lubavich are reluctant to discuss the practical implications of the lack of an heir, and it is often suggested that a possible solution will be coming of the messiah. When the zaddik himself was asked who was to be the successor, he replied: "The messiah will come, and he will take all these troubles and doubts. He could come while I am here. Why postpone his coming?"[32]

When the Satmar zaddik, Yoel Teitelbaum, died in August 1979, some of the mourners compared the event to the Holocaust. Rebbe Teitelbaum left no heirs and no formal method of succession, and although his followers recognized that there will eventually be a successor, they refused to discuss the matter.[33] When there is no clear immediate successor, some time can pass before a new zaddik is chosen, and during the interregnum the cult of the zaddik often focuses on pilgrimages to the grave of the late zaddik. After the death of Aron Rokeah, the Belz zaddik, in 1957 his followers made regular pilgrimages to his tomb in Jerusalem, principally on the anniversary of his death. The rituals on the day began at the Belz Yeshivah in Jerusalem, the major rallying point, where Hasidim from a number of countries prayed together and renewed acquaintances. A little way before the tomb a small hut was erected where pilgrims could ask for their kvitls to be drawn up in exchange for a pidyan. It was believed that a kvitl drawn up by the petitioner was contrary to custom and lacked efficacy. Both before and after the pilgrims placed their kvitls together with some pebbles on the tomb, they pronounced their personal supplications. The men prayed silently while the women cried, gestured, and implored loudly for intercession. After the visit to the cemetery the women and children went to the house of the widow of the zaddik for a meal while the men assembled in the yeshivah. Several men assembled in the apartment of the widow, where they lit commemorative candles and demonstrated an intense fervor in their belief that the spirit of the zaddik had entered the room. Finally, in a large hall the men participated in a joyous banquet to praise and honor the zaddik.

The Belz Hasidim are widely dispersed, and the pilgrimage helped reassert family and social ties and provided an opportunity for matrimonial agreements. The pilgrimage also had the function of asserting the distinctive identity of the Belz within Hasidism. After 1965, when the young nephew of Aron Rokeah was appointed as the new zaddik, the pilgrimage was celebrated more modestly. The cult of the zaddik returned to its more usual form, focusing on a living personality, and although some of the Belz Hasidim refused to recognize such a young man as their zaddik, by 1969 the new leader had fully assumed the spiritual and thaumaturgic roles of the zaddik.[34]

An additional mechanism of commitment among some groups of Hasidim is participation in proselytization. Although most Hasidic groups are against proselytization because of the dangers involved in contacts with the non-Hasidic world, a few communities have attempted to reach out to other Jews in recent years. The Bratslav, for example, attempt to spread the Torah and the works of Nahman, and they predict that they will become the largest Hasidic group.[35] The "Bostoner Rebbe," Levi Yitzhak Horowitz, leads a community in a suburb of Boston and seeks to attract Jewish students from Harvard, M.I.T., and other campuses on the New England coast.[36]

But by far the largest and most organized proselytizing campaign is that undertaken by the Lubavich. The major stated goal of this proselytizing program is not to add to the ranks of the Lubavich but to draw Jews into orthodoxy. Thus, they have no prolonged, sustained indoctrination period to process converts into the movement. Their campaign is based on the Lubavich teachings on the need to love all fellow Jews, regardless of their degree, or lack, of religious observance, and the need to prepare as many Jews as possible for the coming of the messiah.

The most widespread and best-known proselytizing activity of the Lubavich is the tefillin campaign, which was started shortly before the outbreak of the Six Day War in 1967, on the initiative of the zaddik. A notice stated that the practice of tefillin was essential as a divine commandment and for its protective quality. Moreover, it would also help "to vanquish the enemy in the course of battle." Since then the practice of laying tefillin has been seen as an effective device to start nonorthodox Jews on the road to observance. Unlike other precepts (dietary laws, Sabbath observance), it is relatively simple to observe, it requires little time, and it does not involve any initial changes in a person's lifestyle. In the United States, in particular, the tefillin campaign involves many devices, including bumper stickers ("Do your thing. Wear tefillin.") and mobile vans with tefillin booths, which park at airport terminals, on college campuses, and on Manhattan street corners with the message, "Are you Jewish? Have you put on tefillin to-day?" The Lubavich hope that once a man begins to lay tefillin regularly, the observance of additional mitsvot will follow. The Lubavich recommend a gradual adoption of other observances, for they recognize that recruits who try immediately to conform to a completely orthodox way of life will experience difficulties in their personal relationships. Each recruit is dealt with on an individual basis, depending on his interest and level of orthodoxy.

All Lubavich are encouraged to become involved in the campaign, but it is mostly the older yeshivah students who are responsible for the major activity of setting up the tefillin booths and persuading Jewish men who pass the location to lay tefillin. Women contribute to the campaign by raising money for the distribution of free tefillin. Shaffir makes the important point that proselytizing is likely to increase the commitment and reinforce the identity of the proselytizers: as they attempt to convince and influence nonobserving Jews, the yeshivah students are influencing and convincing themselves, and the yeshivah students, between fifteen and twenty years old, are at a stage in their lives when their beliefs may require strengthening.[37]

The commitment of the Hasidim to their own group has often been expressed as antagonism toward other Hasidic sects and their zaddikim. In recent years the major tension has been between the Lubavich and the Satmar. The Satmar look with dismay on the willingness of the Lubavich to interact with secular Jews, but the major issue has been over the appropriate orthodox stance toward the state of Israel. The Satmar abhor the friendly relationship of the Lubavich to the state, which they see as a blasphemy and an abomination. Actions of the Satmar against the Lubavich have included distributing leaflets attacking the Lubavich zaddik, hanging an effigy of the zaddik from a post during Purim, ransacking and later burning the offices of a Yiddish newspaper that was sympathetic to the Lubavich, and burning a candy store in Williamsburg that carried the newspaper. The Satmar were incensed when, in the context of a halachic discourse, the Lubavich zaddik praised the Israeli rescue at Entebbe airport, Uganda, of air passengers captured by terrorists as a miracle from heaven. In a sermon one Satmar likened the Israeli operation to the rescue of Mussolini by the Nazis. In 1977 the Satmar stoned the "Torah tanks" of the Lubavich when they came into Williamsburg, and fights broke out on the last day of Passover 1977 when, despite warnings from the Satmar, the Lubavich arrived en masse in Williamsburg to continue their custom of visiting prayer houses of the area on that day.[38]

Social Control

Social control is facilitated in the Christian introversionist sects by the small size of their communities. Among the Amish, who have thirty to forty households in each community, failure to participate in religious activities is easily noticed. When a Hutterite community reaches 150 members, it divides, and one section establishes a new community. Sanctions against deviance include public admonition and confession, and for graver offenses the deviant is forbidden to communicate with other members, including his own family. "Shunning" is most formalized in the Old Order Amish communities and somewhat less strictly applied among the Hutterites. There are institutionalized procedures for reinstatement, but if the offender does not show proper repentance or if the offense is too grave, he may be banished.

The Hasidim have a system of rewards and sanctions to ensure conformity within the community, but in contrast to the Christian introversionist sects, community size is not regulated, the urban residential pattern does not allow a strict control over participation, and there is no formalized equivalent to "shunning." The use of the *cherem* (excommunication) is a possibility, but it is almost never used. A persistent deviant is, however, likely to experience in less formal ways the rejection of his family and community, and this is a powerful constraint in an inclusive world where the individual is ill prepared for living in the wider society.

Important contexts of social control in the Hasidic community are the synagogue and the mikveh, where deviants are harshly treated through gossip, ridicule, and other treatment. In Satmar synagogues lists of names are occasionally put on the walls to warn worshipers about those currently out of favor. The most damaging gossip is often initiated in the mikveh. Since the individual is part of a dense social network and can only find esteem within the community, gossip can be a very effective means of social control.

Social control is also conducted through material channels. The community assumes responsibility for its poor and sick, and the system of charity applies pressures on both the givers and the recipients. Requests for charity are made individually, and since it is roughly known what each individual earns, members feel compelled to give the stipulated amount. The charity organizations distribute goods and services to needy members, but only to those who conform to Hasidic norms.

Conformity is constantly rewarded by support within the extensive network of social relationships, and, more formally, by ritual honors in the synagogues and at the gatherings of the zaddik. There is a close relationship between social control and social status, since status is dependent on the level and intensity of observance and scholarship. Nonreligious criteria of status, such as wealth, become relevant only if they are connected to religious behavior. Among the Satmar there is also a relationship between status, social control, and separation from the outside world. A person's status is indicated by the Hasidic clothes he wears, especially on Sabbaths and religious holidays. Those who have the highest status wear "extremely Hasidic clothes," which are most distant from non-Hasidic clothes. The process of gaining recognition in a higher social stratum is a gradual one, dependent on raising one's level of religious behavior, and those who display a higher level of religious observance will be permitted to put on more elaborate Hasidic garments.[39]

It is somewhat ironic that the Hasidim, who in the eighteenth century were accused of deviance and heresy, should have become the major carriers of a traditional form of Judaism. Traditional expressions of Jewish messianism are today also found mainly among the Hasidim, especially in the Lubavich sect. Despite his advanced age the Lubavich zaddik increased his activities in the 1970s in the belief that the Redemption was near and that it was necessary to prepare Jews for the coming of the messiah. The Lubavich made a parallel between Moses as the seventh generation after Abraham and Menachem Mendel as the seventh zaddik of their movement. They argued that the seventh leader received the spiritual strength of the first and that the seventh would bring to materialization the mission of the first. This was taken to indicate that Menachem Mendel would lead the people to redemption.

12. The Secularization of Millenarianism

THE TRANSPOSITION of beliefs based on supernatural assumptions into beliefs that emphasize human creation and responsibility is an important dimension of secularization. This chapter describes the three major secular transformations of Jewish millenarian beliefs and relates them to the social contexts in which they arose: first, the "progressive" universalistic version, which abandoned the notions of a personal messiah and the ingathering of the exiles and envisaged a messianic era of peace and harmony as a consequence of human progress; second, the secular revolutionist version, which foresaw a socialist revolution followed by a period of equality and happiness; third, the secular nationalist version, which argued that the Jews would overcome the evils of the diaspora by establishing their own state. The first proposed an accommodation to non-Jewish society, the second an overthrow of the total society, and the third an escape from non-Jewish society.

"Progressive" Millenarianism

This belief appeared mainly among western Jews (of central and western Europe and the United States). The cultural and religious accommodation of western Jews to non-Jewish society was a consequence of the breakdown of their legal, vicinal, and economic separation. Citizenship was granted to all French Jews in 1791, and legal emancipation was subsequently extended to many other European communities by the French occupation. After Napoleon's defeat the central European states reintroduced legal restrictions on Jews, but although the attainment of full legal and political equality was a slow process in many European states, the segregation of Jews was much reduced from the beginning of the nineteenth century. The central European Jews were subject to civil disqualifications and excluded from a number of occupations until late in the century, but they were no longer isolated in ghettos, excluded from the major towns, or limited to a few despised occupations. The abolition of restrictions on residence enabled an increasing number of Jews to migrate from the rural areas, where the traditional Jewish occupations were declining as a result of the urbanization of industry and the extension of markets, to the growing towns and capital cities. Within the cities many Jews moved from Jewish areas to predominantly Christian residential districts. Economic and occupational mobility often accompanied vicinal mobility, and the Jewish occupational structure became more heterogeneous and less distinctive.

With the lowering of the barriers between Jews and non-Jews the majority of western Jews expressed a desire to be accepted within non-Jewish society, and to achieve this they claimed that they did not differ from their countrymen in their "non-religious" culture and national identity. Despite their abandonment of a large part of the traditional pattern of religious observance the majority insisted that their Jewishness was limited to the specifically religious sphere and did not extend to their nationality. They were no longer simply Jews but "Germans of the Mosaic Faith," "Englishmen of the Jewish Persuasion," and so on. The majority of East European Jews, however, remained unemancipated and economically and socially distinctive in the nineteenth century, but a very small minority of wealthy "privileged" Jews who were exempt from residential and other legal disqualifications sought to identify with the dominant nationality.[1]

The reformulation of Jewish identity in strictly religious terms and the importance given to loyalty to the nation of birth or adoption were seen by many, both Christians and Jews, to be inconsistent with the traditional prayers for the coming of the messiah and the return to Zion. Christian opponents to Jewish emancipation pointed to Jewish messianic beliefs to support their case that Jews could not be loyal citizens. One response of the Jews in the emancipation debates was to make a distinction between their concrete loyalty to a country and their metaphysical and religious faith in the messiah and the return to Zion. They argued that that faith had no consequence for their everyday lives and loyalties. Moreover, they pointed out the spiritual similarities between Jewish and Christian messianism, which they said differed only in that the Jews still awaited their messiah, but stated that they had no desire or power to hasten the coming of a Jewish messiah.

For the majority of western Jews the traditional messianic and millenarian beliefs lost their importance and meaning, but the western Jewish communities did differ in the extent to which they sought explicitly to abandon or reformulate their beliefs. In Germany and the United States many congregations adopted prayer books in which the messianic prayers were omitted or reformulated. In France the messianic prayers were retained in the prayer books, but there was some development of a secular version of millenarianism. In England the traditional prayers remained, and the whole issue was almost completely ignored.

Reinterpretations of the millenarian beliefs began among the exponents of the Haskalah, in Germany in the second half of the eighteenth century. The early maskilim combined an orthodox pattern of religious observance with an identification of Judaism with the "religion of reason." They did not attempt to change the messianic doctrines, but they downplayed their importance. Moses Mendelssohn (1729–86), the most famous early exponent of the Haskalah, argued that the return to Zion remained part of Judaism, but that it had no bearing on the everyday life of the Jews. Most of the maskilim made little reference to religious salvation; they saw it as a distant event, and they put their faith in a strengthening of toleration among the gentiles.[2]

The reformulation of the messianic prayers was undertaken in the Reform religious movement in Germany. The first Reform temple was established in 1810, but the first Reform services did not take a consistent stand toward the messianic prayers: a few were omitted, the German translations of some blurred the message, and others were retained in Hebrew.[3]

The innovations of the Reform Jews were strongly opposed by the orthodox, and in 1835 the Bavarian government issued a decree calling for assemblies of Jewish representatives to present their differences in beliefs and practices. One district Jewish synod declared that the belief in the coming of the messiah was to be understood in a spiritual and not in a political sense. It stated that the Jews did not expect to return to Palestine or reestablish a Jewish state and resolved that all passages in the prayer book which petitioned for the coming of the messiah and return to Zion should be removed. The revised prayer book of the Hamburg Temple issued in 1841 expressed the hope for the coming of a messianic time without any reference to Palestine, but some vacillation was still apparent: some prayers referring to a personal messiah and the rebuilding of the Temple in Jerusalem were retained. The compilers recognized the inconsistency and defended it: one argued that the belief in the restoration of a Jewish land did not mean that all Jews would live there, and another said that a thorough consistency would have involved a complete severance from the rest of the Jewish community.

A number of radical Reform laymen established a Reform society in Frankfurt in 1842. They declared that Germany was their only fatherland and that they neither expected nor desired a messiah to lead them back to Israel. One founding member of the association argued that "we owe it to our Christian fellow-citizens" to reject the very notion of a messiah. The society aroused great opposition, including the opposition of some reformers who rejected the notion of the German fatherland as the realization of Jewish messianic hopes. Ludwig Philippson (1811–89) argued that they could not hide their lack of freedom in Germany by emotive phrases. For him the Jewish concept of the messiah was a universalistic one, denoting an era of peace and justice for all men, and it could not be restricted to Germany.[4]

At the Frankfurt Rabbinical Conference in 1845 the Reform rabbis expressed a variety of opinions which called for the elimination or reformulation of the messianic beliefs. Some argued that since the majority of German Jews had repudiated the belief in a personal messiah and Israel's political restoration, the prayers should be removed from the liturgy. Others argued that the messianic prayers should be formulated to express the hope for a spiritual rebirth and union of all peoples. Some claimed that they were now entering the period of a "messianic era," of the emancipation of mankind and the coming of justice and brotherhood. The conference resolved that "the Messianic idea should receive prominent mention in the prayers, but all petitions for our return to the land of our fathers and for the restoration of a Jewish state should be eliminated from the prayers." This policy was followed by the German Reform congregations, and the issue received much less attention in Germany in the second half of the century.[5]

Reform Judaism became the dominant religious stream among the socially mobile German immigrants and their descendants in the United States in the nineteenth century. The traditional millenarian beliefs were seen to be in contradiction with the conception of America as the New Zion, a belief that was prevalent among both Christians and Jews. Max Lilienthal, a rabbi of the Cincinnati synagogue from 1855, told his congregation: "We Israelites of the present age do not dream any longer about the restoration of Palestine and the Messiah crowned with the diadem of earthly power and glory. America is our Palestine; here is our Zion and Jerusalem; Washington and the signers of the glorious Declaration of Independence—of universal human rights, liberty and happiness—are our deliverers, and the time when their doctrines will be recognized and carried into effect is the time so hopefully foretold by our great prophets. When men will live together united in brotherly love, peace, justice and mutual benevolence, then the Messiah has come indeed."[6]

A conference of American Reform Jews in Philadelphia in 1869 adopted the following resolution: "The Messianic aim of Israel is not the restoration of the old Jewish state under a descendant of David, involving a second separation from the nations of the earth, but the union of all the children of God in the confession of the unity of God." Among the declarations of the Pittsburgh Conference of American Jews in 1885 was the following: "We recognize in the modern era of universal culture of heart and intellect, the approaching of the realization of Israel's great Messianic hope for the establishment of the kingdom of truth, justice, and peace among all men. We consider ourselves no longer a nation, but a religious community, and [do not expect] a return to Palestine."[7]

In Germany and the United States the abandonment of the traditional messianic doctrines was part of the program of Reform Judaism, which also insisted on the necessity for decorum during services and introduced prayers in the vernacular, regular sermons, mixed choirs, and organs. English and French Jews also made changes in the form of the synagogue services (decorum, choirs, and so forth), but the great majority of English and French congregations retained the Orthodox Prayer Book with only minor modifications in its content. The French Jews became the most secularized: in fact, one reason why they made little change in the prayer book was that they had little interest in religion and rarely attended synagogue.[8] Michael Marras writes that for most French Jews the messianic idea was a vague conception, "purely theoretical without any immediate or proximate application." Some French Jews proclaimed that the time of the messiah had already begun with the French Revolution and saw the messiah as a symbol of social justice. A widely used prayer book, which first appeared in 1857 and was reissued in 1898, contained a prayer in which France was declared "a second Promised Land" in which the Jewish people could thrive.[9]

Like other acculturated western Jews, English Jews identified their Jewishness in religious terms, but they made no attempt to omit or reformulate the messianic prayers. In 1900, Solomon Schechter, the Jewish scholar who later became president of the Jewish Theological Seminary of America, wrote: "The now fashionable cry . . . of our being Anglo-Saxons or Englishmen of the Jewish persuasion is but a sickly platitude. We can only be Jews of the Jewish persuasion." Simeon Singer, the minister who compiled the authorized British Orthodox Prayer Book, wrote in reply to Schechter: "I am an Englishman professing the Jewish faith. I refuse to recognize a classification according to which my neighbor ranks as an Englishman and I as a Jew." Israel Zangwill, the novelist, quoted passages from Singer's prayer book which appeared inconsistent with Singer's proclamations of his Englishness. For example, the prayer for the royal family included the passage "In her days and in ours may Judah be saved and Israel dwell securely and may the Redeemer come unto Zion."[10]

The success of Reform Judaism in Germany and the United States was related in part to the importance and status of liberal forms of Protestantism, which served as religious references and models for Jews who wished to demonstrate their acculturation to the wider society. Anglicanism in England served as a model for decorum for English Jews, but like Catholicism in France, its symbols and beliefs were too distant from Judaism to serve as appropriate models for changes in the content of the services. A more important factor accounting for the different orientations of the Jewish communities to the messianic prayers were the variations in the social pressures on Jews to emphasize and make explicit their identities with the various national cultures.

The German communities experienced a relatively high level of status deprivation: the movement out of the ghettos and the high rate of economic mobility were not paralleled by social acceptance into non-Jewish circles or by a rise in social honor. The full legal emancipation of the German Jews was slow and erratic, and even when progress was made in legal equality, social discrimination continued. The Germans felt a strong need for a homogeneous culture and strong national identity to integrate an otherwise nonunified nation, and even the Christian advocates of Jewish emancipation argued that the Jews' messianic beliefs were an obstacle to Jewish identification with the German nation and culture. Many German Jews concluded that the omission or reformulation of the messianic prayers would at least facilitate their integration into German society.

In the United States Jews also felt considerable pressure to deny explicitly what could be construed as an alternative national identity. The tendency of many immigrant groups to protect and strengthen their ethnic culture in separate communities and organizations was opposed by those Americans who emphasized the need for a single American culture that would encompass all groups, whatever their national or ethnic origins. Some Americans proposed a "melting-pot" in which all the ethnic cultures would fuse and form a distinctly new culture, but more common was the demand for "Anglo-conformity," the demand that immigrants should adopt the dominant values and behavior patterns that were defined, for the most part, by Protestants of English origin.

The Jews found greater opportunities for occupational and social advancement in the United States than in Europe, and their desire to take advantage of those opportunities made them particularly susceptible to the demands for conformity to the dominant culture. The absence of clearly defined social class distinctions and the emphasis on equality of opportunity produced ambiguity and uncertainty of social position, and in order to secure acceptance and status, Jews strongly asserted their American identity. Discrimination made native American Jews more self-conscious of their status and more sensitive to the demands for conformity than other Americans. In the first half of the nineteenth century American Jews found acceptance in non-Jewish groups, but social discrimination in the form of exclusion from WASP clubs began to appear about mid-century.

Exclusion of Jews from hotels, clubs, summer resorts, and college fraternities began to rise considerably in the 1870s and became more widespread from the early 1880s during the period of mass immigration of East European Jews.

Nationalism was an important force in France and England, but national identities there were more established and secure than they were in central Europe and North America, and English and French Jews felt less pressure to make explicit statements of their national identities in the religious sphere. The rich English and French Jews, who provided the lay leaders of the communities, were accepted within aristocratic circles. Social acceptance was particularly extensive in England, where the aristocracy retained its dominant position by incorporating and absorbing the haute bourgeoisie, gentile and Jew, and where middle-class Jews also mixed socially with gentiles. In this situation there was little pressure on Jews to prove their Englishness by removing the particularistic prayers from the religious services. In France the few titled Jews were accepted into the upper class, but the situation of the nontitled wealthy and middle-class Jews was more ambiguous: they were more accepted than they were in Germany, but they were not accepted quite as openly as they were in England. French Jews, however, had a respectable secularist option: the majority paid little attention to the content of the religious services, and they expressed their French identity by emphasizing their commitment to the secular ideals of the French Revolution.[11]

The conservative religious and political environment of East European Jews (Galicia under Austria, Poland, and Russia) was not conducive either to Reform Judaism or to the highly secular identity of the French Jews. The small circles of "privileged" Jews in eastern Europe sought accommodation to the dominant society through the Haskalah, but although they retained a higher level of religious observance than most western Jews, their stand toward messianism was similar to that of German Reform Jews. In a statement in 1837 to the Austrian government, Joseph Perl, a leading maskil in Galicia, wrote: "The truly educated Jews by no means picture the messiah as a real definite personality, but see in him only a symbol of the idea of redemption and universal peace which awaits its realization when Israel, free of all oppression, will be accepted into the family of nations. . . . The messianic era is, therefore, to the clearly thinking Israelite, nothing else than a time of love, respite and peace."[12] For the Galician maskilim there was no such problem as the diaspora: Austria was their fatherland, and the solution to the Jewish problem was the education and acculturation of the Jewish masses.

The small wealthy section of the Jewish merchant class in the commercial centers of eastern Europe was the major social carrier of the Haskalah.

Mahler has shown that in Galicia the Haskalah was found almost exclusively in the three major trading cities—Lemberg, Tarnopol, and Brody. The rich merchants were joined in their support of the Haskalah by their bookkeepers and clerks, as well as some tax farmers and professionals, especially secular teachers and physicians. There were a few poor Jews among the intelligentsia of the Haskalah, but in their writings they expressed the interests and outlook of the wealthy merchants and others who were linked to the government. The maskilim put great emphasis on their loyalty to the absolutist monarchy; they strongly opposed revolutionaries and expressed enthusiasm for the few concessions that they obtained in civil rights from the "gracious monarch." They looked upon the Jewish masses with disdain, viewed poverty as a consequence of indolence and inertia, and saw their greatest enemy in the Hasidim, whom they regarded as ignorant fanatics.[13]

Secular Revolutionism

In both western and eastern Europe the prominence of Jews in the radical socialist movements was out of proportion to their numbers in the population. The economic mobility of western Jews in the nineteenth century meant that there was no western Jewish proletariat to provide a mass base for a revolutionary movement, and the western Jewish revolutionaries were mainly intellectuals who represented a tiny minority of the comfortable middle class. The Jewish revolutionary leaders in eastern Europe were also mainly intellectuals from the middle class, but in the last decades of the nineteenth century an increase in Jewish factory workers and proletarianized artisans provided a social base for Jewish socialist movements.

A number of historians have argued that the relatively high Jewish involvement in revolutionary movements is explained, in part at least, by the influence of traditional messianism. This argument has been applied to Jewish revolutionaries in both western and eastern Europe. Nicolas Berdyaev, a philosopher of history and an ex-Marxist, wrote of Karl Marx:

> But the most important aspect of Marx's teaching concerning the proletariat's messianic vocation is the fact that he applied to the proletariat the characteristics of God's chosen people. Marx was a Jew; he had abandoned the faith of his fathers, but the messianic expectation of Israel remained in his subconsciousness. The subconscious is always stronger than the conscious; and for him the proletariat is the new Israel, God's chosen people, the liberator and

builder of an earthly kingdom that is to come. His proletarian Communism is a secularized form of the ancient Jewish chiliasm. A Chosen Class takes the place of the chosen people. It was impossible to reach such a notion by means of science. It is an idea of a religious kind. Here we have the very marrow of the Communist religion. For a messianic consciousness is surely always of ancient Hebrew origin.[14]

The passionate socialism of Russian revolutionary Jews has also been interpreted as a secularized expression of messianism. Moshe Mishkinsky wrote that the "Jewish labor organization received socialist doctrines as revelation, as a messianic vision which had been nourished to some extent by Jewish eschatalogical traditions and universal ideas of redemption."[15]

As far as the Jewish revolutionary intellectuals and leaders are concerned, the foregoing argument is not convincing. In both western and eastern Europe the Jewish revolutionary intelligentsia came from highly acculturated, middle-class families who had removed themselves from the Jewish community and who had not socialized their children in the Jewish religious traditions. Marx's grandfather was a rabbi and a descendant of a line of rabbinic scholars, but his father, a lawyer, had converted to Lutheranism for occupational reasons and he had had all his children baptized. Karl Marx was baptized at six years of age and did not receive any education in Judaism. Other Jewish socialists in the German-speaking countries, such as Ferdinand Lassalle, Eduard Bernstein, Viktor Adler, and Otto Bauer, typically came from families that had embraced German culture and were either Reform Jews or took no interest in the Jewish religion.[16] The Jewish revolutionaries in Russia came from families that had embraced the Haskalah, which had led them to reject the messianic beliefs.

It is true that Jewish socialists articulated with particular intensity a climate of imminent revolutionary expectations. This was especially the case in western Europe in the first half of the nineteenth century, prior to the revolutionary outbursts in 1848,[17] and in eastern Europe at the end of the nineteenth century. But the reason for the "secular millenarianism" of Jewish socialist intellectuals is to be found not in the influence of religious millenarianism, which few had experienced, but in their particular social experiences and locations.

Like many non-Jewish revolutionary intellectuals from middle-class backgrounds, the Jewish revolutionaries rejected the "bourgeois conformism" of their family backgrounds. The more intense forms of rejection and revolutionary expectation among Jewish socialists were related to their rejection of both the "pariah" ethnic group, in which they had been raised, and the general society, which refused to accept that group. It is necessary, however, to distinguish those who tried to escape their Jewish background by an identity with a non-Jewish revolutionary movement from those who attempted to radicalize Jewish workers and lead their movements. In western and central Europe, where there was no large Jewish proletariat, the great majority of Jewish revolutionaries were highly assimilationist, rejected the preservation of Jewish culture as reactionary, and refused to recognize the Jews as a separate national minority. This was particularly the case among the German-Jewish revolutionaries, who experienced the exclusion of educated, middle-class Jews from a number of prestigious occupations and from political and social life. In France, where Jews were able to enter the bureaucracy, the army, and higher academic posts, there were fewer Jewish revolutionaries than there were in Germany,[18] and in England, where acceptance of Jews into gentile social circles was widespread, native-born Jewish revolutionaries were unknown.

The radicalization of Jews from acculturated, middle-class backgrounds in Russia can also be attributed to the barriers against assimilation into the Russian middle class. The Russian-Jewish revolutionary intellectuals were raised in families that were no longer embedded in the Jewish community, but were unable to integrate into Russian society. A law passed in 1861 gave Jews with a higher education the right to live outside the Pale of Settlement, and in the 1860s Jewish youth began to enter the Russian school system in significant numbers. The number of Jewish university students grew from 129 in 1864 (3.1 percent of all university students) to 1,857 in 1886 (14.3 percent of the total), but in 1887–88 a quota system was imposed, and the number declined. The universities were centers of radicalism, but the quota system increased the radicalization of the acculturated, middle-class youth still further. Even those who received a university education were frustrated by the lack of employment opportunities for educated Jews. Estranged from the Jewish community and unable to penetrate the Russian middle class, many sought to become part of a working-class movement.[19]

The first Jewish revolutionaries of the 1860s and early 1870s had no connections with Jewish workers, and they attempted to remove themselves as far as possible from the Jewish community. They followed the example of the Russian populists (*narodniki*) from the upper stratum who sought to free themselves from the mentality of their class of origin by joining the life of the peasants. The Russian radicals saw the peasants, rather than the growing urban proletariat, as the carrier of a revolution, and the early Jewish radicals joined them in their contempt for the Jewish masses, mainly artisans and tradesmen, whom they defined as parasites. Many of the Russian revolutionaries were fervid Christians who believed that the revolution would have deep religious meaning, and some of the Jewish narodniki converted to Russian Orthodoxy to strengthen their identification with the Russian people. They found, however, that their efforts to become united with the Russian peasantry were of little avail: they came from an urban background, they were unfamiliar with peasant life, many spoke Russian with an accent, and they came from a religious group that was hated by the peasants. The final disillusionment of the Jewish narodniki came in 1881 when Russian populists justified the large-scale pogroms as a legitimate expression of true revolutionary fervor.[20] The pogroms and the anti-Jewish measures that followed led some Jewish radicals to intensify their efforts at assimilation into the Russian revolutionary movements, but others turned their attention to the radicalization of Jewish workers.

The emergence of specifically Jewish socialist movements, of which the most important was the General Jewish Workers' Bund, founded in Vilna in 1897, was related to the urbanization and growth of Jewish factory workers and proletarianized artisans in eastern Europe in the last decades of the nineteenth century. The emancipation of the serfs in 1861 and the slow but significant encroachment of modern capitalism resulted in the disintegration of the Jewish economic structure, which had been embedded in the feudal system. The growth of industrial production, and the manufacture of ready-made clothes and household goods in particular, displaced the Jewish artisans; the expansion of the railways and the growth of large-scale commercial enterprises undercut small-town Jewish shopkeepers and reduced the economic importance of fairs and market days; and the development of modern banking and loan associations reduced the importance of private moneylenders.[21]

The majority of Jews who suffered from the breakdown of the feudal economic structure were unable to incorporate themselves into the emerging capitalist system. The largest, most productive, and fastest-growing factories in Russia were situated outside the Pale, where only 8 percent of the Russian Jewish population lived. Moreover, within the Pale, most Jews in industry worked in small establishments that were often forced out of business as the competition increased. Trying to cope with the changing economic structure, many Jews became peddlers, hawkers, and small shopkeepers and thus were not attracted to the socialist movements. The Jewish factory workers and proletarianized artisans who provided the social base of the Bund were never more than a substantial minority: at the end of the century, out of a total Jewish population in the Pale of five million, there were about five hundred thousand artisans and fifty thousand factory workers. Robert Brym has shown that whereas the original leaders of the Bund came from acculturated families, they lived in the northern part of the Pale, Vilna and the neighboring Lithuanian provinces, where the proportion of Jewish factory workers was higher than in other regions. The Jewish Bolsheviks and Mensheviks, in contrast, usually lived in industrial regions outside the Pale, where they were relatively isolated from other Jews.[22]

Most Jewish socialist leaders were antireligious, but many workers remained religious after joining the Bund, and the influence of religious styles of expression became more apparent with the entrance into the movement of former students of the more modern type of yeshivah. The early Bund leaders were from Russified families, and some had to learn Yiddish, but their recruitment of former yeshivah students for leadership roles provided a link with the Jewish masses. One early socialist leader, Aaron Lieberman, believed that the students and former students of the yeshivot were the major source of Jewish revolutionaries. Lieberman, himself a former yeshivah student, wrote in the style of the sacred literature, especially that of the prophets, and even imitated the order of prayer.[23]

Yiddish newspapers carried socialist articles as the "portion of the week," and quotes from the religious texts, especially from the prophets, were used to support the revolutionary message. The Bund hymn, "The Oath," was sung as a ceremonial act, akin to Jewish ritual, and some sang it wearing a prayer shawl.[24] Messianic and millennial symbols were also used. A Passover eve colloquy of East European immigrants in the United States identified the Day of Deliverance, the messianic coming, with the social revolution. Like the preachers who concluded their sermons with the words "and come the redemption of Zion," the socialist Abraham Cahan concluded his newspaper articles with the words "and come the proletarian redemption." A song which was sung in many assemblies of the Bund included the following:

> The messiah and Judaism are dying, expiring
> A new messiah is appearing,
> The Jewish worker who the rich man exploits,
> Is raising the miracle of rebellion.[25]

The use of traditional messianic symbols did not mean that most Jewish socialists expected an imminent revolution. The hopes raised by the revolutionary events in Russia in 1904–5 were dashed by a series of pogroms, and in the years prior to World War I the activities of the Bund were directed toward raising funds for strikes.[26] In the late 1890s there was some disillusionment with social messianism among the Jewish socialists in the United States, and by the turn of the century a decline in revolutionism was evident.[27] This was probably the result of the economic mobility of the immigrants, as well as their acculturation to American society, with its less radical, more wage-oriented workers' movements.

Zionism

Jacob Katz writes that Zionism was "Jewish messianic belief . . . purged of its miraculous elements, and retain[ing] its political, social and some of its spiritual aspects."[28] Some of the important ideas of Jewish secular nationalism were first formulated by men from the tradition of religious millenarianism. In 1834, in the booklet *Hear O Israel*, Yehudah Alkalai (1798–1878), a preacher of a small Sephardi community in Semlin near Belgrade, argued that the establishment of Jewish colonies in the Holy Land was a necessary preparation for the Redemption. The traditional view is that the settlement of the land will follow the miraculous coming of the messiah, but Alkalai wrote that the Redemption would begin with the efforts of Jews in settling the land, and he supported his arguments with reference to the notion of the Messiah ben Joseph, who would conquer the Holy Land prior to the coming of the Messiah ben David. Alkalai was a tarnik, a believer in 1840 as the year of redemption. The failure of the messiah to appear and the contemporaneous rescue by leading French and English Jews of the Jewish community in Damascus, which had been charged with ritual murder, convinced Alkalai that human action would initiate the process of redemption.

Rabbi Zvi Hirsh Kalischer (1795–1874) of Posen, a border region between the traditional eastern European culture and the acculturated western culture, expressed ideas similar to those of Alkalai. In a letter to a member of the Rothschild family in 1836, Kalischer wrote: "The beginning of the Redemption will come through natural causes by human effort and by the will of the governments to gather the scattered of Israel into the Holy Land." Kalischer gave greater consideration to these ideas in his later years, and in his book *Seeking Zion* (1862) he wrote that the Redemption would not occur as a sudden miracle but would begin when influential Jews gained the consent of the nations for the Jewish settlement of the Holy Land.[29]

However, the writings of Alkalai and Kalischer made little impression, and when the Zionist movement emerged in the 1880s, its leaders and following were mostly secularized Jews. A "secular millenarianism" or utopianism was evident among at least some of the East European Zionists, who believed that the regeneration of the Jewish people would be achieved by their emigration from Europe and the founding of an entirely new type of Jewish society in the Land of Israel.

A few Zionist writers expressed their hopes and expectations in the symbols and phrases of traditional messianism. An early secular Zionist of this type was Eliezer Ben-Yehudah (1858–1923), who received a traditional education, but left a yeshivah for a scientific high school in Dvinsk, where he was influenced by the revolutionary ideologies of the period. After periods of supporting the narodniki and the nihilists, Ben-Yehudah turned in the 1870s to Jewish nationalism, and in 1881 he made his home in Jerusalem. Ben-Yehudah's traditional background was evident in his expression of his secular nationalism. He argued that the Jews had to end their peculiar history by becoming a modern, secular nation, and that to reside in Israel and speak Hebrew "is the meaning of the hope of redemption." The Jews could save themselves only by reviving the nation and returning to the fatherland: "We must turn our attention to what this people will be in 'the end of days', lest the miraculous day that I envisage come and find us unprepared."[30]

The socialist Zionists were particularly antireligious, but one of the early ideologists of socialist Zionism, Nachman Syrkin, tried to show a link to the Jewish religion and its messianic tradition. Syrkin distinguished between "rabbinic Judaism," which he argued held the people in chains, and "prophetic Judaism," which incorporated the socialist vision and positive national elements. He saw Zionist Socialism as the full materialization of prophetic values, and he expressed those values in the symbols of the messiah, the last days, and the Redemption. He announced that "the hope for a Messiah, always the basic sentiment of the *Galut* Jew, will be converted into political fact."[31]

A utopian orientation was particularly prominent among the second *aliyah*—the second wave of Zionists to settle in Palestine—which began in 1904 and lasted until World War I. These highly idealistic immigrants saw themselves as the vanguard of a future Jewish society based on a life of labor in communion with nature. The settlers of the first aliyah (1882–1903) had also wished to create a society based on social justice, Jewish labor, and the absence of economic exploitation, but they were less radical than the second aliyah in their rejection of the religious tradition, and they became conventional farmers who enjoyed a comfortable living by Palestinian standards.[32] For the second aliyah manual labor was an absolute moral value which was to redeem the Jewish people from all the evils of Jewish life in the diaspora. The values of the "conquest of labor" and self-sacrifice were all important: Jews had to return to a normal life in nature, and the self-sacrifice of the select few who qualified for the national battle would bring about an entirely new era for the Jewish people. Aharon David Gordon (1856–1922), an elder ideologist of the second aliyah, argued that nationality had a cosmic element, a blending of the natural landscape with the spirit of the people who lived there. As a nation in exile, the Jews had become separated from their corporate and individual souls, and they would become whole again only by returning to a life of nature in their homeland.[33]

Katz argues that early Jewish nationalism was not "a mental expression of material needs" and that it "emerged not as an ideology covering the interest of any distinct class but rather as a national utopia to be followed because of its being prefigured by traditional Messianism." There is some truth in Katz's argument that a "social necessity" did not create the nationalist idea, but he overstates his case when he writes that "the idea created the social unit" (that is, the Zionist movement).[34] Although the early Zionist writers of the 1860s gained some support and founded a loose society of sympathizers, they failed to achieve a settlement of Jews in Palestine, and a full-fledged Zionist movement did not begin until the 1880s in eastern Europe after the pogroms and intensified discrimination. It would be an exaggeration to argue that Zionism became the ideology of one particular class, but its major support did come from particular social strata within the Jewish community.

The widespread pogroms in 1881 led to disillusionment among secularized Jews of widely divergent political orientations. Many assimilationists who had looked forward to reform from the czar's regime were shocked by the approval and even the encouragement that a number of highly placed persons gave to the pogromists. Jews who had believed in the possibilities of liberal and democratic developments in Russia were upset by the support for pogromists by leading newspapers and men of education. The Jewish radicals were disillusioned by the response of the populists, who placed the Jews among the oppressors of the peasants and justified peasant violence against them.[35] Following the pogroms and new decrees of discrimination against Jews, groups of "Lovers of Zion," as they came to call themselves, emerged spontaneously and independently in many localities in Russia, especially in the principal cities where the secularized intellectuals were found. Some of the local groups joined in a loose association, the Hibbat Zion movement, founded in 1884, but after some expansion throughout the Pale in the 1880s the movement waned, and a general mood of pessimism set in among its leaders. In 1895 the total membership of the movement was between eight thousand and ten thousand, and even if peripheral supporters are included, the total did not represent more than 1 or 2 percent of all adult male Jews in the Russian Empire.[36] Of the two and one-half million Jews who emigrated from Russia and Rumania between 1880 and 1914, only seventy thousand settled in Palestine.[37]

Prior to World War I, Zionism failed to attract the masses in eastern Europe. The majority of those who stayed in Russia retained their adherence to religion, especially Hasidism, and the more secularized working-class Jews were more likely to support the Bund. In its initial stages, in the 1880s and 1890s, the members of the Zionist groups were generally disillusioned maskilim whose ties to the Jewish community were stronger than the ties of those who had gravitated to one of the socialist movements. Zionism had a pronounced middle-class character, and it tended to influence non-middle-class Jews only in those areas where Jews from the working class were relatively few in comparison with non-working-class Jews and working-class non-Jews (that is, in the southern Pale and Minsk province).[38] Zionism became an increasing concern of the Bund around the turn of the century, when Zionists actively sought the support of workers, and the leaders of the Bund attacked Zionism as an ideological tool of the Jewish bourgeoisie, who wished to divert workers from their true class interests to a nationalist viewpoint.[39]

A growing interest in socialism among Zionists developed independently in several areas, and a number of socialist Zionist movements emerged, the most important of which was Poale Zion. The formation of socialist Zionist groups was a response, in part, by the sons of middle-class Zionist families to the rise in the number of Jewish workers in factories in the two decades following the emergence of the Zionist movement in the 1880s. The mass base of the Poale Zion movement was not, however, the Jewish proletariat but rather the middle class, the more educated, and the master craftsmen. Poale Zion was stronger than the Bund only in those areas where Jewish workers were fewer in proportion to both non-working-class Jews and non-Jewish workers. Like the Bund, Poale Zion was centered in the more developed part of the Pale, but its most important recruitment base was Minsk, the least industrial province of the northern Pale.[40]

While Zionism in eastern Europe was not a direct product of religious millenarianism, part of its appeal was that it presented a secular solution that had similarities to millenarianism: the problems of the Jewish people were to be solved by the negation of the diaspora and the establishment of a completely new way of life, based on a fundamentally different set of values from those of diaspora Jews, in the Land of Israel. The millenarian element was largely absent in the Zionism of western Jews. Before World War I, the majority of western Jews were opposed to Zionism on the grounds that it contradicted their identification with their native countries. Support for Zionism in the West came in large part from a minority of East European immigrants, and only a tiny proportion of native western Jews gave their unqualified support to the movement.

Western support of Zionism often took a philanthropic approach; financial support was given to enable at least some East European Jews to escape persecution and settle as farmers in Palestine. At the end of the century there also appeared among western Jews a political form of Zionism. The best-known exponent of this movement was Theodor Herzl, an acculturated German-speaking Hungarian Jew who had only a superficial knowledge of Judaism. Herzl made no direct appeal to East European Jews, and his political Zionism was slow to make an impact among them. He did not support immediate settlement, but sought to secure a charter for Jewish colonization in Palestine through diplomatic negotiations and with the support of prominent western Jews. When his pamphlet *The Jewish State: An Attempt at a Modern Solution of the Jewish Question* appeared in 1896 it met hostility or indifference from most wealthy and prominent western Jews.[41]

While support for Herzl was not extensive, he did inspire great enthusiasm among some followers, who alluded to his fulfilling a messianic role and the coming of a messianic era. The German rabbis who voiced their opposition included some who feared that he would openly declare himself the messiah. Herzl became interested in Sabbatai Zvi, and his conversations and letters included references to the messiah and Zvi, but he regarded himself as a rational, realistic statesman who was proposing another secular state, and he divorced himself from the miraculous expectations of religious millenarianism.[42] Max Nordau, a disciple of Herzl, wrote in 1902 that political Zionism differed from the traditional religious expectations "in that it disavows all mysticism, no longer identifies itself with messianism, and does not expect the return to Palestine to be brought about by a miracle."[43]

The distance of western Zionists from the traditional notions of religious messianism was demonstrated by their support of schemes to establish a Jewish state outside the Land of Israel. Although Herzl recognized the arguments for the Jewish state to be located in Palestine, he tended at first to favor a relatively unpopulated area in Argentina. Later he came to favor more the possibility of location in Palestine, but after a number of disappointments he proposed at the Sixth Zionist Congress in 1903 that a commission of inquiry be sent to East Africa to consider a scheme for colonization in that area (the "Uganda Plan"). The proposal created a heated debate, and after the resolution was passed, its opponents, who included most of the Russian delegation, sat down on the floor in the traditional ritual mourning of the ninth day of the month of Av, the day of the destruction of the Temple. A threatened secession of the Russians, who called themselves "Zion Zionists," was avoided when the Seventh Zionist Congress in 1905 rejected the East Africa scheme after hearing a report that found the territory unsuitable for colonization. This, in turn, produced a reaction among western, particularly English, Zionists, who formed the Jewish Territorial Organization to work for an immediate territorial solution, even one outside Zion.[44]

Zionists born in the West do not appear to have differed from other western Jews in their social and cultural characteristics: they came from middle and upper socioeconomic strata and were highly acculturated to their societies. However, they had reacted differently from the majority to the renewed expressions of anti-Semitism in the last decades of the nineteenth century. While the majority regarded the new anti-Semitic outbreaks as temporary aberrations and continued to believe that their native lands would finally accept them as equals, the Zionists had become disillusioned with the assimilationist position and sought a redefinition of their Jewish identity. This was especially apparent in Germany, where, from the 1870s, new forms of political and racial anti-Semitism appeared, in addition to the already prevalent social discrimination. The German Zionists did not, however, reject their native country or seek redemption by migration to Palestine. The early German Zionists made no pretense that they saw the major benefit of Zionism for East European Jews and that their own personal destinies were still in Germany. The second generation was more radical and in 1910 passed a resolution which made aliyah, migration to the Land of Israel, an obligation for all Jews. The resolution had little actual effect on aliyah, and as Stephen Poppel has shown, the major function of Zionism for its German supporters was to enhance their self-images and provide a resolution to their problems of German-Jewish identity. In Zionism they found a suitable foundation for remaining in Germany.[45]

From the late 1920s the Zionist movement in the West grew considerably. The growth of racial anti-Semitism in Europe and the United States and the struggle against the Arabs and the British administration in Palestine convinced an increasing number of Jews that the assimilationist position was not viable and that the Jews needed their own state. The movements of acculturated Jews, such as Reform Judaism, which had strongly opposed Zionism, revised their positions and passed new resolutions in support of a Jewish state.[46] Zionism expressed a stronger Jewish identity among many western Jews, but with the exception of the German community in the late 1930s, few had any intention of settling in Palestine. Western Zionists remained principally concerned with the settlement and financial support in Palestine of Jews from persecuted communities, and it was only in Poland that a secular Zionist movement with an apocalyptic and messianic message emerged.

Polish Jews came to despair of remaining in Poland, and in the interwar years Zionism became the predominant Jewish political movement, appealing to a wide range of Polish Jews who differed in class, degree of acculturation, and political viewpoint. The social and cultural heterogeneity of Polish Zionism accounts for the numerous splits and parties in the movement.[47] Vladimir Jabotinsky, the leader of the Revisionist party, prophesied a coming apocalyptic catastrophe for European Jewry and advocated mass migration to Palestine, a Jewish majority on both sides of the

Jordan River, and the achievement of the movement's objective through a paramilitary organization. The movement received much of its support from middle-class Zionists in Poland and Palestine who opposed the ideologies of socialist Zionism, but who sought a more radical and military policy than that of the General Zionists. The most explicitly apocalyptic of the groups to emerge from Revisionism in Palestine was the Lehi (Freedom Fighters of Israel), which, under the leadership of the poet Abraham Stern, split from the movement in 1940. In one poem, Stern described himself as a soldier of the King Messiah from the generation which would "force the end." His followers expected a final apocalyptic battle against the British, and the establishment of the Jewish state under the socialists appeared to them as an anticlimax.[48] Following the achievement of the major aim of political Zionism, the focus of Zionist activity was directed to the protection and building of the state, and the messianic forms of secular Zionism lost their appeal.

13. Religious Zionism in Israel—A Return to Messianism

Orthodoxy and Zionism

Prior to World War I the leading rabbis and zaddikim in eastern Europe perceived Zionism as a vehicle of secularization and a major enemy of Judaism. One of the major aims of Agudat Yisrael, founded in 1912, was to protect orthodoxy against Zionism. A religious Zionist movement, Mizrachi ("Spiritual Center"), was founded in 1902 as a faction of the World Zionist Organization, but it remained a small and marginal sector of the Zionist movement.

Religious Zionists had to cope with the conflicting pressures from traditionalist and secular groups, and their attempts to harmonize two world views created a number of paradoxes that they were unable to reconcile. They were attacked by anti-Zionist traditionalists, Hasidim and mitnagdim, who saw them either as Sabbatians, followers of a false messianic promise, or as maskilim who had surrendered to the falsehoods of modernity. They were accused of delaying the Redemption and of deviating from true messianism, which counseled a passive waiting for the messiah. The followers of Mizrachi adhered strictly to the Halachah, but the anti-Zionists, attempting to discredit them, cast doubt on their religious observance. At the same time, the religious Zionists had to withstand the pressures of the secular Zionists who wished to display to the world the rational components of a modern national movement.[1]

These tensions were particularly acute in Palestine, where the traditionalists and the Zionists had fundamentally different conceptions of the Land of Israel. The traditionalists saw Israel as a holy land where everything had to be in conformity with the Halachah, and many orthodox Jews migrated to Palestine in the nineteenth century to escape the encroaching modernism of the West. The secular Zionists, on the other hand, saw settlement in the Land of Israel as an opportunity for the "normalization" of Jewish society. Exacerbated by competition over financial aid from the diaspora, the conflict reached its peak during the period of the second aliyah; the settlers of the second aliyah saw the Old Yishuv (Settlement) as representative of a deformed Jewish way of life, while the religious Jews saw the second-aliyah pioneer as a symbol of everything that was dangerous in Zionism.[2]

The few religious Zionists in Palestine were caught in a conflict that they were in no position to resolve. Their orthodox way of life and belief that a Jewish state should be founded on the principles of the Halachah alienated the secular pioneers, and their desire to create a premessianic Jewish state was seen as a profanation by the anti-Zionists. The latter argued that, quite apart from the religious question, Herzl's idea of a Jewish state lacked any basis in reality, for the Ottoman Empire and the Great Powers would never agree to its foundation. The only "realistic" solution was the messianic one, since it set the return of all Jews to Israel within a framework of a change in relations between the Jews and other nations.

The religious Zionists encountered a major paradox when they attempted to absorb a new system of beliefs, modern nationalism, into traditional orthodoxy, which denied the legitimacy of innovation within its system of beliefs. One of their problems was to reconcile their involvement in a modern, secular movement, which distinguished between a religious identity and a national identity, with the traditional perception of Judaism and the Jewish people as an organic whole. They were influenced by modern nationalism, but their fear of secularism and modernity inhibited any expression or acknowledgment of that influence. The religious Zionists could have sought to legitimate their activities by defining the period as the beginning of the Redemption, but this view was seldom expressed, for it further exposed them to the accusations of heresy by the anti-Zionist orthodox and the ridicule of the secular Zionists.

The Mizrachi tried to meet the religious criticisms by clearly distinguishing between political nationalism and the messianic promise, and in their support of the former they presented arguments similar to those of the secular Zionists: an independent Jewish state was a solution to the economic, social, and cultural problems of the Jewish diaspora. Political Zionism was also presented as a means of fulfilling the traditional mitsva of settling in the Land of Israel. In these terms, there was no need to present a radically new religious interpretation of Zionism.

An alternative stream of religious Zionism rejected the notion of Zionism as a political nationalist movement, which was denounced as a non-Jewish conception, and defined the whole of the Zionist movement as a sacred phenomenon. According to this view Zionism was an expression of a fundamental spiritual essence which was founded upon the covenant between God and his chosen people.[3] The most important exponent of this view was Rabbi Abraham Isaac Kook, who arrived in Palestine in 1904. He first served as chief rabbi of Jaffa, later became the Ashkenazi chief rabbi of Jerusalem, and from 1921 was in effect the chief rabbi of

Palestine. Kook's ideas require some discussion, not so much because of his position as chief rabbi, but because some aspects of his messianism have found a social carrier and been expressed in an influential religious movement in recent years.

Kook was certain that the days of the messiah were close and that the new settlement in Palestine of mainly secular Zionists was advancing the date of the Redemption. He perceived what was for him a complex paradoxical reality: the young Jews who were building the country, battling against a wicked administration, and living a life of deprivation in order to redeem the Jewish people from galut were at the same time contemptuous of religion and heretics in relationship to the Halachah. In contrast to the orthodox anti-Zionists, Kook saw religion and nationalism as two facets of one phenomenon, but he was faced with the paradox of social idealism among the antireligious nationalists. The traditional distinction between believers and sinners could not solve the paradox, and Kook had to introduce a third category to encompass the secular Zionists—the *chuzpanim* (insolent or impudent).

Kook argued that the revolutionary young who desired and fought for a better world but did not keep the mitsvot were at a higher level of sacredness than the inactive orthodox Jews. Redemption was preordained and would materialize even when its carriers were not aware of it—or were even, on the surface, unfit for the role. The contradiction between the sacred root of the secularists' souls and their religious sins was the inevitable consequence of an attempt to build a perfect world in a premessianic reality. Nevertheless, they were bringing the Redemption nearer, and finally they would recognize their true souls and repent.

The appointment of Kook as chief rabbi was a sign of the advancement of the New Yishuv, but among the circles of important religious scholars, Kook was highly isolated. His blurring of the distinction between the religious and the secular caused consternation among the orthodox, who were engaged in a hard struggle with the nationalists and socialists, who condemned the traditional way of life. Kook believed that opposition of the religious Jews to Zionism derived from the fact that the secularists were dominant in the national movement, and he sought to establish a movement that would give a sacred impetus to the building of the nation, but would not be politically and economically dependent on the secularists. Among the institutions that Kook wished to establish was a yeshivah for the best students and scholars of world Jewry.[4] His vision of a yeshivah in Jerusalem which would provide a spiritual center and religious leadership for world Jewry was not realized, but from the late 1950s the yeshivah under his son, Rabbi Zvi Yehuda Kook, taught a number of students who were later to become leaders of Gush Emunim, a messianic Zionist movement.

During World War I the position of the Old Yishuv was undermined: the Balfour Declaration undercut the political arguments of the traditionalists, and their material support was cut by the Revolution in Russia and the economic crisis of other East European Jews. By the end of the war the raising of money from the diaspora to support the community in Palestine was in the hands of Zionist organizations, and the Old Yishuv had become almost completely dependent on this aid. The beginning of the period of the British mandate was also the beginning of compromise and interdependence between the orthodox rabbinate and the Zionist leaders; the rabbinate needed the economic support of the Zionists, and the Zionists sought the legitimation of the rabbis to emphasize the historical and spiritual ties of the Jews to the Land of Israel.[5] Agudat Yisrael began to cooperate with the official Zionist institutions of the Yishuv in the 1920s, but until 1935 it continued to seek social and political separation from the Zionist community. After that date a new policy of economic integration and some degree of political integration with the Zionists was introduced by orthodox immigrants from Poland and Germany. The modus vivendi of Agudat Yisrael with Zionism was opposed by an anti-Zionist group, Neturei Karta (Keepers of the Gate), which eventually seceded to form a separate community.

Although the tendency among orthodox leaders during the British mandate period was to cooperate with the Zionists, they saw no positive religious meaning in Zionist activities, and they continued to believe that redemption would come solely from the divinity. Kook's teachings were not widely known, and even among the religious Zionists his influence was not great. The Mizrachi movement continued to be guided by a pragmatic stance which emphasized the need for a Jewish state to save the Jewish people and the Torah. The movement was largely an outgrowth of the rational Judaism of Lithuania, with a strong representation of mitnagdim. The social and religious background of the members of ha-Po'el ha-Mizrachi (the Mizrachi Worker), founded in 1922 in Palestine, made them more receptive to Kook's ideas. This group was from the lower strata and Hasidic milieus of eastern Europe and was part of the third aliyah (1919–23), in which the pioneering element predominated. It opposed the rationalism, conservatism, and bourgeois character of the Mizrachi. The movement advocated "Torah and Labour," the need to unite orthodox Judaism with a productive life on the land. A cabbalistic Hasidic influence was evident in the belief that the Jewish pioneer, in his struggle with nature, was performing a tikkun, contributing to the perfection of the creation, and cooperating with the Creator in preparing for the period of the Redemption.[6]

The Holocaust, the foundation of the state of Israel, and the Arab-

Israeli wars brought the vast majority of Jews, both religious and nonreligious, to the support of Zionism. Attitudes of religious Jews toward Zionism and messianism may be described as anti-Zionist, non-Zionist or pro-Zionist. The anti-Zionist position is represented in Israel by Neturei Karta, the members of which are concentrated in the ultra-orthodox quarter of Jerusalem. They argue that God alone will redeem Israel in a miraculous way, and until the end of history the people of Israel should remain passive and submit to the yoke of exile. Any endeavor of man to hasten the process of redemption is considered futile and represents a break in faith which will only delay the coming of the messiah. The repentance of the people is seen as an essential precursor to redemption, and the Neturei Karta find it inconceivable and absurd to believe that God would use those who deny him to bring about redemption. As sources of irreligion, Zionism and the Israeli state are obstacles to the coming of the messiah and should, therefore, be dissolved.

The non-Zionist position, represented by Agudat Yisrael and some other orthodox groups, is that while Jewish sovereignty over the Holy Land is a positive development and brings happiness, it is not a sign or a part of the process of redemption. These groups see the messianic idea as much higher than a Jewish state and stress the need for Jews to perform the mitsvot.

The pro-Zionist position argues that Zionism represents a continuation of the messianic idea, that redemption can be furthered by human effort, and that such events as the foundation of the state, the ingathering of the exiles, and the capture of Jerusalem are part of the beginning of the period of the Redemption. This view has been expressed by leaders of the largest religious party in Israel, the National Religious party (Mafdal), and by the chief rabbis, the chief chaplains, and others with high official positions in the religious and educational institutions of the state. The position of Benei Akiva, the largest religious youth movement, is that full redemption requires that the full geographical territory of Israel, as written in the Torah, be under Jewish control.[7] Members of the Benei Akiva have provided much of the active support for Gush Emunim, the most vocal and activistic of the religious Zionist movements.

Gush Emunim (Bloc of the Faithful)

Gush Emunim was officially established in February 1974, when it emerged from a pressure group within the National Religious party. The group had urged the party to reject any territorial concessions, and for a short time the leaders of Gush Emunim continued the struggle within the party. They found, however, that they attracted support across party boundaries, and they decided that a loose organizational framework, without any close ties to a particular party, would be most advantageous to their cause.

The leaders and spokesmen of Gush Emunim argue that the messianic process has begun, that the Jews have an essential part in bringing about the Redemption, and that the most important mitsva at this time is the settlement of the Land of Israel in its fullest biblical boundaries. They point to the actualization of a number of signs of the messianic period as predicted in the sacred writings: the fertility of the land, the success in agriculture, and the ingathering of Jews from all parts of the world. The foundation of the state and the conquest of the whole of Jerusalem in 1967 were clear steps in the process, and the movement celebrates Independence Day and Jerusalem Day as full religious holidays. The Holocaust, the wars, the international support for the Arabs, and the internal confusion in Israel are seen as the birth pangs of the messiah, which can be reduced only by human action.

The millennial beliefs of Gush Emunim are discussed below using the categories delineated by Yonina Talmon to differentiate millennial movements.[8] It should be emphasized, however, that the leaders of Gush Emunim have not presented a systematic account of their millennial beliefs and that their program of settlements has attracted many supporters and sympathizers who disregard, or are even unaware of, the millennial beliefs of the religious core of the movement.

History or myth. The members of Gush Emunim maintain that the process of redemption is occurring within a framework of natural events and human history. Unlike the traditionalists, who place redemption outside of history and emphasize mythological events, Gush Emunim declares that the phrase "days of the messiah" refers to concrete historical events such as the reappearance of an independent Jewish government, the wars with the Arabs, and the extension of Israel's borders. In accordance with this "rational" form of millenarianism, Gush Emunim does not have an apocalyptic or cataclysmic vision of a period to precede the Redemption. The Arab-Israeli wars are given a religious interpretation, but they are not identified with the cosmic wars that signify an end to history.[9]

Temporal or spatial. Gush Emunim is not a millennial movement in the sense of expecting an imminent completion of the process of redemption, and its members make no attempt to calculate the dates or describe the nature of the future stages in the process. They focus on the security of the whole of the Land of Israel through settlement as the present decisive stage in the attainment of redemption. Further stages are known only to God, who will continue to indicate, in the form of historical events, what he requires from his people. The absence of a focus on a personal messiah is in accordance with the belief that full redemption is not imminent. Members believe that the full unity of the Jewish people with the Torah is only possible in the Land of Israel, and in the present stage toward redemption this spatial dimension is the all-important one. They proclaim that the Jewish people have a sacred right to the land and that it is their sacred duty to repossess every portion of the land that was promised to Abraham, Isaac, Jacob, and the children of Israel. Conquest and war are considered legitimate means to defend this ancestral inheritance. In the words of one leader, the fulfillment of the process of redemption is more important than "hypothetical peace." The bond between the people and the land is seen to derive from God's election of the Jews and his vision of their destiny in the Holy Land. The holiness of the land determines the boundaries of the state, not considerations bearing on the relationships with the Arabs and the international scene. The intrusion of non-Jewish western politicians who demand compromise on the land question is completely rejected, and when Henry Kissinger was the major American negotiator, he was seen as a traitor to his people ("the husband of the *goyah* [non-Jewish woman]").

Particularistic or universalistic. Members of Gush Emunim emphasize the role of the entire Jewish people, secular as well as religious, in the process of redemption, but they are radically particularistic in their orientation toward non-Jews. They emphasize that Zionism differs from other modern nationalist movements in that it represents a continuation of an ancient spiritual reality and is derived from the messianic promise to the chosen people. The belief in the sacred tie of the Jews to the Land of Israel legitimates the appropriation of land from Arab Palestinians, who are seen as analogous to the ancient Canaanites. Peace between Israel and the Arab nations is seen to be dependent on the Arabs' acceptance of the Jewish right to the Land of Israel, but in the present stage of history this will not occur. Thus, the followers of Gush Emunim have no confidence in the peace negotiations and agreements with Arab nations. Real peace will be one of the signs of the messianic redemption.

The particularistic orientation of Gush Emunim is expressed further in its rejection of western culture which is perceived as a threat to the distinctive values of Judaism. The demand for compromise from the West is believed to be a consequence of the degeneracy of western ideas and culture, which can only harm the spirit of Israel. Since the leaders of Gush Emunim wish to gain support from the wider Israeli public, they do not announce publicly their opposition to western culture, and they have no wish to associate their movement with antiimperialistic, anticolonialist movements of the Third World. In public forums they limit their criticisms of western culture to the signs of "decline," such as widespread crime, drug usage, and materialism.

Restorative or innovative. Gush Emunim is a restorative movement in its emphasis on a renewal of an ancient Jewish sovereignty and settlement in the Land of Israel. Members do not concern themselves with the characteristics of a future messianic kingdom, and they make no attempt to remold or perfect the individual or society. In contrast with the Zionist pioneers of the second and third aliyot, secular and religious, who aimed at revolutionalizing the life of the Jew through work on the land, Gush Emunim has not suggested new patterns of community life. The whole question of the social character of the settlements has arisen only after their foundation, and many settlers continue in their former occupations, often commuting from the settlements in the West Bank to the urban centers of Israel.

Hypernomian or antinomian. Some religious opponents of Gush Emunim describe the movement as neo-Sabbatian and believe that it constitutes a great danger to Judaism. But since Gush Emunim does not expect an ontological break in history or an imminent millennial kingdom, there would appear to be little reason to expect an antinomian outburst. The leaders and most active members of Gush Emunim are orthodox Jews who assume that adherence to the Halachah will continue in the future stages of redemption. They do not believe, however, that redemption depends on a return to religion by the Jewish people, and they make no attempt to convert their secular supporters to orthodoxy.[10]

Active or passive. It is not so much Gush Emunim's messianic interpretation of the Jewish state that is new, but its insistence on the great importance of the borders in the historical process and its enthusiasm and dedication in settling the land. According to one spokesman for Gush Emunim, the tragedy of the secular Zionist movement was that it saw itself as similar to other national movements, and it lost its moral force once national sovereignty was achieved. Settlement of the land will remedy the weak moral condition of the people, and the members of Gush Emunim are spearheading the renewal, creating the conditions of redemption through sacrifice and suffering.[11]

Amorphous or cohesive. Gush Emunim has a cohesive core of leaders and highly committed members, but the support of secular Jews has meant that the movement lacks clear boundaries. The movement's leaders rarely express their views of redemption in public forums, but attempt to persuade the secular population by arguments that emphasize the importance of the conquered territories for military security, the need for Jews to defend themselves against anti-Jewishness, and the danger in depending on the "decadent" societies of the West. One obvious center of support by non-orthodox Jews came from the Land of Israel Movement, which was established in 1967 when its members called for the immediate annexation of, and the beginning of Jewish settlement in, all the areas captured in the war. The movement has also attracted support from some members of nonreligious agricultural settlements, the *kibbutzim* and *moshavim*, who see Gush Emunim as a continuation of basic Zionism and as a renewal of the *halutz* (pioneering) spirit, which has been lost in their own established settlements.[12]

The Social Carrier

Although Gush Emunim has found support among wide secular circles, the core of the movement is a religious one. Most of the leaders of Gush Emunim were, at one time or another, students or staff members of the yeshivah Mercaz HaRav in Jerusalem, headed by Rabbi Zvi Yehuda Kook. The older leaders of Gush Emunim were students at the yeshivah in the 1950s when, in contrast to the advice given to students in other yeshivot, they were encouraged by Rabbi Kook to join the armed forces. A considerable increase in the number of students in the yeshivah occurred after the 1967 war when the yeshivah began to attract not only a greater number of the youth from Benei Akiva but also some converts from secular backgrounds. The appeal of the yeshivah was a response to the prominence of the religious, "knitted skullcap" soldiers in actions of valor during the war, and during the Yom Kippur War in 1973 the participation of religious youth received even greater attention.[13]

The knitted skullcap has become the symbol of a new type of religious youth who combine an adherence to an orthodox form of Judaism with support of Zionism and participation in modern life. They are not an entirely recent phenomenon, but in the last two decades their numbers have increased considerably. The majority came from modern orthodox homes, participated in the Benei Akiva youth movement, and attended religious schools. Many are students or graduates of high school yeshivot whose principals and teachers recognized that they would attract students only if they taught secular subjects in addition to the Torah. Religious and secular studies were kept separate (the latter usually taught in the afternoon), and an emphasis was put on secular subjects that did not compete with the religious world view (engineering, mathematics, physics, and so forth). The secular studies are perceived primarily as necessary to making a living, but it is the religious part of the curriculum which is valued and the source of satisfaction. Many Gush Emunim supporters complete their education in yeshivot that combine advanced Torah education with service in the army.

The high school yeshivot teach strict adherence to the Halachah, but their students and graduates have accommodated to many areas of modern life. They provide a striking contrast to the life-styles of the non-Zionist and anti-Zionist ultra-orthodox. They dress in contemporary fashions, and their leisure-time activities are little different from those of secular youth: they watch television, go to mixed parties, and go to the cinema and theater. It is against this background of compromise between the religious and the secular that a strong nationalist tendency has developed.[14]

The Social and Historical Context

The prominence of a modernized religious youth and a messianic religious Zionism may be set against the background of a wider social phenomenon in Israeli society: the decline in the significance of secular Zionist and socialist symbols and belief systems and the concomitant penetration of religious symbols into the national culture or civil religion. Examples of the latter trend include the focus on the Western Wall as a religious shrine, the increasing number of popular songs with religious content, the greater use of religious ceremonial in Memorial Day observances, and the emphasis on the Bible not merely as a book which contains the historical record of the ancient Israelites but as an essentially religious document. Charles Liebman has pointed to a number of causes for this development: the entry into the country and integration into the society of religious immigrants; the unification of the educational system, which involved the disappearance of schools with a Zionist-socialist ideology; the forging of links with western (particularly American) Jews based on the common religious heritage; and, finally, the response of political leaders to the problem of legitimacy. In the prestate period the political elite had little need for religious legitimation: the secular Zionists and socialists were confident of their goals, and they had their own founders, martyrs, ideologies, and symbols. The achievement of the major goal of political Zionism—the foundation of the state—and the failure of the more idealistic Zionist-socialist visions to materialize created a greater need for the legitimation of the Zionist endeavor. After 1967, when the survival of the country appeared more secure, the acquisition and control of territory that was disputed by the indigenous populations was justified not only on grounds of security but more and more by references to "historical rights" that have religious associations. The losses of the Yom Kippur War and the sacrifices that were demanded of Israelis in its aftermath reinforced the tendency toward a religious legitimation.[15]

The major historical events (the creation of the state, the Six Day War, the Yom Kippur War) and the changing values of Israeli society have had important influences on the direction of religious Zionism. The foundation of the Jewish state exacerbated the tensions and paradoxes within religious Zionism. The religious Zionists faced a contradiction between their desire for a halachic state and their cooperation with nonreligious politicians who ruled a secular state. The achievements of the religious Zionists appeared minimal compared with those of the secular Zionists, and the attempts of the religious Zionist politicians to straddle the breach between the secularists and the ultra-orthodox non-Zionists often made them appear to have little direction or purpose. Many young religious Zionists disliked the political haggling, bargaining, and compromises of the religious Zionist politicians, and they were attracted to messianic ideas, which, for them, gave religious Zionism a clear focus and program of action.

From the 1950s the value of agricultural labor, which had been adopted from secular socialist Zionism and given a religious meaning by Po'alei Mizrachi and Benei Akiva, declined among both secular and religious Zionists. Religious kibbutzim had been set up in the 1930s and 1940s alongside the much larger secular kibbutz movements, but with the decline of the prestige of the kibbutzim in Israeli society fewer young Zionists from the Benei Akiva movement chose to join them. Many went instead to attend yeshivot, and it was within the Zionist yeshivot, particularly the Mercaz HaRav of Zvi Yehuda Kook, that the focus of religious Zionism was narrowed down to the messianic element.[16]

Adumbrations of the ideology of Gush Emunim can be traced to the first religious Zionist writers in the middle of the nineteenth century, but its leaders refer to the writings of Rabbi Abraham Kook and the interpretations of his son as their major ideological sources. Religious opponents have argued that Gush Emunim has distorted the thought of Abraham Kook in failing to follow Kook's concern with all aspects of life and in focusing solely on his writings on the beginning of the Redemption. The Oz Veshalom movement, founded in 1975 to counter what its members regard as the misinterpretations of religious doctrine by Gush Emunim, argues that although the Jews have a right to the Land of Israel, there is a need to compromise on this value for another—peace and justice.[17] The correct interpretation of Abraham Kook's writings is not of concern here, but it does appear that Gush Emunim has found an elective affinity with certain of Kook's ideas, which are used to justify their actions in establishing settlements in the land taken from Jordan in the 1967 war—the West Bank, or Judea and Samaria.

The rapid victory of the Israeli forces in the Six Day War, which many religious Jews described as a miracle, gave an important impetus to the development of religious messianic Zionism. The conquest of Judea and Samaria gave a new dimension to the sacredness of the whole of the Land of Israel and its relationship to the messianic hope. Soon after the war a group of religious Zionists met to discuss the religious significance of the victory, and some referred to the beginning of the Redemption. The euphoria following the victory encouraged some to believe that they could convert the secular Jews to their beliefs and build a united movement which would prepare for the Redemption. After some hesitant overtures to secular groups, these hopes were discarded, but the messianic tension remained among young religious Zionists, and a few who were instrumental in the foundation of new settlements later became leaders of Gush Emunim.[18]

The ideological and organizational roots of Gush Emunim considerably predate the Yom Kippur War, but its success as a social movement can be understood only in relation to the consequences of that war. From a strictly military point of view the war ended with a victory, but the initial gains by the Arabs, the twenty-five hundred Israeli lives lost, and the political repercussions dealt an enormous blow to the triumphant confidence that had characterized post-1967 Israel. Following the war many sought to explain the "failure" by questioning many aspects of Israeli life—military, political, social, and cultural. Janet O'Dea has gone as far as to refer to a state of anomie in this period: the former confidence was broken, the consensus on values was lost, and the very meaning of Zionism was questioned.

The war also posed a problem of meaning for the religious Zionists: they had seen the expansion of Israel in the 1967 war as a confirmation of the messianic process, but since the land was already in the hands of the Jews, it was difficult to justify another war. Gush Emunim countered the prevailing discontent, doubts, and fears of the population by interpreting the war as one of the birth pangs of the messiah and as a warning to the Jewish people to take their part in the process of redemption. The spokesmen for Gush Emunim saw the government as lacking an understanding of the situation and saw the members of the movement as a spiritual elite whose actions, though often in opposition to the government and sometimes involving a struggle with Israeli soldiers, were justified by their appreciation of the urgent need to reduce the birth pangs and accelerate the redemption process. The political isolation of Israel was yet another sign of messianic times: it was a fulfillment of the ancient prophecies of the Jews as "a people that dwells alone." Thus, Gush Emunim derived its strength from the malaise that followed the Yom Kippur War. In place of doubt and uncertainty, they substituted certainty and idealism, and in face of the foreign political pressure, they preached defiance and the necessary separateness of the Jewish people.[19]

14. Conclusions

THE RELIGIOUS movements discussed in this work varied considerably in size and duration. Three types may be distinguished. The first type includes ephemeral millenarian outbursts that did not extend beyond a local community or limited area. Most of the incidents during the crusades and some at a later date in Spain were of this type. The second group is composed of millenarian outbursts that encompassed larger numbers in a region or nation. These outbursts were less ephemeral than the first type, but they rarely lasted more than a decade or two. Examples of this type include the movements in Persia in the eighth and eleventh centuries, in Spain at the ends of the fourteenth and fifteenth centuries, and in Italy at the beginning and end of the sixteenth century. The third type comprises movements that spread considerably beyond the area of origin and continued for an extensive period (a century or more). The movements in this category were Sabbatianism, the only Jewish millenarian movement to continue for such a long period, and Hasidism, the only popular mystical movement to develop within the context of rabbinic Judaism. Differences in the scale and longevity of religious movements should be kept in mind in assessing theoretical perspectives. A particular perspective may, for example, address itself to the origins of movements, but ignore the problems of growth and consolidation.

The Remedy-Compensation Perspective

The most common perspective found in studies of religious movements is the remedy-compensation perspective. Explanations within this perspective may be distinguished by their relative emphases on oppression, disaster, relative deprivation, and social disorganization and anomie.

Oppression. Millenarian movements have often been interpreted as protests of a social class or people against their economic and political oppressors. Interpretations of the effect of oppression on Jewish movements may be summarized in two hypotheses: the first states that the movements represented a symbolic revolt of lower-strata Jews against their wealthier brethren, whereas the second maintains that the movements represented a symbolic revolt of entire Jewish communities against their gentile oppressors.

The first hypothesis finds little support: the movements included adherents from the wealthier strata, and although some found their greatest appeal among the poorer strata, very few showed traces of an element of social protest against the Jewish upper class. Jewish millenarian movements emphasized the unity of the Jewish people, and although some early Hasidim criticized the scholarly elite for their indifference to the people, the economic and status divisions within the community did not become major issues. Only Jewish revolutionary socialism, which was not an outcome of Jewish millenarianism, directed attacks specifically against the Jewish bourgeoisie. In that case the Jewish bourgeoisie was also seen as part of the wider ruling class, which was to be overthrown.

Jewish millenarians directed their anger mainly against gentiles, and the desire for national independence was an important element in their movements. Economic and political subordination cannot, however, account for the historical and geographical locations of the movements. The Jews were subject to many legal restrictions, but judged by medieval and early-modern standards, they enjoyed a relatively high level of freedom: they lived under the protection of sovereigns and had considerable corporative autonomy and independence. Discrimination limited Jewish economic activities and their range of occupations, but they were economically no worse off, and often considerably better off, than the great majority of the population. Although political subordination and economic discrimination were persistent features of Jewish life in the diaspora, the economic and political measures taken against Jews varied greatly over different cultures and periods. These are best considered within the explanations that consider disaster and relative deprivation.

In comparison with many non-Jewish millenarian movements Jewish millenarians gave relatively little attention to the element of social revolutionism in the millennium. Their prophecies often included expectations of a radical alteration in the political relationship between the Jewish nation and other nations, but the future social organization of Jewish society and other societies received little consideration. Revolutionism is a prominent feature in the millenarian movements of colonized peoples who wish to destroy or expel the colonialists and in the movements of economically subordinate classes who seek to overthrow the ruling class. With the exception of the Frankists, who did have a revolutionary stance, the major concern of Jewish millenarians was to escape from the dominant society, not change it. In contrast to those of most non-Jewish millenarians the sacred places of Jewish millenarians were located far from their areas of residence. The importance of the theme of the redemption of all Jews from the diaspora and the ingathering of the exiles meant that social divisions within the Jewish communities or the features of the societies from which the Jews wished to escape received less attention.

Disaster. Many widespread millenarian outbursts arose during or following instances of acute persecution, massacre, or exile: in Spain in 1391; following the exile from Spain in 1492; among the conversos in Spain and Portugal; and in Italy at the end of the sixteenth century. Sabbatianism in the seventeenth century was not an outcome of a dramatic instance of persecution (the 1648 massacres in Poland cannot account for the distribution of the movement), but memories of persecution among the former marranos, many of whom were recent refugees from the Iberian peninsula, was no doubt one factor. Renewed persecution in southeast Poland in the eighteenth century was one element in the background of Frankism and Hasidism. The rise of Zionism in eastern Europe followed the widespread pogroms in 1881, and the success of Gush Emunim followed the "disaster" of the Yom Kippur War.

Persecution was not a necessary condition for millenarianism: instances of millenarianism occurred with no clear relationship to persecution, and persecution occurred without being followed by millenarianism. The influence of persecution on millenarian outbursts was variable, dependent on other factors. One important cultural dimension which influenced the association between persecution and millenarianism was the presence or absence of other established explanations of, and compensations for, persecution. Messianic beliefs were as much a part of the religious tradition of Ashkenazim as they were of that of the Sephardim, but in the medieval period the Ashkenazim were far less prone to use those beliefs to account for the disasters that befell them. The Ashkenazim accounted for persecution as a consequence of the sins of the Jewish people, and they found solace in the belief that in accepting death rather than conversion they were proving their righteousness and would be rewarded by a blissful afterlife. The Sephardim and the Italian Jews explained the exile from Spain and persecution as part of the birth pangs of the messiah and looked forward to the revenge that would be exacted by his forces.

The different responses of the Sephardim and Ashkenazim to persecution were related to more general differences in their cultural orientations toward the countries in which they lived and to the whole notion of galut. During most of the medieval period the situation of the Sephardim in the Iberian peninsula was considerably better than that of the Ashkenazim, and although the Sephardim accepted galut as part of their religious tradition, they formed a strong attachment to the Spanish kingdoms and their culture. Galut was less prominent in the consciousness of the Sephardim, and they turned to messianism when their pride and identity were shattered by the massacres and exile. The Ashkenazim felt little or no attachment to the host societies, and it was precisely because they felt in galut and saw it as normative that they were less attracted to millenarianism. Galut was a state of being to which they had to adjust so that sometime in the unforeseen future they would be redeemed.

The religious necessity of galut has been expressed in recent times in Israel by the Neturei Karta, who stem from the traditional Ashkenazi society. They condemn Zionism and the state of Israel because they believe that the Jews were exiled by divine decree and that the ingathering of the exiles and national independence can legitimately occur only by divine decree. Like the Ashkenazim in the medieval period, they glorify the Jewish martyrs who accepted the persecution of the gentile world in a passive manner. Their models are not the partisans of the Warsaw Ghetto uprising or the heroes of the Israeli army but the millions of religious Jews in Europe who, for their love of the Torah and "for the sanctity of the name," accepted suffering and death without rebellion.[1]

The medieval Ashkenazim and Sephardim differed markedly in their reactions to persecution, but their explanations of events were not mutually exclusive. It was possible to account for disaster as both a punishment for the sins of the Jewish people and as part of the process of redemption. In recent times Gush Emunim has interpreted the Yom Kippur War as a warning and trial to help cleanse and purify the Jewish people before the advent of the messiah. As far as the relationship between messianism and Jewish action is concerned, Gush Emunim is at the opposite end of the religious spectrum from Neturei Karta: they argue that the Jews can reduce the sufferings of the pangs of the messiah by taking up the fight against the gentiles.

Relative deprivation. The distinction between absolute and relative deprivation has been a common one among sociologists. If they do not make a comparison with an alternative state of affairs, persons may undergo considerable hardship yet demonstrate little response or reaction. A person feels relative deprivation when he compares his situation disfavorably with that of another, and this gives rise to such feelings as dissatisfaction, resentment, injustice, and a desire for compensation and revenge. He may compare his situation in any of several areas: comparison with members of his own group, comparison with another group, comparison of the present with the past, or comparison of the present with expectations of the future.

The best-known typology of relative deprivation in the sociology of religion was made by Charles Glock, who distinguished economic, social (status), organismic, ethical, and psychic forms of deprivation.[2]

This perspective has drawn considerable criticism, which argues that the perspective explains either too much or too little. It explains too much because if the investigator looks hard enough he is almost certain to find some form of deprivation. It explains too little because the perspective cannot account for the type of movement that will arise under conditions of relative deprivation. Glock went some way toward meeting this criticism when he made a number of hypothetical correlations between type of relative deprivation and type of movements. He argued, for example, that millenarian and revolutionary movements were likely to arise under conditions of economic deprivation, whereas religious movements of accommodation and secular movements of reform were likely to arise under conditions of status deprivation. He acknowledged that the factor of relative deprivation did not itself explain why in some cases the response might be a religious one and why in others it might be secular, and he wrote that the religious response was more likely when the causes of deprivation were not accurately perceived and when those affected were not in a position to eliminate the causes. One can add that the type of response also depends on the availability of religious or secular belief systems, which vary according to the society and the historical period. In the medieval and early-modern periods, when the religious world view was taken for granted, a religious response was likely. Even if people accurately perceived the causes of their deprivation, they were likely to believe that the situation would change only with supernatural help.

A whole number of questions need to be asked if the predictive power of the relative deprivation perspective is to be improved and the possible responses narrowed down: What type of deprivation was it, and how extensive? How did it arise? How was it accounted for? How were the possibilities of remedying the situation perceived? Answers to such questions are likely to require an analysis of social, cultural (including religious), and, possibly, personality factors that are unrelated to relative deprivation.

The limitations of relative deprivation as a general explanation have been widely recognized, but critics of the approach have argued that there are crucial problems even if it is used as only part of an explanation. Roy Wallis argues that the type of evidence used by relative deprivation theorists does not support their theses. First, if one is to prove relative deprivation, one must provide evidence that the deprivation was actually felt or experienced, but investigators have often produced accounts of objective circumstances, which are presumed to have affected the participants, rather than the participants' interpretations of their situation. Second, investigators have used the ideology of a movement to demonstrate that there was deprivation, but this risks tautology, since it is concluded that relative deprivation was the cause of the movement and its ideology. Wallis writes that any explanation of why people join movements must begin with the peoples' accounts, and if these cannot be obtained, the search for causes must be abandoned.[3] These points can be applied to other explanations within the remedy-compensation perspective.

There can be no argument against the view that participants' accounts should be sought, and it is possible that these will provide evidence of relative deprivation. The historical records of a number of groups discussed in this book demonstrate clearly that they compared their situation unfavorably with their past: the Sephardi exiles compared their situation with the past glory of the Jews in Spain; the Jews of Salonika in the late seventeenth century compared their economic distress with their past prosperity; and the Jews of Poland in the eighteenth century bemoaned the disintegration of their communities and the declining standards of moral and religious behavior. These accounts do not generally show or imply that people became millenarians or mystics because of their relative deprivation, and, in fact, very few participants' accounts directly address this problem. But even if participants' interpretations of their adoption of millenarianism or mysticism were available in abundance, this would not overcome the problem of causal analysis. Wallis recognizes that the reliability of participants' accounts may also be questioned and that the accounts should be evaluated in the context of the role of participants and the operation of the collectivity. What is meant by reliability here is presumably not just that the accounts are truthful but also that the accounts reflect the actual motivations of individuals who joined the movements. It is of course possible that the accounts were given in good faith, but that actual motivations were unconscious and unrecognized. In fact, it is unlikely that accounts by members will take the investigator very far in a causal analysis of the emergence and success of a movement. The accounts are obtained after the people have joined the movement, and they often have a stereotyped character that repeats the symbols, concepts, and ideology of the movement.

Wallis writes that an essential step in *explaining* a movement is *understanding* participants' accounts, but he gives little indication how the investigator can move from understanding to explanation. Does the investigator simply build upon the participants' accounts or does he go beyond them by relating the participants' actions to conditions that they have not acknowledged as determining their action? This question has involved many writers in complex philosophical and methodological arguments,[4] but only a few brief remarks are presented here to indicate the present author's position. A person's view of his own action is not necessarily a reliable guide to the causes, consequences, or social significance of the action. Sociologists would severely restrict the range and findings of their investigations if they did not accept the principle that an informed observer can often have a better understanding of participants' actions and their determining conditions than the participants themselves. In some cases the participants' interpretive meanings, however truthful, may give an entirely misleading account of the determining conditions of action, and one problem for the investigator is to account for the discrepancy between his interpretations and the participants' accounts.

The absence or paucity of participants' accounts does not necessarily mean that the investigator has to abandon the task of explanation. If the investigator finds a number of instances of a certain type of movement appearing under similar circumstances, he may presume, on the basis of psychological principles that people experienced the circumstances in a way that made the movement attractive to them. This study has found that a number of millenarian outbursts and movements occurred among Jews who had suffered a sharp decline in wealth, status, and security:[5] these include the Sephardim at the end of the fourteenth and fifteenth centuries, the conversos in Spain and Portugal, the Italian Jews in the last decades of the sixteenth century, and certain Sephardi and former marrano communities in Italy and the Ottoman Empire in the second half of the seventeenth century. Thus, it is reasonable to assume that, in these instances, feelings of deprivation encouraged millenarian activity.

Social disorganization and anomie. The rejection of the Spanish and Italian Jews by societies in which they had formerly been accepted and the loss of valued cultural ties suggest that elements of social disorganization and anomie were also present, but these appear far less acute when we compare them with the background of many non-Jewish millennial movements. If we exclude from consideration Jews who converted to Christianity, we are left with no evidence that Jewish millenarians suffered from the absence of a community or the lack of a normative order. Most Jews were strongly integrated into kin groups and semiautonomous communities, and their lives were strictly governed by religious values and ritual. In contrast, as Norman Cohn has shown, many Christian millennial movements in the medieval period held little appeal to peasants and artisans integrated into cohesive communities and governed by traditional values. Major support for these movements came from the insecure populations of landless peasants, journeymen, and unskilled workers, who lacked strong networks of social relationships and for whom traditional values held little relevance. Disasters, such as plagues and famines, fell with particular sharpness on these disorganized, atomized populations who had no material or emotional support to fall back on.[6]

The breakdown of the society and culture of the American Indians, who turned to the millennial Ghost Dances of 1870 and 1890, provides an even sharper contrast to the circumstances surrounding Jewish millenarianism. The destruction of the buffalo and the move to reservations robbed tribal organizations concerned with war and hunting of their functions, brought on the decline of the traditional patterns of reciprocity and hierarchy, and made traditional religious beliefs and practices, such as the lore of the medicine man, irrelevant.[7] The experience of expulsion may suggest a comparison between American Indians and the Jews who were exiled from Spain, but there is an important difference: the move to the reservations was an exile from the Indians' sacred land, whereas the Sephardim were expelled from a host society, which was itself an "exile" in the terms of the religious tradition.

The disruption of the Spanish and Italian Jewish communities was partial: it affected their social relationships with, and cultural orientations to, the dominant non-Jewish society, but the Jewish culture remained largely intact. Elements of anomie and a more pervasive social disruption were found among the conversos, marranos, and former marranos, who demonstrated a greater adherence to millenarianism than most Jewish communities. The search for community often appears an important element in religious movements, and it has been argued that outsiders or marginals are likely to focus on the unity and stability of community. Jews were outsiders in relationship to the dominant gentile societies, but in the medieval and early-modern periods the great majority were strongly integrated within their own corporate, semiautonomous communities. Conversos, in contrast, had been forced to break with the Jewish community, but many had been unable to find acceptance within gentile society. In addition to social marginality many felt conflicting pressures (internal and external) to conform and identify with two radically divergent religions. The marrano religion became an attenuated Judaism syncretized with elements from Catholicism.

Many former marranos found a discrepancy between their expectations of Judaism prior to their "return" and their experience of Judaism after it. Some former marranos had problems of assimilation into established Jewish communities, and those communities where the former marranos were in the majority were concerned to build unified and integrated communities and avoid tendencies toward deviance and heresy. Millenarian movements offered an end to problems of a lack of social integration and cultural confusion. The desire for a strong community was also a factor in the early development of Hasidism at a time when the kehillot had lost many of their functions and were proving unable to cope with the demands upon them.

Thus, it is possible to argue that religious movements which vary greatly in beliefs and practices provide compensation against disaster and deprivation, a new system of beliefs and practices in a situation of anomie, or a unified community to overcome social disorganization. A correlation may be apparent between a form of deprivation and a movement's religious focus. For example, it can be argued that the emphasis of early Hasidism on ecstatic prayer rather than religious learning appealed to nonscholarly Jews who held little status in a hierarchy based on religious knowledge.

Symbolic Congruency

The remedy-compensation perspective can make a contribution toward an explanation of the rise and success of religious movements, but it has explained little about the specific content of religious beliefs and practices. An alternative perspective, which is directed more to the question of specific cultural content, is that of the neo-Durkheimians, who propose a parallelism or congruency between social structure and religious beliefs and behavior.[8] It is proposed that religious conceptions are constituted from experience within society, and if social change involves important new forms of social experience which are not consonant with the existing religion, new religious conceptions will emerge to express those experiences.

The neo-Durkheimian perspective has been more prominent in the anthropology than in the sociology of religion, and the debate on its merits and limitations has been conducted largely by anthropologists. Criticism of the perspective points out that interpretations of the symbols are those of the anthropologist and not of the native. The neo-Durkheimians presume that from the viewpoint of the native the process of the symbolic expression of social experience is an unconscious one. Other anthropologists argue that their analytical frameworks admit no unconscious principles and that they can discuss only the symbolic meanings that are imputed and understood by the natives. The neo-Durkheimians have been criticized for their lack of psychological data on natives, which might make it possible to find the meaning of a symbol, and they have been accused of making arbitrary analyses in which they only guess at symbolic meanings. The link between the symbol and the phenomenon that it is presumed to symbolize is often tenuous, and there appears to be no explanation of why the natives should not express their social experience in a more direct manner.

These arguments bring us back to the debate over first principles in social scientific investigation, which was touched upon in the discussion of the remedy-compensation perspective: how far and in what ways can the investigator go beyond the accounts and interpretations of the people he is studying? Many anthropologists argue that they can interpret a society's religious symbols in greater depth than the natives. The native's understanding of the meanings of the symbols he uses is limited by his particular interests, goals, and sentiments, which are related to his specific position within the society. The native is also inclined to take for granted the experiences and values that are expressed in his religion. The anthropologist, on the other hand, tries to study the religious system within the total milieu without the preconceptions of the native and, with, one hopes, some awareness of his own preconceptions. The criticism that neo-Durkheimians merely guess at symbolic meanings is not entirely fair: a hypothesis of a link between types of symbols and types of social forms can be made by a cogent argument based on theoretical principles, and the hypothesis finds some support if the symbols and social forms are found together in a number of societies.

A prominent neo-Durkheimian is the anthropologist Mary Douglas, who has argued that different positions on religious issues are related to levels of social control and organization.[9] She uses two dimensions to discuss the social order: group, which refers to the strength of the boundaries of the social unit, and grid, which refers to the extent that roles are clearly articulated and determine behavior. The validity of three of Douglas's hypotheses are considered here with regard to Hasidism. The Hasidic movement provides a better test of Douglas's approach than do most of the millenarian outbursts, which were too short-lived to express an important change in the social structure. A test on one religious movement will not prove or disprove her hypotheses, but it can reinforce or cast doubt on the applicability of her ideas to a religious context that is not among her examples.

The first hypothesis is that a high level of ritualism is found where group and grid are strong and that an anti-ritualistic position, emphasizing internal states, is found where group and grid are weak. The reasoning behind this hypothesis is that a high level of social control requires that the supernatural be mediated through the institutionalized rituals of the group. A low degree of social control is expressed in an emphasis on religious spontaneity and individual expression and a denigration of the standardized forms of mediating institutions.

The second hypothesis is that there is a concordance between social experience and bodily style of the participants in the movement's ritual: a strong group and grid is associated with bodily control, and a weak group and grid is symbolically expressed in forms of bodily dissociation, such as trance, glossolalia, and ecstatic practices.

The third hypothesis is that a group's belief concerning the relationship between the material and the spiritual will correspond to its orientation to social control. If, as Durkheim argued, the idea of the sacred is derived from an image of society, the relationship of spirit to matter or mind to body can provide a condensed statement of the relationship of the society to the individual. An emphasis on the unity of spirit and matter implies that the individual must be subordinate to society; an argument for the separation of spirit and matter implies an insistence on the independence of the individual. Thus, heresies in Christianity that have rejected the social control of the church have often refuted the incarnational doctrine of Christ as a perfect union of godhead and manhood.

The first two hypotheses find some support in early Hasidism. Like Douglas's examples, the pygmies and the hippies, the early Hasidim emphasized the value of joy and internal states against routinization and formalization. The Hasidim retained the traditional ritual, but some did not keep the fixed times of prayer, and in general, they appealed to spontaneity and individual expression in religious action. Certain Hasidic groups demonstrated a freedom in bodily expression: the achievement of devekut in ecstatic prayer was expressed in shaking, trembling, shouting, and violent movements of the body. In accordance with Douglas's argument, Hasidism arose in a social context where there was a weakening of social organization: the kehillot were no longer strong agencies of social control; some decline in moral and religious standards was reported; communities were weakened by pogroms and economic impoverishment; and movement in and out of communities increased as a result of legally enforced and economically motivated migration.

Douglas argues that a religious movement's early phase of "effervescence," in which emotionalism runs high, can be sustained if the boundaries and roles of the movement remain unstructured. Hasidism proves this out to some extent. At least some Hasidic groups retained highly ecstatic forms of prayer for some time, and this may have depended on the loose structure of their organization; in many instances movement in and out of the prayer rooms and court centers was little regulated, and apart from the relationship between the zaddik and his followers there was little internal division or articulation of roles among members. The abandonment of ecstatic practices and the return to a more formalized ritual by most Hasidic groups coincided with the routinization of the movement centered on the intermediary role of the zaddik.

Douglas's third hypothesis is not supported by the Hasidic example. In fact, an opposite correlation to that predicted by Douglas is found. Traditional Judaism presented the spiritual and the material as dichotomous realms, entirely separate from each other. Hasidism, in contrast, proposed that the distinction between the spiritual and the material was ultimately an illusion and that it was appropriate to worship God in everyday bodily functions and activities. The doctrine of the unity of the spiritual and the material was especially prominent in the early stages of the movement, at a time when the instituted religious leadership saw the movement as a challenge to their authority and prior to the full crystallization of the authority of the zaddikim within the movement.

Hasidism does not support the hypothesis that people who are alienated from the social order will adhere to a doctrine of separation between the flesh and the spirit, but this does not undermine the usefulness of the neo-Durkheimian approach.[10] Social control is not the only social experience that can provide a referent for religious beliefs, and an alternative hypothesis, in line with the neo-Durkheimian perspective, might be suggested in this context. The traditional doctrine of the separation of the spiritual and the material was presented by rabbinic scholars whose ideal was to remove themselves from material concerns, such as earning a living, and to devote themselves exclusively to the spiritual occupation of sacred study. The idea of "worship through corporeality" among the early Hasidic leaders was more in accordance with the life-style of men who were close to the masses and who had no choice but to be involved in the material world.

Relative Autonomy of Religion

Whether religion is analyzed as compensation or as symbolic expression, the impact of social forces will depend, in part, on the religious context itself. Weber illustrated this point when he argued that the religion of the disprivileged acquired the character of resentment only in particular religious contexts. He wrote that the Jews resented political and social disprivilege because they believed in a collective salvation that would involve fundamental changes in social and political relationships. Resentment was less common among disprivileged Hindus, since they believed that their position in this world was the consequence of their religious behavior in previous lives and that their caste position in future lives and their ultimate salvation were dependent on conformity to the ritual requirements of their present position.[11]

Weber's notion of elective affinity includes the important point that although a group tends to select beliefs that are congruent with its interests and social experience, the selection takes place within the boundaries of a religious tradition and its historical development. Deprivation does not give rise to millenarian movements in Hindu environments because, quite simply, Hinduism does not have a millenarian tradition, and the emphasis on rebirth mitigates against such a development.[12] The incidence of millenarian movements among colonized populations and the forms that the movements take depend not only on the impact of colonization and Christianity but also on the traditional religious beliefs. The cargo cults in Melanesia can be understood only in relation to the traditional religion, which placed great emphasis on equitable, material exchange between men and gods,[13] and the Ghost Dance movements of the North American Indians have to be seen in connection with the traditional beliefs in the return of the ancestors.[14]

The importance of the role of the leader or prophet may also be dependent on the religious context. In his examination of millenarian movements in a number of colonized societies, Michael Adas writes that a millenarian tradition was not necessary to the rise of the movements: the religious beliefs in some areas contained no apparent millennial elements. He points to the rise of prophetic figures as the critical determinant of the mode of protest that was adopted. It was the prophet who molded and articulated millenarian tendencies into a persuasive ideology of protest against the colonialists.[15] In a religion with a strong millenarian tradition, such as Judaism, the importance of a prophet may not be so great. Our knowledge of most of the messianic and prophetic figures in the Jewish movements is limited, but the majority do not appear to have taken a major role in the formulation of beliefs or the mobilization of support. The beliefs were already available, and under certain circumstances, Jews required little prompting or encouragement to activate them. Nathan of Gaza was important in the articulation of messianic expectations, but the spread of enthusiasm in 1666 went far beyond his sphere of influence.

Another consequence of a strong millenarian tradition is that millenarian outbursts may occur without any apparent cause in the immediate environment. A comparison of Jewish millenarian outbursts suggests that while social factors were among the necessary causes of large and widespread movements, small, local incidences occurred in communities that had not directly experienced persecution, deprivation, or disruption. In a few cases the news of an event or series of events elsewhere in the world was sufficient to activate the millenarian beliefs.

In all societies the religious context will influence the extent and type of influence that social forces have in the rise and development of religious movements. The relative autonomy of the religious sphere is likely to be greater in literate societies where movements are able to draw their beliefs from a religious tradition whose development is chartered and analyzed by members of the society. Religious ideologists formulate religious ideas not only in accordance with their own social experience but also in the context of a knowledge of the intellectual tradition. This means that there can be no one-to-one relationship between social experience and religious ideas.

Important aspects of social experience may exist for long periods before religious ideas emerge to express them, or they may never find expression in religious forms. The development of the Lurianic cabbalah, which expressed the experience of exile in its conceptions of creation and the godhead, was no doubt influenced by the exile from Spain and its repercussions, but exile had been a fundamental condition of Jewry for a considerable period without giving rise to such a clear expression in basic conceptions of the divinity. Even when members of an intellectual elite formulate religious ideas that express a widely and deeply felt experience in life, the diffusion and adoption of the ideas are not inevitable. Luria and his immediate disciples did not attempt to spread their doctrines, and only a very few of Luria's followers took it upon themselves to propagate their beliefs. The extent to which the Lurianic cabbalah filtered down into popular religion, and the extent of its importance as a determinant of the Sabbatian movement, is a matter of some dispute. We have argued that although the diffusion of Lurianism was one factor in the distribution of messianic excitement, it was less important than the association with the former marranos.

The particular form that a religious response takes under certain social conditions may depend on the evaluation of previous religious developments. One reason for the success of Hasidism was that it was a mystical movement which in its early phases "neutralized" messianism. The debacle of Sabbatianism and the antinomian and radical developments within the movement diminished the appeal of millenarianism, which, in any case, had rarely been expressed in a popular movement among the Ashkenazim. The Hasidic leaders repeated the traditional formulas of collective salvation, but their appeal was in the promise of individual salvation, both in this world and the next.

The Processual Perspective

A religious movement should be analyzed as a system in process: members construct and reconstruct a movement's beliefs, practices, and organization in ways that may be unrelated to the social conditions of the emergence of the movement, but that contribute to its growth, spread, and consolidation. Historians of Hasidism have often treated the prominence of the zaddikim from the third generation on as representing a decline in the authentic religious spirit of the early movement, but from the sociological point of view, it was that routinization of the movement, centered on the zaddikim, that accounted for its growth and diffusion. The strain and disruption in the Russian feudal system was an important external factor in the spread of Hasidism, but the combination of magical and mystical roles in the person of the zaddik, the sense of community achieved in the prayer houses and the courts of the zaddikim, and the forms of charismatic succession were internal developments conducive to success that went on quite apart from changes in the movement's environment.

As a mystical and thaumaturgical movement, Hasidism avoided the specific problem of millenarian movements, which is that in order to survive they need to adjust to the failure of their prophecies. Internal developments within a millenarian movement are likely to be of great importance in determining its continuation beyond the disconfirmation of prophecy. Successful adjustment requires intellectual innovations that provide convincing rationalizations of the failure of prophecy and social innovations that engage members in a range of activities. Most millenarian movements do not survive the failure of prophecy, but a few not only survive the crisis or crises of disconfirmation but grow in their aftermath. John G. Gager argues that the cognitive dissonance created by the death of Jesus, which appeared in traditional Jewish terms to disconfirm the belief that he was the messiah, was overcome by missionary zeal, which in turn led to Christianity's survival and spread.[16] Many of the more organized Christian millenarian movements of advanced societies, such as the Jehovah's Witnesses, Christadelphians, Seventh Day Adventists, and Catholic Apostolics, have persisted after the initial disappointments, and sometimes for long after.[17]

The only Jewish millenarian movement to survive for a lengthy period was Sabbatianism, but the persecution of the movement effectively reduced proselytizing activities after Zvi's conversion. Sabbatianism survived by focusing on the spiritual status of its members, and this was reinforced when the members believed that their present leader was an incarnation of God. The Doenmeh were particularly successful in evolving a community life that encompassed a large part of their social world, but they were unable to survive the disruption of the community when they were forced to leave Salonika and relocate as small groups in Turkish towns. Hasidism, a much larger movement, was able to survive the destruction of the majority of its members and its relocation in modern, secularized societies. By strengthening their boundaries, constructing effective agencies of commitment, and maintaining social control, a number of Hasidic sects adjusted to radically different environments in the post-World War II period.

The perspectives discussed here address questions that both overlap and differ in their emphases. No single perspective pretends to account for all the aspects of the religious movements that have been discussed in this work—origins, beliefs, diffusion, routinization, and consolidation. But even within the range of questions on which they focus, the limitations of some of the perspectives are apparent. Each perspective and subperspective emphasizes certain causal interrelationships, and the findings of this work suggest that few, if any, of those interrelationships are invariant or universal. The consequences of each of the major causal dimensions discussed in this study (disaster, relative deprivation, anomie, social control, religious beliefs, and movement organization) have been seen to be dependent on the particular contextual complex of the other dimensions.

No one cause or particular combination of causes can account for all the movements. One of Durkheim's rules of sociological method, that every instance of a particular social phenomenon will have the same set of social causes, has been called into question. Although each religious movement may to some extent be considered unique, their similarities appear to be greater than the various combinations of causes that gave rise to them. This does not mean that every set of circumstances was so unique and fortuitous as to make comparisons pointless and uninteresting; the important alternative causes were relatively few, and certain combinations of causes were found to occur with some frequency. Nevertheless, the diversity of social experiences appears greater than the variety of religious symbols in which they were expressed. This points to the power of messianic and mystical symbols and beliefs to encompass, to condense, and to provide a focus for, the complexities of the human condition.

Notes

Chapter 1

1. The following paragraphs were informed by Biale, *Scholem.*
2. Durkheim, "Individual and Collective," p. 31.
3. Durkheim, *Elementary Forms.*
4. Weber, *Economy*, pp. 494, 468–518, 934–35, *Methodology*, pp. 63, 68–71, and *Protestant Ethic*, p. 91.

Chapter 2

1. Yinger, *Scientific Study*, pp. 1–23.
2. Robertson, *Sociological Interpretation*, pp. 34–51; Campbell, *Irreligion*, pp. 123–44.
3. Spiro, "Religion," pp. 85–126.
4. Malinowski, "Role of Magic," pp. 102–12.
5. Radcliffe-Brown, "Taboo," pp. 112–23. See also, Homans, "Anxiety and Ritual," pp. 123–28.
6. Frazer, *Golden Bough*; Goode, *Religion*, pp. 50–54.
7. Weber, *Economy*, pp. 399–439.
8. Durkheim, *Elementary Forms*, pp. 57–63.
9. Goody, "Religion and Ritual," pp. 142–64.
10. Weber, *Economy*, pp. 425–27.
11. Wilson, *Magic.*
12. Y. Talmon, "Pursuit of the Millennium," pp. 125–48, and "Millenarian Movements," pp. 159–200. Other general discussions include Pereira de Queiros, "Messianic Myths," pp. 78–99; LaBarre, "Crisis Cults," pp. 3–44; Lanternari, "Socio-Religious Movements," pp. 483–503.
13. A sociology of mysticism hardly exists. The classic statements are Troeltsch, *Social Teaching*, pp. 377, 381, 734–36, 743–49, 795–800; Weber, *Economy*, pp. 544–51. Several discussions on the formulations of Troeltsch and Weber are found in *Sociological Analysis* 36, no. 3 (1975). There is, of course, a large literature in religious studies on mysticism, but an appreciation of the social context is rare. An exception is S. Katz, "Language," pp. 22–74.
14. These orientations, together with the thaumaturgical and revolutionary (millenarian), are delineated by Bryan Wilson in his typology of religious

responses to the world. His other types are the manipulationist, the utopian, and the reformist. Manipulationists seek esoteric religious knowledge (a gnosis) which will give them the means to attain worldly goals. Utopians seek to change the world by establishing separate communities which will demonstrate to the world the advantages of a radically different life-style. While the ultimate aim of utopians may be to change the world, the means they use often leads them to a greater emphasis on withdrawal from society. Reformists seek to change selected aspects of the world (Wilson, *Magic*, pp. 22–26). Wilson does not include mysticism as a separate type, but I would argue that without the inclusion of this type, the major features of the Hasidic movement cannot be adequately described.

15. Malinowski, "Role of Magic," pp. 102–12.

16. Radcliffe-Brown, "Taboo," pp. 112–23.

17. Tylor, *Primitive Culture*.

18. Horton, "Neo-Tylorianism," pp. 625–34. See also, Ross, "Neo-Tylorianism," pp. 105–16.

19. Merton, *Social Theory*, p. 64.

20. Beattie, "Understanding Ritual," pp. 240–68.

21. Worsley, *Trumpet Shall Sound*; Lanternari, *Religions of the Oppressed*.

22. Barkun, *Disaster*.

23. O'Dea and Publeto, "Anomie," pp. 180–98; Glock, "Role of Deprivation," pp. 24–36. Aberle, "Relative Deprivation," pp. 209–14.

24. Turner, *Dramas*.

25. Lofland and Stark, "Becoming a World Saver," pp. 862–75.

26. Adas, *Prophets of Rebellion*.

27. Beckford, *Trumpet of Prophecy*.

28. Weber, *Economy*, pp. 502–6.

29. Wilson, *Religious Sects*, chap. 5.

30. O'Dea and Publeto, "Anomie."

31. C. Hill, "Immigrant Sect Development," p. 221–30.

32. Gerlach and Hine, *People, Power, Change*.

33. Wilson, *Magic*, esp. chap. 11.

34. Durkheim, *Elementary Forms*; Swanson, *Birth of Gods*; Douglas, *Natural Symbols*.

35. Spiro, *Burmese Supernaturalism*; Weber, *Economy*, pp. 468–518; Swanson, *Religion and Regime*.

36. Weber, *Economy*, chaps. 3, 14.

37. Gerth and Mills, *Max Weber*, pp. 53–55.

38. Stark, *Sociology of Religion*, 4:31–36.

39. Friedland, "Charisma," pp. 18–26; Worsley, *Trumpet Shall Sound*, pp. 285–97.

40. For defenses of Weber see M. Hill, *Sociology of Religion*, pp. 140–82; Bensman and Grant, "Charisma and Modernity," pp. 570–614.

41. Wilson, *Noble Savages*, pp. 10–11.

42. Parsons, *Structure*, chap. 15.

43. Shils, "Charisma," pp. 199–213.

44. Worsley, *Trumpet Shall Sound*.

45. Wilson, *Noble Savages*, p. 20. Weber stressed the capacity of charismatic authority to transform society in accordance with ideal factors, but revolutionary change was not part of his definition, and there is no reason why charismatic authority should not be directed to the conservation and reinforcement of tradition. For empirical examples see, Oommen, "Charisma," pp. 85–99.

46. Tucker, "Charismatic Leadership," pp. 731–56; Worsley, *Trumpet Shall Sound*, p. 325.

47. Weber, *Economy*, p. 1135.

Chapter 3

1. For a short account of the development of official Judaism see, Epstein, *Judaism*.

2. Patai, *Jewish Mind*, p. 131.

3. Trachtenberg, *Jewish Magic*, pp. 19–22.

4. Skorupski, *Symbol*, pp. 128–31.

5. Trachtenberg, *Jewish Magic*, pp. 23–24.

6. *Encyclopaedia Judaica*, 4:5–7.

7. The categorization of a religious system used here follows, in part, that of Wallace, *Religion*.

8. Weber, *Economy*, p. 415.

9. P. Berger, *Sacred Canopy*, pp. 110–25.

10. Scholem, *Kabbalah*, pp. 88–122, 144–52, and *On the Kabbalah*, pp. 5–157; Raphael Patai, *Hebrew Goddess*; Sperling, Simon, and Levertoff, trans., *Zohar*.

11. Blumenthal, "Methodological Reflections," pp. 111–14.

12. Scholem, *Kabbalah*, p. 237.

13. Ibid., pp. 182–87, 194.

14. Patai, *Hebrew Goddess*, pp. 158–59.

15. Weber, *Economy*, pp. 416, 419.

16. Trachtenberg, *Jewish Magic*, chaps. 3–6; *Encyclopaedia Judaica*, 3:788–95, 5:1521–33; Scholem, *Kabbalah*, pp. 356–61.

17. For detailed accounts of the traditional Jewish society see, J. Katz, *Tradition and Crisis*, and Zborowski and Herzog, *Life is with People*. The novels and short stories of Isaac Beshevis Singer give a feeling for the enchanted world of east European Jews.

18. Weber, *Economy*, pp. 518–26. For a critical discussion see, Obeyesekere, "Theodicy," pp. 7–40.

19. Millgram, *Jewish Worship*, pp. 411–15. A collection of documents on the Resurrection and the Last Judgment is found in Patai, *Messiah Texts*, pp. 197–219.

20. Cohn Sherbok, "Doctrine of Hell," pp. 196–209.

21. Scholem, *Kabbalah*, pp. 344–50.

22. Millgram, *Jewish Worship*, esp. chaps. 4, 6–13.

23. Trachtenberg, *Jewish Magic*, chaps. 7–13; Pollack, *Jewish Folkways*; Zimmels, *Magicians*; Schrire, *Hebrew Amulets*; Marmorstein, "Popular Traditions," pp. 75–89, 138–50; Bernstein, "Two Remedy Books," pp. 289–305; *Encyclopaedia Judaica*, 3:788–95, 5:1521–33, 6:999–1000, 11:703–15.

24. Spiro, *Burmese Supernaturalism*, pp. xxx–xxxvi, 264–71; Ames, "Magical-Animism," pp. 21–52; Tambiah, *Buddhism and Spirit Cults*.

25. The Prayer Book included prayers for rain in the winter and dew in the summer, but these were formulated in ancient Palestine and were related to the weather conditions of that area. In the diaspora the prayers signified the Jewish tie to the Holy Land rather than an attempt to control the immediate environment; they were recited even in lands where there was an abundance of rain and where rain was needed in summer rather than in winter.

26. Thomas, *Religion*.

Chapter 4

1. Jarvie, "Cargo Cults," pp. 299–312.

2. Lerner, "Medieval Prophecy," pp. 3–24.

3. Sarachek, *Doctrine of Messiah*, pp. 301–3; Scholem, *Messianic Idea*, pp. 30–33; Baer, *Jews in Christian Spain*, 1:249. According to one rationalist scholar, R. Abraham Bivach, the messiah would be succeeded by his offspring, and people would not live eternally in the messianic kingdom (Ben-Sasson, "Middle Ages," p. 618).

4. On the development of Jewish messianism in the ancient period see Klausner, *Messianic Idea*; Mowinckel, *He That Cometh*; Isenberg, "Millenarism," pp. 26–46; Rivkin, "Meaning of Messiah," pp. 383–406; *Encyclopaedia Judaica*, 6:860–86, 11:1497–98; Manuel and Manuel, "History of Paradise," pp. 83–128. On Jewish messianic ideas in the medieval period see Sarachek, *Doctrine of Messiah*; Scholem, *Messianic Idea*, pp. 1–36; Glatzer, "Zion," pp. 83–100. Collections of texts are found in Patai, *Messiah Texts*; Buchanan, *Revelation and Redemption*.

5. Silver, *Messianic Speculation*, pp. 25–30; Baron, *History*, 5:167–68.

6. In Pumbedita, Mesopotamia, circa 643–47, during the disintegration of the Sassanian Empire, a Jewish messianic pretender gathered "a vile crowd of weavers, barbers and fullers, about four hundred strong, who burned down three sacred edifices and killed the local governor." It is thought that the majority of his followers were not Jewish (Baron, *History*, 5:184; Sharf, *Byzantine Jewry*, pp. 62–63).

7. Sharf, *Byzantine Jewry*, p. 63; Starr, "Movement Messianique," pp. 81–92; Baron, *History*, 5:184, 193–94, 381. Baron argues that Starr goes too far in denying the spread of the movement to Spain and Gaul at the time of the Muslim conquests in Spain and southern France. Baron writes that Severus's agitation probably started about 721–22 and continued into the reign of Hisham (724–43).

8. Baron, *History*, 5:193–94; Aescoly, *Messianic Movements*, pp. 102–3, 130–33; Mahler, *Karaites*, p. 121.

9. The theme of the concealment and reappearance of the messiah is an old aggadic notion. Baron argues that it influenced the Muslim sectarians who referred to the concealment and reappearance of the Mahdi (Baron, *History*, 5:185). Friedlaender, in contrast, argued that the Shiite belief in the concealment of the Mahdi influenced the Jewish millenarians (Friedlaender, "Jewish-Arabic Studies," 1:196, 2:485–90). The hidden messiah is a common theme in many millennial movements, and it is not necessary to postulate the influence of one religious tradition on another.

10. According to Muslim sources, Abu-Isa acknowledged that Jesus and Mohammed were prophets and advocated the study of the Gospels and the Koran.

11. Baron, *History*, 5:185–94; Friedlaender, "Jewish-Arabic Studies," 1:183–215, 2:481–516, 3:235–99; Mahler, *Karaites*, pp. 119–23; Aescoly, *Messianic Movements*, pp. 100–102, 117–30; Nemoy, "Al-Qirqisani's Account," pp. 328, 382–83.

12. Mann includes under his list of movements a messianic pretender in 1122 in north Israel, where there were very few Jews at the time. The man was a Karaite who announced that redemption would occur in two and a half months, but there is no evidence that he found a following (Mann, "First Crusades," pp. 336–39).

13. Halkin, *Maimonides' Epistle*, p. xx. Most historians have taken it for granted that the location was Lyons, but some have preferred León: both cities are spelled in the same way in Hebrew, both were important towns, and Arab geographers referred to Christian Spain as the land of the Franks (Baron, *History*, 5:199, 383).

14. Sharf, *Byzantine Jewry*, pp. 124–26; Starr, *Byzantine Empire*, pp. 74, 203–6.

15. Halkin, *Maimonides' Epistle*, p. xx.

16. Goitein, "Messianic Troubles," pp. 57–76, and "Meeting in Jerusalem," pp. 43–57.

17. Halkin, *Maimonides' Epistle*, p. xix.

18. Polack, "David Alroy," pp. 404–6; Mann, "First Crusades," pp. 341–49; Aescoly, *Messianic Movements*, pp. 145, 164–78.

19. Halkin, *Maimonides' Epistle*, pp. xvi–xvii.

20. Cohn, *Pursuit of Millennium*.

21. Poliakov, *Anti-Semitism*, 1:33–49. A non-Jewish source, which cannot be relied upon, mentions a Jewish messiah in England in 1140. According to the source, many Jews supported the pretender and only the scholars were opposed. This was a time of troubles for English Jews: pogroms began in 1100, in 1130 a heavy tax was imposed on the Jews in London, and in 1144 there was a ritual blood accusation against the Jews in Norwich (Aescoly, *Messianic Movements*, pp. 163–64).

22. This is suggested by Mann, "First Crusades," p. 253. See also Silver,

Messianic Speculation, p. 58; Eidelberg, *Jews and Crusades*, pp. 21, 79.

23. Eidelberg, *Jews and Crusades*, p. 13.

24. Ibid., p. 10.

25. Zimmels, *Ashkenazim and Sephardim*, pt. 2, chap. 9; Shulvass, *Rhine and Bosporus*, pp. 5–13.

26. Chazan, "Hebrew Chronicles," pp. 235–54.

27. Scholem, *Major Trends*, pp. 87–90.

28. Mann, "First Crusades," p. 252. Since Maimonides wrote that the incident in "Linon" occurred 105 to 110 years prior to his writing in 1172, there is no reason to date the movement in 1087–88.

29. Aescoly, *Messianic Movements*, p. 154.

30. Starr, *Byzantine Empire*, p. 74; Mann, "First Crusades," p. 259.

31. Baer, *Jews in Christian Spain*, 1:60–64. Most of the poems of Judah ha-Levi (1080–1141), who witnessed the destruction of Jewish communities by Christian reconquerors and the flight of the Jews from the Almoravides, end on an apocalyptic note. At one time ha-Levi foretold the appearance of the messiah in 1130 (ibid., pp. 71–72). Baer mentions the influence of the events on the scholar Abraham bar Hiyya (1065–1143) (ibid., p. 66), but most of Hiyya's messianic predictions were not imminent ones. He predicted 1136, but he thought 1230 was more probable. He also calculated 1358 and 1403, with 1448 as the outmost date. The dates 1358 and 1403 became favorites among the speculators (Silver, *Messianic Speculation*, p. 68). On the speculations and calculations of the period see Kochan, *Jew and History*, pp. 23–47.

32. Hirschberg, *Jews in North Africa*, pp. 120–22.

33. Mann, "First Crusades," p. 340. Mann wrote that Tumart's movement was important in Fez in 1128, which he dates as the time of the Jewish millennial outburst.

34. Ibid., p. 344.

35. Polack, "David Alroy," pp. 404–6.

36. Mann, "First Crusades," p. 349.

37. Ibid, p. 351.

38. Baron, *History*, 5:205–6.

39. Harris, *Cows, Pigs*, pp. 160–212.

40. Thrupp, *Millennial Dreams*, pp. 16–17; Spier, Suttles, and Herskovitz, "Aberle's Thesis," pp. 84–88; Lerner, "Medieval Prophecy," pp. 3–24.

Chapter 5

1. A. Berger, "Abraham Abulafia," pp. 55–61; Aescoly, *Messianic Movements*, pp. 194–213; Neuman, *Jews in Spain*, 2:114–15; Scholem, *Kabbalah*, pp. 53–55.

2. Baer, *Jews in Christian Spain*, 1:277–80.

3. Ibid., 2:159–62; Scholem, *Kabbalah*, pp. 65–66; *Encyclopaedia Judaica*, 4:1268–69; Aescoly, *Messianic Movements*, p. 226. At the same time many marranos tried to leave Spain and migrate to Israel, believing that this would

contribute to the coming of the redemption (Dinur, "Emigration from Spain," pp. 161–74.).

4. Ben-Sasson, "Exile and Redemption," pp. 216–27. An undated document describes millennial excitement in Catania, a port in Sicily. Mann writes that the document must have been written between 1282 and 1516. Aescoly argues that all the signs indicate that the incident occurred at the time of "the generation of the expulsion." Sicily was under the authority of Spain, and the rights of the Jews there were similar to the rights of those in Spain. The document describes a Jewish prophetess who after being pregnant for nine months and not giving birth stood outside a synagogue and summoned the congregation to witness manifestations of the coming of the messiah. Various miraculous signs were reported, and there was great excitement. The excitement increased when a gentile from southern Greece told the Jews that ambassadors of the messiah had been received by the Spanish monarch. (Mann, *Texts and Studies*, 1:34–35; Aescoly, *Messianic Movements*, pp. 240–46).

5. Roth, *Jews of Italy*, p. 179. Shulvass, *Rome and Jerusalem*, pp. 41–67.

6. Netanyahu, *Abravanel*, pp. 200–240; Barzilay, *Between Reason and Faith*, pp. 122–31; Baer, "Messianic Movement in Spain," pp. 71–77.

7. Shulvass writes that the majority of Italian Jews believed in Lamlein's prophecies (*Rome and Jerusalem*, p. 45). The prophet's name is spelled in a variety of ways in the literature: apart from Lamlein, also Lämlein, Lammlin, and Laemmlein.

8. Ibid., pp. 44–45; Shulvass, *Renaissance*, pp. 9, 210; Marx, "Le Faux Messie," pp. 135–38.

9. Shulvass, *Rome and Jerusalem*, pp. 45–48; Aescoly, *Messianic Movements*, p. 250.

10. Conversos were former Jews, the majority of whom had been forcibly converted to Christianity. Those converts who continued to practice Judaism in secret are also known as marranos.

11. Aescoly, *Messianic Movements*, pp. 251–78; Shulvass, *Rome and Jerusalem*, pp. 54–64; Roth, "Zionist Experiment," pp. 76–81. For an English translation of a diary purported to be written by Reubeni, see Adler, ed., *Jewish Travellers*, pp. 251–328. Reubeni's origins are unknown, but from his writings and other evidence historians have argued that he was an Ashkenazi, a Yemenite, an Indian, and a Falasha (Ethiopian Jew) (Aescoly, "David Reubeni," pp. 1–45; Shohat, "Notes," pp. 96–116; Birnbaum, "Indian Origin," pp. 3–30; Cassuto, "David Reubeni," pp. 339–58). There is also dispute on the circumstances of Reubeni's death (Rodriguez-Moñino, "Les Judaisants," pp. 73–86; Roth, "David Reubeni," pp. 93–95; Révah, "David Reubeni," pp. 128–35).

12. Aescoly, *Messianic Movements*, p. 251; Roth, "Zionist Experiment," pp. 78–79; Shohat, "Notes," pp. 96–116.

13. Shulvass, *Rome and Jerusalem*, pp. 55–61; Aescoly, "David Reubeni," pp. 26–27, 35–37.

14. Aescoly, *Messianic Movements*, pp. 266–78; Shulvass, *Rome and Jerusalem*, pp. 61–64.

15. Shulvass, *Rome and Jerusalem*, pp. 79–82; Tamar, "Messianic Expectations,"

pp. 61–88. The date 1575 was based on the numerical value of Shiloh, which had for some time been interpreted as a reference to the messiah. The date was also linked to prophecies in Daniel. There was also hope for this date in Salonika.

16. G. Cohen, "Messianic Postures," p. 143.

17. Baer, *Jews in Christian Spain*, 1:129–31, 137; Neuman, *Jews in Spain*, 2:244–47.

18. Baer, *Jews in Christian Spain*, 1:198.

19. Ibid., 2:97–112; Poliakov, *Anti-Semitism*, 2:157–58; Wolff, "1391 Pogrom," pp. 4–18.

20. Baer, *Jews in Christian Spain*, 2:434–39; Poliakov, *Anti-Semitism*, 2:200–201; Minkin, *Abrabanel*, pp. 143–51.

21. Lamlein's prophecies also spread among Ashkenazim who had been expelled from parts of Germany and had settled in Istria and other towns of the Venetian Republic (Shulvass, *Renaissance*, p. 12).

22. Reeves, *Influence of Prophecy*, pp. 354, 358, 430–35; D. Weinstein, *Savonarola*, pp. 62–63, 112–15, 166.

23. Krauss, "Espérances messianiques," pp. 87–96. Krauss speculates that the unknown prophet made his calculations during Lamlein's movement.

24. D. Weinstein, *Savonarola*, pp. 142–47, 167–69, 374–76.

25. Netanyahu, *Abravanel*, pp. 247–78. Netanyahu notes the parallels between the prophecies of Savonarola and Abravanel. Often the only substantial difference is that one is referring to the Florentines and Florence while the other is referring to the Jews and Jerusalem. However, the parallels are common features in millenarianism and are not sufficient to conclude that Savonarola had a direct influence on Abravanel.

26. Roth, *Jews in Italy*, pp. 289–94; Baron, *History*, 14:114–46.

27. Sharot, *Judaism*, pp. 25–29; Poliakov, *Anti-Semitism*, vol. 1, chaps. 2–7.

28. G. Cohen, "Messianic Postures," pp. 125–42.

29. Zimmels, *Ashkenazim and Sephardim*, pt. 2, chap. 2.

30. Ibid., chaps. 7, 9, 10.

31. Baer, *Jews in Christian Spain*, 2:245–46, 253–59.

32. Ben-Sasson, "Kiddush Ha-Shem," pp. 209–16; Chazan, "Hebrew Chronicles," p. 253; G. Cohen, "Messianic Postures," pp. 148–56; Poliakov, *Anti-Semitism*, 2:73–95.

33. Sonne, "On Baer," pp. 61–80.

34. G. Cohen, "Messianic Postures," pp. 144–47.

35. Zimmels, *Ashkenazim and Sephardim*, pt. 1, chap. 1.

36. The "practical" cabbalah of Abulafia, stressing the mystical qualities of sacred names, numbers, and letter combinations, was highly magical (Scholem, *Kabbalah*, pp. 53–55; Aescoly, *Messianic Movements*, pp. 194–213; A. Berger, "Abraham Abulafia," pp. 55–61). The cabbalah of Moses Botarel also had a "practical" bent (Scholem, *Kabbalah*, pp. 65–66).

37. Scholem, *Major Trends*, p. 188.

38. Baer, *Jews in Christian Spain*, 1:198.

39. Scholem, *Major Trends*, p. 186; Baer, *Jews in Christian Spain*, 1:249, 269. Baer notes similarities between the cabbalah and the works of the Franciscan

Spirituals in their apocalyptic descriptions and messianic computations.

40. The Zohar glorified poverty as a religious value, making it a quality of the Shechinah (divine presence). This was a striking innovation in Judaism and possibly reflects the influence of the Christian environment. Poliakov is wrong, however, to link the mysticism of the cabbalah with the poor (*Anti-Semitism*, 2:138). Baer wrote that among the foremost masters of the cabbalah were men of wealthy families as well as others from the lower social strata (*Jews in Christian Spain*, 1:243). He noted the parallels between the Franciscan Joachimites of the thirteenth century, who attacked the worldliness of the church, and the cabbalists who attacked the Jewish communal leaders for their neglect of the Torah and their exploitation of the poor (ibid., pp. 261–77, 367–73). Like the Franciscans, the cabbalists did not themselves come from the poor but were from comfortable families who rejected involvement in the world. On the Franciscans and Joachimist prophecy in Spain, see Reeves, *Influence of Prophecy*, pp. 221–24, 247, 446.

41. Marx, "Le Faux Messie," pp. 135–38. The influence of the cabbalah is seen in Lamlein's arguments that the sinner has to be reincarnated to provide him with the opportunity to become righteous and that the messiah has to come to repair the sin of the first man, of whom the messiah was the last reincarnation.

42. Tamar, "Messianic Expectations," pp. 61–88; Barzilay, *Between Reason and Faith*, pp. 63–65.

43. Scholem, *Kabbalah*, p. 76.

44. Shulvass, *Renaissance*, p. 212.

45. Sharot, *Judaism*, pp. 14–17, 25–32.

46. Poliakov, *Anti-Semitism*, vol. 2, chaps. 5–7; Neuman, *Jews in Spain*, 1:161–69, 2:182–274; Castro, *Spaniards*, pp. 532, 544–47.

47. Baer, *Jews in Christian Spain*, 1:177–80.

48. Ibid., 1:308, 364–68, 2:24–25, 31; Poliakov, *Anti-Semitism*, 2:140–56.

49. Baer, *Jews in Christian Spain*, 2:244–51; Poliakov, *Anti-Semitism*, 2:163–68; Wolff, "1391 Pogrom," pp. 40–44.

50. Baer, *Jews in Christian Spain*, 2:322, 433; Poliakov, *Anti-Semitism*, 2:189–99; Haliezer, "Castilian Urban Patriciate," pp. 35–58.

51. Baer, *Jews in Christian Spain*, 2:434–49.

52. Ben-Sasson, "Exile and Redemption," pp. 216–27, "Generation of Spanish Exiles," pp. 23–64, and "Middle Ages," pp. 691–92.

53. Netanyahu, *Abravanel*, pp. 87–88, 226–34.

54. Shulvass, *Renaissance*, pp. 195–99, 207–10, 328, 333–36, 346–47, 350.

55. Tamar, "Messianic Expectations," pp. 63, 70–72.

Chapter 6

1. Baer, *Jews in Christian Spain*, 2:124–25, 166–69; Beinart, "Converso in Fifteenth-Century Spain," pp. 425; Poliakov, *Anti-Semitism*, 2:157–59, 167–68.

2. Baroja, *Los Judios*, 1:189–90. Baroja estimates that in 1541 there were 250,000 conversos in a Spanish population of 7.4 million.

3. Oliveira Marques, *Portugal*, 1:287.

4. Dinur, "Emigration from Spain," pp. 161–74.

5. Baer, *Jews in Christian Spain*, 2:292, 294–95.

6. Ibid., pp. 356–58, and "Messianic Movement," pp. 61–77; Beinart, "Converso in Sixteenth- and Seventeenth-Century Spain," pp. 235, 248–49.

7. Reeves, *Influence of Prophecy*, p. 446; Castro, *Spaniards*, p. 78; Bataillan, *Erasme*, pp. 65–75.

8. Reeves, *Influence of Prophecy*, pp. 359–60.

9. Castro, *Spaniards*, pp. 344–45; Baroja, *Los Judios*, pp. 411–12.

10. Lea, *Religious History*, pp. 222–36, 251.

11. Hornik, *Collected Studies*, pp. 8–9; Dominguez Ortiz, "Spanish Conversos," pp. 79–81.

12. Kamen, *Inquisition*, pp. 71–82.

13. Roth, *Marranos*, pp. 146–48.

14. Shulvass, *Rome and Jerusalem*, p. 60.

15. Adler, *Jewish Travellers*, pp. 286–88, 296–300.

16. Shulvass, *Rome and Jerusalem*, pp. 61, 66.

17. M. Cohen, trans., *Samuel Usque's Consolation*.

18. Yerushalmi, *From Spanish Court*, pp. 305–6. Among the marranos in Mexico, the messiah was expected in 1642 or 1643 (Roth, *Marranos*, p. 172).

19. Beinart, "Converso in Sixteenth- and Seventeenth-Century Spain," p. 472.

20. Yerushalmi, *From Spanish Court*, pp. 306–9; Oliveira Marques, *Portugal*, 1:319; Nowell, *Portugal*, pp. 137–39.

21. MacKay, "Popular Movements," pp. 33–67; Marquez Villanueva, "Converso Problem," pp. 317–33; Baer, *Jews in Christian Spain*, 2:270–81; Kamen, *Inquisition*, pp. 22–23.

22. Kamen, *Inquisition*, pp. 26–32, 35–53.

23. Révah, "Marranes," pp. 36–37; Roth, *Marranos*, pp. 64–66, 69–79; M. Cohen, trans., *Samuel Usque's Consolation*, pp. 6–8; Gilman, "Conversos," pp. 127–36.

24. Netanyahu, *Marranos*, pp. 75, 190, 204–5.

25. Baer, *Jews in Christian Spain*, 2:272–73; Beinart, "Converso in Sixteenth- and Seventeenth-Century Spain," pp. 464–66.

26. Netanyahu, *Marranos*; Dominguez Ortiz, "Spanish Conversos," pp. 64–66; Marquez Villanueva, "Converso Problem," pp. 318, 321, 326.

27. G. Cohen, "Marranos," pp. 178–84.

28. Roth, *Marranos*, pp. 168–94, and "Religion of Marranos," pp. 1–33; Beinhart, "Converso in Sixteenth- and Seventeenth-Century Spain," pp. 463–72; Braunstein, *Chuetos*, pp. 94–114, 194–202; Moore, *Street*, pp. 128–30.

29. Sokolow, *Spinoza*, pp. 255–59; Zinberg, *Jewish Literature*, 5:121.

30. Baer, *Jews in Christian Spain*, 2:273–77; Netanyahu, *Marranos*, pp. 75–76, 121; Marguez Villanueva, "Converso Problem," p. 327.

31. Révah, "Marranes," pp. 35, 40. In Mallorca, the community of conversos, the Xuetas, gave up their secret practice of Judaism by 1700, but they remained a distinct group in their community life and economic activity. The Inquisition broke their will to continue the marrano religion, but the stigma attached to

them, their specialized economic functions, their organization in a guild, and the hostility of the larger society resulted in their continuation as a pariah people for more than two centuries. They had almost no possibility of marrying outside the group, and it was only in the twentieth century, especially with the advent of industrial tourism in the 1950s, that they assimilated into the general population (Moore, *Street*, pp. 137–77, 202–4).

32. Yerushalmi, *From Spanish Court*, pp. 5–9; Roth, *Marranos*, pp. 54–63; Révah, "Marranes," pp. 37–41.

Chapter 7

1. Scholem, *Sabbatai Sevi.*

2. Biale, *Scholem*, p. 155.

3. Weinryb is a notable exception. He provides an important critique with regard to Poland (*Jews of Poland*, chap. 10).

4. Scholem, *Sabbatai Sevi*, pp. 206–354, 468–72.

5. Ibid., pp. 238–67, 354–447, 606–7.

6. Ibid., pp. 633–57.

7. Ibid., pp. 477–602.

8. Ibid., pp. 472–75, 477, 531, 573–75.

9. Weinryb, *Jews of Poland*, pp. 218–19.

10. Scholem, *Sabbatai Sevi*, pp. 546–66. Scholem writes, for example, "Throughout Germany the penitential revival embraced the rabbinic scholars as well as the masses" (p. 552).

11. Weinryb, *Jews of Poland*, pp. 219–20.

12. Scholem, *Sabbatai Sevi*, p. 592.

13. Ibid., pp. 591–601. Digging to the bottom of the barrel for references to Zvi in Poland, Scholem presents an exchange of letters on halachic matters between two leading rabbis in Zamot and Vilna in which the "renewal" is inquired about "in passing" (p. 598).

14. Weinryb, *Jews of Poland*, pp. 224, 230. Weinryb reviews the major pieces of documentary evidence of support among Polish Jews and concludes that they "would be thrown out of a court of law in thirty seconds for lack of probative" (p. 372). Waugh writes that Weinryb too quickly dismisses a polemical tract by an orthodox monk. The tract received attention in Muscovy in 1669, but there is nothing to suggest that the Muscovite government knew of unrest in Poland in 1666 (Waugh, "News of False Messiah," pp. 301–22).

15. Scholem, *Sabbatai Sevi*, pp. 123–38.

16. Ibid., p. 118.

17. Ibid., pp. 138–44, 201–33, 251–52, 464–67.

18. Weinryb, *Jews of Poland*, pp. 151, 181–205.

19. Scholem, *Sabbatai Sevi*, pp. 1–3, 88–93, 139, 461, 591–92.

20. Weinryb, *Jews of Poland*, pp. 171–72, 200–201, 205.

21. Scholem, *Sabbatai Sevi*, pp. 3–6, 391–93, 435, 463–64.

22. Ibid., pp. 539–40.

23. Ibid., pp. 485–90, 518–45.

24. Ibid., p. 462. Katz writes that the consciousness of exile gave rise to messianic movements, and that the emergence of the Sabbatian movement in 1666 "constituted mere historical chance. The movement could have made its appearance at a much later date or not at all" (J. Katz, *Tradition and Crisis*, pp. 217–18). Needless to say, this is not a viewpoint accepted here.

25. Scholem, *Sabbatai Sevi*, pp. 7–71, and *Major Trends*, pp. 244–88.

26. Scholem, *Sabbatai Sevi*, pp. 251–52, 268–81, 302–24, and *Major Trends*, pp. 244–85.

27. Scholem, *Sabbatai Sevi*, pp. 68–77, and *Kabbalah*, pp. 76–78.

28. Scholem, *Sabbatai Sevi*, pp. 18–20, and *Major Trends*, pp. 244–49.

29. Schechter, "Safed," pp. 202–85.

30. *Encyclopaedia Judaica*, 1:563–64.

31. Ibid., 8:231–32.

32. Nehama, *Salonique*, 2:19–32, 125–30, 162–68, 3:15–22, 93–97.

33. Scholem, *Sabbatai Sevi*, p. 77.

34. Weinryb, *Jews of Poland*, pp. 225–26.

35. Scholem, *Sabbatai Sevi*, pp. 80–85; Weinryb, *Jews of Poland*, pp. 227–28.

36. Scholem, *Kabbalah*, p. 79.

37. Scholem, *Sabbatai Sevi*, pp. 538, 570. On the distance between the cabbalist elites and the masses, see J. Katz, *Tradition and Crisis*, pp. 221–24.

38. The most important opponent of the movement was Jacob Sasportas, a cabbalist in Hamburg, who represented, in Scholem's words, the conservative aspect of the cabbalah (*Sabbatai Sevi*, p. 570).

39. Ibid., pp. 485–86, 496, 570.

40. *Encyclopaedia Judaica*, 11:1019–25.

41. Rivkin, *Jewish History*, pp. 142–49.

42. In the middle of the seventeenth century, Salonika had about 30,000 Jews, 10,000 Greeks, and 20,000 Turks (Nehama, *Salonique*, 5:22).

43. Roth, *Marranos*, pp. 195–235, and *Jews of Italy*, pp. 333–35, 346–50; Rivkin, *Leon Da Modena*, pp. 21–23; *Encyclopaedia Judaica*, 2:895–98, 7:1225–26, 10:1571; Dubnov, *History*, 3:471–73, 482, 627–31.

44. On economic links, see Arkin, *Aspects*, pp. 45–46, 96; Gross, ed., *Economic History*, pp. 187, 216–17, 254.

45. Lea, *Inquisition*, 3:303; Roth, *Marranos*, p. 172.

46. Yerushalmi, *From Spanish Court*, p. 44.

47. Jacob, "Millenarianism and Science," pp. 335–41.

48. Roth, *Menasseh ben Israel*.

49. Scholem, *Sabbatai Sevi*, pp. 152–54.

50. Capp, *Fifth Monarchy Men*, pp. 26, 213.

51. McKeon, "Sevi in England," pp. 131–69.

52. Scholem, *Sabbatai Sevi*, pp. 333–34, 545; Capp, *Fifth Monarchy Men*, p. 214; Toon, *Puritans*, pp. 137–53.

53. Scholem, *Sabbatai Sevi*, p. 154.

54. Popkin, "Historical Significance," pp. 18–27; Petachowski, *David Nieta*,

pp. 33–36; Rivkin, *Leon Da Modena*, pp. 5–6.

55. Yerushalmi, "Conversos," pp. 201–9.

56. Yerushalmi, *From Spanish Court*, pp. 44–47.

57. Yerushalmi, "Conversos," p. 202.

58. Nehama, *Salonique*, 5:17–19.

59. P. Berger, *Invitation to Sociology*, pp. 51–52.

60. Nehama, *Salonique*, 5:14–20.

61. Rivkin, *León Da Modena*, pp. 7–16; Sonne, "León Modena," pp. 1–28; Révah, "Spinoza," pp. 173–218.

62. Yovel, "Spinoza," pp. 46–52.

63. Aston, *Crisis in Europe*, especially Hobsbawm, "Crisis," pp. 5–58. For a recent summary of work on the economic aspects of the crisis see Wallerstein, *Modern World-System*, pp. 3–34. For an account which gives greater consideration to cultural aspects see Rabb, *Struggle for Stability*.

64. Hobsbawm, "Crisis," p. 11. As noted in the text, a number of Christian millenarian prophecies were centered on the year 1666. Rabb writes that the subsidence of prophecies after that date was one indication that the crisis was passing. Rabb, *Struggle for Stability*, p. 51.

65. Braudel and Spooner, "Prices in Europe," pp. 374–486.

66. Lewis, "Reflections on Decline," pp. 215–34; Pennington, *Seventeenth-Century*, pp. 368–72; Olson, "Jews in Ottoman Empire," pp. 75–88; Gibb and Bowen, *Islamic Society*, pt. 2, pp. 239–41.

67. Nehama, *Salonique*, 5:7–8, 55–98.

68. Cipolla, "Decline of Italy," pp. 196–214.

69. Rivkin, *Leon Da Modena*, pp. 18–39.

70. Roth, *Jews of Italy*, pp. 333–35, 348–50.

71. Price, *Dutch Republic*, pp. 42–53, 211–12; Barbour, *Capitalism in Amsterdam*; Wallerstein, *Modern World-System*, pp. 37–71.

72. Rabb, *Struggle for Stability*, esp. pp. 35–59, 107–15.

73. Scholem, *Sabbatai Sevi*, pp. 651–52. The messianic tradition was particularly strong among the Yemenite Jews. See Ratzahbi, "Apocalypses," vol. 1. The Yemenite messiah of the twelfth century, mentioned by Maimonides, had a close parallel in the nineteenth. Shukr Salim Kuhayl (c. 1840–63) claimed that the prophet Elijah had ordered him to prepare the people for redemption. Kuhayl gained a large following among the Yemenite Jews and was considered sufficiently dangerous to be assassinated on the order of the king. The belief that he would be resurrected served the purpose of an heir, who also gained considerable influence (*Encyclopaedia Judaica*, 10:1286).

74. Freimann and Kracauer, *Frankfort*, pp. 108, 113–17.

75. *Encyclopaedia Judaica*, 13:967–68.

76. Scholem, *Sabbatai Sevi*, p. 561.

77. Grunwald, *Vienna*, pp. 91–95.

Chapter 8

1. Scholem, *Sabbatai Sevi*, chaps. 7, 8.
2. Festinger, Riecken, and Schachter, *When Prophecy Fails.*
3. Zygmunt, "Prophetic Failure," pp. 926–48.
4. Festinger, et al. discussed the Sabbatian movement as one of their historical examples of disconfirmation. Their reliance on Graetz as their source led them to give a somewhat misleading account of the movement's development. They placed too much emphasis on Zvi's announcement in 1648 that he was the messiah (Festinger, Riecken, and Schachter, *When Prophecy Fails*, pp. 8–12; Graetz, *History*, 5:118–67). A similar perspective to the account presented here is found in Zenner, "Apostate Messiah," pp. 111–18. Zenner's account does not go beyond the believers' explanations for Zvi's conversion.
5. Scholem, *Kabbalah*, pp. 262–64.
6. Scholem, *Sabbatai Sevi*, pp. 688–702, 749–53, *Kabbalah*, pp. 265–66, and *Messianic Idea*, pp. 61–63.
7. Scholem, *Sabbatai Sevi*, pp. 703–4, 710, 720–21, 800–805, *Kabbalah*, pp. 266–67, *Major Trends*, pp. 310–12, and *Messianic Idea*, pp. 87–89, 94–99.
8. Scholem, *Sabbatai Sevi*, pp. 703, 760–61, 889–99, *Major Trends*, pp. 302–3, and *Kabbalah*, pp. 272–75; Kaplan, "Attitude of Leadership," pp. 198–216.
9. Scholem, *Sabbatai Sevi*, pp. 794–95, *Major Trends*, pp. 309–10, and *Messianic Idea*, p. 95.
10. Yerushalmi, *From Spanish Court*, pp. 312–41.
11. Tishby, "Documents," pp. 106–7. Quoted in Zenner.
12. Scholem, *Sabbatai Sevi*, pp. 893–98.
13. Yerushalmi, *From Spanish Court*, p. 339.
14. Festinger, Riecken, and Schachter, *When Prophecy Fails*, p. 12.
15. Scholem, *Sabbatai Sevi*, pp. 920–23, and *Kabbalah*, pp. 276, 396–400, 441–42, 452–53; *Encyclopaedia Judaica*, 12:311.
16. Benayahu, *Sabbatian Movement*, chap. 2, and "Holy Society," pp. 133–82; *Encyclopaedia Judaica*, 10:373; Scholem, *Kabbalah*, pp. 277, 429–31.
17. Tishby, "Messianic Ferment," pp. 374–97; *Encyclopaedia Judaica*, 11:599–604.
18. Scholem, *Sabbatai Sevi*, pp. 714–19, 724, 740, 746–47, 832, 856, 867, 872–73, *Major Trends*, p. 302, and *Studies and Texts*, pp. 78–83.
19. Scholem, *Major Trends*, pp. 312–18, and *Messianic Idea*, pp. 100–126.
20. Scholem, *Sabbatai Sevi*, pp. 859–62, *Kabbalah*, pp. 274, 327–32, and *Messianic Idea*, pp. 142–66; Benayahu, *Sabbatian Movement*, chaps. 2–5. A few Polish Sabbatians visited Salonika and later introduced antinomian ideas in Poland. After his return from Turkey to Poland, Molach promoted the idea that in order to subjugate the *kelippot*, it was necessary to go through forty-nine gates of uncleanliness; the highest and truest levels of purity were attained by the soul that had descended into the depths of filth (Zinberg, *Jewish Literature*, 6:171–72). Jacob Frank, to be considered in the following chapter, also stayed in Salonika for a period.

21. Scholem, *Sabbatai Sevi*, pp. 147, 799, and *Major Trends*, p. 293.
22. Benayahu, *Sabbatian Movement*, chap. 2; Nehama, *Salonique*, 5:181–83.
23. Scholem, *Kabbalah*, pp. 327–32; Ben-Zvi, "Salonica," pp. 131–51.

Chapter 9

1. Scholem, *Kabbalah*, pp. 287–309; Weinryb, *Jews of Poland*, chap. 11; Duker, "Frankism's Duration," pp. 287–333.
2. The literature on Hasidism is large, but there is no major work which provides a comprehensive history of the movement. For a good short account, see Tishby and Dan, "Hasidism," pp. 756–821. Prior to the Hasidic movement, the term *hasid* was used to denote a saintly man who met the highest standards of piety, observance, and ethical behavior. The earliest reference to a group calling themselves hasidim is in the Book of Maccabees. A famous group in the middle ages was the Haside Ashkenaz, "the saints of Germany."
3. In the partitions, Prussia annexed the mainly German areas adjoining its territory, Austria annexed Galicia, and Russia annexed the Ukrainian districts, Belorussia, and Lithuania.
4. Benes and Pounds, *Poland*, pp. 61–63.
5. The census found a total of 587,236 Jews: 171,382 in the Polish ethnic areas, 258,205 in the Ukrainian areas, and 157,649 in Lithuania and Belorussia. Since the census was undertaken for tax purposes, Jews did not report their total numbers. The true number of the total Jewish population was probably over 750,000 (Mahler, *Jewish People*, vol. 1, bk. 2, p. 269).
6. Mahler, *Jews in Poland*, pp. 238–45.
7. Ibid., pp. 249–88.
8. Weinryb, *Jews of Poland*, pp. 202–5; Dubnov, *History*, 4:83–167, 357–69; J. Katz, *Tradition and Crisis*, pp. 227–34; Mahler, *Modern Jewry*, chap. 9; Dinur, "Hasidism," pp. 83–139.
9. In the dispute, although the Frankists made no explicit reference to Jesus, they emphasized the similarities between their beliefs and Christianity. They included in their arguments that the Talmud taught that the Jews need Christian blood for their rituals. It is most likely that this was a tactic in the dispute and not a real belief among the Frankists.
10. Weinryb, *Jews of Poland*, pp. 240–57; Scholem, *Kabbalah*, pp. 287–303; Mandel, *Militant Messiah*.
11. Scholem, *Studies and Texts*, pp. 47–62, 116–39, and *Kabbalah*, pp. 288, 293–94, 303; Weinryb, *Jews of Poland*, pp. 242–43.
12. An English translation is now available: Ben-Amos and Mintz, trans. and ed., *In Praise*.
13. Horodezky notes similarities in the stories about the Besht and Jesus: miraculous elements in their births, their capacity to heal the sick, their ability to walk on water, and so on (Horodezky, *Hasidism*, vol. 4). The legendary biography of the Besht is told in many works: ibid., vol. 1; Dubnov, *Hasidism*, pp. 41–52, 59–69; Zinberg, *Jewish Literature*, 9:28–34.

14. Schipper, "Ba'al Shem Tov," pp. 525–26, 531–32, 551–52. The contention that a certain Joel Ba'al Shem, and not Israel Ba'al Shem, was the original leader is based on one piece of slender evidence and much speculation. It ignores the references to the Besht that have come down to us from his disciples.

15. Aescoly, *Hassidisme*, pp. 23–53.

16. Scholem, "Historical Image," pp. 335–56.

17. Scholem, *Messianic Idea*, pp. 203–27, and *Major Trends*, pp. 325–50; Weinryb, *Jews of Poland*, pp. 271–72, 322–24; Dubnov, *Hasidism*, pp. 53–57; Horodezky, *Hasidism*, vol. 1; Shochat, "On Joy," pp. 30–43; Weiss, "Kavvanoth," pp. 163–92; Jacobs, *Hasidic Prayer*, chaps. 1–8; Schatz, "Contemplative Prayer," pp. 209–26; *Encyclopaedia Judaica*, 7:1403–13; Rapoport-Albert, "God and Zaddik," pp. 296–325.

18. Ben-Amos and Mintz, trans. and ed., *In Praise*.

19. Scholem, "Historical Image," pp. 335–56; Rapoport-Albert, "God and Zaddik," pp. 310–11.

20. Scholem, "Two First Testimonies," pp. 228–44; Rubinstein, "Chapters," pp. 241–42.

21. Ben-Amos and Mintz, trans. and ed., *In Praise*, pp. 173–75.

22. Dinur accepted the story that the Besht was accepted by a scholarly circle in Brody, but, in fact, the group, which began in the 1740s, opposed the Besht (Dinur, "Hasidism," p. 159; Scholem, "Historical Image," pp. 302–3; Ben-Amos and Mintz, trans. and ed., *In Praise*, p. 31). The Besht also had little success among a circle in Kosov, but a story from the "Praises" tells how one member of the circle, Nahman of Kosov, who initially opposed the Besht, was won over after the Besht demonstrated that he was able to read Nahman's thoughts (Ben-Amos and Mintz, trans. and ed., *In Praise*, pp. 234–35; Weiss, "Circle of Pneumatics," pp. 199–213).

23. Prior to his contact with the Besht, Dov Baer was a strict ascetic whose way of life had made him ill and bedridden. Hasidic legend tells that Dov Baer became a disciple after the Besht recited a passage from a cabbalistic work with such mystical fervor that the whole room was filled with light and angels appeared (Jacobs, *Hasidic Thought*, pp. 3–5).

24. Jacobs, *Hasidic Prayer*, pp. 23, 29–32; Schatz (Uffenheimer), *Mysticism*, pp. 78–110; Horodezky, *Hasidism*, vol. 1; Dubnov, *Hasidism*, pp. 87–93; Zinberg, *Jewish Literature*, 9:64–76; *Encyclopaedia Judaica*, 6:180–84.

25. Scholem, *Studies and Texts*, pp. 60, 120, and *Kabbalah*, p. 300; Weinryb, *Jews of Poland*, p. 242.

26. Scholem, "Historical Image," pp. 313–14.

27. Dinur, "Hasidism," p. 142; Mahler, *Modern Jewry*, pp. 446–48.

28. Shmeruk, "Arendars," pp. 182–92.

29. The argument that the Russian Christian sects had a direct influence on the Hasidim finds support in at least two specific practices that were common among Christian sectarians and Hasidim: the wearing of white clothes and the wearing of a gartel, a sash-type belt worn during prayer. The latter practice is noted in ancient Jewish law, but in the eighteenth century Jews saw it as an innovation. Opponents of the Hasidim recognized that ecstatic behavior was common among

Christian sects and compared the Hasidim to them (Eliach, "Jewish Hasidim," pp. 147–66). Eliach's contention that the Besht's teachings originated with a Greek Orthodox clergyman has been described by Bernard Weinryb as "pure fiction" (Eliach, "Dissenting Sects," pp. 57–83; Weinryb, "Reappraisals," pp. 971–74). See also Weinryb, *Jews of Poland*, pp. 237–38, 243, 272. A recent attempt to emphasize the Christian influence has been made by Patai, *Jewish Mind*, chap. 8. Billington claims Jewish influence on Russian sectarianism (Billington, *Icon and Axe*, pp. 153–54, 178). On the Russian sects, see Conybeare, *Russian Dissenters*.

30. Dinur, "Hasidism," pp. 148–53; Dresner, *Zaddik*, pp. 80–109.

31. Dinur, "Hasidism," pp. 134–47; Weiss, "Beginnings," pp. 46–106. Weiss suggests a continuity with the opposition elements in the underground Sabbatian circles which also contained "wandering" preachers (pp. 128, 131–32). He emphasizes the frustrations and feelings of failure among the preachers because of their failure to influence the people to repent (pp. 134–35, 147). Piekarz doubts that this was an important factor in the development of Hasidism. He argues that such frustrations are typical of preachers at all times, and that there is no reason to assume an increase in such feelings prior to the beginnings of Hasidism (Piekarz, *Beginning of Hasidism*, pp. 170–71).

32. Ettinger, "Hasidic Movement," pp. 251–66.

33. One of the few ritual modifications made by the Hasidim was their use of polished knives in *shechitah* (ritual slaughtering). The Hasidim were dissatisfied with the inspection of shechitah by the kehillah and they used polished knives to make sure that the slaughtering was properly performed. The practice was also related to their belief in the transmigration of souls into animals and the "correction" of such souls by proper shechitah (Shmeruk, "Shechitah," pp. 47–72).

34. Dinur, "Hasidism," pp. 181–83.

35. Scholem, *Messianic Idea*, pp. 176–202.

36. Tishby, "Messianic Idea," pp. 1–45.

37. Scholem, *Messianic Idea*, pp. 176–202. Dinur also recognized that the Hasidic emphasis on the redemption of the individual departed from the messianic tension of the Lurianic cabbalah (Dinur, "Hasidism," p. 184). It is difficult, therefore, to make sense of Dinur's description of Hasidism as a millennial movement.

38. Schatz (Uffenheimer), "Self-Redemption," pp. 207–12; Werblowsky, "Mysticism and Messianism," pp. 305–14.

39. Scholem, *Texts and Studies*, pp. 103–8, 113–14.

40. Ibid., p. 115.

41. Rubinstein, "Hasidism and Sabbatianism," pp. 182–97.

42. Ben-Amos and Mintz, trans. and ed., *In Praise*, pp. 86–87. Another Hasidic story includes a reference to the Frankists as a "wicked sect that converted to Christianity" (p. 58). There is also a legend that the Besht took part in the public dispute with the Frankists (Dinur, "Hasidism," p. 199; Scholem, "Historical Image," p. 305).

43. Tishby and Dan, "Hasidism," pp. 785–86; Piekarz, *Beginning of Hasidism*,

pp. 271–73; Weiss, "Beginnings," pp. 165–76.

44. Tishby and Dan, "Hasidism," p. 787; Piekarz, *Beginning of Hasidism*, pp. 178–244.

45. Dresner, *Zaddik*, pp. 148–221; Rubinstein, "Hasidism and Sabbatianism," pp. 193–96; Piekarz, *Beginning of Hasidism*, pp. 281–87; Weiss, "Beginnings," pp. 149–56, 164. In rabbinic, Jewish ethical, and cabbalistic literature the term *zaddik* generally designated a man who conformed to normative standards of piety and the term *hasid* was used for a man of exceptional piety and saintliness. It has been argued that since all the members of the movement were called hasidim, the meanings of the two terms were exchanged. However, in some rabbinic sources there are indications that the term *zaddik* was used for exceptional men.

46. Piekarz, *Beginning of Hasidism*, pp. 35–95, 383. On the opposition to Hasidism, see Wilensky, *Hasidim and Mitnaggedim*.

Chapter 10

1. Jewish population: Russia, 1818, approximately 1,000,000; 1851, 1,750,000. Galicia, 1830, 250,000. Congress Poland, 1827, 377,754; 1851, 563,970.

2. Sharot, *Judaism*, chaps. 2, 3.

3. In 1828, in the Pale of Settlement, 124 of the 673 industrial plants were owned by Jews, and Jews made up 27 percent of the factory workers.

4. Mahler, *Jewish People*, vol. 2, bk. 1, pp. 13–42, 147, 196–97, and *Hasidism and Haskalah*, pp. 16, 211–14.

5. Mahler, *Hasidism and Haskalah*, pp. 13–15, 25–26; Dubnov, *History*, 4:668–73, 5:142–99.

6. Mahler, *Hasidism and Haskalah*, pp. 17–24; Brym, *Jewish Intelligentsia*, pp. 24–28.

7. Weber, *Economy*, pp. 446–47.

8. This development can be traced in the stages of the history of the Hasidic story (Dan, *Hasidic Story*, pp. 34–35). Eliach argues that the zaddik was modeled after that of the Christs, the leaders of the Russian Christian sects. The sects believed in the reincarnation of Christ in their leaders, and that after the death of a leader the Christhood would pass into the body of another. The Christhood could be inherited by a son of the former leader or transferred to another member of the sect (Eliach, "Jewish Hasidim," pp. 176–96). The influence of the Christian sects cannot be ruled out here, but the parallels in leadership are of such a general nature that they can be found in a great number of religious movements in many societies. Eliach's argument that the model for the zaddik was adopted by the Besht from the sectarian Christs does not take account of the stages in the development of the institution within Hasidism, and the fact that the zaddik became the focus of the movement only from the third generation on.

9. Dubnov, *Hasidism*, pp. 57–58; Tishby and Dan, "Hasidism," pp. 779–80; Zinberg, *Jewish Literature*, 9:58–59; Weiss, "Beginnings," pp. 159–61.

10. Dresner, *Zaddik*, pp. 117–239.

11. Dubnov, *Hasidism*, pp. 91–92; Horodezsky, *Hasidism*, vol. 1; Zinberg, *Jewish Literature*, 9:77–79; Tishby and Dan, "Hasidism," p. 783; Weiss, "Contemplative Magic," pp. 137–47.

12. Dan, *Hasidic Story*, pp. 53–54.

13. Dubnov, *Hasidism*, pp. 178–84; Tishby and Dan, "Hasidism," pp. 783, 797; Schatz (Uffenheimer), "Essence of Zaddik," pp. 365–78; Zinberg, *Jewish Literature*, 9:94–99.

14. Weber, *Economy*, pp. 544–50.

15. Troeltsch, *Social Teaching*, pp. 377, 381, 734–36, 743–49, 795–800; Campbell, "Clarifying the Cult," pp. 375–88.

16. Dan, *Hasidic Story*, pp. 34–35, 55–58; Mintz, *Legends*, p. 110.

17. Wilson, *Magic*, esp. chaps. 3–6.

18. Weber, *Economy*, pp. 249–51, 253.

19. The house of the zaddik Schneur Zalmon occupied an area of twenty-five by twelve meters and had two floors. The ground floor included Zalmon's living quarters and a small synagogue (the "Lower Garden of Eden") which also served as a waiting room for those who had been granted an audience with the zaddik. The upper floor contained a private study and a second reception room in which the zaddik received his followers (the "Upper Garden of Eden") (Mindel, *Schneur Zalmon*, pp. 136–38).

20. Green, "Zaddiq as Axis Mundi," pp. 327–47.

21. Three ritual meals on the Sabbath were already required by the rabbis in the talmudic period. The fourth meal was a Hasidic innovation (Wertheim, *Laws and Customs*, pp. 151–53).

22. Mintz, *Legends*, pp. 5, 95–98; Zborowski and Herzog, *Life Is with People*, pp. 166–79; Langer, *Nine Gates*, pp. 4–20; Wertheim, *Laws and Customs*, pp. 157–68.

23. Turner, *Dramas*, pp. 166–230.

24. Minkin, *Romance*, pp. 324–25.

25. Langer, *Nine Gates*, pp. 14–15.

26. Weber, *Economy*, p. 1140.

27. Ibid., pp. 252–53.

28. Ben-Amos and Mintz, trans. and ed., *In Praise*, p. 258.

29. Dresner, *Zaddik*, pp. 48, 59–61. Jacob Joseph was described as a harsh, officious man, aloof from the people and given to frequent outbursts of anger. Pinhas Shapiro of Korets, a close disciple of the Besht, did not accept Dov Baer and came into conflict with Dov Baer's disciples.

30. Ben-Amos and Mintz, trans. and ed., *In Praise*, p. 84.

31. Dubnov, *Hasidism*, pp. 213–14; Horodezsky, *Hasidism*, vol. 2.

32. Baruch was the son of Adel, the Besht's daughter. Another son of Adel, Moses Hayyim of Sadylkow (c. 1740–1800), did not attract a large following (*Encyclopaedia Judaica*, 3:2–9, 12:430).

33. A useful chart of the relationships of the leading Hasidic dynasties is provided in the *Encyclopaedia Judaica*, 1:160–67.

34. A prominent example was Jacob Isaac, "the Seer" of Lublin (1745–1815),

who had no hereditary successor, but had twelve disciples who became zaddikim. A son-in-law became a successor to one of his disciples.

35. Dov Baer of Lubavich had two brothers, but neither was believed to have his experience or capabilities.

36. Jacobs, *Seeker of Unity*, pp. 12–13, 23–25.

37. In Congress Poland, Jacob Isaac Ben Asher of Przysucha (1766–1814) left three sons, but most of his followers chose as their zaddik his disciple Simheh Bunem of Przysucha (1765–1825). Simheh Bunem was followed by a son, but the real leadership was taken by Menahem Mendel of Kotsk (1787–1859), who had been a disciple of both Jacob Isaac and Simheh Bunem. Five of Bunem's disciples became zaddikim after his death. Of these, one had no successor, three had hereditary successors only, and one had both a disciple-successor and hereditary successors. Menahem Mendel had no hereditary successors, but two of his disciples who had previously been disciples of Simheh Bunem became zaddikim. One of these, Mordecai Joseph Leiner of Izbica (died 1854), was succeeded by a son, and the hereditary dynasty continued for a further three generations. The other, Isaac Meir Rothenberg Alter of Gur (1789–1866), had thirteen children, all of whom died during his lifetime; he was succeeded by a disciple, Hanrkh of Alexander (1798–1870), who was in turn succeeded by a grandson of Isaac Meir. Another disciple of Isaac Meir, Judah Leib Eger of Lublin (died 1888), became a zaddik and was succeeded by a son.

38. Weber, *Economy*, p. 1137.

39. Ibid., p. 1139.

40. Rubin, *Satmar*, pp. 34–38.

41. Rabinowitsch, *Lithuanian Hasidism*, pp. 223–30; Mintz, *Legends*, pp. 120–21.

42. The dynasty established by Sabbatai of Raszkov (died 1745), a disciple of the Besht, continued for a further six generations; each time one son followed his father as zaddik.

43. Gerlach and Hine, *People, Power, Change*, pp. 38–40.

44. Ibid., pp. 41–55.

45. Green, *Tormented Master*, pp. 101–13.

46. The following section on religious differences within Hasidism is a synthesis of many sources. The most important sources are: Dubnov, *Hasidism*; Horodezsky, *Hasidism*; Mahler, *Jewish People*, vol. 2, bk. 2, pp. 19–85, and *Hasidism and Haskalah*, chaps. 1, 9; Rabinowitsch, *Lithuanian Hasidism*; Mindel, *Schneur Zalmon*; Schatz (Uffenheimer), "Essence of Zaddik," pp. 365–78; Green, "Rabbi Nahman," pp. 141–57; Rabinowicz, "Music and Dance," pp. 252–57; Weiss, "Contemplative Mysticism," pp. 19–29. Also the individual entries under the names of zaddikim and dynasties in the *Encyclopaedia Judaica*.

47. Menahem Mendel was succeeded by Isaac Meir Rothenberg Alter (died 1866), who tried to win the masses and involved himself in their daily problems.

48. Zalmon and other Habad teachers distinguished between the zaddik and the "average man," but they were not consistent in presenting the differences between these two types. In many parts of Zalmon's most popular work, *Tanya*, the raising of divine sparks is seen as the task of the zaddik alone, but in other

writings the average man also had an important role in this process. Whereas in the *Tanya* there is an emphasis on the essential differences between the zaddik and the average man, in other writings the differences are made relative and it is considered possible for the average man, by constant effort, to reach the heights of the zaddik.

49. On their part, the maskilim were attracted to Nahman because of his personality, artistic expression, and his conflict with other Hasidic leaders. They believed that he might, consciously or otherwise, serve their purposes.

50. The Bratslav grew considerably in the late nineteenth century, and between the two world wars they broke out of their isolation from other branches of Hasidism and attained considerable social recognition, especially in Poland.

51. Among the zaddikim known for their ecstatic prayer were Israel ben Sabbetai Hapstein of Kozienice, Uri ben Phinehas of Strelisk (died 1826), Abraham Joshua Herchel of Apta (died 1828), Kolonymus Kalman Epstein (died 1823), Joseph Meir Weiss of Spinka, and Solomon of Karlin.

52. The Hebrew letters for TAR are numerically equivalent to the Hebrew year in 1839–40. There was also some speculation concerning 1860; the letters of that year were interpreted to mean "crown" (Duker, "Tarniks," pp. 191–229).

53. Aryeh Leib of Shpola (1725–1812), Mordecai Joseph Leiner of Izbica (died 1854), Issachar Baer of Radarshikser (1764–1843).

54. In 1852, the average amount of capital per Jewish family was 4,151 rubles in the northwest areas (mainly Lithuania and Belorussia) of the Pale, 3,579 in the southwest areas (mainly the Ukrainian areas that had been annexed from Poland), and 9,378 in the southeast areas, where there were far fewer Jews. In Podolia the average was 2,691 rubles. The Jewish merchants in the southeast had twice the capital of the merchants in the northwest and three times the capital of the Jewish merchants in the southwest (Mahler, *Jewish People*, vol. 2, bk. 1, p. 29).

55. Ben-Sasson, "Lithuania," pp. 167–83.

56. Mahler, *Hasidism and Haskalah*, chaps. 2, 8, 9.

Chapter 11

1. Rabinowicz, *Legacy of Polish Jewry*, pp. 126–47; Meldelsohn, "Dilemma of Jewish Politics," pp. 203–19.

2. Mintz, "Ethnic Activism," pp. 449–50.

3. Simon, *Continuity and Change*, pp. 1, 29, 31.

4. Wallach, "Chasidim of Stamford Hill," pp. 11–19, 68. According to Wallach, in Stamford Hill there are about 200 Belz families, 200 Lubavich, 200 Gur, 350 Satmar, 100 Bobov, 100 Vishnitz, and some Trisk, Zanz, and others.

5. Gutwirth, *Vie juive traditionnelle*, p. 51. The Belz are the most numerous Hasidim in Antwerp. The others include Satmar, Vishnitz, and Gur.

6. Wilson, *Religious Sects*, pp. 118–40; Hostetler, *Amish Society* and *Hutterite Society*.

7. Much of the following is informed by four community studies of the Hasidim: Gutwirth, *Vie juive traditionnelle*; Poll, *Williamsburg*; Rubin, *Satmar*; Shaffir, *Montreal*.

8. Levy, "Shifting Patterns," pp. 32–34.

9. Shaffir, *Montreal*, p. 101.

10. Levy, "Shifting Patterns," pp. 36–37.

11. Mintz, "Ethnic Activism," pp. 454–55.

12. Poll, *Williamsburg*, pp. 153–247.

13. Rubin, *Satmar*, chap. 9.

14. Poll, *Williamsburg*, pp. 101–7, 214, 250–51.

15. Shaffir, *Montreal*, pp. 97–98.

16. Rubin, *Satmar*, chap. 9; Poll, *Williamsburg*, pp. 89–90, 93–96, 246–47.

17. Gutwirth, *Vie juive traditionnelle*, pp. 53, 424. A survey of ultra-orthodox in Israel found that 55 percent of the men were employed in a synagogue or religious school, 13 percent had small shops, 11 percent were clerks in government agencies, 15 percent were skilled craftsmen, and 6 percent were laborers (Simon, *Continuity and Change*, p. 80).

18. Rubin, *Satmar*, chaps. 10, 11.

19. Mintz, "Ethnic Activism," pp. 453–63.

20. Poll, *Williamsburg*, pp. 256–57.

21. Mintz, "Ethnic Activism," pp. 455–64; *Ma'ariv*, 11 July 1977; *New York Times*, 26 October, 1 December 1979.

22. Pinsker, "Piety as Community," p. 243.

23. Isaacs, "Brooklyn," pp. 189–94; Steinberg, "New Square," pp. 195–201.

24. Rubin, *Satmar*, p. 66.

25. Levy, "Shifting Patterns," pp. 29–30; Shaffir, *Montreal*, pp. 73–75.

26. Rubin, *Satmar*, chap. 8.

27. Levy, "Shifting Patterns," pp. 39–42.

28. Shaffir, *Montreal*, pp. 110–40.

29. Pinsker, "Piety as Community," pp. 230–46.

30. Levy, "Shifting Patterns," pp. 35–37; Rubin, *Satmar*, chap. 12.

31. Rubin, *Satmar*, chaps. 4, 5.

32. Shaffir, *Montreal*, pp. 52–70.

33. *New York Times*, 27 August 1979.

34. Gutwirth, *Vie juive traditionnelle*, pp. 277–96.

35. *Ma'ariv*, 26 September 1975.

36. *Jerusalem Post*, 19 September 1975.

37. Shaffir, *Montreal*, pp. 180–203.

38. Mintz, "Ethnic Activism," pp. 460–61; *Jewish Chronicle*, 25 February 1977.

39. Rubin, *Satmar*, chap. 12; Poll, *Williamsburg*, pp. 59–82.

Chapter 12

1. Sharot, *Judaism*, pp. 63–69, 72–74.
2. Dinur, "Question of Redemption," pp. 229–354.
3. Mevorah, "Messianism," pp. 189–218.
4. Philipson, *Reform Movement*, pp. 75–124; Carlebach, *Karl Marx*, pp. 44–45.
5. Philipson, *Reform Movement*, pp. 173–80.
6. Plaut, *Reform Judaism*, p. 145.
7. Philipson, *Reform Movement*, pp. 350–55.
8. Sharot, *Judaism*, pp. 74–87.
9. Marras, *Politics of Assimilation*, pp. 112, 116–18.
10. *Jewish Chronicle*, 12, 19, 26 October 1900; Sharot, *Judaism*, pp. 120–21.
11. Sharot, *Judaism*, pp. 87–100, 117–31.
12. Mahler, "Haskalah in Galicia," pp. 75–76.
13. Ibid., pp. 64–85, and *Hasidism and Haskalah*, pp. 47–77, 247–86.
14. Berdyaev, *Russian Revolution*, pp. 69–70. Quoted in Wistrich, *Revolutionary Jews*, p. 4.
15. Mishkinsky, "Jewish Labor Movement," p. 228. Peter Lavrov, a Russian who knew many of the first generation of Russian Jewish socialists, included the following words in a speech to Jewish workers from eastern Europe in Paris on 1 May 1886: "The traditional Jews expected in their fanatical belief a messiah who would rule all the peoples. Did this belief not prepare unintentionally for a more rationalistic belief? Did the new socialist Jew not change the mythical messiah for a real messiah by raising the banner of the workers' kingdom and by destroying the golden calf of capitalism?" (Erez, "Bible and Jewish Tradition," p. 141).
16. Wistrich, *Revolutionary Jews*, pp. 4–29, 47, 60, 99, 116.
17. J. L. Talmon, "Jews," pp. 17–21.
18. Wistrich, *Revolutionary Jews*, pp. 6–21, 131–45.
19. Brym, *Jewish Intelligentsia*, pp. 47–56.
20. Levin, *Socialist Movements*, pp. 26–37; J. L. Talmon, "Jews," pp. 30–38; Erez, "Bible and Jewish Tradition," pp. 118–20.
21. Antonovsky and Tcherikower, *Labor Movement*, pp. 12–15.
22. Brym, *Jewish Intelligentsia*, pp. 63–64, 69–70.
23. Erez, "Bible and Jewish Tradition," p. 123.
24. Tobias, *Jewish Bund*, pp. 41, 44–45.
25. Erez, "Bible and Jewish Tradition," pp. 123–25, 129, 137; Rischin, *Promised City*, pp. 157–58.
26. Tobias, *Jewish Bund*, pp. 335–36; Johnpoll, *Politics of Futility*, p. 34.
27. Rischin, *Promised City*, p. 159.
28. J. Katz, "Jewish National Movement," p. 130.
29. Hertzberg, ed., *Zionist Idea*, pp. 103–14; J. Katz, "Jewish National Movement," pp. 131–34.
30. Hertzberg, ed., *Zionist Idea*, pp. 159–65.
31. Erez, "Bible and Jewish Tradition," pp. 138–40; Levin, *Socialist Movements*, p. 385.

32. Vital, *Origins of Zionism*, pp. 85–86; Laqueur, *Zionism*, p. 278.

33. S. Weinstein, "Pioneers with a Passion"; Laqueur, *Zionism*, p. 281; Knaani, *Labour Second Aliyah*.

34. J. Katz, "Jewish National Movement," pp. 135, 139, 141.

35. Vital, *Origins of Zionism*, pp. 54–56, 116–17, 125; Hertzberg, ed., *Zionist Idea*, pp. 168–70, 179–80.

36. Vital, *Origins of Zionism*, pp. 144–58.

37. J. Katz, "Jewish National Movement," p. 142.

38. Brym, *Jewish Intelligentsia*, pp. 76–77, 81.

39. Tobias, *Jewish Bund*, pp. 127–28.

40. Brym, *Jewish Intelligentsia*, pp. 45, 68–69, 77–78.

41. Vital, *Origins of Zionism*, pp. 233–70, 316–17.

42. Neclava, "Herzl," pp. 9–26.

43. Blau, *Judaism*, pp. 141, 144.

44. Gonen, *Psychohistory*, pp. 75–85.

45. Poppel, *Zionism in Germany*; Reinharz, *Fatherland or Promised Land*.

46. Siegel, "Reflections," pp. 63–84.

47. Heller, *Edge of Destruction*, pp. 265–66.

48. Biale, *Scholem*, pp. 177–78, 269.

Chapter 13

1. Raanan, *Gush Emunim*, pp. 18–23.

2. Friedman, *Non-Zionist Orthodox*, pp. 1–3, 22–28.

3. Raanan, *Gush Emunim*, pp. 19–29.

4. Friedman, *Non-Zionist Orthodox*, pp. 93–102.

5. Ibid., pp. 33–34, 53–55.

6. Raanan, *Gush Emunim*, pp. 30–31.

7. Ahlberg, *Messianism*. Benei Akiva was founded in 1929 as the youth movement of Po'alei Mizrachi with Rabbi Abraham Kook as its spiritual leader. In 1969 the movement had a membership of twenty-five thousand (*Encyclopaedia Judaica*, 4:490–91).

8. Y. Talmon, "Millenarian Movements," pp. 159–200. The following account of the beliefs of Gush Emunim applies to the movement in the 1970s, when religious leaders and activists of the movement showed a high degree of agreement over both ends and means. With regard to means, this consensus has now broken down. See notes 10 and 11.

9. Raanan, *Gush Emunim*, pp. 63–65, 72–73, 168. Members of Gush Emunim refer to the writings of Maimonides on messianism to support their rational form of messianism, but unlike Maimonides, they interpret contemporary events in messianic terms.

10. Ibid., pp. 58–59, 75–77, 117–18; O'Dea, "Gush Emunim," pp. 39–50; Kohn, *Gush Emunim*, pp. 34–35; Goldman, "Messianic Interpretation," pp. 37–41. There has now emerged a section in Gush Emunim who believe that,

having established their presence in the territories, they should undertake a campaign "to return" the people to religion. Another section argues that they should seek the cooperation of secular settlements outside the pre–June 1967 borders in a common front against political opposition to the settlements. They maintain that, in order to obtain this cooperation, they should be careful not to emphasize their religious beliefs.

11. Livneh, *Elon Moreh.* At least half of the approximately five thousand adult settlers in the West Bank identify with Gush Emunim (*Jerusalem Post Magazine,* 30 January 1981, pp. 4–5). While the entire movement agrees on the central importance of settlements in Judea and Samaria, there is now a division over tactics. While one sector argues for the continuing creation of settlements, another urges a pause in settlement activities and a focus instead on a propaganda campaign among the Israeli public to counteract those groups opposed to settlement in the occupied territories (*Jerusalem Post Magazine,* 27 February 1981, p. 6).

12. Kohn, *Gush Emunim,* pp. 11–20. At the time of this writing (February 1981), the Gush leadership has not convened for some time. Gush Emunim continues as an ideological frame of reference, but as an organizational entity, it may have ceased to exist. Its political and organizational activities appear to have devolved on Amana, the settlement movement, the Yesha Council, the body representing the settlements in Judea, Samaria, and Gaza, and the regional councils (*Jerusalem Post Magazine,* 13 February 1981, p. 8).

13. Kohn, *Gush Emunim,* pp. 28–30.

14. *Haaretz,* 6 October 1978 (summary of doctorate by M. Bar-Lev); Raanan, *Gush Emunim,* pp. 50–53. The dependence of Gush Emunim for its major support on Benei Akiva and yeshiva students and graduates has set limits to its growth, and the number of possible additional recruits from this reservoir is small. Some orthodox Jews from the United States have joined the Gush settlements, and hopes for further expansion of the settlements appear to be based on expectations of attracting more from this group.

15. Liebman, "Religion," pp. 17–27.

16. Raanan, *Gush Emunim,* pp. 37–40.

17. Kohn, *Gush Emunim,* pp. 22–24; Raanan, *Gush Emunim,* pp. 67–70.

18. Raanan, *Gush Emunim,* pp. 43–45, 80–81.

19. O'Dea, "Gush Emunim," pp. 35–50, and "Religious Aspect," pp. 39–41; Kohn, *Gush Emunim,* p. 30; Raanan, *Gush Emunim,* pp. 41, 49; Rotenstreich, "Religious Conviction," pp. 34–36.

Chapter 14

1. On a Jewish-Christian millenarian movement, which was a response to the Holocaust, see Sharot, "Adventist Movement," pp. 35–45.

2. Glock, "Role of Deprivation," pp. 24–36.

3. Wallis, *Salvation and Protest,* pp. 3–7.

4. See, for example, the articles in Wilson, ed., *Rationality*.

5. This form of deprivation has been termed decremental deprivation: expectations remain relatively constant, but position and opportunities decline (Gurr, *Why Men Rebel*, pp. 46–52; Morrison, "Relative Deprivation," pp. 675–90).

6. Cohn, *Pursuit of Millennium*, esp. pp. 54–66, 281–83.

7. Wilson, *Magic*, pp. 274–308.

8. For a general discussion of this approach see Winter, "Metaphoric Parallelist Approach," pp. 212–29.

9. Douglas, *Natural Symbols*, and "Social Preconditions," pp. 69–80.

10. In his book on the Reformation, Guy Swanson adopts a neo-Durkheimian perspective to explain why some societies adopted Protestant transcendentalism while others retained Catholic immanentism. His independent variable is the degree of penetration and control of government by interests that are external to the central concerns of government (Swanson, *Religion and Regime*). The immanence-transcendence dimension was an important one in the differences between Hasidism and other Jews, but even with considerable modification it is difficult to see how Swanson's independent variable can be applied to the Jewish context.

11. Weber, *Economy*, pp. 492–99.

12. For the Buddhist case, see Malalgoda, "Buddhism," pp. 424–31.

13. Lawrence, *Road Belong Cargo*.

14. Spier, Suttles, and Herskovitz, "Comment," pp. 84–88.

15. Adas, *Prophets of Rebellion*.

16. Gager, *Kingdom and Community*.

17. For examples see Wilson, *Sects and Society*, and *Sectarianism*.

Bibliography

Aberle, David. "A Note on Relative Deprivation Theory as Applied to Millenarian and Other Cult Movements." In *Reader in Comparative Religion*,
edited by William A. Lessa and Evon Z. Vogt, pp. 537–41. New York,
1965.

Adas, Michael. *Prophets of Rebellion: Millenarian Protest Movements against the
European Colonial Order*. Chapel Hill, 1979.

Adler, Elkan Rathan, ed. *Jewish Travellers*. New York, 1966.

Aescoly, Aaron Zeev. "David Reubeni in the Light of History." *Jewish Quarterly
Review* 28 (1937–38): 1–45.

———. *Jewish Messianic Movements* (Hebrew). Jerusalem, 1956.

———. *Le Hassidisme*. Paris, 1928.

Ahlberg, Sture. *Messianism i staten Israel: En Studie om Messiastankens nutida
forekomst, formoch funktion bland orthodoxa judar*. Stockholm, 1977.

Ames, Michael M. "Magical-Animism and Buddhism: A Structural Analysis of
the Sinhalese Religious System." *Journal of Asian Studies* 23 (1964): 21–52.

Antonovsky, Aaron, and Tcherikower, Elias. *The Early Jewish Labor Movement in
the United States*. New York, 1961.

Arkin, Marcus. *Aspects of Jewish Economic History*. Philadelphia, 1975.

Aston, Trevor. *Crisis in Europe, 1560–1660*. London, 1965.

Baer, Yitzhak. *A History of the Jews in Spain*. 2 vols. Philadelphia, 1961, 1966.

———. "The Messianic Movement in Spain in the Period of the Expulsion"
(Hebrew). *Zion* 5 (1933): 71–77.

Barbour, Violet. *Capitalism in Amsterdam in the Seventeenth Century*. Ann Arbor,
1963.

Barkun, Michael. *Disaster and the Millennium*. New Haven, 1974.

Baroja, Julio Caro. *Los Judios en la Espana moderna y contemporanea*. Vol. 1.
Madrid, 1961.

Baron, Salo Wittmayer. *A Social and Religious History of the Jews*. Vols. 5, 14. New
York, 1957, 1969.

Barzilay, Isaac E. *Between Reason and Faith: Anti-Rationalism in Italian Jewish
Thought, 1250–1650*. The Hague, 1967.

Bataillan, Marcel. *Erasme et l'Espagne*. Paris, 1937.

Beattie, J. H. M. "On Understanding Ritual." In *Rationality*, edited by Bryan R.
Wilson, pp. 240–68. Oxford, 1970.

Beckford, James A. *The Trumpet of Prophecy*. New York, 1975.

Beinhart, Haim. "The Converso Community in Fifteenth-Century Spain." In *The*

Sephardi Heritage, edited by R. D. Barnett, vol. 1, pp. 425–46. London, 1971.

―――――. "The Converso Community in Sixteenth- and Seventeenth-Century Spain." In *The Sephardi Heritage,* edited by R. D. Barnett, vol. 1, pp. 457–78. London, 1971.

Ben-Amos, Dan, and Mintz, Jerome R., trans. and eds. *In Praise of the Ba'al Shem Tov.* Bloomington, 1970.

Benayahu, Meir. "The Holy Society of R. Yehuda Hasid and the Aliya to Israel" (Hebrew). *Sufunot* 3–4 (1960): 133–82.

―――――. *The Sabbatian Movement in Greece* (Hebrew). Jerusalem, 1973.

Benes, Vaclav L., and Pounds, Norman G. J. *Poland.* London, 1970.

Ben-Sasson, H. H. "Exile and Redemption through the Eyes of the Spanish Exiles" (Hebrew). In *Yitzhak F. Baer Jubilee Volume,* pp. 216–27. Jerusalem, 1960.

―――――. "The Generation of the Spanish Exiles and Its Fate" (Hebrew). *Zion* 26 (1961): 23–64.

―――――. "Kiddush Ha-Shem." In *Trial and Achievement: Currents in Jewish History,* pp. 209–16. Jerusalem, 1974.

―――――. "Lithuania." In *Trial and Achievement: Currents in Jewish History,* pp. 167–83. Jerusalem, 1974.

―――――. "The Middle Ages." In *A History of the Jewish People.* Cambridge, Mass., 1976.

Bensman, Joseph, and Grant, Michael. "Charisma and Modernity: The Use and Abuse of a Concept." *Social Research* 42 (1975): 570–614.

Ben-Zvi, Itzhak. "The Sabbateans of Salonica." In *The Exiled and the Redeemed,* pp. 131–53. Jerusalem, 1957.

Berdyaev, Nicolas. *The Russian Revolution.* Ann Arbor, 1961.

Berger, Abraham. "The Messianic Self-Consciousness of Abraham Abulafia." In *Essays on Jewish Life and Thought,* edited by Joseph L. Blau, et al., pp. 55–61. New York, 1959.

Berger, Peter L. *Invitation to Sociology.* New York, 1963.

―――――. *The Sacred Canopy.* New York, 1967.

Bernstein, Mordecai. "Two Remedy Books in Yiddish from 1474 and 1508." In *Studies in Biblical and Jewish Folklore,* edited by Raphael Patai, et al., pp. 289–305. Bloomington, 1960.

Biale, David. *Gershom Scholem: Kabbalah and Counter-History.* Cambridge, Mass., 1979.

Billington, James H. *The Icon and the Axe: An Interpretative History of Russian Culture.* New York, 1966.

Birnbaum, Ervin. "David Reubeni's Indian Origin." *Historia Judaica* 20 (1958): 3–30.

Blau, Joseph L. *Modern Varieties of Judaism.* New York, 1966.

Blumenthal, David R. "Some Methodological Reflections on the Study of Jewish Mysticism." *Religion* 8 (1978): 111–14.

Braudel, F. P., and Spooner, F. "Prices in Europe from 1450 to 1750." In *The Cambridge Economic History of Europe,* vol. 4, pp. 374–486. Cambridge, 1967.

Braunstein, Baruch. *The Chuetos of Majorca*. Scottdale, Pa., 1936.

Brym, Robert J. *The Jewish Intelligentsia and Russian Marxism*. London, 1978.

Buchanan, George Wesley. *Revelation and Redemption: Jewish Documents of Deliverance from the Fall of Jerusalem to the Death of Nahmanides*. Dillsboro, N.C., 1978.

Campbell, Colin. "Clarifying the Cult." *British Journal of Sociology* 28 (1977): 375–88.

――――. *Toward a Sociology of Irreligion*. London, 1971.

Capp, B. S. *The Fifth Monarchy Men*. London, 1972.

Carlebach, Julius. *Karl Marx and the Radical Critique of Judaism*. London, 1978.

Cassuto, M. D. U. "Who Was David Reubeni" (Hebrew). *Tarbiz* (1962–63): 339–58.

Castro, Américo. *The Spaniards*. Berkeley, 1971.

Chazan, Robert. "The Hebrew First Crusade Chronicles." *Revue des études juives* 133 (1974): 235–54.

Cipolla, Carlo M. "The Economic Decline of Italy." In *The Economic Decline of Empires*, edited by Carlo M. Cipolla, pp. 196–214. London, 1970.

Cohen, Gerson D. "Messianic Postures of Ashkenazim and Sephardim (Prior to Sabbatai Zevi)." In *Studies of the Leo Baeck Institute*, edited by Max Kreutzberger, pp. 117–56. New York, 1967.

――――. Review article of B. Netanyahu's "The Marranos of Spain." *Jewish Social Studies* 29 (1967): 178–84.

Cohen, Martin A., trans. *Samuel Usque's Consolation for the Tribulations of Israel*. Philadelphia, 1965.

Cohn, Norman. *The Pursuit of the Millennium*. New York, 1961.

Cohn Sherbok, Daniel. "The Jewish Doctrine of Hell." *Religion* 8 (1978): 196–209.

Conybeare, Frederick C. *Russian Dissenters*. Harvard, 1921.

Dan, J. *The Hasidic Story: Its History and Development* (Hebrew). Jerusalem, 1975.

Dinur, Benzion. "The Beginnings of Hasidism and Its Social and Messianic Elements" (Hebrew). In *At the Turning of the Generations*, pp. 83–227. Jerusalem, 1955.

――――. "The Emigration from Spain to Eretz Yisrael after the Disorders of 1391" (Hebrew). *Zion* 32 (1967): 161–74.

――――. "The Question of Redemption at the Beginning of the Haskalah and the First Emancipation Dispute" (Hebrew). In *At the Turning of the Generations*, pp. 229–354. Jerusalem, 1955.

Dominguez Ortiz, Antonio. "Historical Research on Spanish Conversos in the Last Fifteen Years." In *Collected Studies in Honour of Américo Castro's Eightieth Year*, edited by M. P. Hornik, pp. 79–81. Oxford, 1965.

Douglas, Mary. *Natural Symbols: Explorations in Cosmology*. New York, 1970.

――――. "Social Preconditions of Enthusiasm and Heterodoxy." In *Forms of Symbolic Action*, edited by Robert F. Spencer, pp. 69–80. Seattle, 1969.

Dresner, Samuel H. *The Zaddik: The Doctrine of the Zaddik According to the Writings of Rabbi Yaakov Yosef of Polnoy*. New York, 1974.

Dubnov, Simon. *History of Hasidism* (Hebrew). Tel Aviv, 1932.

————. *History of the Jews*. London, 1971.

Duker, Abraham G. "Polish Frankism's Duration." *Jewish Social Studies* 25 (1963): 287–333.

————. "The Tarniks (Believers in the Coming of the Messiah in 1840)." In *The Joshua Starr Memorial Volume*, pp. 191–229. New York, 1953.

Durkheim, Emile. *The Elementary Forms of the Religious Life*. London, 1915.

————. "Individual and Collective Representations." In *Sociology and Philosophy*, pp. 1–34. Glencoe, 1953.

Eidelberg, Shlomo. *The Jews and the Crusades: The Hebrew Chronicles of the First and Second Crusades*. Wisconsin, 1977.

Eliach, Yaffa. "Jewish Hasidim, Russian Sectarian Non-Conformists in the Ukraine." Ph.D. dissertation, City University of New York, 1973.

————. "The Russian Dissenting Sects and Their Influence on Israel Ba'al Shem Tov, Founder of Hassidism." *Proceedings of the American Academy for Jewish Research* 36 (1968): 57–83.

Encyclopaedia Judaica. Jerusalem, 1972.

Epstein, Isidore. *Judaism: A Historical Presentation*. London, 1959.

Erez, Yehuda. "The Bible and the Jewish Tradition in the Jewish Workers Movement" (Hebrew). In *Jewish Socialism and the Jewish Labor Movement in the Nineteenth Century*, edited by M. Mishkinsky, pp. 117–41. Jerusalem, 1975.

Ettinger, S. "The Hasidic Movement—Reality and Ideals." *Cahiers d'histoire mondiale* 11 (1968): 251–66.

Festinger, Leon; Riecken, Henry W.; and Schachter, Stanley. *When Prophecy Fails*. Minneapolis, 1956.

Frazer, James George. *The Golden Bough*. 12 vols. London, 1911–15.

Freimann, A., and Kracauer, F. *Frankfort*. Philadelphia, 1929.

Friedlaender, Israel. "Jewish-Arabic Studies." *Jewish Quarterly Review*, n.s. 1 (1910–11): 183–215; 2 (1911–12): 481–516; 3 (1912–13): 235–99.

Friedland, W. H. "For a Sociological Concept of Charisma." *Social Forces* 43 (1964): 18–26.

Friedman, Menahem. *Society and Religion: The Non-Zionist Orthodox in Israel, 1918–1936* (Hebrew). Jerusalem, 1977.

Gager, John G. *Kingdom and Community: The Social World of Early Christianity*. Englewood Cliffs, N.J., 1975.

Gerlach, Luther P., and Hine, Virginia H. *People, Power, Change: Movements of Social Transformation*. Indianapolis, 1970.

Gerth, H. H., and Mills, C. Wright, trans. and eds. *From Max Weber*. New York, 1946.

Gibb, H. A. R., and Bowen, Harold. *Islamic Society and the West*. Oxford, 1957.

Gilman, Stephen. "The Conversos and the Fall of Fortune." In *Collected Studies in Honour of Américo Castro's Eightieth Year*, edited by M. P. Hornik, pp. 127–36. Oxford, 1965.

Glatzer, Naham N. "Zion in Medieval Literature." In *Zion in Jewish Literature*, edited by Abraham S. Halkin, pp. 83–100. New York, 1961.

Glock, Charles Y. "The Role of Deprivation in the Origin and Evolution of

Religious Groups." In *Religion and Social Control*, edited by Robert Lee and Martin E. Marty, pp. 24–36. New York, 1964.

Goitein, S. D. "Meeting in Jerusalem: Messianic Expectations in the Letters of the Cairo Geniza." *AJS Review* (Association for Jewish Studies) 4 (1979): 43–57.

———. "A Report on Messianic Troubles in Baghdad in 1120–21." *Jewish Quarterly Review*, n.s. 43 (1952–53): 57–76.

Goldman, Eliezer. "Messianic Interpretation of Current Events." *Forum* 26 (1977): 37–41.

Gonen, Jay Y. *A Psychohistory of Zionism*. New York, 1975.

Goode, William J. *Religion among the Primitives*. New York, 1954.

Goody, Jack. "Religion and Ritual: The Definitional Problem." *British Journal of Sociology* 12 (1961): 142–64.

Graetz, H. *History of the Jews*. Philadelphia, 1895.

Green, Arthur. "Rabbi Nahman Bratslaver's Conflict Regarding Leadership." In *Texts and Responses*, edited by Michael A. Fishbane and Paul R. Flohr, pp. 141–57. Leiden, 1975.

———. *Tormented Master: A Life of Rabbi Nahman of Bratslav*. University, Ala., 1979.

———. "The Zaddiq as Axis Mundi in Later Judaism." *Journal of the American Academy of Religion* 45 (1977): 327–47.

Gross, Nachum, ed. *Economic History of the Jews*. Jerusalem, 1975.

Grunwald, Max. *Vienna*. Philadelphia, 1936.

Gurr, Ted Robert. *Why Men Rebel*. Princeton, 1970.

Gutwirth, Jacques. *Vie juive traditionnelle: Ethnologie d'une communauté Hassidique*. Paris, 1970.

Haliezer, Stephen H. "The Castilian Urban Patriciate and the Jewish Expulsions of 1480–92." *American Historical Review* 78 (1973): 35–58.

Halkin, Abraham S., ed. *Moses Maimonides' Epistle to Yemen*. New York, 1952.

Harris, Marvin. *Cows, Pigs, Wars, and Witches*. New York, 1975.

Heller, Celia S. *On the Edge of Destruction*. New York, 1977.

Hertzberg, Arthur, ed. *The Zionist Idea*. New York, 1977.

Hill, Clifford. "Immigrant Sect Development in Britain: A Case of Status Deprivation." *Social Compass* 18 (1971): 221–30.

Hill, Michael. *The Sociology of Religion*. London, 1973.

Hirschberg, H. Z. *A History of the Jews in North Africa*. Leiden, 1974.

Hobsbawm, E. J. "The Crisis of the Seventeenth Century." In *Crisis in Europe, 1560–1660*, edited by Trevor Aston, pp. 5–58. London, 1965.

Homans, George C. "Anxiety and Ritual: The Theories of Malinowski and Radcliffe-Brown." In *Reader in Comparative Religion*, edited by William A. Lessa and Evan Z. Vogt, pp. 123–28. New York, 1965.

Hornik, M. P., ed. *Collected Studies in Honour of Américo Castro's Eightieth Year*. Oxford, 1965.

Horodezky, S. A. *Hasidism and Hasidim* (Hebrew). Jerusalem, 1953.

Horton, Robin. "Neo-Tylorianism." *Man* 3 (1968): 625–34.

Hostetler, John A. *Amish Society*. Baltimore, 1963.

_____. *Hutterite Society.* Baltimore, 1974.

Isaacs, Stephen. "Hasidim of Brooklyn." In *A Coat of Many Colors: Jewish Subcommunities in the United States,* edited by Abraham D. Lavender, pp. 189–94. Westport, 1977.

Isenberg, Sheldon R. "Millenarism in Greco-Roman Palestine." *Religion* 4 (1974): 26–46.

Jacob, Margaret C. "Millenarianism and Science in the Late Seventeenth Century." *Journal of the History of Ideas* 37 (1976): 335–41.

Jacobs, Louis. *Hasidic Prayer.* New York, 1973.

_____. *Hasidic Thought.* New York, 1976.

_____. *Seeker of Unity: The Life and Works of Aaron of Starosselje.* New York, 1966.

Jarvie, I. C. "On the Explanation of Cargo Cults." *Archives européenes de sociologie* 7 (1966): 299–312.

Johnpoll, Bernard K. *The Politics of Futility: The General Jewish Workers Bund of Poland, 1917–1943.* Ithaca, 1967.

Kamen, Henry. *The Spanish Inquisition.* London, 1965.

Kaplan, Y. "The Attitude of the Leadership of the Portuguese Community in Amsterdam to the Sabbatian Movement, 1665–1671" (Hebrew). *Zion* 39 (1974): 198–216.

Katz, Jacob. "The Jewish National Movement: A Sociological Analysis." In *Emancipation and Assimilation,* pp. 130–45. Farnborough, Hants., 1972.

_____. *Tradition and Crisis: Jewish Society at the End of the Middle Ages.* New York, 1961.

Katz, Stephen T. "Language, Epistemology, and Mysticism." In *Mysticism and Philosophical Analysis,* edited by Stephen T. Katz, pp. 22–74. London, 1978.

Klausner, Joseph. *The Messianic Idea in Israel.* New York, 1955.

Knaani, David. *The Labour Second Aliyah and Its Attitude toward Religion and Tradition* (Hebrew). Tel Aviv, 1975.

Kochan, Lionel. *The Jew and His History.* New York, 1977.

Kohn, Moshe. *Who's Afraid of Gush Emunim.* Jerusalem, 1976.

Krauss, Samuel. "Le Roi de France Charles VIII et les espérances messianiques." *Revue des études juives* 51 (1906): 87–96.

LaBarre, Weston. "Materials for a History of Studies of Crisis Cults: A Bibliographic Essay." *Current Anthropology* 12 (1971): 3–44.

Langer, Jiri. *Nine Gates to the Chassidic Mysteries.* New York, 1961.

Lanternari, Vittorio. "Nativistic and Socio-Religious Movements: A Reconsideration." *Comparative Studies in Society and History* 16 (1974): 483–503.

_____. *The Religions of the Oppressed.* New York, 1965.

Laqueur, Walter. *A History of Zionism.* New York, 1976.

Lawrence, Peter. *Road Belong Cargo.* Manchester, 1964.

Lea, Henry Charles. *Chapters from the Religious History of Spain.* Philadelphia, 1890.

_____. *A History of the Inquisition of Spain.* New York, 1922.

Lerner, Robert E. "Medieval Prophecy and Religious Dissent." *Past and Present* 72 (1976): 3–24.

Levin, Nora. *Jewish Socialist Movements, 1871–1917.* London, 1978.

Levy, Sydelle Brooks. "Shifting Patterns of Ethnic Identification among the Hassidim." In *The New Ethnicity: Perspectives from Ethnology,* edited by John W. Bennett, pp. 25–50. St. Paul, Minnesota, 1975.

Lewis, Bernard. "Some Reflections on the Decline of the Ottoman Empire." In *The Economic Decline of Empires,* edited by Carlos M. Cipolla, pp. 215–34. London, 1970.

Liebman, Charles S. "Religion and Political Integration in Israel." *Jewish Journal of Sociology* 17 (1975): 17–27.

Livneh, Eliezer. *Toward Elon Moreh* (Hebrew). Jerusalem, 1976.

Lofland, John, and Stark, Rodney. "Becoming a World Saver: A Theory of Conversion to a Deviant Perspective." *American Sociological Review* 30 (1965): 862–75.

MacKay, Angus. "Popular Movements and Pogroms in Fifteenth-Century Castile." *Past and Present* 55 (1972): 33–67.

McKeon, Michael. "Sabbatai Sevi in England." *AJS Review* (Association for Jewish Studies) 2 (1977): 131–69.

Mahler, Raphael. *Hasidism and Haskalah in Galicia and the Congress Kingdom of Poland in the First Half of the Nineteenth Century* (Hebrew). Merhavya, 1961.

―――. *History of Jews in Poland* (Hebrew). Merhavya, 1946.

―――. *A History of Modern Jewry, 1780–1815.* London, 1971.

―――. *History of the Jewish People in Modern Times* (Hebrew). Vol. 1, bk. 2; vol. 2, bk. 1; vol. 2, bk. 2. Merhavya, 1954–76.

―――. *Karaites: A Medieval Jewish Movement for Deliverance* (Hebrew). Merhavya, 1949.

―――. "The Social and Political Aspects of the Haskalah in Galicia." *Yivo Annual of Jewish Social Science* 1 (1946): 64–85.

Malalgoda, Kitsiri. "Millennialism in Relation to Buddhism." *Comparative Studies in Society and History* 12 (1970): 424–31.

Malinowski, Bronislaw. "The Role of Magic and Religion." In *Reader in Comparative Religion,* edited by William A. Lessa and Evan Z. Vogt, pp. 102–12. New York, 1965.

Mandel, Arthur. *The Militant Messiah.* Atlantic Highlands, N.J., 1979.

Mann, Jacob. "Messianic Movements at the Time of the First Crusade" (Hebrew). *ha-Tequfah* 23 (1925): 243–61; 24 (1928): 335–58.

―――. *Texts and Studies in Jewish History and Literature.* 2 vols. New York, 1972.

Manuel, Frank F., and Manuel, Fritzie P. "Sketch for a Natural History of Paradise." In *Myth, Symbol and Culture,* edited by Clifford Geertz, pp. 83–128, New York, 1971.

Marmorstein, A. "The Place of Popular Traditions in the History of Religions" (Hebrew). *Edoth* 1 (1946): 75–89, 138–50.

Marquez Villanueva, Francisco. "The Converso Problem: An Assessment." In *Collected Studies in Honour of Américo Castro's Eightieth Year,* edited by M. P. Hornik, pp. 317–33. Oxford, 1965.

Marras, Michael R. *The Politics of Assimilation.* Oxford, 1971.

Marx, A. "Le Faux Messie Ascher Laemmlein." *Revue des études juives* 61 (1911): 135–38.

Meldelsohn, Ezra. "The Dilemma of Jewish Politics in Poland: Four Responses." In *Jews and Non-Jews in Eastern Europe, 1918–1945*, edited by B. Vago and G. L. Mosse, pp. 203–19. New York, 1974.

Merton, Robert K. *Social Theory and Social Structure*. Glencoe, 1949.

Mevorah, Baruch. "Messianism as a Factor in the First Reform Controversies" (Hebrew). *Zion* 34 (1969): 189–218.

Millgram, Abraham. *Jewish Worship*. Philadelphia, 1971.

Mindel, Nissan. *Rabbi Schneur Zalman*. New York, 1969.

Minkin, Jacob S. *Abrabanel and the Expulsion of the Jews from Spain*. New York, 1938.

————. *The Romance of Hasidism*. New York, 1932.

Mintz, Jerome R. "Ethnic Activism: The Hasidic Example." *Judaism* 28 (1979): 449–64.

————. *Legends of the Hasidim*. Chicago, 1960.

Mishkinsky, M. "The Jewish Labor Movement and European Socialism." In *Jewish Socialism and the Jewish Labor Movement in the Nineteenth Century*, edited by M. Mishkinsky, pp. 225–37. Jerusalem, 1975.

Moore, Kenneth. *Those of the Street*. Notre Dame, 1976.

Morrison, Denton D. "Some Notes toward a Theory of Relative Deprivation, Social Movements, and Social Change." *American Behavioral Scientist* 14 (1971): 675–90.

Mowinckel, Sigmund. *He That Cometh*. Oxford, 1956.

Neclava, Joseph. "Herzl and Messianism." *Herzl Year Book* 7 (1971): 9–26.

Nehama, Jos. *Histoire des Israelites de Salonique*. Paris, 1935.

Nemoy, Leon. "Al-Qirqisani's Account of the Jewish Sects and Christianity." *Hebrew Union College Annual* 7 (1930): 317–97.

Netanyahu, B. *Don Isaac Abravanel*. Philadelphia, 1953.

————. *The Marranos of Spain*. New York, 1966.

Neuman, Abraham A. *The Jews in Spain*. Philadelphia, 1942.

Nowell, Charles E. *A History of Portugal*. New York, 1952.

Obeyesekere, Gananath. "Theodicy, Sin, and Salvation in a Sociology of Buddhism." In *Dialectic in Practical Religion*, edited by E. R. Leach, pp. 7–40. Cambridge, 1968.

O'Dea, Janet. "Gush Emunim: Roots and Ambiguities." *Forum* 25 (1976): 39–50.

————. "The Religious Aspect." *Forum* 26 (1977): 39–41.

O'Dea, Thomas F., and Publeto, Renato. "Anomie and the Quest for Community: The Formation of Sects among the Puerto Ricans of New York." In *Sociology and the Study of Religion*, by Thomas F. O'Dea, pp. 180–98. New York, 1970.

Oliveira Marques, A. H. De. *History of Portugal*. New York, 1972.

Olson, Robert W. "Jews in the Ottoman Empire in the Light of New Documents." *Jewish Social Studies* 41 (1977): 75–88.

Oommen, T. K. "Charisma, Social Structure, and Social Change." *Comparative Studies in Society and History* 10 (1967): 85–99.

Parsons, Talcott. *The Structure of Social Action*. New York, 1949.

Patai, Raphael. *The Hebrew Goddess*. New York, 1978.

———. *The Jewish Mind*. New York, 1977.

———. *The Messiah Texts*. New York, 1979.

Pennington, D. H. *Seventeenth-Century Europe*. London, 1970.

Pereira de Queiros, Maria Isaura. "Messianic Myths and Movements." *Diogenes* 90 (1975): 78–99.

Petachowski, Jakob J. *The Theology of Haham David Nieta*. New York, 1970.

Philipson, David. *The Reform Movement in Judaism*. New York, 1967.

Piekarz, Mendel. *The Beginning of Hasidism: Ideological Trends in Derush and Musar Literature* (Hebrew). Jerusalem, 1978.

———. *Bratslav* (Hebrew). Jerusalem, 1971.

Pinsker, Sanford. "Piety as Community: The Hasidic View." *Social Research* 42 (1975): 230–46.

Plaut, W. Gunther. *The Growth of Reform Judaism*. New York, 1965.

Polack, A. "David Alroy" (Hebrew). In *World Congress of Jewish Studies*, vol. 1, pp. 404–6. Jerusalem, 1947.

Poliakov, Léon. *The History of Anti-Semitism*. Vols. 1 and 2. London, 1965 and 1974.

Poll, Solomon. *The Hasidic Community of Williamsburg*. New York, 1962.

Pollack, Herman. *Jewish Folkways in Germanic Lands (1648–1806)*. Cambridge, Mass., 1971.

Popkin, Richard H. "The Historical Significance of Sephardic Judaism in Seventeenth-Century Amsterdam." *American Sephardi* 5 (1971): 18–27.

Poppel, Stephen M. *Zionism in Germany, 1897–1933*. Philadelphia, 1977.

Price, J. L. *Culture and Society in the Dutch Republic during the Seventeenth Century*. London, 1974.

Raanan, Tsvi. *Gush Emunim* (Hebrew). Tel Aviv, 1980.

Rabb, Theodore K. *The Struggle for Stability in Early Modern Europe*. New York, 1975.

Rabinowicz, Harry M. *The Legacy of Polish Jewry: A History of Polish Jews in the Inter-War Years, 1919–1939*. New York, 1965.

———. "Music and Dance in Hasidism." *Judaism* 8 (1959): 252–57.

Rabinowitsch, Wolf Zeev. *Lithuanian Hasidism*. London, 1970.

Radcliffe-Brown, A. R. "Taboo." In *Reader in Comparative Religion*, edited by William A. Lessa and Evan Z. Vogt, pp. 112–23. New York, 1965.

Rapoport-Albert, Ada. "God and the Zaddik as the Two Focal Points of Hasidic Worship." *History of Religions* 18 (1979): 296–325.

Ratzahbi, Yehuda. "Apocalypses and Reckoning of the End of Days among Yemenite Jews" (Hebrew). In *Folklore Research Center Studies*, edited by Dov Noy and Issachar Ben-Ami, vol. 1. Jerusalem, 1970.

Reeves, Marjorie. *The Influence of Prophecy in the Later Middle Ages*. Oxford, 1969.

Reinharz, Jehuda. *Fatherland or Promised Land: The Dilemma of the German Jew, 1893–1914*. Ann Arbor, 1975.

Révah, I. S. "David Reubeni: Exécuté en Espagne en 1538." *Revue des études juives*

117 (1958): 128–35.

———. "Les Marranes." *Revue des études juives* 118 (1959–60): 29–77.

———. "Spinoza et les hérétiques de la communauté judéo-portugaise d'Amsterdam." *Revue de l'histoire des religions* 154 (1958): 173–218.

Rischin, Moses. *The Promised City*. New York, 1964.

Rivkin, Ellis. *León Da Modena and the Kol Sakhal*. Cincinnati, 1952.

———. "The Meaning of Messiah in Jewish Thought." *Union Seminary Quarterly Review* 26 (1971): 383–406.

———. *The Shaping of Jewish History*. New York, 1971.

Robertson, Roland. *The Sociological Interpretation of Religion*. Oxford, 1970.

Rodriguez-Moñino, A. "Les Judaisants à Badajoz de 1493 à 1599." *Revue des études juives* 115 (1956): 73–86.

Ross, Gillian. "Neo-Tylorianism—A Reassessment." *Man* 6 (1971): 105–16.

Rotenstreich, Nathan. "Religious Conviction and Political Behaviour." *Forum* 26 (1977): 34–36.

Roth, Cecil. *The History of the Jews of Italy*. Philadelphia, 1946.

———. *A History of the Marranos*. Philadelphia, 1932.

———. *A Life of Menasseh ben Israel*. Philadelphia, 1934.

———. "Le Martyre de David Reubeni." *Revue des études juives* 116 (1957): 93–95.

———. "The Religion of the Marranos." *Jewish Quarterly Review* 22 (1931): 1–33.

———. "A Zionist Experiment in the Sixteenth Century." *Midstream* 9 (1963): 76–81.

Rubin, Israel. *Satmar: An Island in the City*. Chicago, 1972.

Rubinstein, Avraham. "Chapters in Hasidic History" (Hebrew). In *Studies in Hasidism*, edited by Avraham Rubinstein, pp. 241–49. Jerusalem, 1977.

———. "Between Hasidism and Sabbatianism" (Hebrew). In *Studies in Hasidism*, edited by Avraham Rubinstein, pp. 182–97. Jerusalem, 1977.

Sarachek, Joseph. *The Doctrine of the Messiah in Medieval Jewish Literature*. New York, 1968.

Schatz (Uffenheimer), Rivka. "Contemplative Prayer in Hasidism." In *Studies in Mysticism and Religion Presented to Gershom G. Scholem*, edited by E. E. Urbach, R. J. Zvi Werblowsky, and Ch. Wirszubski, pp. 209–26. Jerusalem, 1970.

———. "Essence of the Zaddik in Hasidism" (Hebrew). *Molad* 18 (1960): 365–78.

———. *Hasidism as Mysticism* (Hebrew). Jerusalem, 1968.

———. "Self-Redemption in Hasidic Thought." In *Types of Redemption*, edited by R. J. Zvi Werblowsky and C. Jouco Bleeker, pp. 207–12. Leiden, 1970.

Schechter, S. "Safed in the Sixteenth Century." In *Studies in Judaism*, pp. 202–85. Philadelphia, 1908.

Schipper, I. "R. Israel Ba'al Shem Tov and His Image in the Early Hasidic Literature" (Hebrew). *Hadoar* 39 (1960–61): 525–26, 531–32, 551–52.

Scholem, Gershom. "The Historical Image of R. Israel Ba'al Shem Tov" (Hebrew). *Molad* 18 (1960): 335–56.

_____. *Kabbalah*. Jerusalem, 1974.

_____. *Major Trends in Jewish Mysticism*. New York, 1961.

_____. *The Messianic Idea in Judaism and Other Essays on Jewish Spirituality*. New York, 1971.

_____. *On the Kabbalah and Its Symbolism*. New York, 1969.

_____. *Sabbatai Sevi: The Mystical Messiah, 1626–1676*. Princeton, 1973.

_____. *Studies and Texts Concerning the History of Sabbatianism and Its Metamorphosis* (Hebrew). Jerusalem, 1974.

_____. "The Two First Testimonies on the Relations between Hasidic Groups and the Ba'al Shem Tov" (Hebrew). *Tarbiz* 20 (1949): 228–44.

Schrire, Y. *Hebrew Amulets: Their Development and Interpretation*. London, 1966.

Shaffir, William. *Life in a Religious Community: The Lubavitcher Chassidim in Montreal*. Toronto, 1974.

Sharf, Andrew. *Byzantine Jewry: From Justinian to the Fourth Crusade*. London, 1971.

Sharot, Stephen. "A Jewish Christian Adventist Movement." *Jewish Journal of Sociology* 10 (1968): 35–45.

_____. *Judaism: A Sociology*. New York, 1976.

Shils, Edward. "Charisma, Order, and Status." *American Sociological Review* 30 (1965): 199–213.

Shmeruk, Ch. "The Hasidic Movement and the Arendars" (Hebrew). *Zion* 35 (1970): 182–92.

_____. "The Social Significance of the Hasidic Shechitah" (Hebrew). *Zion* 32 (1967): 1–45.

Shochat, A. "On Joy in Hasidism" (Hebrew). *Zion* 16 (1951): 30–43.

Shohat, Azriel. "Notes on the David Reubeni Affair" (Hebrew). *Zion* 35 (1970): 96–116.

Shulvass, Moses A. *Between the Rhine and the Bosporus*. Chicago, 1964.

_____. *The Jews in the World of the Renaissance*. Leiden, 1973.

_____. *Rome and Jerusalem* (Hebrew). Jerusalem, 1944.

Siegel, Laurence. "Reflections on Neo-Reform in the Central Conference of American Rabbis." *American Jewish Archives* 20 (1968): 63–84.

Silver, Abba Hillel. *A History of Messianic Speculation in Israel*. New York, 1927.

Simon, Rita James. *Continuity and Change: A Study of Two Ethnic Communities in Israel*. Cambridge, 1978.

Skorupski, J. *Symbol and Theory*. New York, 1976.

Sokolow, Nahum. *Baruch Spinoza and His Time* (Hebrew). Paris, 1928–29.

Sonne, Isaiah. "Leon Modena and the Da Costa Circle in Amsterdam." *Hebrew Union College Annual* 21 (1948): 1–28.

_____. "On Baer and His Philosophy of Jewish History." *Jewish Social Studies* 9 (1947): 61–80.

Sperling, H.; Simon, M.; and Levertoff, P., trans. *The Zohar*. London, 1931–34.

Spier, Leslie; Suttles, Wayne; and Herskovitz, Melville J. "Comment on Aberle's Thesis of Deprivation." *Southwestern Journal of Anthropology* 15 (1959): 84–88.

Spiro, Melford. *Burmese Supernaturalism*. Philadelphia, 1978.

————. "Religion, Problems of Definition, and Exploration." In *Anthropological Approaches to the Study of Religion*, edited by Michael Banton, pp. 85–126. London, 1968.

Stark, Werner. *The Sociology of Religion*. Vol. 4. New York, 1970.

Starr, Joshua. *The Jews in the Byzantine Empire, 641–1204*. Athens, 1939.

————. "Le Mouvement messianique au début du VIIIe siècle." *Revue des études juives* 102 (1937): 81–92.

Steinberg, Harry. "New Square: Bridge Over the River Time." In *A Coat of Many Colors: Jewish Subcommunities in the United States*, edited by Abraham D. Lavender, pp. 195–201. Westport, 1977.

Swanson, Guy. *The Birth of the Gods: The Origin of Primitive Beliefs*. Ann Arbor, 1960.

————. *Religion and Regime: A Sociological Account of the Reformation*. Ann Arbor, 1967.

Talmon, J. L. "Jews between Revolution and Counter-Revolution." In *Israel among the Nations*, pp. 1–87. London, 1970.

Talmon, Yonina. "Millenarian Movements." *Archives européennes de sociologie* 7 (1966): 159–200.

————. "Pursuit of the Millennium: The Relation between Religious and Social Change." *Archives européennes de sociologie* 3 (1962): 125–48.

Tamar, David. "The Messianic Expectations in Italy for the Year 1575" (Hebrew). *Sufunot* 2 (1958): 61–88.

Tambiah, S. M. *Buddhism and the Spirit Cults in North-East Thailand*. Cambridge, 1970.

Thomas, Keith. *Religion and the Decline of Magic*. London, 1971.

Thrupp, Sylvia L., ed. *Millennial Dreams in Action*. The Hague, 1962.

Tishby, I. "Documents on Nathan of Gaza in the Writings of Rabbi Joseph Hamis" (Hebrew). *Sufunot* 1 (1956): 80–117.

————. "The Messianic Ferment in the Circle of Moses Hayyim Luzzatto in the Light of the Marriage Contract and Messianic Poems" (Hebrew). In *Yitzhak F. Baer Jubilee Volume*, edited by S. W. Baron et al., pp. 347–97. Jerusalem, 1960.

————. "The Messianic Idea and Messianic Trends in the Growth of Hasidism" (Hebrew). *Zion* 32 (1967): 1–45.

————, and Dan, J. "Hasidism" (Hebrew). In *Hebrew Encyclopaedia*, vol. 14, pp. 756–821. Jerusalem, 1959.

Tobias, Henry J. *The Jewish Bund in Russia: From Its Origins to 1905*. Stanford, 1972.

Toon, Peter, ed. *Puritans, the Millennium, and the Future of Israel: Puritan Eschatology, 1600–1660*. Cambridge, 1970.

Trachtenberg, Joshua. *Jewish Magic and Superstition*. Cleveland, 1961.

Troeltsch, Ernst. *The Social Teaching of the Christian Churches*. London, 1931.

Tucker, Robert C. "The Theory of Charismatic Leadership." *Daedalus* (1968): 731–56.

Turner, Victor. *Dramas, Fields, and Metaphors*. Ithaca, 1974.

Tylor, Edward Burnett. *Primitive Culture: Researches into the Development of My-

thology, Philosophy, Religion, Art, and Custom. 1871. Reprint. London, 1958.

Vital, David. *The Origins of Zionism*. Oxford, 1975.

Wallace, Anthony F. C. *Religion: An Anthropological View*. New York, 1966.

Wallach, Michael. "The Chasidim of Stamford Hill." *Jewish Chronicle Magazine* (27 May 1977): 11–19, 68.

Wallerstein, Immanuel. *The Modern World System II: Mercantilism and the Consolidation of the European World Economy, 1600–1750*. New York, 1980.

Wallis, Roy. *Salvation and Protest: Studies of Social and Religious Movements*. New York, 1979.

Waugh, Daniel Clarke. "News of the False Messiah: Reports on Sabbatai Zevi in Ukraine and Muscovy." *Jewish Social Studies* 41 (1979): 301–22.

Weber, Max. *Economy and Society*. Edited by Guenther Roth and Claus Wittich. New York, 1968.

———. *The Methodology of the Social Sciences*. Chicago, 1949.

———. *The Protestant Ethic and the Spirit of Capitalism*. New York, 1958.

Weinryb, Bernard D. *The Jews of Poland: A Social and Economic History of the Jewish Community in Poland from 1100 to 1800*. Philadelphia, 1972.

———. "Reappraisals in Jewish History." In *Salo Wittmayer Baron Jubilee Volume*, edited by Saul Lieberman, vol. 2, pp. 939–74. Jerusalem, 1974.

Weinstein, Donald. *Savonarola and Florence*. Princeton, 1970.

Weinstein, Stephen L. "Pioneers with a Passion: A Study of Secularization and the Second Aliyah." Unpublished paper, Jerusalem, 1975.

Weiss, J. G. "The Beginnings of Hasidism" (Hebrew). *Zion* 16 (1957): 46–106.

———. "A Circle of Pneumatics in Pre-Hasidism." *Journal of Jewish Studies* 8 (1957): 199–213.

———. "Contemplative Mysticism and Faith in Hasidic Piety." *Journal of Jewish Studies* 4 (1953): 19–29.

———. "The Great Maggid's Theory of Contemplative Magic." *Hebrew Union College Annual* 31 (1960): 137–47.

———. "The Kavvanoth of Prayer in Early Hasidism." *Journal of Jewish Studies* 9 (1958): 163–92.

Werblowsky, R. J. Zvi. "Mysticism and Messianism: The Case of Hasidism." In *Man and His Salvation: Studies in Memory of S. G. F. Brandon*, edited by Eric J. Sharpe and John R. Hinnells, pp. 305–14. Manchester, 1973.

Wertheim, Aaron. *Laws and Customs of Hasidism* (Hebrew). Jerusalem, 1960.

Wilensky, Mordecai. *Hasidim and Mitnaggedim: A Study of the Controversy between Them in the Years 1772–1815* (Hebrew). Jerusalem, 1970.

Wilson, Bryan R. *Magic and the Millennium*. London, 1973.

———. *The Noble Savages: The Primitive Origins of Charisma and Its Contemporary Survival*. Berkeley, 1975.

———. *Religious Sects*. New York, 1970.

———. *Sects and Society*. London, 1961.

———, ed. *Patterns of Sectarianism*. London, 1967.

———, ed. *Rationality*. Oxford, 1970.

Winter, J. Alan. "The Metaphoric Parallelist Approach to the Sociology of Theistic Beliefs: Theme, Variations, and Implications." *Sociological Analysis*

34 (1973): 212–29.

Wistrich, Robert S. *Revolutionary Jews from Marx to Trotsky.* London, 1976.

Wolff, Philippe. "The 1391 Pogrom in Spain: Social Crisis or Not." *Past and Present* 50 (1971): 4–18.

Worsley, Peter. *The Trumpet Shall Sound.* London, 1970.

Yerushalmi, Yosef Hayim. "Conversos Returning to Judaism in the Seventeenth Century: Their Jewish Knowledge and Psychological Readiness" (Hebrew). *Proceedings of the Fifth World Congress of Jewish Studies*, pp. 201–9. Jerusalem, 1972.

_____. *From Spanish Court to Italian Ghetto.* New York, 1971.

Yinger, J. Milton. *The Scientific Study of Religion.* London, 1970.

Yovel, Yirmiahu. "Why Spinoza Was Excommunicated." *Commentary* 64 (November 1977): 46–52.

Zborowski, Mark, and Herzog, Elizabeth. *Life Is with People: The Culture of the Shtetle.* New York, 1962.

Zenner, Walter P. "The Case of the Apostate Messiah: A Reconsideration of the 'Failure of Prophecy.'" *Archives de sociologie des religions* 21 (1966): 111–18.

Zimmels, H. J. *Ashkenazim and Sephardim.* London, 1958.

_____. *Magicians, Theologians, and Doctors.* London, 1952.

Zinberg, Israel. *A History of Jewish Literature.* New York, 1975–76.

Zygmunt, Joseph F. "Prophetic Failure and Chiliastic Identity: The Case of Jehovah's Witnesses." *American Journal of Sociology* 75 (1970): 926–48.

Index

Sharot, Stephen

MESSIANISM, MYSTICISM, AND
(A Sociological Analysis of
Religious Movements)

University of North Carolin
Chapel Hill 1982
Studies in Religion series